WHAT IS GOVERNMENT GOOD AT?

What Is Government Good At?

A Canadian Answer

DONALD J. SAVOIE

McGill-Queen's University Press

Montreal & Kingston · London · Chicago

© McGill-Queen's University Press 2015
ISBN 978-0-7735-4621-9 (cloth)
ISBN 978-0-7735-9794-5 (ePDF)
ISBN 978-0-7735-9795-2 (ePUB)

Legal deposit third quarter 2015
Bibliothèque nationale du Québec

Printed in Canada on acid-free paper that is 100% ancient
forest free (100% post-consumer recycled), processed chlorine
free.

This book has been published with the help of a grant from
the Canada Research Chair in Public Administration and
Governance at the Université de Moncton.

McGill-Queen's University Press acknowledges the support of
the Canada Council for the Arts for our publishing program.
We also acknowledge the financial support of the Government
of Canada through the Canada Book Fund for our publishing
activities.

Library and Archives Canada Cataloguing in Publication

Savoie, Donald J., 1947–, author
    What is government good at? : a Canadian answer /
Donald J. Savoie.

Includes bibliographical references and index.
Issued in print and electronic formats.
ISBN 978-0-7735-4621-9 (bound). – ISBN 978-0-7735-9794-5 (pdf). –
ISBN 978-0-7735-9795-2 (epub)

    1. Public administration – Canada. 2. Federal government –
Canada. I. Title.

HJL75.S389 2015   351.71   C2015-903010-2
                                         C2015-903011-0

This book was typeset by True to Type in 10.5/13 Sabon

*This book is dedicated to all Canadians
and the pursuit of their common good.*

At the bottom of all the tributes paid to democracy is the little man, walking into the little booth, with a little pencil, making a little cross on a little bit of paper – no amount of rhetoric or voluminous discussion can possibly palliate the overwhelming importance of that point.

Winston Churchill

Contents

Preface   ix

1 Introduction   3

PART ONE: THE CONTEXT

2 From Parish Picnics to Facebook   19

PART TWO: WHAT HAS CHANGED AND WHAT
MATTERS IN GOVERNMENT

3 Institutions under Attack   53

4 Different Ways to Get What You Want   73

5 Fixing Bureaucracy: Please Mind the Gap   97

6 I Could Never Find the Culprit   119

7 *Apologia Pro Vita Sua*   139

8 Inside Government   169

9 Why Are Things So Complicated?   191

10 Regulations: You Can Feed the Animals   211

PART THREE: ANSWERING THE QUESTION

11 Good at What?   237

12 Upstairs, Downstairs   261

Notes   281

Index   335

Preface

The idea for this book grew out of a discussion with Professor Martin Lodge at the London School of Economics. In July 2013, together with several colleagues, we presented papers at a conference on public spending sponsored by the British Academy. Francis Maude, the minister responsible for the British civil service, was poised to unveil a reform package that would put permanent secretaries, the top civil servants in government departments, on five-year contracts, while at the same time expanding the size of ministerial offices. Over coffee I asked Martin Lodge why Maude was taking this action. Wishing to be deliberately provocative, he replied, "If the minister had his way, he would do away with the civil service altogether." My puzzled look no doubt prompted him to add, "You know, it's only a slight exaggeration. Month after month he has come out with highly negative comments about the civil service." "But what about hospitals, schools, the local police force?" I asked. Lodge said, "Francis Maude considers those to be operations and are different from what he is talking about. He is talking about the central civil service." A good part of the government of Canada's bureaucracy functions essentially as a central civil service. It does not, with some exceptions, run hospitals and schools.

The next day the *Financial Times* ran a story on the government's intention to privatize the Royal Mail, which has been a public sector icon for some 500 years. The government explained, "In the public sector its hands are tied, while those of competitors are not."[1] The *Financial Times* supported the decision on the grounds that, although "the universal postal service is a cherished part of Britain's civic life," to succeed in the years ahead, it is important to establish "greater distance between the company and politicians."[2] The minister of state for business and enterprise simply concluded that Britain could no longer "afford the Royal Mail" and added that "selling shares in the Royal Mail would give it commercial freedom."[3] The political class was saying that the problem with the Royal Mail is political.

This turn of events prompted me to ask colleagues at the conference, is government good at anything these days? What is it that the public sector can do better than the private sector? It was the right place to ask these questions. Participants included two friends who are arguably the leading scholars of public administration of my generation: Christopher Hood, the Gladstone Professor of Public Administration at All Souls College, Oxford, and Christopher Pollitt, Research Professor of Public Management at Leuven University.

They were intrigued by my questions, and both had given them a great deal of thought over the years. To be sure, the questions are ambitious, and both Hood and Pollitt, wiser than I, likely decided that it was not possible to provide definitive answers. Pollitt suggested that I should start by rereading Herbert Simon's widely acclaimed 2000 Gaus lecture in which he argued that "a basic tenet of democratic theory ... is that self-interest is such a strong motive that no fraction of society can be entrusted with the freedom and welfare of others who do not participate in the decision-making processes."[4] Simon wrote that there was "no need to reinvent government," but he did not explore what government was good at.[5] He did, however, outline a very persuasive argument that the private sector, in order to prosper, needs strong public sector organizations. I cannot help but think that Simon would be deeply disappointed with the perception, if not the reality, of the state of today's public sector.

I decided to give the questions a go, knowing full well that there are many contestable ways to answer them. I am also well aware that this book will leave many readers *sur leur faim*. Students of government will be looking for a more definitive answer to the question, what is government good at? But we need to start somewhere, and my hope is that this book will encourage others to explore the question further.

It is hardly original to write that the state of the public sector, particularly in Anglo-American democracies, is confronting serious challenges that go to the very heart of what it stands for. My sense is that the public administration community writ large has been unable to defend itself, relying on a self-serving narrative to make its case. I hold that we need to step back, take a broad view of the public sector, and explore where it has been and where it is going if we are to make progress in sorting what ails it, if we are to come up with proper prescriptions. In short, we need a better understanding of what government is good at.

To be sure, there has been no shortage of attempts to fix government in recent years. I have written a great deal about these efforts, and I revisit some of them in this book. It is necessary at times to return to my earlier work, to lay the groundwork for assessing what government is good at. However, here my focus is on the broader question: what is government good at? I also draw extensively from my own experience as advisor to federal and provincial governments.

I have no illusion that I can possibly provide answers to questions outlined in the introduction that would meet with everyone's approval. I suspect that no one could answer them conclusively. Several of my colleagues in the public administration field insist that the issue I am tackling is too broad, too fraught with methodological pitfalls, and far too ambitious. Best, they argue, to divide the research into several parts and design a detailed research plan for each.

I decided to press on, knowing full well the limitations. Our political institutions, government and government bureaucracies, have lost both credibility and public support in recent years, and we need to explore what has gone wrong. I see nothing more important for the public administration community than to explore what government does well and less well. Some of the lessons learned may be painful for government officials to hear, but one must address them in the interest of good public administration. My hope is that this book will encourage others to explore further the question, what is government good at?

I also hope that this book will encourage the next generation of students of public administration to focus their efforts on the larger questions. We have all too often in the past – and the "we" incudes me – dealt with narrow issues that hold limited interest for practitioners and Canadians. We have also too frequently overlooked the more pressing, the more demanding, and the more important challenges.

Admittedly, working from a narrow perspective holds advantages. One can delve into the details of a subject and explore it from various angles. I was not able to do this, particularly when reviewing certain issues. But the price is well worth paying, given the state of our public institutions.

I want, with more than usual emphasis, to express my sincere thanks to three anonymous reviewers of the manuscript. To be sure, it was not an easy manuscript to assess, but they produced insightful and very helpful observations and recommendations. They forced me to go back to the drawing board and make substantial revisions to several chapters. The book is much improved as a result, and I am in their debt.

I once again want to thank two outstanding women who have always been there for me: my wife Linda for her patience, support, and continued willingness to put up with my insatiable appetite for work, and Ginette Benoit for her unfailing competence, good cheer, and uncanny ability to read my handwriting. Céline Basque made an important contribution in incorporating final revisions to the manuscript. I take responsibility for any defects in this book, and I am fully responsible, answerable, and accountable for all of them.

Donald J. Savoie
Canada Research Chair in Public Administration and Governance
Université de Moncton

WHAT IS GOVERNMENT GOOD AT?

I

Introduction

The theory of comparative advantage dates back to Adam Smith's *Wealth of Nations* (1776).[1] Others, from David Ricardo to Paul Samuelson, followed to refine it.[2] The theory has stood the test of time and has of late witnessed a revival of sorts. For example, one of the best-selling business books in recent years, *Now Discover Your Strengths*, borrows heavily from the theory of comparative advantage.[3] Common sense alone tells us that both individuals and institutions will try to make the most of their strengths and focus their efforts on what they excel at.

But what are the comparative advantages for the public sector? What is it that government does better than the private sector? We know that public sector managers operate in a political marketplace, while private sector managers operate in an economic marketplace. But what of it? Mark Moore explains that the goal of "managerial work in the public sector is to create public value," while in the private sector it is "to create private value."[4] How does creating public value differ from creating private value?

The creation of public value requires an emphasis on process and probity. It also requires that initiatives be politically and legally supported. Traditionally, at least, one equates the public sector with equality, efficiency, merit, fairness, and justice. Citizens expect to be treated the same before the courts and to have equal access to government employment and government programs.

Public participation is central to the public sector. Citizens vote, they join political parties, and many engage in public debates in the hope that their efforts will make a difference. Albert Hirschman's classic *Exit,*

Voice and Loyalty: Responses to Decline in Firms, Organizations and States highlights the difference between the public and private sectors.[5] At the risk of oversimplification, the public sector deals with "voice" while the private sector deals with "exit." Unhappy citizens can express their displeasure in many ways – by voting or not voting, by participating in public demonstrations, and by voicing criticism in the media or through membership in associations. Exit, meanwhile, is associated with the private sector, where customers can move easily between competing firms. Buyers can always shop elsewhere. Not so with the public sector, where one has to deal with a single tax-collection agency, passport office, or immigration department. Voice is not as neat and tidy as is exit. It can be messy and confrontational and often is.

I have argued elsewhere that the public sector is different from the private sector in both important and unimportant ways.[6] No matter, observers tend to compare the performance of the two sectors and debate which one is more productive, efficient, and effective.[7] The public sector no longer seems to measure up, at least when compared with the private sector. Something has gone wrong. Voice has become louder, clearer, and more tenacious against the public sector in recent years. Why?

Voter turnout is down in Western democracies, morale in government remains low, and many governments are fighting stubborn deficits and debt problems. A public service employee survey revealed in 2012 that specific segments of the Canadian public service "had shown that low morale was prevalent among executives and knowledge workers and that many employees felt that workplace conditions were not conducive to confidence in management and job satisfaction."[8] This situation, it appears, is no better elsewhere. A similar survey in Britain in 2012 revealed that "two-thirds of the top civil servants are so demoralised that they are considering leaving their jobs."[9]

The perception is that the public sector is slow, inefficient, and costly, while the private sector is dynamic and efficient. One could even ask, is government better than the private sector in managing anything? The view is widely held in the Western world that the way to make an economy more dynamic and more competitive is to reduce the role of government. In brief, the private sector is regarded as the dynamic force while the public sector as the inertial one.[10]

Fifty years ago this was not the case. Political leaders declared war on poverty and spoke about building a Great Society and a Just Society.[11] Government expanded on all cylinders, and in the 1960s and 1970s university graduates flocked to government departments and agencies, eager to make a difference.

Today, political leaders have a vastly different take on the role of government. We no longer hear about a Just Society. Rather, political leaders talk about downsizing or managing government operations more efficiently. Britain's David Cameron argues, "Public services should be open to a range of providers competing to offer a better service. Of course, there are some areas, like national security services or the judiciary, where this wouldn't make sense. But everywhere else should be open to real diversity. This is a transformation. It ends the state's monopoly over public services. Instead of having to justify why it makes sense to introduce competition in individual public services – as we are now doing with schools and in the NHS – the state will have to justify why it should ever operate a monopoly."[12] Accordingly, there are functions that belong to the public sector not because government is better at delivering them but rather because it would not make sense to have others responsible for them.

Those who think that only right-of-centre politicians have turned on the public sector should think again. Jean Chrétien, Bill Clinton, and Tony Blair, among others, echoed the views of their predecessors, right-of-centre politicians, on the superiority of private sector management practices. Tony Blair, for example, said, "Some parts of the public sector were not as efficient, dynamic and effective as the private sector."[13] It poses the questions, What parts are governments not very good at and why are governments still in them? How do we know and what can be done about it? It may be that left-of-centre politicians held this discourse to defend the public sector in a political culture that is vehemently anti-government.[14]

To be sure, the private sector holds considerable appeal when compared to the public sector. It knows better how to downsize, how to measure performance, how to compete, and how to innovate. Private sector firms know that they have to focus on a bottom line or die. Harrison McCain, who, together with his brother, built a multi-billion-dollar frozen food empire from scratch, often argued that "if you cannot measure it, you cannot manage it."[15] It is possible and often relatively straightforward to measure performance in the private sector. The *Globe and Mail*, for example, regularly ranks Canada's most profitable companies, simply by measuring their after-tax profits, excluding extraordinary gains or loses.[16] Try that for size in the public sector. The public sector houses ambiguity in terms of goals, responsibilities, and relationships that are difficult, if not impossible, to measure.

Values associated with the private sector include managing risk, competitiveness, personal accountability, individual performance, and close attention to outcomes. By contrast, public sector values include impartiality, honesty, loyalty, risk-aversion, probity, equity, hierarchy, integrity, accountability, and fairness. Public servants are expected to accept the legitimacy of political structure and be committed to implementing policy or major initiatives without reference to their own views. That, at least, is the theory. They are also expected to operate within a complex and at times contradictory set of loyalties to their departments, central agencies, political leaders, country, citizens, institution, statutes, and constitution. The public sector manager is expected to pursue the public interest or the public good, however defined, in contrast to the private sector manager, who is expected to deliver a return on shareholders' investment. Given this, is it fair to compare the performance of the two sectors?

Public opinion surveys reveal that only one in three Canadians trusts the government of Canada, only 30 per cent believe that the federal government is doing enough to improve its operations, and 50 per cent believe that the ethical standards of the federal public service have slipped in recent years.[17] Canadians also believe that public servants have less influence in shaping policies than in years past.[18] Trust in political institutions does not fare better. Indeed, trust in the Canadian Parliament and members of Parliament is among the lowest of some twenty-six countries surveyed, and we have also seen a twenty-point drop in democratic satisfaction in Canada over an eight-year period. We have reached the point where only 55 per cent of Canadians report being satisfied with the way their democratic institutions work, down from 75 per cent in 2004.[19]

Signs that Canadians are not satisfied with government are everywhere. During the first week of January 2014, the leading newspaper in my province, a slow-growth province, ran a front-page article above the fold with the headline "Think-tank: Grow Economy by Shrinking Government," and ran an editorial, "The Case for Less Government." On the very same day, the Toronto *Globe and Mail* ran two articles: "Time to Renew Canada's Cowed Bloated Bureaucracy" and "Audit Takes Transport Canada to Task on Wasteful Spending."[20]

Canadians can take some comfort in that things are not different in other Western countries. The challenges for governments appear to be the same everywhere but particularly so in Anglo-America democracies: trust in government has been in sharp decline in recent years, as has voter turnout, fewer and fewer citizens believe that their national governments have the consent of the governed, and public servants are perceived to be overpaid and inefficient.[21] The challenges are clear but solutions less so. Consumers can always take their business elsewhere when they are not satisfied with the product, as BlackBerry quickly discovered. However, as Peter H. Schuck puts it, "Discontented citizens are stuck with the government they have."[22]

So what happened? Why has the public sector fallen on such hard times? Why has bureaucracy-bashing been on the rise in Anglo-American democracies for the past thirty years or so? There is no shortage of answers. Gavin Newsom maintains that "in the private sector and in our personal lives, absolutely everything has changed over the past decade. In government, very little has."[23] The argument goes that the public sector is top-down, producer-centred, while the private sector is bottom-up, consumer-driven: hence the latter is more open to innovation and change.

People also increasingly tend to divide the world into taxpayers and tax-eaters. Tax-eaters are the undisciplined politicians and bureaucrats. The thinking is that politicians are interested only in the short term and doing what is politically necessary to win the next election. There is also a widely held view that there are too many bureaucrats for the work at hand, with the result that, in the opinion of some observers, we have too many government regulations, too many programs, and too much government spending. It appears that at least some public servants agree. One senior government official told me that he manages his department as if it were a business and so cuts in spending and staffs have to be implemented "just like in the private sector."[24]

It was not always thus. The public service in Anglo-American democracies enjoyed a golden age – or at least an age a good deal more golden than it does now. I have argued elsewhere that the Canadian public service did indeed have a golden age of sorts in the mid-twentieth century, when it was held in high esteem and its work was valued by both politicians and the public.[25]

Others have made the same observation with regard to other countries. Barry J. O'Toole writes that in Britain "there was an ideal of public service; and, however imperfect from the perspective of the actual world, this acted as a guide to public servants." He adds that, from the postwar period up until the 1960s, most "had a genuine desire to be good public servants. In this they largely had the trust of their ministers, each of whom, as the personification of the department in which the civil servants worked, relied on their loyalty and support. This relationship was mutually beneficial: civil servants remained largely anonymous, and thus able to be free and frank in their advice; ministers could reject and accept that advice and take either the credit or blame for its fruit. The effect was one of collegiality and mutual respect."[26] Coincidentally or not, I, and others, have noted the same for the same period in Canada.[27]

But what about the private sector? Again, the perception persists that the private sector is both more dynamic and more successful at whatever it attempts than is the public sector and that governments should look to the business community for inspiration. This has been the dominant political narrative since the early 1980s. The *Economist* magazine encapsulated the situation when it reported, "Most politicians now believe that businesses are better than bureaucracies at generating growth. Prime ministers and finance ministers flock to Davos not to lay down the law to businesspeople but to court their favour."[28]

The worst criticism one can throw at an organization is to label it bureaucratic. When a group of university students tried to leave the Canadian Federation of Students, the media, after consulting the students, said the organization was "an out-of-touch, money-squandering bureaucracy."[29] Government bureaucracy has few friends these days.[30]

Britain's David Cameron promised in February 2011 to deliver "a public sector revolution" by turning to the private sector for solutions.[31] Margaret Thatcher had of course made precisely this commitment over thirty years earlier.[32] In fact, the private sector may well at the moment be enjoying its own golden age.

This is so, despite the many bad calls made by large businesses of late and growing income disparity. There was the BP oil fiasco, the 2008 financial meltdown, and the SNC-Lavalin scandal, there was the North American automobile industry going to government cap-in-hand in order to survive, the tragically flawed opinions of major private sector agencies and accountancy firms in the United State on the banking industry's financial health, and the list goes on.[33] It is quite revealing that 64 per cent of Americans thought in 2011 that big government was the biggest threat to their country's future while only 26 per cent identified big business – this, only three years after the economic meltdown.[34] Much has also been written about a worrying shift in wealth away from the middle class.[35] Still, the political narrative is that the public sector is in worse shape. It may well be that the private sector's golden moment is due less to its accomplishments and more to the failings of the public sector.

Again, it has not always been thus. Government in Western democracies demonstrated that it could lead and accomplish great things, as they did during the Second World War. The public sector had to enjoy considerable public support over the past fifty years, since public spending rose from 27 per cent of GDP to 46 per cent over the last century in OECD countries.[36]

Think back to the day in 1961 when President John F. Kennedy laid down a daunting goal for the nation: "I believe that this nation should commit itself to achieving the goal, before this decade is out, of landing a man on the moon and returning him safely to the earth."[37] Contrast that with President Obama's commitment to reform health-care coverage, making it an important theme of his 2008 and 2012 election campaigns.[38] In November 2013 Obama "apologized" to the American people for the serious flaws in implementing the reforms.[39] Kennedy promised Americans the moon and delivered, while Obama promised health-care reform and could not deliver on time.

This is not to suggest that governments have not tried to fix things. The United States government sought to reinvent itself under Al Gore, while Britain has, since the Thatcher days, launched one reform measure after another, and the government of Canada, among other initiatives, introduced *La Relève*, the 1994–97 program review exercise and the multifaceted accountability reform act (circa 2006). In brief, politicians in Anglo-American democracies have, over the past thirty-five years, sought to dress the public sector to look like the private sector. This, in turn, has given rise to new accountability and transparency requirements.

In response, blame-avoidance has become an important part of the decision-making process in the public sector. Managing blame-avoidance has also shifted the locus of decision-making. Heads of government and their advisors now dominate government to a much greater extent than they did forty years ago. The thinking is that, to be successful in the era of a twenty-four-hour news cycle and the social media, it is important not to have government departments and agencies run off in different directions with their own narratives. The influence of heads of governments and their advisors today extends to virtually all facets of government operations, well beyond simply shaping new policies. On the face of it, at least, one sees a contradiction. Governing from the centre does not easily square with attempts to make the public sector look like the private sector, where the empowerment of managers is highly valued.[40]

At the risk of repetition, the great majority of the public sector reforms introduced in Anglo-American countries since the 1980s borrowed heavily from the private sector.[41] They were all introduced with the promise of finally fixing government. None have lived up to expectations.[42] This has served to make the public sector look weaker still, when compared to the private sector. Reform in private firms succeeds or the firm suffers consequences in the marketplace.

Notwithstanding the many attempts to dress the public sector to look like the private sector, the fundamental differences between the two sectors have remained intact. One can easily distinguish the public from the private sector by looking at ownership, source of financial resources, and model of control and accountability. The question is, can the public sector operate like the private sector without altering the predominant criteria distinguishing public organizations from private ones?[43] I think not.

At the same time as attempts were underway to make the public sector look like the private sector, new oversight bodies appeared, as did a more aggressive twenty-four-hour news media. The phenomenal rise of social media, a better-educated population, and public-private partnership arrangements have all had a profound impact on the public sector. It may not have brought about the kind of change that some had hoped for, and it may not have been successful in making the public sector operate like the private sector, but it has generated change. It is wrong to argue that "very little has" changed in the public sector, even though the changes may not have had the kind of positive impact that public sector managers and others wanted.

There have been three broad phases in the development of the machinery of government in much of the Western world. The first phase was designed to develop a country's basic infrastructure, from roads to canals to the post office.[44] Keynesian economics, the desire to smooth out demands in the economy, and the willingness to intervene in many sectors gave rise to the second phase. We are currently living the third phase as governments are trying, with mixed results, to rationalize their operations and deal with stubborn deficits and growing debt.[45]

There are very few sectors in which the government of Canada is not an active player. It has carved out a role for itself in health care, social services, and education, through transfer payments. Among other things, it manages an elaborate regulatory regime, issues passports, incarcerates prisoners, and even operates the CN Tower at a profit in downtown Toronto, declared by the American Society of Engineers to be one of the modern seven wonders of the world.[46]

We have seen in recent years numerous studies on the rise of the New Public Management (NPM), on the self-interest of politicians and public servants in understanding how government decides, and on the challenges in motivating one party to work in the best interest of the other.[47] We have not, however, seen much on the question, what is government good at?

It is odd, given the ubiquitous role of government in society, that so few students of government have taken an interest in assessing what government is good at. I maintain that understanding what government is good at and conversely what it is not good at should be the basis for good public policy. Yet our political and public policy debates, for the most part, are concerned with what – if anything – governments should do about problems in our society. They very rarely stop to ask, what is government good at? It may well be that the reason we lack an adequate theory of what government is good at is that government itself has become so unattractive in the eyes of many observers, including politicians, even those on the government side.[48]

Understanding what government is good at – and how it may become better at it – is the responsibility of policy-makers. It is, however, also the responsibility of citizens to ensure that their government is as good as it can be in shaping policies and delivering programs and services.

There are several reasons why the public sector has fallen on hard times. I argue that government is no longer as able to define the broader public interest as it once could or as accessible to the average citizen as it once was. Political and economic elites dominate when new policies are struck and major initiatives are planned. Those with the resources can pursue their agenda before the courts or with the assistance of lobbyists and dedicated associations and organized interest groups.

Things are even more difficult when it comes to implementation. In government, notwithstanding over thirty years of efforts to dress the public sector to look like the private sector, implementation remains a poor cousin. In business, implementation is key to success. In government, as we shall see, the fault-line theory prevails, and that makes implementation uncertain.

In business, establishing strategic direction is the responsibility of a few, but implementation is the responsibility of everyone.[49] In government, establishing policies and shaping new initiatives is the responsibility of a few operating above the fault line, while those below the line, perceived as the less gifted, are responsible for implementation. In business, senior executives in successful firms constantly assess their organization's capabilities to deliver an ambitious strategy. In government, those with the power and influence – the prime minister and his courtiers – are much too busy navigating a politically volatile environment and managing the blame game to focus on the organization's capabilities below the fault line. There are also too many constraints inhibiting the ability of political and public service leaders to assess the organization's capacity to deliver and do much about the shortcomings.

THE QUESTIONS

I set out to answer a number of questions, all designed to help us understand better what government is good at. How do national political institutions define the common interest? Has it been possible to reconcile governing from the centre and blame-avoidance with new public management measures? Have efforts to make the public sector look like the private sector been successful? How have governments been able to reconcile New Public Management measures with new accountability and oversight requirements? How can we explain the growth of citizen disenchantment with government over the past thirty years? Is the disenchantment tied to failing government performance? How do governments know if their activities have been successful? Were governments in Western democracies better at getting things done fifty years ago than they are today? If so, why? Answers to these questions feed into the central question that permeates this book: what is government good at – or put in another way, not good at?

Peter Drucker went to the heart of the matter when he wrote, "We do not have a theory of what government can do. All political theory, from Locke on through the *Federalist Papers* and down to the articles by today's liberals and conservatives deal with the process of government, with constitutions, with power and its limitations, with methods and organizations. None asks what the proper functions of government might be and could be. None asks what results government should be held accountable for."[50] Drucker concluded that the state "has not delivered" and that the various efforts to "reinvent government" have failed. He explained, "Able people are getting nowhere fast because their basic approach is wrong. They are trying to patch and to patch and to spot – well, here, there, and yonder – and that never accomplished anything."[51] If patching does not work, what does?

This book avers that the various reforms of the past thirty-five years have essentially overlooked the important question, what is government good at? To be sure, the question is not an easy one to answer. At the conference on public spending I refer to in the preface to this book, I asked a number of participants why we did not have an answer. One said, "Because it is not answerable," while another maintained that "political ideology always answers that question," and yet another threw it back in my lap: "Go for it, you have my best wishes!"[52] Political ideology is, of course, an important guide in deciding what government should be doing, but it is of limited value in answering what government is good at.

I had much less difficulty getting answers to my questions from friends and acquaintances in my community in eastern Canada, a region long associated with government intervention. A businessman said, "That's easy. Government is good at spending money," and another said, "Why bother answering the question? Government officials are not interested in answers." Meanwhile, a well-known Canadian journalist maintained, "The problem with democracy? It's biased toward the incompetent."[53] A leading local businessman suggested that I should ask, "What is government *not* good at? – it would be a much longer book."[54] Another, from Prince Edward Island, had a similar take. He said, "Jeez, that is going to be a very short book."[55] Others, however, thought differently. One said, "Government has to be good at something. Can you imagine a society without government? Think of Somalia."[56]

My questions would have drawn a far different response had I asked them when I first became interested in public administration in the 1970s. Harrison McCain, a leading entrepreneur of his generation, for example, often spoke out in favour of a strong role for government in society, and he hired senior public servants to occupy executive positions in his firm.[57]

When I put the question to actual players, former Canadian prime minister Jean Chrétien said, "You can start from the premise that government can be a force for good. That's my position. Others on the right of the political spectrum have a different view. I can give you many, many examples where government became an instrument for the good. But an instrument to do good can wear out. Government is good at coming up with instruments to do good. Government is not as good at deciding that the instrument has done the job and when it should be done away with."[58]

I also put my questions to Ed Clark, one of Canada's business leaders of the past twenty years and a highly respected former senior public servant. His response: "Government should focus on putting in place the right policy framework. Government is not very good at operations, at delivering programs, and there are reasons for this."[59] I discuss these reasons more fully later as I seek to answer the question, what is it that government is good at?

This book offers both a diagnostic and prescriptive perspective. It argues:

- Society and politics have changed to the point that they have knocked public administration off its moorings. The changes are forcing us to re-examine what government is good at, even asking if good government is still possible with the existing machinery of government.
- The perception, if not the reality, is that the public sector is no longer able to express the public interest as well as it once could and is now left to manage conflicts between factions or interest groups. This favours the more powerful in society.
- Governments, since the 1940s, have simply added one activity on top of another without asking, what is it that government is good at?

- Various public sector reforms have made government less capable of delivering programs and services by bringing new problems and a wide array of new activities to government operations.
- There are areas where government has to play a direct role, whether it is good at it or not.
- There are also areas where it can never be as efficient as the private sector. Citizens need to recognize this.
- There has been a shift from accountability based on procedures to one based on performance in the public sector, a shift that has made governing more difficult and the public sector less efficient.
- The public sector, as currently organized, is incapable of dealing with an overload problem, and some of its institutions can never measure up when compared with private sector firms.
- The machinery of government was not designed to cope with today's complex policy environment and demanding transparency requirements.
- To those inside, particularly where it matters increasingly in central agencies and in the Prime Minister's Office (PMO), government is 90 per cent ideas and 10 per cent implementation. To those outside, government should be 90 per cent implementation and 10 per cent ideas.
- There is a fault line in government that separates those responsible for generating new policies and managing the blame game from those responsible for implementation. This explains, at least in part, why government is not as good as it once was in delivering programs and services.

OUTLINE OF THE STUDY

I have divided the book into three parts. Part One provides the context within which we seek to answer the question, what is government good at? We explore the context in which the government of Canada has operated over the past seventy years. It has evolved greatly during this period and has made it more difficult for government, not only to perform but also to establish the common good. The demands on politicians, the new media, the age of transparency, the changing role of religion in our communities, the rise of interest groups, a more active court, and a better informed public – among other developments – have had a profound impact on government and on governing.

We look at how our political and administrative institutions now operate, the various efforts to modernize government operations, and at new accountability requirements. We look inside government bureaucracy to see how it decides and what truly matters at different levels of the public service. We explore the growing influence of the judiciary, not only on government policy but also on operations.

We review how two government agencies, with which I have had a close association, operate in order to explore further what matters to politicians and to public servants. The objective is to shed more light on how the government's expenditure budget takes shape and how and why management decisions are struck in government. We also assess recent reform measures to the government's regulatory regime against our central question: what is government good at?

In Parts One and Two, I draw on the literature, on my earlier work in public administration and economic development, on my own experience as a senior public servant with the government of Canada, and as an advisor to federal and provincial governments and abroad. I also consulted a limited number of officials, and I identify them in the endnotes.

In Part Three we seek to provide answers to the central question – what is government good at? – from a Canadian perspective. Though we draw from British, American, and Canadian literature and look to some provincial governments in the study, the focus is on the government of Canada. We also do not address what markets are good at – clearly an important question in understanding better what government is good at in comparison with the private sector.

There are things that governments do and have to continue to do, whether they are good at it or not. But the role of government has expanded considerably beyond these activities. How government decides has also evolved considerably in recent years, and this in turn has wide implications on the ability of government to deal with citizens. The argument is that government is not as good as it once was in designing policies and in implementing them. The government is also not as good as it needs to be in dealing with citizens. The requirements of contemporary politics and deficiencies in public administration explain in large measure why government is not as good as it once was or needs to be in several areas if it is to enjoy the support of citizens.

PART ONE

The Context

From Parish Picnics to Facebook

I grew up in a hamlet some thirty miles north of Moncton, in a relatively small village, even by Canadian standards. Good Catholics, we attended mass every Sunday, never ate meat on Friday, and partook in prayers every evening in May at the local chapel to celebrate the Virgin Mary. We made sacrifices throughout the four-week Advent period before Christmas and again during the six weeks of Lent before Easter.

Every Sunday at mass, I stared at a fresco on the church ceiling. The fresco depicted hell, with the devil standing tall over a raging fire, where tormented souls were reaching out in agony. He had sharp horns, was burning red, and had a long rat-like tail. He also had a metal pitchfork, which, for some reason, never melted. The devil happily employed his pitchfork to push souls back in the fire. The souls were doomed for eternity, and here was the evidence. The priest often talked about hell. I believed in hell then, and, as far as I could tell, so did everyone else in the community.

No matter how hard one tried, one could not hide from God or the devil. I remember well the first page in our catechism, where a large All-Seeing Eye stood in the middle of a triangle. The triangle represented the Father, the Son, and the Holy Spirit, while the Eye was the eternal watchfulness of God. You could lie to yourself or to others but never to God, who saw your every move and even knew your every thought. The one certain way to avoid hell was to attend church, pray often, avoid all occasions of temptation, and confess your sins. I recall well going into a small dark closet-like room to confess my sins. I resolved at a very young age that I would not go to hell. Time will tell.

The church was much more explicit about hell than it was about heaven. Those who went to hell would suffer physical, mental, and spiritual pain for eternity, more pain than anyone could possibly imagine. Government authorities considered the threat of hell to be an asset in helping to reduce crime and in promoting a more obedient society, one of many links between organized religion and government. In fact, history tells us that, as fear of hell declined, the role of governments expanded.[1] Government officials had considered hell to be a particularly powerful deterrent against crime, and as belief in hell fell away, more statutes and more legal penalties were introduced.

There is evidence to suggest that private firms located in regions where residents are still religious are also more ethical and less likely to withhold bad information from shareholders, thus having to restate their financial reports at a later date. One author of a study on the subject reports that unethical behaviour is frowned upon in these communities, and "the more religious the milieu you are in, probably the greater the cost in terms of social stigma."[2] Both the public and private sectors thus have an interest in having citizens and clients believe in the tortures of hell.

It is hardly possible to overstate the power of the parish priest some forty years ago – he was to be obeyed always, never to be questioned. He lorded over a tight-knit community where everyone, generation after generation, knew his or her place. For the most part, people left life not much better off than when they entered it. All families in my community were frugal because they had to be. It was not a choice. The community lived within itself, and many families grew their own food.

Neighbours helped neighbours to the extent they could, and extended families looked after family members. I recall visiting a relative crippled by polio, unable to leave his bed. His family looked after him with no government help. For the family, it was the right thing to do. The parish would help the poor with food and shelter and organized a summer picnic to raise money. Almost everyone in the parish attended the picnic, paid a very modest entrance fee, and paid to play various games or to purchase trinkets. Nuns ran the local hospital on a shoestring. They took care of the sick, even if they could not afford hospital care.

Volunteer work was part of the community culture. I recall my mother knocking on doors, asking for financial contributions, however modest, to help La Société Nationale des Acadiens (SNA). The organization's goal was to promote the interests of Acadians, before anyone who would listen, including governments.

The federal government, and even the provincial government, was far removed from our community – but politics was not. The local MP and member of the Legislative Assembly were highly respected. Politicians were warmly welcomed when they came to our community. Residents had their favourite political party, of course, and were not always impressed by what some politicians had to say. But elected politicians enjoyed a status of sorts in our community, and many people would turn out at meetings to hear them speak.

Today, things are vastly different. The last parish picnic in the hamlet where I was born was held some thirty years ago. Church attendance is down, the priest has lost credibility and influence, the fresco on the church ceiling is no longer there, special-care homes take care of senior citizens and the disabled, and no one goes door-to-door raising money for the SNA. Nor do politicians enjoy the standing that they once did.

The parish summer picnic gave way to government programs. The small village chapel was torn down at about the same time that the parish priest was asked to look after several other parishes. Priests no longer command much respect in the community. The debate around the Roman Catholic Church in my community, as elsewhere, today centres on past sexual transgressions of parish priests.[3] Nuns no longer operate hospitals, and in fact few are now to be seen anywhere. The small hamlet I grew up in has lost over half its population in recent years.

Today, the Roman Catholic Church is in crisis. The *National Catholic Reporter* described it as "the largest institutional crisis in centuries, possibly in church history." In the United States, church membership continues to fall (400,000 alone in one year), the number of priests dropped from 49,000 to 40,000 between 1995 and 2010, and more than 1,000 parishes have closed during the same period.[4] As I was working on this book, the Roman Catholic Church in my province declared that it could no longer maintain all its churches and was turning to the government for funds, making the case that the churches had some heritage value and that government should lend a helping hand.[5]

The Roman Catholic Church, however, is hardly alone in dwindling membership. The United Church, the largest Protestant denomination in Canada, has been closing one church every week in recent years, and the Anglican Church is "hemorrhaging members."[6] Before 1971, fewer than 1 per cent of Canadians ticked the "no religion" box on national surveys. However, two generations later, 23 per cent report that they are not religious.[7] Canada continues to make the transition from religion to secularization. For many, rewards are no longer in the next life. This has far-reaching implications for civil society, for the role of government, and for a willingness of citizens to pursue a common or collective interest.

Growing up in a small rural hamlet and later in a mid-size city, my classmates lived with two parents at home. The father of one of my friends worked as a mechanic, another as a bus driver, another had a taxi and yet another was a carpenter. My father had a small business. Few families I knew experienced serious poverty. Fathers and some of the mothers of my friends had permanent jobs. Single-parent families were rare. Today, nearly 20 per cent of children live in single-parent families.[8]

All my friends expected to surpass their parents in education and in careers, as did their parents, who saw education as the road to better jobs for their children. Looking back, all my friends did go to university and all surpassed their parents in career attainment.

We all participated in church activities. We also all believed that education was the key to success and that tomorrow's economy would be better than today's. Everyone expected a steady job after graduation, and that proved to be the case. Government was viewed as a force for good and many wanted to join its ranks. Many did. Friends and families visited one another regularly and stayed in touch by telephone. Community organizations, in addition to the church, were visible and helped the less fortunate in society. I recall friends and family members joining the Rotary and Lions Clubs and Le Club Richelieu. If all of the above are key building blocks for greater social cohesion, then we had it.

The purpose of this chapter is to take stock of civil society and its impact on the public sector. Robert Putnam put social capital on the political agenda in the United States with his book *Bowling Alone*. Neil Nevitte did the same in Canada.[9] Both books discuss the substantial decline of social capital since the 1950s and maintain that this development undermines the kind of civil engagement needed for a strong democratic culture and for securing support for pursuing the common good. Putnam maintains that social capital contributes to democracy by creating "community bonds that keep individuals from falling prey to extremist groups" and by providing a forum "for thoughtful deliberations over vital public issues."[10]

Putnam provides a long list of indicators that document the sharp decline in civil society between the 1960s and 1990s: attendance at a public meeting down 35 per cent; serving on a local service committee down 39 per cent; member of parent-teacher associations down 61 per cent; and membership in men's bowling leagues down 40 per cent while the number of individual bowlers rose by 10 per cent between 1980 and 1993, hence the title of his book. His point is that people are increasingly disconnected from both one another and their community.[11] Niall Ferguson, among others, has also lamented the further decline of civil society since Putnam published *Bowling Alone* in 2000.[12]

FROM RELIGION TO GOVERNMENT

Religion and politics are only partially separated. One does not have to speculate for very long, for example, to conclude that Canadian values that gave rise to the call for a Just Society in the 1960s derived from Judeo-Christian sources. As R. Johnstone explains, "Inasmuch as both religion and politics are social institutions and consist of subgroups, norms, and people, they interact with one another; they sometimes overlap in their functions; they often involve the same people; they seek commitment and involvement from the same people."[13] Church leaders of yesteryear may have become the political leaders of today, but they are not driven by the same goals, values, and culture. The church is concerned with spiritual matters and government with earthly things.

As the Roman Catholic Church began to withdraw from providing health care and social services in my community, the public sector expanded, or perhaps it was the other way around. Indeed, in Canada, both senior levels of government introduced program after program to deal with all manner of socio-economic challenges. Families no longer have to look to their own resources or to the church to care for family members who cannot function in society. They can now turn to government programs. The SNA is now essentially a state-sponsored organization. In fact, there are now two state-sponsored Acadian advocacy groups – the SNA and La Société de l'Acadie du Nouveau-Brunswick (SANB).

Among many other initiatives introduced between the 1950s and the 1980s, the Canadian government decided to strengthen francophone communities outside Quebec by turning local associations into pressure groups, by financing them to pursue all kinds of endeavours, and by supporting groups representing virtually every segment of Acadian society. Thus began the governmentalization of the Acadian movement. Volunteerism, for the most part, gave way to paid advocacy. "Have federal funds, will travel" gave rise to parallel bureaucracies at home, staffed by Acadians but funded by Ottawa. A colleague at the Université de Moncton recently observed that the federal government now supports directly or indirectly some 300 francophone associations or events outside Quebec, though in some cases the funding is very modest.[14]

Acadian associations soon began to exhibit some of the same characteristics as government bureaucracies. Protecting their own turf and expanding their expenditure budgets became important, and they learned that one does not bite the hand that feeds them. They challenged government policies, but only up to a point. Martin Normand, who has carried out several studies in the sector, maintains that the associations are reluctant to admit that their funding comes from government and are also hesitant to criticize government departments for fear of losing their source of funding.[15] The associations became, however, as expected, more assertive and demanded better government services in both official languages. But then what? What do you do with advocacy associations after they have served their initial purpose?

I don't mean to suggest that the SNA, the SANB, or other associations have not had a positive impact or that there are no longer challenges confronting Acadians and their society. They have had an impact and continue to have one. To be sure, government programs played an important role in the Acadian renaissance, especially in its early years. You can't throw millions of government dollars at associations or causes without having some impact. The point, however, is that Acadians, no less than others in society, can become overly dependent on government programs. Why worry about language rights, promoting economic development, or an education strategy when there are people paid to do that? We now have government programs, lawyers, some even paid by the government, and the courts doing what volunteers once did. As many have argued, there is a strong link between volunteerism and social capital, and the link appears weaker today than forty-fifty years ago.[16]

Governmentalization is hardly limited to Acadian associations. It is evident in many communities. A veteran advocate of Aboriginal interests reports, "In many instances the administrative structure and functions adopted by Aboriginal communities, both at the local and regional levels, replicate structures within Aboriginal Affairs and Northern Development Canada."[17] The government has been able to export its organizational model to non-government groups with mixed results.

The above raises other important questions about government. Have governments created an overload problem? Do they ponder how best to deliver initiatives as they plan them? What has happened to civil society? What impact have social media had on civil society and on government?

OVERLOADING GOVERNMENT

Think back to when Pierre E. Trudeau was sworn in as Canada's fifteenth prime minister on 20 April 1968. He entered politics with a clear purpose – to keep Quebec in the Canadian family, to bring the constitution home, and to strengthen French Canada's presence from coast to coast. This, he was convinced, would strengthen national unity and make for a stronger Canada, the common good as he saw it. He was also able to secure a majority mandate to pursue these goals.

Trudeau and his advisors decided that one of the ways to achieve their goal was to turn minority-language associations into paid advocacy or pressure groups. Trudeau wanted English-speaking associations in Quebec and French-speaking ones outside Quebec to be more assertive and demand better government services in both official languages.[18]

If Trudeau's vision of a strong French Canada from coast to coast was to be given life, it required government intervention. Volunteers were not enough, nor would a simple call to citizens to strengthen the French-Canadian community from British Columbia to Newfoundland and Labrador. The solution was to develop new policies and new programs. This, in turn, would add units to government departments to assume new responsibilities – in this case, Secretary of State and, later, Canadian Heritage.

The policies and programs were not without political risks, and so they both required new political and administrative oversight.

Growth in departmental units and new spending in turn required a capacity in central agencies to monitor and assess the work of the new units. The prime minister and ministers were not to be outdone, and they too expanded their offices to ensure some level of political oversight was in place to protect their partisan political interests.

Provincial governments, meanwhile, were not about to be left on the outside looking in, as the federal government was defining a role for itself in their communities. They too established units to keep an eye on what the federal government was doing and, whenever necessary, negotiate agreements with Ottawa.[19] Thus, the machinery of government became thicker and decision-making much more complex.

Few at the time questioned the ability of the machinery of government to integrate new units and deliver new programs. They had no reason to do so. The government was in a growing mode and the public service had just lived through a golden age of sorts. Both the British and Canadian public services had had their best years in the post–Second World War period. Lord Wilson of Dinton, a former Cabinet secretary and head of the Home Civil Service in Britain, summed it up well when he wrote, "Though it would be wrong to glorify the mandarin period, their heyday was in the postwar years when the performance of the service was strong."[20]

By the end of the Second World War, the public's belief in the ability of government was high in Canada, Britain, and even the United States. Not only had the Allies won the war, but the governments had planned the war effort and run the economy very well indeed. Unemployment had fallen to zero and yet prices had been held down, at least when the goods were available. It became clear that national governments were able, in moments of crisis and when moved by an overriding goal, to lead their countries and accomplish great things. The concern now turned to the postwar economy, with many fearing that the end of the war would trigger a recession, if not another depression. However, the confidence of Canadians in the ability of government to lead and accomplish great things could not have been stronger.

The Canadian government presented a major policy paper to Parliament towards the end of the Second World War that was clearly Keynesian in outlook. It said that "the Government will be prepared, in periods where unemployment threatens, to incur deficits and increases in the national debt resulting from its employment and income policy ... in periods of buoyant employment and income, budget plans will call for surpluses."[21] When the war ended, everyone was prepared for measures to avoid a return to the Depression years. But the expected severe economic downturn did not materialize and the measures proved unnecessary. Still, the Canadian government was now convinced that it possessed a new arsenal of economic policies to achieve high employment and generally manage the economy.[22] If governments could successfully manage a war effort and avoid another economic depression, they could do almost anything. Adding programs and new units to the machinery of government was viewed as the easy part, because government departments and agencies had accomplished great things during the war years and in the postwar period.

The war years, if anything, only solidified Keynesian economics in government treasuries and growth in government programs. Keynes and a strong number of his disciples on both sides of the Atlantic served in key positions in government. Classical economists were on the defensive everywhere. They proved unable to come up with solutions for the expected postwar recession or to compete with the new intellectual force increasingly being felt on university campuses. Keynesian economists, meanwhile, did not hesitate to come forward with fresh thinking and take centre stage in government offices. They also did not hesitate to expand the role of government.

In Canada, Bob Bryce was promoting the message of Keynes's General Theory inside government. He had studied at the feet of Keynes while at Cambridge and had returned to Canada via Harvard, where he introduced Keynesian economics to both faculty and students.[23] Bryce went to work in the Department of Finance in October 1938 on the eve of the Munich crisis. He found the department very small, congenial, and preoccupied with routine tasks and financial and administrative details.[24] He discovered that "some limited policy work" was being done in the office of the deputy minister and by a handful of senior clerks (six in all) there and in the Treasury Board. This was about to change dramatically in both central agencies and line departments. Some thirty-five years later, there were 2,374 economists in the Canadian public service.[25]

Between the postwar period and the 1970s the government of Canada expanded in all sectors: units were added in line departments, new departments and agencies were created, new Crown corporations were established, and central agencies expanded. The government could be good at whatever it wanted to be and had the track record to prove it.

Governments in Canada were able to carve out new roles in every sector of the economy in this period. They introduced new programs in health care, social services, industrial development, the environment, post-secondary education, economic development, arts and culture, agriculture, fishery, regional economic development, and the list goes on.

Little, if any, thought was given on possible new organizational models or whether government was well suited to take on new responsibilities in all economic and social sectors. No one asked what government was good at because most felt that it had already established a track record to be good at whatever it tried. Indeed, policy-makers believed that no new activity or new government unit could possibly compare with the complexity of mounting a war effort or developing plans to avoid a depression.

Policy-makers overlooked the fact that the war effort constituted an all-consuming goal and at a time when government was a great deal smaller, when accountability and transparency requirements were at a minimum, and when the blame game had yet to fully kick in. The one thing government demonstrated was that it was very good at designing policies and delivering programs when it was pursuing a goal that had wide public support, at least in English Canada, and when there was a consensus on what needed to be done. Postwar economic plans were just that – plans. The anticipated severe recession or depression did not materialize and the plans remained on shelves.

But government grew and grew. As a proportion of gross domestic product (GDP), the combined expenditure of all three levels of government in Canada increased from 20 per cent in 1951 to 32.5 per cent in 1961 and again to 49 per cent in 1992. Over the past several years It has hovered near 45 per cent.[26] In addition, between 1947 and 1995, total government spending rose 114 per cent faster than did GDP.[27] In 1941 there were 49,709 federal public servants. The number grew to 180,325 in 1951, to 281,834 in 1961, to 382,775 in 1971 and to 427,093 in 2011.[28]

How it grew and what form departments and agencies would take were regarded as secondary issues. The less gifted would look after administrative matters and the details of the day, a pattern that continues to this day. The challenge for ambitious public servants was and remains tied to policy, to coming forward with innovative ideas and policy prescriptions, and identifying measures to meet the expectations of the prime minister, his close advisors, and the more senior ministers.

Public service leaders in Ottawa between the 1950s and late 1970s consistently made the point that working on policy always trumped working on administrative issues. Arthur Kroeger, a former deputy minister in several departments, made it clear: "General management, management with a capital M and management theory never interested me very much."[29] Gordon Robertson, described as the gold standard for clerk of the Privy Council, did not discuss management issues in his memoirs. He did, however, mention that administrative matters frequently left him insufficient time to deal with major policy issues.[30] Al Johnson, in his 1961 article, "The Role of the Deputy Minister," never once employed the word *management*. He wrote, "The role of the deputy minister is to make it possible for the minister and the cabinet to provide the best government of which they are capable – even better if either of them happens to be weak."[31] The dominant culture, among senior public servants and those aspiring to the senior ranks, was to focus on policy and on defining new measures and to leave management issues to the less ambitious and the less talented.

The point is that few were concerned about the machinery of government and how best to manage operations as government expanded on all cylinders. Again, government departments had performed very well in the past, and it was assumed that there was no reason why they should not continue to do so. Adding new departments and a multitude of units did not ring any alarm bells inside government. The administrative class, albeit with less prestige and salary, would look after human and financial resources, and all they had to do was follow centrally prescribed rules and regulations.

THE MACHINERY

All decisions, large and small, on machinery of government questions belong to the prime minister, and the Privy Council Office (PCO). PCO jealously guards this responsibility, no doubt in part because the prime minister prefers it that way. The PCO has also consistently protected the doctrine of ministerial responsibility. This, more than any other reason, has inhibited the development of new organizational forms or changes to the machinery of government. The doctrine ties all government activities to an overriding principle and to a minister.

We need to go back to Earl Grey to appreciate how the doctrine took shape and how it is applied. Grey described the "first principle of our system of government – the control of all branches of the administration by Parliament." As he explained, "All holders of permanent offices must be subordinate to some minister responsible to parliament."[32] Only the minister can speak for the department to the House, which in turn must look to the minister to secure answers about departmental policies and activities. Again, this ties everything to the minister. As Herman Finer explains in his classic essay, "Only the minister has views and takes action."[33]

One can appreciate why PCO officials would wish to guard the doctrine, given its central feature in the Westminster parliamentary system. That said, the doctrine has a lot to answer for in assembling government activities on top of one another and by inhibiting policy-makers from considering new approaches to machinery issues. The thinking was, and for the most part remains, to put in place solid policies and programs and the machinery will do as it's told.

Policy-makers counted on past successes for guidance on machinery of government issues as they pursued plans to expand the role of government. But the future would be vastly different from the past. For one thing, government was a much larger operation. For another, it would not be guided by an overriding goal in which every department, every agency and every public servant knew what was to be the central focus every day, as was the case during the war years.

Policy-makers could also look to religious organizations for guidance on how to structure the machinery of government. In some instances, government organizations would be assuming responsibilities that once belonged to the church. The church also influenced how government organization took shape. Like the church, especially the Roman Catholic Church, but other denominations as well, government organizations are autocratic, positions are established, and their responsibilities are laid down in written form. Much like the church and the military, hierarchy and a well-defined chain of command are key characteristics of the machinery of government.

WHAT IF THERE IS NO HELL?

The Roman Catholic Church, of which I remain a member, is nothing like its former self. As already noted, when I was growing up in the 1950s, the parish priest was master of his parish, commanding tremendous respect and power. The church ran things from education to health care and even, to some extent, the local economy. The church permeated most activities, commercial or otherwise, and had a tremendous hold on all of us. But that was then.

Today, things are vastly different. Indeed, only 32 per cent of Americans believe in hell as "an actual place of torment and suffering where peoples' souls go after death."[34] Less than a third of Canadians now believe that there is a hell.[35]

If there is no hell, then individuals should feel freer to set their own rules. Common rules are set by common institutions and should be respected by its members. If there is no hell, then religious institutions lose at least some of their standing in society, including their ability to establish common rules and make them stick. If religious institutions are in decline, so is their capacity for charitable work. Religious institutions did and, albeit to a much lesser extent, still do promote collective action, volunteer work, public goods provision, and stronger social bonds in communities.[36] But this too is changing. As Anthony Giddens argues, people increasingly see themselves as free to choose the convictions, beliefs, and practices they like. He writes that "even the most reliable authorities can be trusted only until further notice," and life today "offers multiple possibilities rather than fixed guidelines or expected action."[37]

Religion also provided a strong bond between economic classes, but that is less so today. Heaven and hell are the great equalizer.[38] I recall the priest in his Sunday sermons telling us that "it is easier for a camel to go through the eye of a needle than for a rich man to enter into the kingdom of heaven."[39] I actually felt sorry for the few highly successful businessmen in our community. How could one possibly want to sacrifice eternity for a few years of economic success on earth? The community believed that in the end everything would equal out, with the poor having a much greater chance of seeing heaven than the wealthy. There was no need to be cynical or even envious of the well-to-do because we believed that they would pay the ultimate price. But

if hell no longer exists, then it changes the equation. It no longer pays
to be poor and wait for heaven for one's reward.

Still, the owners of the local drugstore, the local restaurant, and the
local grocery store were small entrepreneurs from our community. We
saw them at church every Sunday. They gave to local charities and
helped community causes. Today, the owners are from away, operating
large nationals or multinationals. When they give to charities, like the
United Way, they do so in large urban centres where their head offices
are located. McDonald's has displaced the local restaurant owner,
Shoppers Drug Mart the local pharmacy owner, and Costco the local
merchant.

Even the local bank manager had a much stronger presence and
authority in the community thirty years ago. Today, virtually all decisions of significance are sent to the risk assessment centre at head
office for review and decision. Head office relies almost exclusively on
Equifax's formula to establish a credit score to arrive at decisions, with
the result that local bank managers have lost standing in the community.[40] It is one more factor making the point that social cohesion is
not as strong as it once was. And there are still other factors.

SOCIAL COHESION MATTERS

Social cohesion speaks to the bonds or the glue that holds society
together. The belief is that stronger social cohesion makes it easier to
identify and pursue the public interest and makes it easier for government to function. Strong social cohesion also leads to a more cohesive society, and a more cohesive society may well make society more
tolerant of government and government mistakes.[41]

Scores of new studies on social cohesion have been produced in
recent years, and new websites have been launched to debate the
issue. Indeed, social cohesion is getting such wide currency that even
the credit-rating agency Moody's is now looking at adding social cohesion to its rating of foreign debt.[42]

Though it is beyond the scope of this book to review all the
research on social capital, social cohesion, and civil society, the issue is
important for our purpose. If, as a leading Canadian columnist maintains, "everyone is in it for themselves," and if "the notion of altruistic
public service, which did in fact exist in a certain period of Canadian
history no longer does," then this has a bearing on what government

is good at.[43] If everyone is in it only for himself, then support for collective action, the hallmark of government responsibilities, will enjoy less popular backing. Thus, social cohesion and social capital should matter for both those inside government and those outside.

If social cohesion is on the decline and if even those inside government are in it for themselves, then government officials simply become other self-interested actors in society, unable to command the respect to rise above the fray to be the guardian of the public interest. We noted earlier that there was a golden age of sorts for the public service and national economies from the immediate postwar period to the 1970s. The same can be said about social cohesion and civil society, so one likely reinforced the other.

There is a link between social cohesion and how well political institutions and governments perform.[44] Kenneth Newton and Pippa Norris concluded, after reviewing data from seventeen countries included in the world surveys of 1980 and 1991, that "social trust can help build effective social and political institutions, which can help governments perform effectively."[45] Ralf Dahrendorf maintains that "a certain erosion of civil society has robbed democracy of its social base."[46]

There are many factors that shape social cohesion and, as noted, we now have a plethora of studies underlying the importance of social capital, social cohesion, and civil society to a well-functioning society.[47] For our purpose, we look at public participation, the growing divide between the rich and poor, volunteerism, and the rise of social media.

PUBLIC PARTICIPATION

Public participation is widely accepted as a key foundation of representative democracy.[48] The enthusiasm for participatory democracy in the 1960s and 1970s has waned, and now we increasingly hear about the "democratic deficit."[49] Processes designed to involve citizens in the policy- and decision-making process have never lived up to expectations. Howard Doughty summed it up well when he wrote, "It has been some time since the phrase participatory democracy was uttered in polite company. For many people of a certain age, however, the term evokes fond memories."[50]

There are several fundamental problems with public consultations. First, the perception, if not the reality, is that all too often the government already knows what it wants to do and the consultation process is just for show, a *bella figura* exercise. Second, special interest groups will invariably try to capture consultation processes to promote their own agenda. As the old saying goes, an organized minority will always beat a disorganized majority. Mancur Olson famously made the point that a leaderless mob is no match for an organized army.[51]

Other observers have also made the point that citizens do not have the wit, the will, or the time to govern themselves.[52] There is evidence to suggest that some citizens do not like politics and that they much prefer politicians to get on with what they are elected for, so that they can get on with their own lives. They view the role of politicians as looking after things in government and pursuing the public interest, though they are often disappointed at the outcome, which fuels dissatisfaction and cynicism.[53]

The most common and visible form of citizen participation is voting for representation. Max Weber and Joseph Schumpeter both concluded that citizen participation is limited essentially to selecting elites in competitive elections.[54] But even that process is not as robust as it once was. This may well explain why trust in the ability of elected politicians to articulate and pursue the public interest has declined in recent years throughout the Western world. As Russell Dalton explains, "Most Americans believed that one could trust the government to do what was right, that there were few dishonest people in government ... and that government was run for the benefit of all. These positive feelings remained relatively unchanged until the mid-1960s and then declined precipitously."[55] Dalton sees "the breadth of these patterns across nearly all advanced industrial democracies."[56]

EKOS Research, through extensive public opinion surveys in Canada, comes to the same conclusion as Dalton. It reports on the decline of trust in politicians "for the past forty years."[57] EKOS asked Canadians to rate their trust in some occupations in 2011. The result: 89 per cent said that they had "high level of trust" in nurses, 78 per cent in doctors, 76 per cent in teachers, 33 per cent in journalists and only 13 per cent in politicians – just slightly more than for bloggers, at 8 per cent.[58]

Voter turnout in Canada reflects the increased distrust of politicians. Elections Canada reports that, with only a few exceptions, voter turnout averaged about 75 per cent in the years after the Second World War. In contrast, there has been a prolonged downward trend since the 1972 general election (see figure 1). Elections Canada takes

Figure 1   Voting turnout in Canadian federal elections (1945–2000)

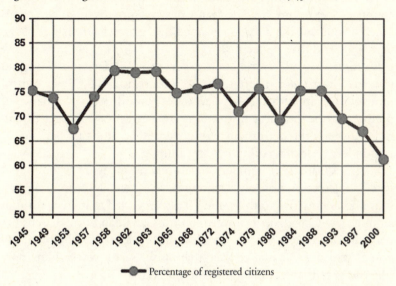

Percentage of registered citizens

Figure 2   Voting turnout in selected foreign countries

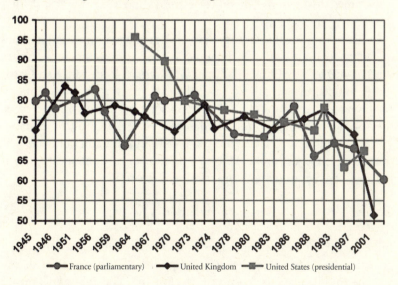

France (parliamentary)   United Kingdom   United States (presidential)

Source: *Explaining the Turnout Decline in Canadian Federal Elections: A New Survey of Non-voters* (Ottawa: Elections Canada, March 2003), 5.

comfort in noting that the same trend is evident in other Western countries (see figure 2). The trend has not improved since 2000.[59] Voter turnout in the 2004, 2006, 2008, and 2011 elections were 60.9, 64.7, 58.8, and 61.1 per cent.[60]

Elections Canada carried out a survey to understand the trend towards lower voter turnout. At the top of the list – 25 per cent of non-voters pointed to negative attitudes toward the performance of politicians and political institutions, 16 per cent had negative attitudes towards the performance of government, and 14.5 per cent of respondents felt that voting was "meaningless."[61]

Statistics Canada also undertook a study on the issue. It found that voter participation was lower among people aged eighteen to twenty-four and twenty-five to thirty-four. It also revealed that voter turnout among new Canadians is lower than for Canadian-born citizens (51 per cent versus 65 per cent). In addition, without providing a breakdown, Statistics Canada reported that public sector workers are more likely to vote than are private sector workers.[62]

Samara, a non-profit group that promotes citizen engagement in Canada, carried out eight focus groups of non-voters. It reports that non-voters "feel a sense of powerlessness" and that they think that they "can't effect change."[63]

Canadian political scientists have also produced important studies on voter turnout and the dynamics of election campaigns. André Blais, Neil Nevitte, Elisabeth Gidengil, Richard Johnston, Ken Carty, Jon Pammett, among others, have all, in one form or another, lamented low voter turnout and its impact on society. Among other factors, they tie the phenomenon to the democratic deficit and to the inability of government to articulate the public interest and generate support for it.[64] Others make the point that lower turnout speaks directly to low civil engagement and social cohesion.[65]

THE GROWING DIVIDE

In more recent years, politicians and observers have looked to the growing divide between the rich and poor and between the wealthy and the middle class to explain the decline in social cohesion. Former prime minister Paul Martin explains, "The ability for succeeding generations to do better than preceding generations is an essential part of the glue that makes democracy work. The gutting of the middle class is more than the canary in the coal mine. It essentially opens your society and your economy to all kinds of fissures."[66]

Princeton economist Alan Krueger speaks about the emerging "winner take all economy and its impact on society."[67] The result is that the middle class is shrinking. The reasons – globalization, a digital revolution, government cutbacks in social programs, reductions in pension plans, and good paying manufacturing jobs leaving for lower salary jurisdictions.

Canada has hardly been immune to this development. Inequality in income has grown faster in Canada than in all but one of the OECD countries. The concentration of income for the richest 1 per cent of Canadians amounted to 10.6 per cent in 2010, up from 7.1 per cent in 1987 with 20 per cent of Canadians now controlling 70 per cent of net worth.[68] Canada's top one hundred CEOs earned an average of $6.6 million in 2009, 155 times more than the average wage earner, up from 104 in 1998.[69]

Public policy has contributed to the growing income inequality by reducing taxes on income and capital gains. Across OECD countries, the personal tax rate dropped from about 66 per cent in 1981 to 41 per cent in 2008.[70]

As income inequality has grown, civil society organizations have weakened. There has been a drop in private sector unionized jobs. Today about 17 per cent of private sector jobs are unionized, compared to 21 per cent as recently as 1997 and about 30 per cent in the 1970s. Globalization and greater efficiency in the manufacturing and resources extraction sectors have not only eliminated hundreds of thousands of unionized jobs, they have also weakened the remaining private sector unions.[71] Private firms tell their workers that if they are to compete in the global economy, they are simply not able to support union jobs. Large global firms can shop jobs to low-wage countries such as China, where factory workers earned $1.74 an hour in 2009, about 10 per cent of North American factory workers.[72] The choice then is between a non-union job and no job.

Keith Banting and John Myles assembled an excellent collection of essays in 2013 on the growing income inequality in Canada and on the reasons for it. They singled out public policies, tax policies, globalization, little appetite for redistributive policies, and a weaker civil society, and concluded on a pessimistic note: "The cumulative message of the volume is that retrenchment has mattered but inaction has

mattered more. A critical part of the story has been the quiet indif-
ference to new social risks and rising inequality. Policy drift, living off
the policy accomplishments of an earlier generation, is not enough."[73]
The point is that the government's commitment to address income
inequality began to weaken at the same time as intellectual and political challenges emerged to the welfare state and the role of government in Western society.[74]

Politicians from all political parties are increasingly making commitments to growing the middle class as a means of dealing with income
inequalities. In doing so, they are reacting to what public opinion surveys are telling them: "Ten years ago, two-thirds of Canadians described
themselves as middle class while today it is just under half."[75] Justin
Trudeau made strengthening the middle class central to his political
agenda shortly after becoming leader of the Liberal Party, Thomas Mulcair, leader of the NDP, claims that his party is the one party that has and
continues to support the middle class, while Stephen Harper maintains
that his Conservative party, more than any other, speaks for the middle
class and its concerns.[76] He insists that only his Conservative party
speaks for the average Canadian, "the cab driver, the small business
owner, the farmers and office workers," not for elites.[77]

Though politicians from all political parties are talking about the
importance of the middle class to social cohesion, it is not at all clear
what they are proposing to do about it. The problem and solutions,
to the extent that they may exist, are likely to be found beyond Canada's borders. The challenges confronting the middle class are hardly a
Canada-only phenomenon. The work of Thomas Piketty and others
suggests that the growing income inequality is a global problem, and
potential solutions include a global tax on wealth and an annual tax
on stocks and bonds.[78] The taxes would inhibit the concentration of
wealth and the flow of income to capital. The catch – to be effective,
the taxes would have to apply in a multitude of countries, not just in
Canada. As is the case with many economic challenges, dealing with
the growing income inequality is beyond the reach of Canadian
politicians and political institutions, a reality that precious few Canadian politicians are prepared to explain to voters. The goal is to win
political power: making political promises and playing the blame
game offers far greater potential than trying to explain why the middle class is shrinking.

Whatever policy prescriptions one may apply to the challenge, many observers stress the importance of a strong middle class to social cohesion. The OECD, for example, underlined the importance of social cohesion and that of the middle class to long-term economic development and stability.[79] Studies also show that high levels of income inequality and the "missing middle class" reduce social cohesion and in turn lead to lower levels of social and political trust, making it more difficult for public institutions to function.[80] Social cohesion and volunteering encourage good citizenship and develop a belief in the social contract that underpins society and collective action.[81]

Social cohesion and public trust in public and private institutions suffered a "severe blow" in the aftermath of the 2008 global financial crisis. As Mark Carney, governor of the Bank of England, explains, "Bankers made enormous sums in the run-up to the crisis and were often well compensated after it hit. In turn, taxpayers picked up the tab for their failures. That unjust sharing of risk and reward contributed directly to inequality but – more importantly – has had a corrosive effect on the broader social fabric of which finance is part and on which it relies."[82] To the average citizen, economic elites have access to political, government, and other economic elites to push and pull the necessary levers to protect their interest.

VOLUNTEERISM

Volunteerism and giving to charities also contribute to social cohesion. Here again there has been a downward trend as well as a decline in trust between givers and charities. The level of trust in the people running charities in Canada had fallen to 71 per cent in 2013 from 80 per cent in 2000. One in four Canadians now reports being unsure that the charities are honest about their spending.[83] Fewer and fewer Canadians are giving to charities. From a high of about 30 per cent of Canadians giving to charities in the early 1990s, the proportion dropped to 23 per cent for 2011. These data are based not on public opinion surveys but on the number of taxpayers claiming charitable donation through income tax.[84]

Volunteerism is also on the decline in Canada. Canada lost 1 million volunteers between 1997 and 2000, or from 7.5 million to 6.5

million. Some observers believe that the decline in people attending church explains in part the decline of volunteers.[85]

In my home province, the Saint John ambulance service announced in the summer of 2013 that it could no longer provide first aid in the Moncton and Fredericton regions "due to a lack of volunteers." Ambulance New Brunswick, a government agency, was asked to expand at least some of its services to accommodate new demands.[86] No one asked whether government could be good at running an ambulance service. Because no volunteers were coming forward to assume responsibilities, people looked to government to do what no one else was prepared to do.

THE MEDIA

The rise of the social media has had an impact on social cohesion and politics. They fuel a fast-paced political environment, making it very difficult for journalists to gain the full knowledge and background to deal with complex issues and to inform citizens. Chris Waddell argues that this makes journalists focus on conflict or personalities rather than on more substantive issues. He writes that "assisted by new technologies" and "focussing on personalities and conflicts" have become the staple of "political reporting." This, he adds, "has helped to alienate the public from politics and public policy."[87]

The twenty-four-hour television news channels and social media have meant a revenue crisis for newspapers, resulting in shrinking newsrooms and fewer resources in trying to cope with more information. Dan McHardie, a veteran print and CBC journalist, writes that "before the emergence of the minute-by-minute online news cycle, a journalist would be assigned a story in the morning, attend a news conference, work sources throughout the day and produce a story for either the evening news or morning newspaper." Today, he adds, "a journalist at a major mainstream news organization will likely be expected to bring a BlackBerry or an iPhone to a news conference so they can send instant headlines out via Twitter, file short paragraphs to the organization's website, prepare radio or television hits that could go on cable networks or radio newscasts and then work on a longer story for the evening news or morning newspaper. There is an amazing pressure on journalists to get the story out accurately and quickly by whatever means necessary. The media and politicians now operate in a news cycle that has quickly become nasty, brutish and short."[88]

Some journalists also maintain that "BlackBerry journalism" has hardly been able to connect journalists to the pulse of the country – rather, it has had the opposite effect. Political spin specialists and journalists in the Ottawa bubble now trade gossip and political strategies with one another on Twitter or their smartphones. One journalist writes, "Instead of using technology to bridge the communications gap between voters in their communities and the media, the media has used it to turn its back on the public, forging closer links with the people reporters cover rather than with the people who used to read, watch, and listen to their reporting."[89]

Still others suggest that social media, most notably Twitter, Facebook, and political blogs, have also contributed to the rise of the permanent election campaigns. Politicians are now in continuous campaign mode and have woven together politics and government.[90] Political operatives are never at rest and now have the tools through social media to remain on the offensive round the clock. The "just visiting" negative ads against Michael Ignatieff ran outside of a national political campaign and they made their way into various broadcasts. They also proved to be effective. The new media tend to focus on personal conduct and personal conflicts rather than on more substantive policy issues. This, in turn, promotes a negative view of those serving in public life.

There is growing evidence that Canadians are turning to the Internet and social media rather than to traditional media for the news and also to communicate with one another.[91] A long-time media participant and observer, Elly Alboim, argues that social media have promoted "decoupling," with users increasingly living in their own isolated media bubbles.[92]

The traditional media have tried to adjust. It is worth quoting Alboim at length on this point.

Market forces are turning what was once a business with a sense of corporate responsibility, one that was providing a public good, into organizations driven by the bottom line that are providing a commodity within the context of an increasingly frail business model … The operative decision-making rules have editors deciding not what people need to know but what they want to know. There is no longer a concept of an overriding civic mandate. There are no "must-carry" stories … Journalists who work for mass media have moved from reporting and evaluating to trying to represent and empower their audience. They have understood that people are alienated and suspicious of most institutions and have begun to pander to those feelings both by reinforcing the reasons for alienation and suspicion and by acting as a voice for the alienated.[93]

People now get the news any time they want, either through the Internet or the social media. Social media have the added benefit of enabling citizens to interact directly with journalists and policy-makers. Ron Nessen, press secretary for President Gerald Ford, maintains that "the internet makes everybody a journalist. You sit at your computer, you type something that is true, not true, partially true, hit the button and it goes around the world. You can't stop that."[94] Former British prime minister Tony Blair took aim at the media in leaving office, declaring that they had turned into a "feral beast, just tearing people and reputations to bits."[95] Michael Ignatieff wrote, after stepping down as Liberal Party leader, "It never ceased to amaze me that the same people who would never have dared insult me to my face did not scruple to engage in the most imaginative kinds of slander in the disinhibited world of the blog and tweet."[96] In short, online news and many social media allow anonymous comments and attacks on individual politicians or policy orientations. Some journalists are questioning why there is one standard for identifying sources in news stories for the traditional media and another for online comments, which can be and often are diverse, offensive, and off-topic.[97]

No matter what is being said, politicians need to respond if the tweets or the observations should gain wide currency or if they are picked up by the mainstream media. Citizens expect quick responses to their questions or perspectives, putting enormous pressure on the machinery of government to react quickly and to get it right, which it was hardly designed to do, given its reliance on hierarchy.

This explains why politicians are able to react quickly to tweets but the machinery of government is much less so. Documents obtained through the Access to Information legislation reveal a high level of bureaucratic control on managing tweets and re-tweets. The documents show how teams of public servants frequently work for weeks to sanitize tweets in a medium that places a premium on spontaneity and informality. The Canadian Press reports that "most 140-character tweets issued by the department of Industry are planned weeks in advance; edited by dozens of public servants; reviewed and revised by the minister's staff; and sanitized through a 12-step protocol, the documents indicate." It adds, "Public servants vet draft tweets for hashtags, syntax, policy compliance, retweeting, French translation and other factors. Policy generally precludes tweeting on weekends, and the minister's personal Twitter handle must be kept out of departmental tweets, though his name and title are often included."[98] This speaks to a highly risk-averse bureaucracy coping as best it can in the era of permanent elections and a machinery of government that has difficulty adjusting to new developments outside of its comfort zone.

What about using social media to hold town hall meetings or to promote public consultations? In the absence of the church picnic, church service on Sunday morning, and social clubs, like the Rotary, the social media appear to fill the void. But they cannot perform the same function in the same manner. The difficulty is that social media enable special interest groups to organize and promote their own policy agenda. The debates can be polarizing and push the concerns of the majority of citizens to the side.[99] Social media also allow unfounded opinions to be voiced without fact-checking and force decision-makers to react to demands without waiting for all the facts. No matter, for politicians the view remains that if you cannot react quickly, you are not in command of the situation.

Social media have also strengthened the hand of the prime minister and his advisors in their attempt to control the government agenda. To control the message and the media spin become paramount in the blame-generating and blame-avoidance games. One faux pas, one major gaffe can push a dozen important success stories off the public agenda. David Frum suggests that if that "was true for politicians before the advent of smartphones, YouTube and Facebook, think how much more true it is today."[100]

All of this explains why the federal government recently issued a tender call seeking continuing "real time monitoring and analysis of social media content," with the potential supplier having the ability to "target key influencers found in blog commentary and social conversations." A keen observer of security and intelligence explains that this is another sign that "governments are working increasingly hard to control the political narrative and public discussions" through the social media and other means.[101] The blame-generating and blame-avoidance games require nothing less.

The PCO has taken the lead in managing the social media. It directed, as far back as 2011, all departments to provide it with their plans to deal with social media. The PCO is directing departments to make full use of social media to promote their initiatives and to monitor developments, but it is also keeping a close eye on departments to ensure that they do not go off their tracks and feed the blame-generating game. Already calls are being heard to have proper oversight procedures put in place to oversee the government's use of social media.[102]

THE POLITICAL ENVIRONMENT IS
ALSO MORE DIFFICULT

The immediate postwar period gave rise to a national consensus. The party structures at the national level in Canada may well have appeared to be frozen between 1935 and 1984, providing stability and an easy working relationship between politicians and public servants.[103] The Liberal Party held power for nearly forty-three of those forty-nine years. Quebec's quiet revolution was born only in the 1960s. Leaving aside the CCF (later the NDP), there was little difference between the two main political parties.

Canada was united by common values that flowed out of shared experiences of the Great Depression, the wartime effort, and the unexpected economic prosperity in the 1950s and 1960s. Notwithstanding a few missteps, national governments were able to manage the national economy well, and they could claim with some legitimacy to have created jobs and to have managed the economic and public finances well over two decades. The generation that lived through the Depression and the war effort had fresh memories of the demanding challenges of those years. Some had served overseas, some in wartime industries, all had to live with food rationing, and a large segment of GDP was allocated to munitions production.[104] That generation welcomed a national consensus and was more tolerant of government initiatives in pursuit of the public interest.

National economies are no longer what they once were, but expectations of what national governments can accomplish have not kept pace. National governments no longer have the levers they once had to influence the pace and location of economic activities. Firms can relocate operations and employment with relative ease in response to changing economic circumstances or lower wages elsewhere. Nike, for example, closed twenty factories and opened thirty-five new ones over a five-year period.[105] This enables corporations to squeeze employee benefits and wages by threatening to relocate activities elsewhere. Corporations will argue before their employees and national governments that they either compete in the global economy or they die. In addition, firms can also adjust their balance sheets to redirect profits to activities located in countries that have lower taxation. Capital is free to move around the global economy in search of a better return, but this ability is much less so for labour. In brief, capital is mobile, it goes where it is wanted and stays where it is well treated, but not so for labour.[106]

All of this has prompted many public policy observers to argue that large multinational private firms are creating an economy beyond the reach of national governments.[107] The rise of the global economy is being "driven by private, not public actors – that is, by firms, not governments."[108] Half of the hundred biggest economies in the world are now private companies.[109] How then do national governments define and pursue the common good in such an environment?

Political and public policy agendas are constantly being influenced by international financial markets and large multinational firms and the persistent call to be competitive. National governments increasingly believe that it is in the interest of a competitive national economy and thus in the national interest to get out of the way and let the private sector lead the way. A sure approach to make a national economy uncompetitive, the conventional argument goes, is to introduce high levels of taxation, generous labour legislation, and demanding regulations.[110]

There is, however, a disconnect between the workings of the global economy and what politicians in national settings are saying. Politicians continue to speak about job creation, managing the national economy, and promoting domestic and regional or community interests. Former French president Nicolas Sarkozy reports that an irritated woman once told him, "My son does not have a job and it's your fault."[111] Sarkozy could have told her that the global economy places a premium on the individual in creating his or her own economic opportunities. He could have added that, under the new economic order flowing from the global economy, her son alone is master of his own life and that he has to derive action from within himself. It is unlikely, however, that it would have satisfied her grievance, if only because politicians are not prepared to admit that they have less influence than they once had to shape the pace and location of economic activity. Governments no longer have the capacity, assuming that they ever did, to match expectations with their ability to deliver.

Big-box stores and online shopping were decades away. Both urban and rural Canadians looked at the same merchandise and at the same prices in their Eaton's and Simpsons-Sears catalogues. As Susan Delacourt writes, these catalogues could "paper over rifts in Canada in a way that politicians and other institutions could only envy."[112]

Social cohesion was easier with the postwar generation, as was the ability to promote social bonds. Political leaders could secure election victories by offering a vision of a "just society" or a "great society." They could more easily equate the common good with a positive role for government in society. Today's political discourse, by contrast, centres on putting in place the conditions to compete in the global economy, and, again, one important way to do so is to get government out of the way.

The media are also vastly different today from their former selves in the 1970s and even the 1980s. In Canada, there were only three television networks, two national radio networks, and local stations. It was relatively easy to reach two cultures and two languages. Contrast this to today's hundreds of cable channels, radio talk shows, the new media, and social media. It only takes a moment's reflection to appreciate that it is considerably easier to speak a common language in defining the national interest when there are only a few national television channels and before the social media arrived.

Politicians could, through CBC, CTV, and Radio-Canada, easily reach the great majority of Canadians. Multi-channel cable television, the Internet, and social media have changed things. Establishing a common understanding leading to a debate about the national interest is far more difficult today. In addition, a strong emphasis on individual rights or, as one leading observer of Canadian politics labels it, "the rights revolution," raises questions about squaring it with collective responsibility and the public interest.[113]

It is hardly possible to overstate the point that the new media and the rise of social media are inhibiting national debates about national interests. Theme-based television has a narrow focus and a narrow content designed to capture a narrow audience. Internet-based communications also tend to turn political and public policy issues into "piecemeal debates among smaller groups concerned about their own issues." The notion that, if it is important for me, it will get to me, speaks to this development. There is less shared or common knowledge than forty years ago because there are fewer common media. Less common knowledge means that it is more difficult to engage Canadians in a debate about the common good.

With the advent of the new media and the social media, a Conservative does not need to hear or read a single Liberal message, and vice versa. One can also now easily access the media to confirm that one's views were right all along.

When Pierre Trudeau campaigned for a Just Society in 1967, Canada's average age was twenty-six. Today, it is forty-three. Today, Canada is also more urban and more secular. Today we talk about declining social cohesion; forty years ago social cohesion was not even part of our political vocabulary.

Many public policy issues have become too complex to engage Canadians in a debate over the common good. How many Canadians understand the workings of the country's equalization program or tax incentive schemes? Both have become highly specialized policy areas. Forty years ago, it was possible to turn to a line department and its minister and ask that they take the lead in shaping a new policy or a new program. Canadians could follow progress by focusing on what the minister had to say. A typical policy issue now involves a multitude of government departments and agencies and at times other orders of government, as well as public-private partnership agreements. We know, for example, that it took no fewer than twenty federal departments and over two years to plan new measures to promote development in Canada's North. Ministers are no longer the lead actor for their policy sectors and are no longer as responsible as they once were for the workings of their departments. Forty years ago, a member of Parliament could grasp the government's budget, zero in on a minister and a specific policy or program, and ask questions about their purpose and contributions. This is much less the case today.[114]

Not only have many policy issues become too complex, the machinery of government has also become complex. One reason the great majority of deputy ministers (the permanent heads of government departments) are drawn from central agencies, notably the Privy Council Office, is their knowledge of the policy-making process and their ability to navigate the system. If a career public servant cannot become deputy minister in his or her line department because of a lack of knowledge of how policy-making works, imagine what it is like for everyone else. It explains, at least in part, why Canadians are looking to single issues, non-government organizations or interest groups, and the courts to pursue what they consider to be in the public interest. In the eyes of many Canadians, both the public policy process and the machinery of government have become too complex, too slow, and too cumbersome to grasp, let alone to get anything done. Best to join a group of like-minded people and take matters into their own hands.

Bureaucracy is expected to play an important role in pursuing the common good. The narrative is that bureaucracy provides scientific neutrality to public policy-making and acts as a counterweight to the excesses of both politicians and the demands of interest groups in society. Bureaucracy should provide for neutral, objective, public-minded administration that can contribute substantially to the public interest. More to the point is that bureaucracy, with its scientific neutrality, should provide an antidote to the shortcomings of representative democracy. The thinking used to be that bureaucracy should be able to determine scientifically what policies would contribute what benefits, which ones would produce results to assist democracy in deciding on the best course of action.[115] This is much less evident today, and much more is said about it in the following chapters. Suffice to note that representative democracy also no longer enjoys the credibility that it once had, as sharp declines in voter turnout reveal.

Schumpeter's view that the sole purpose of representative democratic institutions is to choose leaders through competitive election appears to resonate more with voters now than it did in 1942 when he published his classic *Capitalism, Socialism and Democracy*. Voters do not agree on a common good and then elect leaders to pursue it; rather, they elect leaders in the hope that they will pursue the common good. Groups that exist to pursue group and special interests now have a greater capacity to tailor the public good to their own narrow interest. Added to this is the growing tendency among political parties to tailor their messages with an eye on certain groups to strengthen their chance to win an election.[116]

New theories also emerged to challenge the ability of bureaucracy to assist in pursuing the common good. Many took dead aim at its perceived neutrality. The behaviour revolution led many social scientists to maintain that public servants were acting less for the common good and more for their own interests. If representative political institutions and bureaucracy can no longer give life to a debate about the public interest, then one may ask what is left of them. If they cannot be good at doing this, what can they possibly be good at?

Politicians still evoke the common good when unveiling new measures. Prime Minister Harper told Canadian businesses with Russian dealings to "brace for economic pain for the greater national interest," as he and other G7 leaders contemplated economic sanctions against Russia's invasion of Crimea.[117] Nigel Wright insisted that his decision to cut a $90,000 cheque for Senator Mike Duffy was in "the public interest."[118] Wright did not want taxpayers to be stuck with the bill.

LOOKING BACK

Social cohesion and social capital speak to a sense of sharing a common vocabulary, common interest, mutual responsibility, and commitment to help others. There are several means to address public values conflicts, to assess and embrace public values, and to promote social cohesion.[119] Greater social cohesion makes it easier for politicians, public servants, and governments to be better at what they do.

All in all, the means to address public service values have fallen on hard times. Religion has lost currency as the glue that holds communities together. Trust in public institutions is eroding. Voter turnout has been on a downward trend. Given new information technologies, political parties can focus efforts on specific segments of the population rather than the broader community to tailor their message to get the friendly voters out. This, however, comes at a price for broader public values.

The machinery of government had great success in mounting the war effort and in the immediate postwar period when it took on new responsibilities in all sectors. However, we have since overloaded the machinery with new responsibilities, new programs, new departments, and new units, making it in the process thicker, less responsive, and less competent.

In my lifetime, I saw a world where the parish priest and the Roman Catholic Church were the dominant force. Our rewards were in the next life and we held no resentment towards the political and economic elites. I then saw a shift in which government became the dominant actor where it was regarded as a positive force for those wishing to build a better life and a better community. The church and the expanded role of government had at least one thing in common – both focused on the community. The most recent shift is to a highly competitive global economy where immediate economic rewards for individuals are highly valued. The growing inequality in income, in turn, is making it more difficult to manage conflicts in public values. This and other factors are also generating resentment towards society's elites.

The rise of the social media has not helped matters, accentuating rather than attenuating public values conflicts. It also forces government officials to attempt to monitor the social media and to control activities more closely than in years past, so as to manage the all-important political spin. Changes in societal values, overloading government with myriad responsibilities and the new media have had a profound and largely negative impact on how government decides and operates.

Notwithstanding these challenges, it is still up to our political and administrative institutions to manage public values conflicts, to define and pursue the public interest, and to deliver public services. The next chapters look into the workings of present-day political and administrative institutions.

PART TWO

What Has Changed and What Matters in Government

3

Institutions Under Attack

In Western democracies, it is the role of representative political institutions to debate the public interest and try to give life to it. Representative democracy took shape in the nineteenth century in many Western countries. Citizens began to look to representative institutions to hold politicians accountable for maintaining the public interest and for the spending of public money. In time, representative institutions became a part of a larger process, a process that brings together many actors from different sectors. Many of these actors are non-elected but they do have a hand in shaping, negotiating, defining, and implementing public policies and programs.

The Canadian Parliament is in its essence a collection of voices that connect Canadians across the country, from the smallest community in Newfoundland and Labrador to the smallest in British Columbia. Effective political power is granted to the government by Parliament, and Parliament – in theory at least – holds the government to account for its policies, activities, and spending in the pursuit of the public interest.

Effective power has, in more recent years, been further concentrated in the hands of the prime minister. Nothing new here. Political power has, throughout history, more often than not rested in the hands of an individual or small groups. When communities first took form, power was concentrated in the hands of tribal leaders, rulers, and kings, who were all free to rule as they wished. Their raison d'être was to rule over their territory and to wage war, and to this end their authority was absolute. As Sam Finer writes, in some societies the ruler was "the manifestation of a god and in principle the entire land was his."[1] The state, to the extent that it had an administrative apparatus, existed solely to serve the ruler and his interests. The public interest merged quite nicely with the ruler's personal interests. England's Henry VIII, for example, did not need to consult anyone on what he deemed to be the public interest, and if other institutions, such as the church or the courts, got in his way, he simply sidestepped them and did as he pleased. He held a divine right to rule as he saw fit.

In this chapter we review how political institutions were shaped down through the ages to give life to the public interest. Our focus is on the Westminster model and Canada. The Westminster model was not born in a vacuum and, for this reason, we shall briefly review developments that led to Canada's representative political institutions.

SEARCHING FOR THE PUBLIC INTEREST

As I already pointed out in my earlier work, Athens gave the word *democracy* to the world and a democratic process that involved all citizens (narrowly defined) – no small contribution, to be sure.[2] It experimented with direct democracy through an association of citizens that would, if nothing else, do away with kings, politicians, and even, to some extent, bureaucrats. Some administrative responsibilities were delegated to boards, but officials had to account directly to the assembly for their decisions and their spending.[3]

The Greek polis is not without its critics, with some claiming that it was not democratic at all, since political power remained concentrated in the hands of the minority. Only male citizens could participate in decision-making. Slaves formed a majority of the residents, the ratio of slaves to citizens being about three to one, but they had no say in the running of their communities. In brief, the pursuit of the public interest was undertaken by and for the interest of a minority.

Still, the Greek polis showed us that a society did not have to be ruled by absolute rulers – that alternative forms of government could exist. Yet there were those who harboured a deep suspicion of direct democracy, even of democracy itself. As recently as the eighteenth century, James Madison, in the *Federalist Papers*, issued a strong warning against pure democracy, writing that "such democracies have ever been spectacles of turbulence and contention, have ever been found incompatible with personal security or the rights of property, and have in general been as short in their lives as they have been violent in their deaths."[4] The architects of the American system of government concluded that the will of the people needed to be "tempered by an acute awareness of the potentially negative effects of citizen power, particularly citizens who were not of the chosen body."[5] They were concerned that the "masses" would simply "vote themselves free beer and pull down the churches and country houses." *Democracy*, for a long time, was a pejorative word and became "an affirmative term of pride" only when Thomas Paine took it up in his first volume of the *Rights of Man*.[6] John Dunn writes that for almost two thousand years the term *democracy* "proved grossly illegitimate in theory and every bit as disastrous in practice."[7] The crucial lesson learned, then, was that democracy needed a sober second voice if it were to serve citizens well.[8] In brief, the people could not be fully trusted to define the public interest, and institutions with carefully built checks and balances had to take charge. This has had a profound impact on how our institutions took shape.

Rome, meanwhile, was ruled by aristocrats and could not claim to be a democracy. Military leaders and aristocrats determined the public interest, which conveniently meshed with their own interests. That said, the Romans did introduce important checks and balances in their system of government. In the Greek democracy, all male citizens could vote, while in Rome, only men with money and property could do so. Though it never produced a written constitution, the Roman Republic, unlike ancient Greece, provided for the three branches of government (circa 287 BCE) that we still see today: the legislative, the executive, and the judicial branches. Romans would provide a key lesson: the public interest, however defined, required checks and balances.

There are two other relevant developments that we need to highlight: Rome's code of laws, and the role of the bureaucracy. Emperor Justinian drew on a long history of law-making in Rome to prepare his "Justinian code." Not only did the code preserve for posterity a unique experience in Roman government, but it also transmitted to Europe and beyond the basis for legal systems now found throughout the Western world. The existence of a body of laws meant that all the power could not, or at least should not, rest in the hands of an absolute ruler. This was in sharp contrast to those systems of government in which an absolute monarch enacted laws that applied to everyone except himself. Since he was the source of all laws, he was thus above them.[9]

THE WESTMINSTER MODEL

The history of the Westminster parliamentary system is a story of the struggle for power between the king and Parliament, then between Parliament and the executive. Some would argue that the struggle has recently been extended to ministers and public servants. Adam Tomkins sums up the earlier struggle well when he writes that "power resides in the authority of the Crown, save for that which has been specifically forced from it by Parliament."[10]

English kings, like their European counterparts, enjoyed a divine right to rule, and until 1701 they were accountable only to God.[11] Other European monarchs, at least those who remained in power, were able to cling to this notion much longer – until the early years of the twentieth century, in some cases. They held a divine right to rule, and the people were their subjects. They were accountable to no earthly authority. Thus, no one could punish them if they broke the law, only God.[12] Yet they were also head of "their" people, and all political power flowed to and from their hands, not from citizens or other institutions. The crown had the authority to call upon its subjects for support in times of war or in raising revenues. King Charles I, though with no success, reminded his accusers that they should remember that they were "born his subjects and born subject to those laws which determined that the king can do no wrong."[13]

It was during the reign of Edward III (1327–77) that the council was actually transformed into Parliament and that the position of Speaker of the Commons was established. The Commons also gained influence, though much of it was short-lived, only to find new life centuries later. It was argued that the king had to demonstrate the need for a new tax, and that it had to be to the benefit of the community or in the public interest, and that Parliament could make presentations or grievances to the king for resolution. This would lay the groundwork for the Westminster parliamentary system.[14]

Political parties and party government became necessary when the government required parliamentary majorities in order to survive, rather than relying on the support of the crown. In Britain, the process began in the mid-eighteenth century and became fully developed between 1832 and 1867, while in British North America it emerged in the 1840s. Thus there is a direct link between the rise of party politics and the development of responsible government in Canada. Political parties became the vehicles through which the public interest was debated and defined.

It is important to stress that in the Westminster parliamentary government, "the people" are represented in and by the House of Commons. The government and its general policy require the confidence and approval of the House, and the sovereign and Cabinet must give way to the Commons. Walter Bagehot wrote succinctly that the "Queen must sign her own death warrant if the two Houses unanimously send it." Political parties appeal to the electorate, and election outcomes decide the composition of the House, which determines the party origin of the Cabinet.[15]

CANADA'S VERSION OF THE WESTMINSTER MODEL

The Fathers of Confederation embraced the British constitution as the model to guide Canada's political development, and the British North America Act (BNA Act) of 1867 was British in intent, spirit, and design. The goal was to write as little as possible in the constitution and to establish representative democracies for the national and provincial governments based on parliamentary principles as defined by the Westminster model. The hope was that Parliament would stand unchallenged to create laws for all aspects of collective life and constitute the one place to provide the continuing source for authoritative action for society.

Canada and the Westminster model, however, were not an easy match. The Westminster model took form over many years in an essentially unitary state. Canada, given its large territory and its regional and linguistic diversity, required a federal system. However reluctantly, the Fathers of Confederation would have to look to the United States for inspiration in designing the federation. Thus, the BNA Act provided for both parliamentary government at the national level and a division of powers between the two levels of government, thereby limiting the supremacy of Parliament. Other developments have further shifted Canada away from the British model. The Constitution Act of 1982 and its Charter of Rights and Freedoms have moved many issues to the courts, where Canadians can test legislation for its constitutionality.

Unlike Britain, Canada would have two senior orders of government to define the public interest.[16] Canada, however, followed Britain in establishing an upper House in Parliament to act as a check on democracy. The "sober second thought" argument was essentially to protect the economic interest of the propertied class.[17] The Canadian Senate, unlike the House of Lords, was also expected to promote a regional perspective within the federal government, a responsibility that it has never been able to fulfil properly.[18]

DID THE CANADIAN PARLIAMENT
ENJOY A GOLDEN AGE?

I am not viewing the past through rose-coloured glasses when I maintain that the Canadian Parliament once had a stronger standing in and greater respect from society than it enjoys today. Nor is this a phenomenon unique to Canada. In Britain, the *Economist* declared that "it is perfectly true that the chamber [the House of Commons] is not what it was."[19]

To be sure, the broad political environment makes it far more difficult for Parliament to perform effectively than was the case some forty years ago.[20] Before the twenty-four-hour news cycle, the great political debates of the day took place in Parliament: the conscription issue, the flag debate, planning the war effort in the 1940s.[21] Parliament also played a more central and meaningful role in holding the government to account, most notably when it came to the budget.[22] But that was then. Today, the search for sleaze, the fifteen-second clip on the evening news, and the work of spin specialists dominate the work of the House of Commons. Parliament is not as good as it once was in holding the government to account and in scrutinizing the government's spending plans.

PARLIAMENTARY DEMOCRACY IS SICK, TATTERED,
AND NEEDS HELP[23]

The heading above comes from a sitting member of Parliament, and many of his colleagues are in agreement with the assessment. Numerous MPs openly despair about the state of their institution. Former MPs are no less critical. Sergio Marchi writes that we have witnessed an "erosion of Parliament as the principal forum for national debate and decision making; a reduced importance of back bench MPs," and insists that this serves to "dissuade talented Canadians from pursuing a stint in public service, further compounding the political malaise."[24] No one, it seems, is happy with the status quo except, perhaps, the sitting prime minister, and yet the status quo remains firmly entrenched.

Michael Chong, a long-serving Conservative MP, tabled a private member's bill in late 2013 designed to wrestle away some of the power held by the prime minister and to transfer it back to MPs. He sought to do so by giving MPs the power to remove their party leader, remove the leader's power to kick an MP out of the parliamentary caucus, and strip party leaders of their power to veto a candidate's nomination to be an MP.[25] The proposals generated a great deal of media interest, but little came of them. In September 2014, Chong revised his proposal one more time, effectively gutting it.[26] After he removed all contentious issues, Harper signalled his support.[27] A veteran Ottawa-based journalist maintains that, since Brian Mulroney, "every prime minister has promised to give MPs more of a say but every government has done the opposite."[28]

The decline of Parliament over the past forty years or so has been well documented, and there is no need to go over that well-travelled territory once again. Suffice to note that I know of no publication claiming that all is well with Parliament and that it is currently living its best moments. However, plenty suggest that Parliament is in urgent need of repair.[29] Two of Canada's leading students of Parliament, Ned Franks and David E. Smith, write that parliamentary "sessions have become less of an assembly for debate and discussion and more of a 'football game,' a contact sport, a fight to the death and a head butting contest than a serious deliberation. They have all the spontaneity and credibility of a professional wrestling event. The purpose of debate and question period has become to defeat, trounce, crunch, pulverize, annihilate the opposition – not to achieve a consensus or to reach a compromise, far less to identify a common purpose."[30]

Samara, a non-partisan, not-for-profit organization, has been carrying out original research for several years about the state of Canada's political institutions, especially Parliament, and on how to improve political participation.[31] It has held exit interviews with MPs, conducted public opinion surveys, and produced valuable reports on the workings of the Canadian Parliament. Samara's findings are worrisome, as they have consistently reported serious shortcomings.

For one thing, Samara reports that a good number of MPs describe themselves as "trained seals."[32] For another, only 27 per cent of Canadians think that Ottawa deals with issues that are important to them. A recurring theme in some of the Samara reports is that some Canadians observed that "politicians are concerned for their own interests" and that politicians "don't really care what people want."[33]

Both ordinary Canadians and MPs themselves lament the decline of Parliament. A bipartisan committee of MPs concluded in 2003 that Parliament "has, in a sense, lost its way."[34] Samara's exit interviews with MPs speak of "frustrations," "confusion," and even "embarrassment" with their institution.[35] The Samara group has thus far published several reports, including one with a revealing title: *Welcome to Parliament: A Job with No Description*. This report reveals that there is little "consistency" among MPs about their proper role. It discusses their arrival in Ottawa "largely unprepared for what lay ahead," and it notes that they have "little initial sense of where to focus" and that "their assignments seemed to be allocated at random."[36]

Studies have pressed home the point that MPs are "unprepared for their roles as parliamentarians" and receive "little or no formal training or orientation."[37] Virtually all jobs in modern society require formal training and periodical skills-development sessions to perform at expected levels. Not so for members of Parliament. There is no question that many MPs are amateurs in understanding the ways of Parliament or government. Indeed, a good number regard their amateur status and their lack of national political experience as an advantage.[38] Many run their election campaigns on an anti-Ottawa theme, pledging to work on changing the culture in the nation's capital and in government.[39]

Once MPs are elected, their training and orientation sessions are thin. One MP explained, "You get there, they take you in the House, they give you a book on constituency rights and responsibilities, the former Speaker talks about being in the House, and that's it. There is no orientation. There is no training. There is nothing on how to be effective." As another MP summed it up, "You learn by the seat of your pants."[40] Little wonder that the Samara study revealed that although two-thirds of the MPs consulted spent at least a portion of their time in Ottawa on the opposition benches, "only a few mentioned holding government accountable as part of their job."[41]

So what is an MP's job description or what should MPs be good at? Traditionally, a member of Parliament was essentially expected to perform three roles: review, refine if necessary, and pass legislation; authorize the spending of public money and hold the government accountable; and decide to support or withdraw confidence in the government. On the face of it, one could conclude that these functions belong to a different era. Unlike in nineteenth-century Britain, MPs are hardly free to decide to support or withdraw confidence in the government. It is a news item of considerable interest when a single MP decides to disregard party discipline, if only because it is so rarely done and because it challenges the party leader openly. Party discipline is alive and well in the Canadian Parliament, and no majority government is at risk of losing the confidence of the House of Commons.

MPs have all but abandoned their roles other than to represent their constituents by promoting local projects in Ottawa and to support their parties in Parliament. Constituency work grows and grows.[42] It is what many MPs want to be good at, because it helps to get re-elected and also because they are allowed to be good at it. It rarely gets in the way of the prime minister and his courtiers' agenda. MPs spend a great deal of time helping constituents deal with what they call uncaring bureaucrats and in bringing home the bacon. MPs do not have the power to review the work of public servants, but some can provide a useful guide on whom to contact in the local government offices or seek remedy through parliamentary questions or appeal to the relevant minister.[43]

For MPs, articulating the public interest is all about promoting the interest of their own constituencies. There is little advantage in speaking to a broader agenda. That, of course, has been the case since Confederation. The difference is that Parliament is less conducive today for MPs to take an interest in the broader policy agenda and in holding government to account for public service.

David Docherty reports that community service is "the strongest motivating factor in many MPs' initial decision to seek office." He adds that, unlike policy work, working on behalf of one's constituency is "encouraged by the Commons preference rule."[44] MPs who run for Parliament to promote the interests of their constituencies are more likely to be successful than those who run to contribute to policy-making or to hold the government to account or who find flaws in the spending estimates.[45] Promoting a local project before government is a great deal easier to understand and to master than is holding the government to account. Understanding how Parliament and government operate has become a field of specialization in its own right.

Keith Martin, a long-serving MP with the Reform and Liberal parties, had this to say about an MP's role: "The tragedy of the Commons is that the public good is sacrificed on the altar of short-term political gain. The system works against independent thought, works against representing the constituents."[46]

Party leaders and their advisors now dictate party positions, new policy initiatives, and communication with the media and citizens. We have leader-centric political parties in Canada. In brief, it is the leader and his or her advisors who shape election campaigns, and all roads lead to the leader. John Meisel and Matthew Mendelsohn maintain that political parties have now become largely ineffective in connecting citizens to their government.[47]

Long-time political activist and former senator Hugh Segal laments the decline of political parties. He writes, "Membership has been devalued, their role in policy has been diminished, and the place of parties as incubators and recruiters of talent has been under merciless attack from various forces. Even the most fundamental role of a political party – to choose the platform and leaders from which voters can then choose policies, direction, and governments – has also been diminished."[48] A Samara-sponsored survey reveals that Canadians believe that political parties are failing to perform their most important roles – making sure that citizens' views are respected and drawing on party members to come up with new ideas and policy prescriptions.[49]

Susan Delacourt writes that Canadian politics has been transformed from public service to the kind of marketing strategy usually found in the private sector. Party leaders and their advisors plan their marketing strategies to win elections, much as large firms design their marketing strategies to gain market share. She maintains that politics as currently practised divides Canada into political "niche" markets. It also abandons the "hard political work of knitting together broad consensus or national vision." She reports that one political strategist, for example, divided the "Canadian-citizen market into six basic groups to sell better the party and the leader."[50]

Delacourt points to a number of developments to make her case. She writes that only 2 per cent of Canadians now belong to a political party, and the bulk of these are over forty years old. Ninety per cent of Canadians believe that politicians are more concerned with money or their own interest than with the people, and that the purpose of political campaigns is not to inform or to educate but to sell the leader and denigrate the other parties. This in turn explains the rise of attack ads and strategies designated to speak to a party's "political base." Delacourt makes the point that the goal now is to feed the base and secure its support at election time, not to lead it. Political parties' marketing strategies and polling expertise are so well refined that they can zero in on the 500,000 votes needed to win.[51] Graham Steele, a former Nova Scotia finance minister, makes the point that "in the new politics, the role of the constituency politician is to feed the party's database, which is used for ever more sophisticated marketing schemes. Our constituency politicians have less impact on governing than ever." He adds, "Politics has become a never ending election campaign and a continuous marketing scheme."[52]

Parliament is no longer the prime theatre where adversarial politics play out. The media have taken on that role.[53] Partisan spin doctors slug it out on national airwaves for one or two hours every day on Newsworld's *Power and Politics*, CTV's *Power Play*, and RDI's *Le national hebdo* or *Les Coulisses Du Pouvoir*. They also go at it on weekends on such programs as CTV's *Question Period*. This world is largely foreign to the private sector – something that observers should keep in mind when comparing the merits of the public sector with the private sector.

Adversarial politics is also more intense in the age of permanent election campaigns and negative ads. This explains why at least some political leaders have compiled an "enemies' list,"[54] which includes journalists, public servants, assorted interest groups, and members of the judiciary.[55] The goal, of course, is to make political enemies look bad and to spin developments to one's advantage. Ministers and their staff will turn to friendly spin doctors, often working as lobbyists in their day jobs, to manage news. We read about political aides in the Prime Minister's Office muzzling Cabinet ministers and employing feel-good announcements to deflect attention from a negative development. They will leak information at the right time and in some cases develop "a parallel news/controversy plan that ... is salacious" to divert attention.[56] Being good at managing permanent election campaigns deters Parliament and political parties from engaging Canadians in a sustained debate about the national interest and holding government to account in delivering programs.

Members of Parliament and local candidates are shunted aside as political strategists plan the election campaign with the leader. MPs are, of course, free to raise concerns in the privacy of caucus meetings. However, by the time they become aware of things in caucus, they see only the final products as prepared by party leaders and their advisors. MPs, whether on the government side or on the opposition bench, sit at the end of the assembly line when decisions have already been struck. They can only react, and even then their suggestions can be easily dismissed, since they are no match for the political and marketing experts around party leaders and their close advisors.

IF WE HAVE TO KEEP OUR PROMISES, IT MEANS WE WON

Dominic LeBlanc, MP for Beauséjour, reports that during general discussions leading up to the 2011 election, a long-serving MP observed, "If we have to keep our promises, it means that we won the election."[57] The goal is to win, end of story. Sound public policy and the capacity of the machinery to deliver commitments are other issues that, if necessary, will be sorted out at another time by somebody else. What government is good at is never part of the discussions.

Meanwhile, the government's budget process is put on hold, and not a word is heard from the fiscal guardians in Ottawa, whether it be Finance, Treasury Board, the comptroller general, or the auditor general. The overriding goal for local candidates and party workers is to win, leaving to a later day and often to others the task of picking up the pieces. The result is that there are a lot of pieces to be picked up or discarded after a general election. MPs on the government side are not easily convinced to give up their campaign commitments once they arrive in Ottawa. They know that they will be held to account by the local media and by their constituents when the next election rolls around, if not sooner. When it comes to the expenditure budget, virtually all MPs walk around Ottawa seeking support for initiatives for their constituencies. How to implement the idea or whether the machinery of government is well suited to deliver the project, that is someone else's problem.

But someone eventually has to pick up the pieces, and this is where the prime minister, the finance minister and the Treasury Board president, together with thousands of public servants in central agencies, come in. It is no coincidence that successful expenditure-reduction exercises are often carried out shortly after a government secures a majority mandate (i.e., the Chrétien-Martin program reviews, 1994–97 and that of Harper in 2012–14).[58] A majority mandate enables the government to get its fiscal house in order and free up spending room to accommodate at least some campaign commitments.

Senior politicians on the government side, together with central agency officials, have to be good at deciding what spending commitments on an MP's "to do" list are to be retained or discarded. To be sure, the pressure from government MPs will be intense, often with a life-or-death argument: "If I don't get this, we can never win my riding again." All the "to do" lists can never be accommodated, and any attempt to do so would only play havoc with the government's budget.

As in so many other things, this function is peculiar to the public sector. No private sector executives have to deal with campaign commitments. It is completely foreign to their work. What about the other roles MPs have? How do they discharge their primary responsibility – to hold the government to account for its policies and its budget?

IT JUST DOES NOT WORK ANYMORE

In government, the budget steals the stage.[59] It decides who wins and who loses, and it lays down government priorities in the most concrete of terms. Two students of public administration have observed that "budgeting is the most important annual ritual of governing – the World Series of Government, or perhaps the Grey Cup of Government, within the Canadian context."[60]

The private sector does not operate anything like government. Budgeting in government and in the private sector is different in virtually all respects. The budget in government is akin to market forces, market share, and the bottom line all rolled into one, but without the market forces, market share, and a bottom line.

If Parliament and MPs are to be good at one thing, it should be at holding the government to account on the budget. On this front, they are failing and failing badly. Sheila Fraser declared, shortly before she stepped down as auditor general, that MPs are "failing Canadians" on one of their most fundamental roles: the scrutiny of yearly spending estimates.[61] Lowell Murray, a highly respected Cabinet minister in the Mulroney government, recently said, "Parliament – specifically the House of Commons – over a period of more than forty years, has allowed its most vital power, the power of the purse, to become a dead letter, their Supply and Estimates process an empty ritual."[62]

The estimates process has become too complex, too convoluted, and too spread out in too many documents for MPs to invest the time to have any impact. It is simply not worth their while. Herb Gray, a veteran MP who knew his way around government and who was well known in Ottawa circles for doing his homework, said, "The Estimates are complex and difficult to analyse and are, for constitutional reasons, difficult to change. In addition, their consideration is subject to a rigorous timetable. As a result, the examination of the Main Estimates has become rather cursory and there has been no focus for parliamentary debate on government spending before its spending priorities are actually set."[63]

The reams and reams of documents sent to Parliament every year are of little help. Shawn Murphy, the former chair of Parliament's Public Accounts Committee, went to the heart of the matter when he met with senior financial officials, including those from the Treasury Board Secretariat, at a retreat in 2008. He challenged them to insert some blank pages in their documents to see if MPs would notice. He felt confident that they would not. He reminded the committee that one year the Department of Justice simply "forgot" to include financial statements for the firearms registry, a controversial initiative widely reported in the media.[64] No one noticed, let alone raised questions about it.

Politicians are not the only ones making the case that Parliament is unable to hold the government to account on budget issues and that the process is now overly complicated. Others outside of government also appear to have thrown in the towel. One student of Parliament writes, "Canadian scholars have almost stopped trying to grasp and explain supply [appropriations] as either part of our type of democracy or in respect to its technocratic managerial aspects, said to be value-free, as executed and explained by appointed officials."[65] One journalist explains, "It used to be many years ago, when a budget came down, the very next day the spending estimates would be introduced. There was a lock-up for the spending estimates. That's because the budget and the spending estimates matched each other, so you knew exactly what the government was spending the very next day. You could comb through that and have a real understanding of how the budget was allocated and how the budget was spent. Those days are gone. That doesn't happen anymore. In fact, it often happens that the spending estimates are tabled before the budget." He adds, "There simply has to be better parliamentary oversight. Do you think that if we had proper parliamentary oversight we would have allowed the government to spend $1.5 million of Canadian taxpayers' money on job grants for a program that didn't even exist? Of course not."[66]

John L. "Jack" Manion maintained that the 1968 changes to the budget process altered Parliament's relationships with the government and with career officials, and that only the government and senior public servants obtained long-term benefits from the change. Because of the fixed calendar for approval, Parliament could no longer delay supply indefinitely and apply pressure to lower spending plans. It goes a long way toward explaining why Parliament's power of the purse has become an empty ritual. Manion revealed that opposition parties accepted the changes in return for some funding to support activities in their constituency and Ottawa offices.

But he argued that this advantage came at a tremendous cost, since it "caused Parliament to lose its main function, i.e., holding the Government to account." In a report to the Office of the Auditor General, he explained,

The new procedures produced significant advantages for the government, principally a fixed supply calendar, greater freedom to advance its legislative program and some reduction of the potential for opposition harassment offered by the Old Supply process. By 1991, opposition MPs were complaining that ministers had reduced attendance at committees to a minimum, often restricting their input to a pro forma opening statement at the commencement of the review of the estimates, then have their officials handle all but policy questions. This practice has continued and reflects an erosion of the principle of ministerial responsibility, while exposing officials to the sometimes hostile treatment of frustrated MPs.

He added, "Within the new committees, there was seldom much interest in expenditures – except to demand more for their constituencies
and ferret out information for partisan political purposes."[67]

Well aware that Parliament now pays only lip service to the budget
process, the government uses it to load it up with all manner of
things that it wants done, that may or may not be related to the budget. The 2013 omnibus budget bill is a case in point. The 322-page
bill not only implements the government's 2013 budget but also
introduces several other important policy and program changes that
are not all directly related to the budget. Here is a list of some of
the changes: the establishment of a new Crown corporation to set
employment insurance rates; changes to employer-immigrant match-
making services; changes to the criteria of who can serve on the
Supreme Court; expanded conflict-of-interest rules; changes to the
Canada Pension Plan; new efforts to tackle tax avoidance; ending
labour-sponsored venture capital tax credit; limitations to the right
to strike for public servants; a more narrow definition of dangerous
work for federally regulated workers; and a reduction in the number
of members on the National Research Council and the Veterans Review
and Appeal Board.[68]

MPs on the government side said nothing about these inclusions,
but many on the opposition benches raised objections, all to no avail.
The government simply said that this practice was done before, and
all MPs were free to raise objections. But the government went further
and announced time allocation for the bill, thus cutting off the
debate. The government House leader explained, "Time allocation is
not a device for eliminating debate but a device for scheduling the
House in an orderly and productive manner … and its use is within
House rules."[69] No matter, with a majority of seats in the Commons,
the government can essentially do what it wishes and employ any
argument to justify it and "spin" the issue to their political advantage.
It is simply not in the government's interest to give Parliament any
advantage as it tries to manage the blame game in the era of permanent election campaigns.

Career officials, meanwhile, are of little help to MPs. Indeed, most
consider MPs to be actual or at least potential adversaries. Given how
the blame game works, they have a point. Public servants seek to tell
standing committees as little as possible, to protect the department, and
to provide as much flexibility as possible in the days ahead. Officials

invariably stick to the specific question, provide a short, to-the-point answer, and volunteer nothing else. Unless MPs have enough information to pursue the issue, the matter will never be fully explored. They ask obvious questions and receive obvious answers. More substantive issues go unattended. This, according to an official who works with MPs and standing committees, "happens a great deal more than is generally assumed."[70]

Robin Butler, secretary to the Cabinet in Britain during the 1990s, told an inquiry that "half an answer" by a civil servant could be accurate in reply to parliamentary questions and that at times it is necessary to give an "incomplete" answer, which "falls short of the whole truth." He explained that "government activity is more like playing poker than it is like playing chess."[71] By the time they make it to the top, many senior public servants have mastered the art of providing incomplete answers and how to play poker. MPs are no match for them.

LOOKING BACK

Trust in Canada's Parliament and its MPs is among the lowest of some twenty-six countries.[72] In preparing for this book, I searched the literature for individuals who saw strengths in our present-day parliamentary system. I found few such voices. I did, however, come across many in the media, in Parliament itself, and from many highly respected observers who believed that the Canadian Parliament has lost its way.

The *Hill Times*, an independent Ottawa-based publication about Parliament, MPs, their staff, and government bureaucracy, ran an editorial on 25 April 2011 declaring that "Parliament is broken" and MPs "should fix it."[73] In a lead editorial, the Toronto *Globe and Mail* argued on the eve of the 2011 election that "the next House of Commons must find new ways to protect Parliament, the heart of our democracy."[74] The editorial was not clear about whom the House of Commons had to protect Parliament from or what had caused Parliament to need protection, but it received the endorsement of many academics and practitioners.

The decline of the role of Parliament in the nation's business has given rise to a variety of studies and task forces in recent years, all with the purpose of making Parliament more relevant. A well-known student of politics wrote an article asking, "Is the decline of Parliament irreversible?" He concluded with a plea for Canadians to "rediscover the relevance of political institutions."[75] No less an authority on the subject than Robert Marleau, former clerk of the Canadian House of Commons, maintains that the Commons has "almost abandoned its constitutional responsibility of supply."[76]

At the heart of the problem is the fact that senior politicians on the government side and senior public servants all too often regard Parliament as a nuisance, an obstacle to be ignored or overcome, an institution whose members are essentially concerned only with scoring partisan political points. The overriding goal of opposition MPs is to cast the government in a bad light on the evening news, and the goal of the prime minister and ministers is to give them little opportunity to do so. If Parliament is not good at pursuing its "most vital power, the power of the purse," then it poses the question, what is Parliament good at? It appears that Parliament, if it is now good at anything, it is at generating blame, avoiding blame, and promoting partisan political spin.

Canadians appear to have given up on political parties and Parliament as avenues to pursue the public interest. A majority of Canadians have concluded that these institutions are not good at carrying out their more important tasks – debating and defining the public interest and holding the government to account. It is worth repeating that a Samara survey reveals that Canadians believe that MPs do a better job pursuing the interest of their political parties than of those they represent, and only 36 per cent of them are satisfied with how MPs do their job.[77]

All of this underlines the point that MPs and Parliament itself are not very good at what they should be good at. They fall short on holding the government to account, scrutinizing and authorizing the spending of public money, reviewing and refining legislation, and acting as an effective forum to debate the important issues of the day. MPs and Parliament also have a responsibility for safeguarding the public interest, the common good. They are falling short on this responsibility as well. This, in turn, has wide implications for the machinery of government and for assessing what government is good at. Political and administrative institutions are joined at the hip and, if one is not as good as it should be, it will have an impact on the other. Political and administrative institutions do not operate in isolation or in a vacuum. If Parliament is not as good as it should be at what it does or should do, then other institutions are also not likely to be as good as they should be at what they do or should do.

Recent developments in society, from globalization to the rise of the new media, have left us with no historical models to draw on to debate and define the public interest. As Ulrich Beck observes, "Those who live in this post-national, global society are constantly engaged in discarding old classifications and formulating new ones."[78] We are formulating new ones on the fly, largely in the absence of a debate on what government is actually good at. Individual public servants, like Edward Snowden, have decided that they, rather than their institutions, are better suited to define the public interest. Snowden has since been described as a hero, a traitor, a dissident, a patriot, and a whistle-blower.[79] Most Western countries now have whistle-blower legislation, a sure sign that public institutions cannot and should not always be trusted.

All this is to say that we may well have reached the point where the common good or the public interest is too complex for anyone outside of government to identify, debate, and pursue.[80] The state no longer seems capable of expressing and pursuing the public interest as well as it once could, for a variety of reasons. As Mark Bevir argues, "Democracy now seems less a means of expressing a common good and more a contest among factions or classes."[81] He adds, "Even as modernism revealed cracks in representative democracy, so it papered over them by appeals to an apparently neutral expertise."[82] In Canada, at least, neutral expertise is no longer valued as it once was. The Canadian government, for example, casually dismissed the near-unanimous expert opinion on the need to retain the long-form census questionnaire in 2010.[83]

Globalization, the fragmentation of the state into a series of self-interested actors or complex policy networks, and the realization that national representative institutions are now only a small part of the larger policy process where "a range of actors, many of whom are unelected and unaccountable, negotiate, formulate and implement policies in accord with their particular interests and norms," are some of the reasons why the pursuit of the public interest has become more difficult.[84] Yet national policy actors cling to "representative ideals" and their institutions "try" to patch things up as best they can by introducing one reform measure after another.[85] If there is a consensus emerging, it is that politicians and officials no longer act in accord with the common good and that they are overly preoccupied with their own interest.

It may well explain why Canadians are turning to other means to pursue their interests and to get government to respond to their wishes. Organized groups, the courts, and, if one can afford it, lobbyists, are better suited at getting things done than are Parliament, MPs, and even some Cabinet ministers. They, however, lack the legitimacy and the accountability requirements found in representative democratic institutions. We explore their work in the next chapter.

4

Different Ways to Get What You Want

Political institutions and government do not operate in the same way they did fifty years ago. As we saw in the previous chapter, Parliament no longer holds the respect of Canadians, and even of its own MPs, that it once did, membership in political parties is down, election campaigns are planned and executed by party leaders and a handful of specialists, Cabinet is more of a focus group for the prime minister than a decision-making body, and individual ministers and departments have less latitude in shaping policies or even taking decisions than they once had.[1] Bureaucracy has also changed substantially in more recent years, and more is said about this in the next chapter. Though government operates differently, new policies are still introduced, and thousands of program decisions are still made every day.

This chapter assesses how groups and individuals now access government decision-makers and programs. If the locus of decision-making has changed inside government, and if, as many have argued, there has been a shift favouring the attributes of individuals over those of the community, then this should be felt both by those inside and outside government.[2] And if, as the new literature of public sector governance suggests, we are moving towards governing by networks and multi-level governance dealing with horizontal issues, then it should raise questions of who has gained or lost influence.[3] This, in turn, brings up the matter of the public sector's defining characteristics and what, traditionally at least, government should be good at, relative to the private sector – namely, equality, efficiency, merit, fairness and justice. This and the following chapters explore whether these characteristics have been compromised. They also explore who wins and who loses under new approaches to decision-making.

Fifty years ago, access points to influence public policy and government programs were few, highly visible, and relatively easy to navigate: basically politicians, political parties, and public servants in relevant line departments were about all one needed. This was true for almost everyone. The worlds of politics, the media, and the machinery of government were relatively simple and straightforward. Not only was the political world and machinery of government far less complex, there were also far fewer actors trying to influence public policy and program decisions. The world of government was also a great deal simpler, and hierarchy still enabled citizens to understand who did what and how to find the right person to approach. A meeting with your local member of Parliament and preferably with the Cabinet minister responsible for your region was often all that was needed to get an effective hearing about your concerns.

Things are vastly different today, and this poses serious challenges for the average citizen, in that a more complex government structure favours the better educated and those with the resources to hire experts with the knowledge to determine the most promising way to influence decisions. As we have seen, the average Canadian has only a limited knowledge of the workings of the machinery of government and can easily get lost trying to navigate it. It will be recalled, for example, that a public opinion survey carried out by the Dominion Institute in 2008 revealed that over half of Canadians believed that the prime minister was directly elected by voters, and 75 per cent could not identify Canada's head of state.[4]

THE COURTS

It is hardly original to write that the courts are increasingly present in various public policy sectors. The Charter of Rights and Freedoms that became part of Canada's constitution in 1982 has had a profound impact on the role of Canadian courts. Canada's chief justice made it clear in a public lecture that law and justice now rest on rational principles and not simply on laws approved by Parliament. She explained that "embedded in the concept of the rule of law is the proposition that there are fundamental and overriding principles of justice binding civilized societies that trump state-made rules where the two come into conflict."[5] State-made rules are struck by politicians, while over-riding principles of justice are decided by appointed judges, essential-ly accountable to one another and ultimately to themselves. Our focus is on the Supreme Court of Canada.

Though they stand above the fray, the courts, notably the Supreme Court, no longer hesitate to shape the country's social agenda and public policies.[6] Politicians, meanwhile, must debate and sell their decisions. Partisan politics is never far from the surface and all oppor-tunities to score political points will be taken. The courts have no such concerns. If the government is no longer as good as it once was in providing clear answers, the courts are now there to do so.

Judicial activism has become a part of Canada's political vocabulary, since the Charter of Rights and Freedoms became part of our consti-tution. Court decisions, after going through all the appeals, are final and, for the most part, do provide clear answers. We now have a fast-growing body of literature documenting the work of the courts in var-ious public-policy issues.

In his study of the impact of the 1982 Charter of Rights and Free-doms on Canada's judiciary, Christopher Manfredi maintains that the Supreme Court has shown "little restraint in building up its own review of judicial review or in asserting its own pre-eminent authori-ty over the development of Charter-related constitutional principles."[7] He reports that interest groups, preferring to pursue their political agenda through the courts rather than through politicians, have con-tributed to the expansion of judicial power. In the process, Canadian politics is being transformed, in that difficult or divisive issues are increasingly being submitted to the courts for resolution rather than through the political process.[8]

In his comprehensive review of the work of Canada's Supreme Court, Donald Songer concluded that "while it is still fashionable in many circles to think of the work of the courts as divorced from the often disdained world of politics, both the empirical analysis of the Court's decisions and the views of the justices expressed in interviews provide strong support for the thesis that one must understand the Court as a court of law and a political court."[9] Put another way, the courts have become political actors, but without having to deal with the constraints politicians have to contend with, such as transparency requirements, having to seek re-election, dealing with opposition par-ties, managing the blame game, and deciding how to fund initiatives.

Allan Hutchinson argues that "the Supreme Court of Canada is as political in its decisions as those of its American counterpart." He adds, "Let there be no mistake, the Supreme Court is a powerful body and, as importantly, an ideological one at that."[10] Former Supreme Court justice Willard Estey is concerned that the court risks becoming "an unelected mini-legislature" and regards interveners as "nothing more than publicity-seeking pressure groups."[11]

Rainer Knopff and F.L. Morton maintain that the Charter of Rights and Freedoms has resulted in a significant transfer of policy-making power to the courts and now labels the courts as "policy-making institutions."[12] Christopher Manfredi and Antonia Maioni have looked at the impact of the Charter and the courts on Canada's health-care policy and have come to the same conclusion.[13] Ian Greene, Carl Baar, Peter McCormick, George Szablowski, and Martin Thomas also looked at the role of Canadian courts of appeal, and they too write about the impact on policy-making. They argue that "sometimes, even when the general will is clear, it appears to contradict an important constitutional principle in the Charter or another part of the constitution and so it cannot be followed."[14] As a result, the general will and even the resolution of public-policy issues are no longer matters for Parliament or even for the prime minister and Cabinet to decide – the courts now have an important say.

To be sure, there is disagreement on the merits of judicial activism but not on its implications for policy-makers. Emmett Macfarlane's *Governing from the Bench* provides important insights on the workings of the Supreme Court and its growing significance to Canada's political institutions and in shaping public policy. He writes, "The Supreme Court of Canada's importance can be measured not only by its rulings on the country's law and the immediate policy issues that come before it but also by the influence its decisions have on government, political culture, and public discourse." He documents the "transfer of power to the courts" and sheds new light on how court decisions are reached.[15]

Macfarlane reviews a number of cases dealing with contentious policy issues where the personal policy preferences of individual justices took over. In one case, the justices accepted the view of a single expert who maintained that allowing private health insurance would not hurt the public system and dismissed the views of six other experts who said it would.[16]

Canada's chief justice explains that the Charter has introduced a new set of constitutional limitations on the legislative and executive branches of government. Canadians, she points out, can "now go to court to challenge laws and government acts not only on the grounds that they exceeded the grants of power, but also on the grounds that they violate fundamental rights." She insists that the Charter has changed the constitutional role of the courts, not only quantitatively but qualitatively: before the Charter, the courts' role in defining the boundaries of power of the legislature and the executive meant that they were mediating between different levels of government and sometimes between the citizen and government; today, the courts are "required to mediate conflicts between individuals and minorities on the one hand and the majority elected government on the other."[17]

Mark Harding and Rainer Knopff recently made the case that the courts have moved beyond Charter provisions to incorporate "Charter values" in their decisions. They point out that sometimes the courts refer "to underlying values such as *human dignity* that do not appear in the Canadian Charter." The concern is that this and other developments are enabling the courts to go beyond the reach of the Charter in their work. In turn, these changes can "threaten the appropriate institutional division of labour between legislatures and courts."[18] Harding and Knopff warn that we run the risk of "constitutionalizing everything."[19] They have a point – female players competing in the 2015 World Cup games to be played on artificial turf in Canada threatened to turn to the courts to argue "gender discrimination" in violation of the Charter of Rights and Freedoms. Male soccer players, they argued, who competed in the 2014 World Cup in Brazil were able to play on "real grass."[20] Interest groups are less concerned about the division of labour between legislature and the courts and far more about achieving the right decision in support of their interests.

Again the debate is no longer whether the courts have power – the point is now widely acknowledged, and judges appear to relish their new-found clout. The courts now rule on such matters as whether Quebec has a constitutional right to secede unilaterally from Canada and whether it is within the legislative authority of the Canadian Parliament to amend the constitution to provide, among other things, fixed terms of nine years for senators.

There have been also many Supreme Court decisions with substantive public policy content. Raymond Bazowski writes about the "judicialization of politics," suggesting that the courts have intruded into the policy-making arena and that political conflicts are being transformed into legal issues to be resolved "in an impenetrable institutional setting."[21] The setting may be particularly impenetrable to individual citizens, but much less so for groups and associations with financial resources. Some observers insist that self-serving special interest groups (feminists, gays and lesbians, Aboriginals, and minority-language groups) have turned to the courts to secure rights that they would not have been able to obtain through the political process.[22]

In some instances, the courts have gone beyond the Charter to stop the government from changing policy direction. When the New Brunswick government decided to eliminate its early French immersion program in March 2008, some parents challenged the decision in court. The judge ruled that the government's decision did not violate the Charter of Rights and Freedoms, but he said that the government had not allowed sufficient time for debate on the issue. He added that the minister's decision "was unfair and unreasonable" and on this basis "quashed" it.[23] The government decided not to appeal but to go back to the drawing board. It initiated a new round of public consultations and subsequently revised its plan by introducing early immersion in grade 3. The important point is that the court essentially ignored the substance of the issue but decided that a democratically elected government had adopted a wrong process in taking a policy decision. It forced the government to initiate a new one.

The New Brunswick government was in for another surprise when it decided to overhaul the delivery of health-care services in the province. Ostensibly to cut costs and eliminate duplication, it planned to reduce the number of regional health authorities from eight to two. Mike Murphy, minister of health, declared that the changes would save nearly $20 million over five years. He explained that the legislation contained a provision (section 17) that denied the right to challenge the proposed reform before the courts. A recently retired Supreme Court judge, known for being a strong advocate of minority-language rights while on the bench, agreed to be part of the citizens' group taking the provincial government to court. He dismissed out of hand the minister's claim, insisting that no legislative body in Canada has such power any longer.[24]

The issue was a machinery-of-government matter and the objective was to streamline operations and reduce spending. The courts do not concern themselves with machinery issues or where the money should come from. They also do not concern themselves with how best to implement a program, thinking that all that really matters is reaching the right decision as they see it. Politicians and public servants are left to implement the decision, no matter the difficulty in doing so. In many cases, including this one, government also has to pay all or nearly all of the legal costs for both sides. When the government pays legal costs for groups pursuing it in court, the groups have nothing to lose and everything to gain.

The Supreme Court, in a unanimous decision, ruled on 10 November 2012 that governments and school boards could not turn to budget constraints or other arguments to avoid providing special programs to help students with special needs to get an education. Justice Abella wrote, "Adequate special education is not a dispensable luxury. For those with severe learning disabilities, it is the ramp that provides access to the statutory commitment to education made to all children in British Columbia."[25] Representatives of the Learning Disability Association declared that they were "ecstatic. Time and time schools districts say – we can't afford this. Well now they can't afford not to."[26]

Once again the courts had nothing to say about where the funding should come from or how the decision should be implemented. That was someone else's problem. Someone else was left to find the necessary funding and to determine how to implement the decision. Someone else will have to raise taxes or cut spending in other areas. The court simply decided that providing special programs to help students with special needs was in the public interest. The court dealt with only one part of the equation, in many ways the easy part. It is no less in the public interest to determine how such initiatives can be financed from the public purse. Someone, not the courts, has to decide if other public services should be cut or reduced or which taxes should be increased.

The Supreme Court also ruled in 2005 that the Quebec government could not prevent individuals from paying for private insurance for health-care procedures covered under medicare. The court found that banning private insurance for a list of services ranging from an MRI test to cataract surgery was unconstitutional since medicare had failed to ensure patients access to those services in a timely manner. Lawyers representing the government argued that the court should not interfere with the health-care system, insisting that it is considered "one of Canada's finest achievements and a powerful symbol of national identity."[27] The court ruled otherwise, and government officials were left to pick up the pieces and figure out how best to implement the decision.

Several lawsuits have also recently been launched across the country arguing that long wait times for surgery and the inability to jump the queue violates the right to life, liberty, and security of the person provisions of Canada's Charter of Rights and Freedoms.[28] The courts will rule and again leave it to government officials to deal with all resource and implementation issues.

The Supreme Court overturned a decision by the Nova Scotia Court of Appeal in 2003 and forced the provincial government to report to the court on progress made in the province's school construction program for French-language students. The ruling served notice that delay in constructing schools for the linguistic minority constituted an infringement on the rights of the minority and would not be tolerated. The argument was that the linguistic minority was increasingly being assimilated into the English majority, and, as a result, delays in implementing the court's decision would put the minority at risk. The Supreme Court ruling also served notice that the court was not only satisfied in simply issuing a ruling without authority, it also wanted to assess the performance of the government in implementing the decision. Two justices of the Supreme Court (LeBel and Deschamps) wrote a dissenting opinion on the grounds that the court should avoid becoming "managers of the public service."[29]

Some judges are simply ignoring or defying the government's legislative and policy agenda. The Harper government's "tough on crime" agenda is a case in point. The government decreed in October 2013 that financial penalties should be instituted on convicted criminals and that the money should be turned over to victims' services, such as rape crisis centres and witness-protection programs. Not all judges are buying into the government's agenda. One judge explained why: "It's bizarre that a piece of legislation like that could go through Parliament. I mean, is no one down there thinking?" He added, "Why aren't victims looked after in our general revenues?"[30] The judge's point: a duly elected government and MPs cannot think properly, while judges can, and drawing new spending from general revenues, at least for judges, is an easy, straightforward solution.

The courts limited the government's ability to shape its own policies and programs when Justice Ann Mactavish ruled in July 2014 that cuts to health care for failed refugee claimants are "unconstitutional." She sounded like a politician from the opposition benches when she turned to section 12 of the Charter of Rights and Freedoms to declare that the government's decision was "cruel and unusual treatment." She gave the government four months to restore funding.[31]

The decision was applauded by Canadian Doctors for Refugee Care, the Canadian Association of Refugee Lawyers, and Justice for Children and Youth. The government meanwhile argued that it had every right to "deter bogus claimants from coming to Canada or over-staying by denying them medical care." The responsible minister, Chris Alexander, explained that the move would have saved taxpayers "hundreds of millions at all levels of government."[32]

Adam Dodek warns that "judges cannot pick and choose which laws they like and which they do not. This undermines the rule of law and public confidence in the administration of justice." One judge recognizes that Dodek "is right," but adds that "the greater principle is one of justice, it's more important to stand up for what is just."[33] Judges, not politicians, now decide in certain circumstances what is the right public policy, and they now have the power, it seems, to decide to apply the law or not. Not only is Parliament no longer su-preme, it is also not allowed to make mistakes.

Those who enter the political arena soon realize governing is about making difficult decisions. One can – and many do – argue over whether politicians are good or not at making these decisions, but it is their responsibility. The trade-offs are never easy, as Michael Ignatieff discovered in his relatively brief sojourn in politics. He writes,

What a person wants from his or her national community often conflicts with what others want. Every community wants recogni-tion of its own distinctiveness but is reluctant to grant it to others. Canadian communities often give the impression of being sealed off from each other. Immigrant communities wanted more immi-gration and unionized workers wanted less; rich people wanted tax breaks and poor folks wanted a better deal. Gun control, of any kind, was poison in any small town or rural district, and yet it was the key to holding the vote in a downtown core. Everywhere people wanted more federal money, but everywhere people want-ed the federal government to stay out of provincial jurisdictions.[34]

The courts are now full participants in the political arena without having to face the electorate or to reconcile one of their decisions with another from a public policy and government spending perspective. This is not to suggest for a moment that members of the judiciary should run for office. It is simply to say that the difficult tasks of allocating scarce resources and actually figuring out how to implement the decision are of little concern to them.

It also leaves the art of political compromise out in the cold. Peter Russell warns that the "great bulk of the citizenry who are not judges and lawyers will abdicate their responsibility for working out reasonably and mutually acceptable resolutions of the issues which divide them."[35] Anne Gilbert and Joseph Yvon Thériault make a similar point, insisting that the courts are replacing public debates on important public policy issues, notably on minority language rights.[36]

THE COURTS AND PUBLIC SERVANTS

Public servants are also singling out the courts as an important factor that has reshaped their work over the past twenty or thirty years; the impact on the machinery of government has been strongly felt in many areas. A senior official at the Department of Fisheries and Oceans (DFO) reports that thirty years ago public servants rarely thought about the courts as they went about their work. Today, he maintains, the courts are never far from people's minds when planning departmental activities. As he explains, "When you launch a new activity or unveil an important decision, you should always make provision for a court injunction to stop the department from moving forward."[37] He adds, "In 1979 there were three lawyers handling all DFO legal issues. Only twenty years later, there were twenty-six lawyers handling our cases. That in itself tells you what has happened inside government."[38]

Another senior line-department official reports that he and his staff are very careful about putting things down on paper for fear that the information will be employed against the department in a future court case.[39] Public servants in the Department of Justice confirm these developments. One senior official there reveals that, despite the ambitious program reviews of the mid-1990s and 2012, the number of lawyers in the department responsible for "litigation" and "litigation avoidance" has more than doubled in recent years.[40]

One can appreciate why some public servants may be reluctant to commit things to paper. The Supreme Court in its 2004 Haida and

Taku River and 2005 Mikisew decisions told the government that it had "a duty to consult and, where appropriate, accommodate when the Crown contemplates conduct that might adversely impact potential or established Aboriginal or Treaty rights."[41] Much ink has already been spilled, turning that decision into a workable framework for public servants. Public servants, or anyone else, for that matter, find it difficult to operate when rules and processes are not clear. In addition, the political blame game does not easily lend itself to such an open-ended process.

The government has issued and updated guidelines to assist public servants in dealing with the court decisions. The most recent update focuses on "the increased need for policy leadership coordination and collaboration, federal accountability strengthening partnerships and strategic and practical guidance, training and support." It is difficult to imagine that this can be of any help to anyone. The guidelines also established a series of guiding principles, including one that reads, "The government of Canada will use and rely on, where appropriate, existing consultations: mechanisms, processes and expertise, such as environmental assessment and regulatory approval processes in which Aboriginal consultation will be integrated, to coordinate decision making and will assess if additional consultation activities may be necessary."[42] The other seven guidelines are written in the same vein, and one can only hope that some public servants find them of some assistance.

The Supreme Court, for its part, had precious little to say in how the government should implement the decisions. It simply passed on that responsibility to the government and likely assumed that the machinery of government would do as it is told. It takes only a moment's reflection to appreciate the impact court decisions have had and continue to have on the machinery of government and public sector management. If nothing else, it makes it more difficult for government managers to be good at planning initiatives and managing operations.

THE COURTS AND MANAGEMENT

The courts have also been drawn even into management issues. A senior manager with Corrections Canada reports that both employees and their unions now turn to the courts about issues that thirty years ago were quietly handled internally. It has never been easy to deal with non-performers in government. It is still more difficult today, as employees and their union representatives go to court if management initiates any action to remove anyone for non-performance. Again, senior officials at Justice reveal that the number of lawyers working on behalf of the employer in personnel-related cases has increased substantially in recent years.[43]

Public servants have turned to the courts to challenge the constitutionality of new labour laws designed to overhaul collective bargaining and health and safety in the workplace.[44] Senior public servants, even the government's own lawyers, have turned to the courts to challenge government decisions. The Supreme Court ruled that the government had to release parts of documents classified as Cabinet secrets to its own lawyers who were suing the Treasury Board for a pay increase.[45]

The Supreme Court publishes a performance report accounting for "cases filed," "applications for leave," and "appeals heard."[46] The court's workload has remained relatively stable in recent years. In 2002, for example, the court considered 523 applications for leave to appeal and seventy-two appeals heard. In 2012 the numbers were 548 and seventy-eight, respectively. Comparing the court's workload between the pre- and post-Charter era is like comparing apples and oranges, given that the Supreme Court now has a much greater say in deciding which cases it will hear.[47]

Yet a case can be made that the appointment process for deputy ministers is more rigorous and demanding than it is for judicial appointments. Leaving aside the failed Nadon appointment, the prime minister still essentially makes the final decision on Supreme Court justices and provincial chief justices, and if he has his eye on a candidate, he will very often get his way, or at least has done so in the past.[48] Merit is in the eye of the prime minister, and a past association with him or her, or with the political party in power, matters. In a recent study of the Supreme Court of Canada, Donald Songer observed a "moderately strong relationship" between the federal party that appointed a judge and his or her policy preferences. He writes that "notwithstanding disclaimers that judicial ideology is not actively considered in judicial selection," three of the Supreme Court justices whom he interviewed confirmed their belief that this is so.[49]

Roméo LeBlanc, a senior minister in the Trudeau government and later governor general of Canada, once told me, "Lawyers are the only people in the world who can regain their virginity; all you have to do is appoint them judges." He explained that overnight, some of them go from being fiercely partisan to having a disdain for politicians and all things political. "You meet them at airports, and they are eager to profess their complete loyalty to you and your party and their willingness to get involved and give a helping hand. You promote their nomination to the bench. Later, when you see them at airports, they will avoid you; some do not want even to make eye contact with you. Overnight, they change. Politics is suddenly unhealthy and to be avoided. I always find it quite amazing and amusing."[50]

The relationship changes, of course, because we expect judges to operate above the fray, to be non-political, and to arrive only at objective decisions rather than the kind that politicians and public servants make. In the eyes of many interest groups, individuals with the required resources, and even public servants, the courts are better at defining the public interest in their decisions than is government. What are citizens to make of this? If it boils down to a popularity contest between the Prime Minister's Office and the Supreme Court, the court will come out on top. It can largely avoid political controversies, partisan politics, Question Period, and the prying eye of the new media.

There is evidence, however, that Canadians are supportive of the Supreme Court and that they see merit in the ability to seek justice through the courts.[51] Public opinion surveys consistently show that a majority of Canadians sides with Supreme Court decisions when in conflict with government policy.[52] To be sure, there are advantages in making public policy decisions and then turning over difficult financial and implementation decisions to others. There is no need for the court to sell its decisions. It simply rules and its voice is final, always insisting that the decision was free of politics. If someone has to pick up the pieces to implement the decision, it is never the judges.

In addition, the courts favour interest groups and the economic elites because they have the resources to pursue justice through the courts. Individual citizens, for the most part, do not have easy access to the courts to challenge government, if only because the effort is much too costly.[53] Chief Justice McLachlin said as much when she wrote, "Do we have adequate access to justice? It seems to me that the answer is no. We have wonderful justice for corporations and for the wealthy. But the middle class and the poor may not be able to access our justice system."[54] Ontario's chief justice echoed the views of Justice McLachlin when he said that "with the best of intentions" the legal system is now inaccessible to many of the people it is meant to serve.[55]

The courts are not the only means for those with the resources to get what they want from government policies or programs. Other important developments over the past fifty years have had a profound impact on how policies are made and decisions are taken in government. The growing concentration of power in the hands of the prime minister and his key advisors and the horizontal nature of decision-making in government have also allowed those with the knowledge or the resources to hire well-connected experts, knowledgeable in the ways of government, to influence decision-making or at least to exert far more influence than others can. In short, this also favours the economic elites.

CONSULTANTS DRIVING DECISIONS

The ability of the courts to shape public policies and to influence program content is limited because they cannot possibly cover all sectors. The federal government expenditure budget, taxation policies, many public policies, and government regulations all have a direct impact on the lives of Canadians and Canadian businesses, and many remain outside of the court's ambit.

Canadians can always turn to their MPs to speak on their behalf before the federal government, and many still do. But there are limits to what an MP can do on behalf of his or her constituents in the role of an ombudsman. For the most part, MPs react to a specific request to deal with a specific problem, and those sitting on the government side of the House stand a better chance of being heard. As we have seen, in the great majority of cases, MPs will focus their efforts and spend whatever political capital they have on high-profile commitments made during the election campaign. They will often hand over specific problems to a staff member who is always partisan, often young, and with little or no experience in government.

Canadians can join an association that squares with their views, and some do. They have opportunities to join such groups as the Canadian Taxpayers Federation, the World Association for the Protection of

Animals Canada, the David Suzuki Foundation, and the list goes on and on. The *Hillwatch.com* counts hundreds of associations with a political advocacy or a public policy content dealing with, among others, such matters as Aboriginal issues, the environment, immigration, tax policy, and here too the list goes on.[56] Some of these associations are well funded, others less so. But all have a policy preference, an axe to grind. They all want to influence public policy to their way of thinking.

The point is that only well-funded associations, organized groups, and economic elites have the knowledge or the resources to penetrate the complex policy-making processes and machinery of government. Government decision-making is not simply a question of accountability after the fact. It is also vitally important to know how to access the process, whom to talk to, when, and what arguments should be marshalled to have an impact.

This at a time when we are also witnessing a "de-statization" of the state as the locus of policy, and even decision-making is shifting to networks, interdepartmental and intergovernmental negotiations, and public-private partnership arrangements. Unless one has the expertise or the resources to retain the expertise, one can hardly navigate this territory with any chance of success. This in turn heightens further the inability of national political and administrative institutions to speak to the public interest. Those with the knowledge or resources to influence government and public opinion will want to speak to their own sectoral or economic interests and rarely to the broader public interest. Those without the resources or membership in an interest group are left virtually voiceless.[57]

In addition, just as politicians were seeking to push back the influence of senior public servants on policy-making and make policy advice more responsive to their views and their policy agenda, policy-making became more complex. Think tanks and research institutes broke the monopoly that career officials held on the provision of advice. Modern technology, including Google searches, has made information on virtually any public issue more accessible to interest groups. Think tanks, lobbyists, consultants, and interest groups are now all able to obtain information quickly, and many can now analyze it as well as anyone in government can. As Patrick Weller argues, "Policy advice, once an effective monopoly of public servants, is now contestable and contested."[58]

Canadian career officials, as we shall explore further in the next chapter, are also being challenged by other developments: the shift towards horizontal policy-making; the growing dominance of the prime minister and his office in the policy process; the pervasiveness of public-opinion polling to provide policy answers; the need to make policy on the run to accommodate "news breaks" from a more aggressive media; policy overload; and the interconnected nature of public policies. A new model is emerging that forces career officials to look outside their departments to shape new policy measures. This, in turn, makes it easier for well-funded and well-organized interest groups to focus their efforts on decision-makers who matter the most inside government.

All in all, to senior public servants of fifty years ago, the current decision-making process would likely appear as a kind of undisciplined free-for-all. It is substantially thicker than it once was and now involves many hands from both inside and outside government.

Consulting firms have grown both in numbers and size over the past forty years. There are now hundreds in economics, program evaluation, and public policy in Ottawa. Many of them employ former federal officials and perform tasks once conducted by public servants. A number of government departments use consultant firms even to prepare Cabinet and Treasury Board submissions – unthinkable fifty years ago. These consultants lack security of tenure and have an economic interest to promote. The next contract may well depend on how they perform on the current one, and so they may well want to present what they think the client wants to hear. They "speak truth to power" at their peril and at a potential personal economic cost. Can consultants, keen to secure new contracts, say no to power? Can they make or want to make the distinction between the public interest and their own immediate economic interest? Can they be as good in pursuing the broader public interest as career public servants?

The government of Canada now spends more than $10 billion a year on consultants. The tendency to turn to them spans the political spectrum. Under Prime Minister Harper's watch, spending on outside consultants has increased by 28 per cent.[59] Consultants are retained by every government department and perform a variety of tasks.

While working on this book, I received an email asking for advice from a consultant who had been retained by the Privy Council Office to prepare a report on prospects for future cooperation between the four Atlantic provinces.[60] I was puzzled why the PCO had not turned to the Atlantic Canada Opportunities Agency (ACOA), a federal agency, for such a report and advice. ACOA, according to its 2013–14 report on plans and priorities, has seventy-two full-time equivalents working in its policy, advocacy, and coordination unit, with a mandate to provide "intelligence, analysis and well-grounded advice on a broad range of issues and topics."[61]

This all suggests that either the PCO is not very good at knowing who does what in the machinery of government or the ACOA is not very good at providing well-grounded advice. It also suggests that, from a PCO perspective, a consultant is better at providing advice than are seventy-two public servants about an issue that goes to the heart of their agency's mandate.

The initiative also stands in sharp contrast to the PCO's role as defined by its former clerk, Gordon Robertson. He insisted that the PCO's mandate was one of "information, coordination, follow-up and support for the Prime Minister." He added that the PCO should not violate a few basic principles, including "staying off the field" that properly belongs to ministers and their departments.[62] That was then. Today the PCO does not hesitate to get on the playing field that properly belongs to line departments.

IT PAYS MORE TO KNOW HARVIE ANDRÉ
THAN TO BE HARVIE ANDRÉ

Harvie André, a former Cabinet minister in Brian Mulroney's government, referring to lobbying in Ottawa, once observed that "it pays more to know Harvie André than to be Harvie André."[63] Fifty years ago, there were virtually no lobbyists in Ottawa. Today, there are thousands of them keeping a close eye on developments. They know, as a former British Cabinet secretary observed, that "power is never constant, it moves around from day to day and somebody who was powerful last week is less powerful this week … reputations rise and fall like a stock exchange."[64] The one constant is that Parliament does not offer much opportunity to influence policy. Though MPs are often lobbied, it remains that lobbyists, interest groups, and even research institutes try to sway the House of Commons only as a last resort, when it is clear that their attempts to influence the government have failed.[65] We are also informed that lobbyists will lobby MPs to "appease clients" or to "pad registry statistics."[66]

Hired guns get things done in Ottawa, and they matter like never before.[67] Large businesses and well-funded associations or interest groups always have interests to promote. They know, or if they do not know, they will be quickly told by lobbyists, that court government (or government by the prime minster and carefully selected courtiers) has replaced Cabinet government in Ottawa.[68] It is thus vitally important not only to identify who in government has influence but also how to access those who do, and this is where lobbyists come in. The importance of that knowledge also explains why many former political advisors and career public servants become lobbyists after leaving government. They have an intimate knowledge of how the system works and who the important players in government are, or at least how to identify them. They also know the importance of being discreet.

The future prosperity of lobbyists often depends on their ability to operate under the radar and to avoid being involved in public controversies. Their purpose is to influence decision-makers on behalf of their clients, but to do so without being seen or heard outside these circles. Drawing media attention to themselves or to their clients is rarely seen in a positive light. Successful lobbyists know that any discussions about the interests of their clients or the public interest are to be held in private, away from public scrutiny.

Lobbying has become an extremely lucrative business. The private sector is not in the business of throwing money around without seeing results. Lobbyists provide a variety of services: they are their customers' eyes and ears in Ottawa; they advance a firm's image and interests before policy-makers; they seek business opportunities in government departments; they can advocate a specific project or develop a public-private partnership agreement; and they can promote a particular point of view. Some even further the interest of the tobacco industry. Whatever the issue, there is a lobbyist in Ottawa always willing to take it on.

Back in 1983, John Kenneth Galbraith wrote that "government and business are widely regarded as mutual enemies."[69] Things are vastly different today. Governments now turn to the business community in good or bad economic times for advice, and the business community has never had a louder or more powerful voice in government. Large businesses have the resources to access those with power in government, and those with power in government are willing recipients of the advice.

The 2008 financial and credit crisis revealed weaknesses in the private sector, especially in the financial sphere. However, when political leaders throughout the Western world decided to establish committees to advise them on dealing with the crisis, many turned to the business community. In Canada, for example, finance minister Jim Flaherty assembled an eleven-member Economic Advisory Council to provide advice to the government. Nine of the eleven were leading members of Canada's business community, and another member, Jack Mintz, is an economist with very close ties to the private sector. Flaherty explained, "In this time of unprecedented economic turmoil, I am bringing some of Canada's best minds together to find solutions and help launch a timely recovery."[70] Best minds are now to be found in the private sector, not in government and not elsewhere. The best minds from the private sector also have quite naturally their own economic interest or those of their shareholders to attend to. Similar committees with a strong private sector bias were set up in other countries, including the United States and Britain.

In any event, many in the business community no longer wait for governments to call for advice. Top Canadian CEOs regularly meet with senior government officials, some of whom, including former ministers and public servants, will, in turn, join their firms on their retirement. Leading representatives of the business community also meet with the minister of finance at an annual retreat. The minister explains that it's "important to hear from Canadian CEOs because of their influence on the economy." He added that he and his department are in regular contact with Canadians from many backgrounds, and one of his advisors explained that "the government pursues some, but not all of the ideas put forward by the business community." At the 2012 retreat, for example, the minister of finance was urged "to adopt measures to reduce the pay of Canadian workers, limit union power by enacting US style right-to-work legislation and allow two-tier health care."[71]

We now know a lot more about the activities of lobbyists. Access-to-information legislation and the Office of the Commissioner of Lobbying of Canada have given us a window on the activities of lobbyists. An access-to-information request, for example, revealed in November 2013 that the Canadian Association of Petroleum Producers lobbied decision-makers to delay climate regulations, insisting that a $40 a tonne carbon tax would drive away investment. It insisted that such a move would leave "Canada far in front of the United States on climate regulations for the oil industry."[72] The lobbying efforts were successful in this case, as they have been in many other cases. Would the industry have been successful without the help of lobbyists? We have no way of knowing. The fact that businesses are prepared to spend a considerable amount of money on lobbyists speaks to their unwillingness to try without their help.

Paid consultant-lobbyists are now required to report communications with government officials, while lobbyists with corporations and interest groups need only to do so if they spend 20 per cent of their time lobbying. The Office of the Commissioner of Lobbying provides a thorough review of lobbying activities.

In 2013, there were 5,256 active lobbyists in Ottawa, including 783 consultant-lobbyists, 1,861 in-house lobbyists with corporations, and 2,612 in-house lobbyists with organizations. There are thus some seventeen lobbyists in Ottawa for every member of Parliament. The office also offers a breakdown of subject matters most frequently identified in order of rank (see tables 1 and 2).

Between January and September 2012, nine of the top ten lobby groups in Ottawa in terms of number of communications with government officials, were leading private sector associations. The top five were Canadian Association of Petroleum Producers, Canadian Bankers Association, Canadian Cattlemen's Association, the Mining Association of Canada, and the Canadian Federation of Independent Business. The more popular topics of discussion included pipelines, tax credits, credit cards, free trade agreement, meat inspection, identity theft, and land claims.[73] The most lobbied ministers include the ministers of industry, finance, and agriculture, which speaks to the interest of the business community and its influence on public policy.[74]

Lobbyists and interest groups know where power lies in government. In the first four months of 2014 alone, firms and interest groups contacted officials in the Prime Minister's Office (PMO) 186 times. One lobbyist explains that the groups "either provide a connection to a voter base or represent vital economic sectors."[75] Representatives of the oil and gas sector contacted the PMO 32 times during the period,

Table 1
Number of individuals registered to lobby, by type

Active lobbyists by type – as of 31 March	2013	2012	2011
Consultant lobbyists	783	814	814
In-house lobbyists (corporations)	1,861	1,786	1,808
In-house lobbyists (organizations)	2,612	2,582	2,507
Total registered individual lobbyists (all types)	5,256	5,182	5,129

Source: Canada, Annual Report 2012–2013 (Ottawa: Office of the Commissioner of Lobbying of Canada, 2013)

Table 2
Number of registrations filed by consultant lobbyists and entities

Active registrations by category— as of 31 March	2013	2012	2011
Consultant lobbyists registrations	2,131	2,123	2,136
Corporations	301	310	311
Organizations	489	492	484
Total active registrations (all categories)	2,921	2,925	2,931

Source: Canada, Annual Report 2012–2013 (Ottawa: Office of the Commissioner of Lobbying of Canada, 2013)

followed by the Canadian Chamber of Commerce, the Canadian Manufacturers and Exporters, and the Canadian Council of Chief Executives.[76] The more popular departments with lobbyists during this period were Industry Canada, Foreign Affairs, Trade and Development, Finance, Natural Resources, and the PMO. Again, these departments all speak to the interest of the country's economic elites.[77]

As noted, former politicians, partisan political advisors, and senior public servants often find employment with lobby groups.[78] Some will also join law firms, though they insist that they do not lobby government officials directly. They do, however, provide advice to clients on how the policy- and decision-making processes work and whom they should talk to. There is now a cooling-off period, which is designed to discourage former government officials from selling their connections immediately after leaving government. Pat Martin, who has supported efforts to strengthen values and ethics in government, insists that the purpose is to ensure that former senior public servants do not "put their own interests ahead of the best interest of the public service."[79] It is no longer sufficient, it seems, to rely on the judgment of career public servants and generous pension plans to guard against improper conduct.

LOOKING BACK

Decision-making is now the product of many hands and many forces. The locus of policy- and decision-making and policy debates has shifted away from Parliament and Cabinet. The prime minister and his close advisors, the courts, the horizontal nature of government operations, and the forces tied to the global economy have reshaped fundamentally how public sector decisions are struck. We now have fuzzy boundaries, and hierarchy in government no longer works, certainly not to the extent that it once did.

One traditional means for citizens to access government programs and to be heard – the local member of Parliament – no longer works well. Not only has the decision-making process become overly complicated for the average MP to influence, it is also difficult for MPs even to know where to turn in order to seek answers or to have influence. One veteran observer of Canadian politics exemplified the extent to which Parliament has been brought low by noting that MPs are increasingly turning to the Access to Information Act in order to get information from the government. This he describes as "ridiculous and an affront to Parliament."[80]

The courts, like all other institutions, once took a back seat to Parliament in the Westminster model. The courts, until the era of the Charter of Rights and Freedoms, could check government only if it acted ultra vires of statutory authority. That was then. At the risk of oversimplification, power first shifted from the king, to Parliament, to Cabinet, to the prime minister, who now needs to share some of his power with the courts.

The courts, as we have seen, now have the luxury of making decisions with important public policy content without having to find the funds to support their decisions or to be concerned about how the machinery of government will deliver what they decide. Judges do not have to make the necessary trade-offs between competing demands, they do not have to reconcile their decisions with the fiscal framework, they never have to cut spending in certain sectors if only to increase funding in other areas, and they never have to increase taxes. The courts are in the envious position of shaping public policy and striking decisions without having to deal with their implementation. That, for the courts, is someone else's problem.

The someone elses are government officials managing a complex horizontal policy process and a management structure overly burdened by accountability and reporting requirements. The courts have little appreciation of the challenges confronting government officials implementing policies and delivering programs and services. It is a world foreign to them, because they are not exposed to it. Judges all too often assume that the machinery of government will do as it is told, and they too think that public policy is 90 per cent ideas and 10 per cent implementation. Reality, however, is quite different, at least when viewed from the perspective of government line managers and citizens.

Viewed from the perspective of citizens, the current system is fundamentally flawed. It does not square with Bernard Crick's treatise on politics: "People act together through institutionalised procedures to resolve differences, to conciliate different interests and values and to make public policies in the pursuit of common purposes."[81] The common purpose has given way to organized narrow interests, and the ability to navigate institutionalized procedures has become the preserve of those with the knowledge or resources to influence them. With fuzzy boundaries and other factors, government officials who can influence decisions are not easily identifiable, let alone accessible. It seems that only those with the knowledge of the system or with the resources to hire that knowledge can influence their work.

In brief, those with the knowledge or resources now have the upper hand in shaping the public interest. The *Economist*, hardly a left-of-centre publication, went to the heart of the matter when it observed, "Government must remember that businesses are self-interested actors who will try to rig the system for their own benefit."[82] The same can be said for organized interest groups. The government is now good at dealing with organized groups and the economic elites with the resources to retain hired guns, often drawn from the ranks of politicians and senior public servants. It is less good at dealing with citizens.

It is becoming increasingly difficult to assess what government is good at, because there are now so many hands shaping decisions. How can one determine, for example, if governments are good at financial management when the courts can instruct a government department not only to launch a new measure but also how it should be implemented?

The public service is the one institution that should be detached from interest groups. If it is to be good at one thing, it is to know how to be objective and to be the guardian of the public interest by giving impartial and evidence-based advice to ministers. In the next chapter, we explore how the public service measures up.

5

Fixing Bureaucracy:
Please Mind the Gap

Margaret Thatcher was "no ordinary politician."[1] Her views were firm and unshakable. She is famously remembered for telling her colleagues, "You turn if you want to. The lady's not for turning!" Thatcher believed that we had to "encourage and reward the risk takers, the entrepreneurs who alone create wealth without which government cannot do anything."[2] At the risk of oversimplification, for Thatcher the public sector was the problem and the private sector was the solution. She once said that she "disliked government bureaucrats as a breed."[3]

Thatcher came to power in 1979, determined to cut government down to size. She was convinced that the civil service was too big, too intrusive in the lives of citizens, wielding too much influence over policy-making, and too much in the way of resources for what it accomplished.

Thatcher believed that she did not need the public service to help define the public interest. She knew what she wanted to be done and had just secured a majority mandate to pursue it. What she wanted from bureaucrats was that they run government operations and programs efficiently, while she and her senior ministers set the policy agenda. In brief, Thatcher felt that politicians should be good at policy-making and bureaucrats at managing programs and delivering services.

Senior public servants, however, are not in the habit of saying that they have too much influence over policy and too many resources. They are also not in the habit of saying that their ability to manage operations is lacklustre. When Thatcher asked senior officials for new approaches to running departments and agencies, she drew a blank. She, her ministers, and senior advisors were left searching for answers outside of the machinery of government, and that is where they went. Senior public servants were and remain convinced that they have a legitimate policy advisory role, with the great majority of them joining the public service for that very reason.

Thatcher would in time have a profound impact on how policy is struck in Britain and how government operates. Moreover, her reforms were also taken up throughout Anglo-American democracies, where they reverberate to this day.

We need to revisit Thatcher-inspired reform measures to assess better what government is good at. This chapter looks at how government bureaucracies have evolved over the past thirty years. It assesses the impact of the managerial revolution on government operations and considers the evolving relationship between politicians and public servants. This and the various management reform measures have had a direct impact on what government is good at.

THINGS WILL BE DIFFERENT

As I reported in my earlier work, Thatcher served notice, from day one, to other politicians and to senior bureaucrats that things would never be the same. The briefing material she received as she assumed office made the case that the 733,000-strong civil service was already stretched to the limit and that "even modest" cuts in staff would inhibit departments from functioning effectively. Some departments asked for more staff. She simply ignored the claim and declared a freeze on hiring the day she came to office. She decided that public servants were not good at establishing the level of financial and human resources required to deliver programs and services.

Early in her first mandate, she directed that the civil service be reduced in size by about 15 per cent. By the time she left office, it had been cut by over 22 per cent, down to 569,000.⁴ Thatcher imposed cuts by simply laying down targets. She stuck to her position and met her objectives. I once asked Sir Robert Armstrong, former Cabinet secretary and one of the authors of the briefing book, if Thatcher had it right when she ignored their claim and imposed cuts by picking a number out of the air. Yes was his answer. "Why then," I asked, "did you attempt to persuade her to hire more public servants?" His answer:

"Permanent secretaries made their claim, and we packaged the various requests and made the case for more resources."[5] Public servants are good at reacting to what government departments and agencies want, but much less so at determining if what they are asking for is warranted. This is no less true in Canada.

Something broke in the relationship between politicians and career public servants in the late 1970s that has never been repaired.[6] This, in turn, has had a profound impact on what government is good at. It is wrong, however, to assume that the relationship first went astray under Thatcher.

Richard Crossman's *Diaries of a Cabinet Minister* sent shock waves throughout the political world in Anglo-American democracies in the mid- to late 1970s. Crossman, a former Oxford don and a leading socialist of his day, favoured an expanded role for government in virtually every policy field. His diaries, however, took dead aim at government bureaucracies, insisting that they took on a life of their own, like an uncontrollable monster. He argued, "Whenever one relaxes one's guard, the Civil Service in one's Department quietly asserts itself ... Just as the Cabinet Secretariat constantly transforms the actual proceedings of Cabinet into the form of the Cabinet minutes (i.e. it substitutes what we should have said if we had done as they wished for what we actually did say), so here in my Department the civil servants are always putting in what they think I should have said and not what I actually decided."[7]

Other left-of-centre politicians also began joining in the criticism. Shirley Williams, another highly respected former British politician and later a professor emerita at Harvard's Kennedy School of Government, had this to say: "My impression of the British Civil Service is that it is a beautifully designed and effective braking mechanism. It produces a hundred well-argued answers against initiative and change."[8] In Canada, Allan J. MacEachen, a long-time senior member of the Liberal Party and an important architect of Canada's welfare state, reported that if Liberals had learned anything during their brief stay in opposition in 1979, it was that his party would no longer rely as much as they had on the policy advice of senior public servants.[9]

If left-of-centre politicians saw problems with government bureaucracy, what were right-of-centre politicians to think? But that was not all. The Crossman diaries gave rise to the popular BBC Television series *Yes Minister*, which attracted nine million viewers in Britain alone and became the favourite television program of the permanent secretaries. Mrs Thatcher urged her senior civil servants to watch the series, which also gained a worldwide audience and became highly popular with many politicians and public servants in Canada, the United States, and Australia. The not-so-subtle message of *Yes Minister* was that public servants were running the country, their deference to politicians was pure pretence, and the Sir Humphreys of the bureaucratic world wielded considerable power. The series actually gave credence to bureaucrat-bashing.[10]

Again, politicians, not simply those on the right, decided that senior public servants should not influence policy-making to the extent that they had in the past. What politicians wanted was for senior public servants to become better managers. If public servants could not identify means to turn themselves into better managers, politicians had the answer: emulate the private sector.

Thus, since the early 1980s, politicians, whether on the right or left of the political spectrum, have essentially all pushed in the same direction: get a firmer handle on the policy-making and turn senior public servants into better managers. If bureaucrats were to be good at something under the new political order, then it was to be at managing operations and delivering programs and services by borrowing best management practices from the private sector.

LOOKING TO THE PRIVATE SECTOR

Margaret Thatcher, Ronald Reagan, and Brian Mulroney all turned to private sector executives to help them review programs. The Rayner (under Thatcher), Grace (under Reagan) and Nielsen (under Mulroney) reviews had varying degrees of success, but all three had strong private sector input.[11] The three political leaders served notice that business would not be as usual in government. Public servants would see their role redefined by stealth. The partnership between politicians and the senior public servants who had managed the war effort and built the postwar Keynesian consensus was fast coming to an end.

Politicians by the 1980s felt that political, policy, and administrative roles could no longer be distinguished from one another. They also believed that this served the interest of public servants, not that of politicians. The thinking was that public servants had a hand in all the roles but, in the end, were not accountable for any of them. Politicians were accountable for all things but believed that they had only limited power over policy and very little over administration. As Mark Bevir writes, "Ministerial responsibility became too obvious a myth to be taken seriously."[12]

The solution for politicians: grasp the political and policy levers and tell public servants to focus on management, the boiler room of government. They wanted public servants to become results-oriented in managing government operations, like their private sector counterparts. In the process they sought to redefine the role of public servants as managers and of citizens as customers, with the intent of making the providers more responsive to customers.[13]

CHANGING THE CHANNEL

How could politicians take hold of the policy levers? How could they turn public servants into better managers? How could they make the case that senior public servants should take a back seat on policy?

History reveals that there is a gulf between politicians wishing to do something in government and actually getting it done. Public servants likely felt that if politicians wanted to control policy, all they had to do was to grasp the steering wheel and drive the government's public agenda. Too often, they claim, politicians talk about change but in the actual event, they balk. More to the point, few senior public servants were then or are now prepared to admit that they have too much power over the policy process, since politicians are always free to accept or reject the bureaucrats' policy advice.

Right-of-centre politicians in the 1980s were not the first to call on public servants to become better managers. Reports of the Glassco Commission in Canada (1963), the Fulton Commission in Britain (1968), and the Hoover Commission in the United States (1949) had all brought forward a series of recommendations to strengthen management in government. All three had also looked to the business community for a model of better management practices. Years later, critics argued that there had been little improvement. They accused public servants of intuitively favouring the status quo, of giving the appearance of change while, in fact, moving very slowly or even standing still.[14]

It was this widely held view that, in part, led politicians in the 1980s to declare that government had become part of the problem rather than the solution. It led Brian Mulroney, for example, to promise that, if elected, he would hand out "pink slips and running shoes to bureaucrats."[15] This may well have given Mulroney a good political line during an election campaign, but it scarcely constituted a plan once in office.

So what to do? Mulroney did not arrive with a plan in hand any more than Margaret Thatcher and Ronald Reagan had done. They would improvise on how to change the policy process and look to the private sector for ideas to overhaul management practices in government. The private sector may offer best management practices, but it has little to offer politicians on how to shape public policy. To be sure, business executives could offer policy advice, and they did and still do. But the public policy apparatus differs in every way from the private sector.

EXPANDING THE POLITICAL APPARATUS

How does the policy process today differ from forty years ago? Have politicians gained the upper hand in shaping policy? If so, how?

Politicians in Canada did what politicians in the United States have long done. They expanded the role and number of partisan political staff. They also expanded the role and number of officials in central agencies, especially in the politically partisan Prime Minister's Office. Politicians also welcomed the arrival of politically friendly consultants and lobbyists who provided a new source of policy advice.

Initially, the objective was to strengthen the governing party's control in determining policy. That has remained the goal but, as new oversight bodies were added, a new objective surfaced: managing the blame game. Politicians, for obvious reasons, feel more comfortable managing blame-avoidance with committed partisans than with career public servants. This alone has given partisan political staffers a greater role in policy and program decisions and in directing the government's communications strategy.

Brian Mulroney set an important precedent in Canadian public administration when he told his ministers that they could appoint a chief of staff in their offices and increase their exempt staff budgets. Salary levels for chiefs of staff were set at the assistant deputy minister level, a level immediately below deputy ministers. Mulroney's decision to have a chief of staff in each ministerial office had one purpose: to check the permanent officials' influence on policy. Government press releases even described the position as an "official in the American style."[16] Jean Chrétien did away with the position when he came to power, but in name only. The chief of staff position has since been re-established and enjoys the same status and salary levels as it did during the Mulroney years. New positions have also been created in ministerial offices of late – director of policy and director of communications.

The power structure in Ottawa has changed substantially over the past forty years or so. Prime ministers in Canada now govern from the centre and have been doing so in varying degrees since the Trudeau years. This, in turn, has strengthened the position of central agencies and a few carefully selected senior ministers. All policy roads now lead to and from the prime minister, who, with his courtiers, decides the substance, scope, and pace of policy changes. There are precious few exceptions, and even these are closely watched by both the Prime Minister's Office and the Privy Council Office.

To be sure, some individual public servants continue to play an important policy role – the clerk of the Privy Council, the deputy minister of finance, and a handful of other deputy ministers who have gained the confidence of the centre. The difference is that before the Thatcher and Mulroney reforms, the public service, as an institution, had substantial influence over policy, while today influence belongs to a carefully selected handful of partisan advisors and senior deputy ministers.

Public servants are adept at reading political tea leaves. That explains why, while preparing briefing books for the 1984 transition to power for the incoming Mulroney government, Gordon Osbaldeston, the clerk of the Privy Council, insisted on a "strict separation of background briefing for advice and administrative matters," or, stated differently, the separation of administration from politics.[17] It was the first of many signs that many senior public servants had decided to step aside and let politicians and their partisan advisors define the government's policy agenda. This, among other factors, pushed deputy ministers to look to the interdepartmental policy process nearly as much as to their own departments. Deputy ministers now know more about the interdepartmental policy process and how to fall on hand grenades to manage political problems than they do the history of their departments.

There was a time when a public servant would rise through the ranks of the department, eventually becoming a director general, an assistant deputy minister, and even a deputy minister, and remain there for a long time. Sir Edward Bridges wrote in 1950 that one of the most important skills a public servant should have is "long experience of a particular field."[18] No more.

Forty years ago, deputy ministers were concerned primarily with their own departments and identified strongly with them. One former deputy minster reports that when he was first appointed in the early 1970s, he would not have recognized one-third of his counterparts, had he come across them on the street.[19] Today, deputy ministers spend nearly as much time with one another reconciling the interdepartmental process as they do with their own senior departmental managers. The deputy minister club has regular meetings, at breakfast, during luncheon, and on retreats. Members identify strongly with the club, and each may well serve over time as deputy minister in three or four departments. Loyalty is as much to the club, if not more so, than to their departments.

Deputy ministers have become as much a part of the centre of government and the interdepartmental process as they are administrative heads of their departments. They are now selected for their knowledge of how the system works rather than for their sectoral expertise or for their knowledge of a department and its policy history. Deputy ministers today come from central agencies, not from line departments, and typically their stay in one department is short. Central agencies are not the place where one develops strong management skills. Deputy ministers have thus hardly become better managers, and one would be hard-pressed to claim that they have learned to focus more on operations and services to clients.

Deputy ministers readily acknowledge that the nature of their jobs has changed in recent years and that today they are more negotiators and networkers than traditional managers. One keen observer writes, "There is no precise job description for deputy ministers. It is a variable, multifaceted job, depending on political schedules, political crises and events arising from both outside and inside the organization."[20] Henry Mintzberg and Jacques Bourgault reveal in *Managing*

Publicly that deputy ministers now spend "sixteen percent of their time dealing with crises and answering emergencies" – more than on managing human resources (i.e., 15 per cent). As well, "they spend twenty percent of their time on strategic files that will move forward or change their organizations."[21] The emphasis is now on networking, brokering, and problem-solving in a fast-moving political context.[22] Deputy ministers "will look for quick fixes and sound risk-takers who are capable of negotiating agreements that can be appreciated in terms of results and impact rather than in the usual vague terms."[23]

A deputy's workday of ten to twelve hours typically consists of dealing with the prime minister's priorities; implementing the government's agenda; protecting the minister; networking with other deputies, the provincial governments, and the department's stakeholders; learning to work with senior business executives; articulating and promoting the department's interests; and managing political crises. These many functions have transformed the role into a kind of buckle linking the political realm, the relevant policy communities, and the key stakeholders to the permanent administration. Deputy ministers know that it is in this role that they can best leave their mark. Promoting the department's policy interests and expanding its scope and mandate are a tangible way to demonstrate success to politicians and central agencies. There are not many other such clear standards of success available to them. Better management practices are not one of them. Being good at managing operations and programs is not as highly valued in government as being good at operating in a highly charged and at times hostile political environment.

INDIVIDUALS HAVE POWER AND INFLUENCE

The *Hill Times* publishes a yearly report on the most influential people in politics and government in Ottawa. *Maclean's* magazine now also ranks the top twenty-five most important people in Ottawa. The focus is on individuals: institutions, government departments, or agencies don't get a mention. In brief, it is now never about the public service, always about individuals.

Both publications always place the prime minister at the top of their respective lists. In 2008, the *Hill Times* included eight consultant lobbyists.[24] In 2012 the prime minister's wife was ranked at twenty, his chief of staff at six, the clerk of the Privy Council at eight, the deputy minister of finance at nine, the top lobbyist for the business community (the voice of "Canada's industrial and financial CEOs") at number twelve, and Canada's chief justice at number nineteen.[25] It is safe to assume that neither the top lobbyist for the business community nor the chief justice would have made it in the top fifty, let alone top twenty, in the 1960s or 1970s. In *Maclean's*, the prime minister placed first in 2012, followed by the chief justice at number two.[26]

Leaving aside a few highly influential public servants, the public service as an institution is taking a back seat in the policy-making process. Politicians have not only been successful in wrestling away at least some of the influence of the public service over policy; evidence-based policy advice is now also out of fashion. Politicians and their partisan advisors have easy access to multiple sources of information and advice and do not hesitate to use them.

We now live in a world of Google searches, focus groups, public opinion surveys, and well-connected lobbyists who can provide any policy answer that politicians want to hear. This is in sharp contrast to yesteryear when the public service could and would follow proper data-gathering procedures and produce analyses with predictive power and would constitute the main and undisputed source of policy advice to the prime minister and ministers.

Anyone looking for proof that politicians no longer much value evidence-based policy advice need look no further than to the government's decision to cancel the mandatory long-form questionnaire as part of the 2011 Canadian census of the population. The long-form questionnaire was the main source of information about key socio-economic matters from income to geographic mobility. The Canadian Research Data Centre Network asked to have the long-form questionnaire reinstated, given its status as a "public good."[27] All in all, over two hundred groups and prominent citizens publicly opposed the change and only three supported it.[28] All efforts to reverse the decision failed. In the end, the government decided what was in the public interest, despite strong opposition to its position.

More recently, the government decided to reduce funding for Statistics Canada to gather labour data and rely more on private sector data based on scans of Internet job boards. The data from this source were found wanting, with the parliamentary budget officer pointing out that the problem lies with double counting when relying on web-sites such as Kijiji for data.[29] Don Drummond, a former senior feder-al government official, explains, "Normally you create an information infrastructure and that informs the policy. But here we've had dra-matic changes in policy with the temporary foreign worker program and the Canada Job Grant, while we undermine the lousy informa-tion infrastructure we already had."[30]

Andrew Griffith, a director general in the Department of Citizen-ship and Immigration, provides an inside look at how policy on mul-ticulturalism took shape under Jason Kenney, a powerful senior min-ister in the Harper government. He describes the transition to a new way of making policy as traumatic for public servants. He reports that Prime Minister Harper gave notice of the change when he observed, "Probably the most difficult job, you know, practical difficult thing you have to learn as a prime minister and our ministers as well, is deal-ing with the federal bureaucracy … It's walking that fine line of, of being a positive leader of the federal public service, but at the same time pushing them and not becoming captive to them."[31]

Brian Mulroney had essentially said the same thing over twenty years earlier, as did Allan J. MacEachen nearly thirty years ago.[32] The differ-ence is that Harper and some of his senior ministers have proved to be more tenacious and have stayed the course in their desire to challenge the status quo and to gain a firm upper hand in shaping new policies.

Griffith explains that getting over the challenge of adjusting to the new reality "was existentialist, demoralizing and even traumatic for many public servants, particularly but not exclusively in multicultur-alism. The Kübler-Ross model of grief applied, consciously or not; many had to pass through varying degrees of the denial, anger, bar-gaining and depression stages. At the same time, the political level grappled with the lack of responsiveness of the public service, per-ceived at times as arrogant or even disloyal, in responding to their pol-icy direction and priorities. The risks for both sides of falling into a pattern of 'rolling one's eyes' and viewing the political-bureaucratic relationship as antagonistic, were high."[33] What is more remarkable is that Griffith made this observation some thirty years after Mulroney, Thatcher, and other senior politicians had served notice that they intended to firmly grab hold of the policy function and turn senior public servants into better managers.

Griffith writes that the minister based his policy preferences on "anecdotes that the minister and his staff would bring back" from their trips. He adds, "Our evidence tended to be large-scale research and surveys, which are very valid, and his evidence tended to be anecdotal, but it was such a large base of anecdotes that it was something that we actually had to take into account." When it came time to rewrite the citizenship guide, *Discover Canada*, the public servants working on it "didn't get it right at all," so the ministerial and political staff "actually wrote it for us," and the department went from there.[34]

This approach is in sharp contrast to when Jack Manion served in a similar capacity in the same department. Manion spent much of his career in the Department of Citizenship and Immigration, going up through the ranks to serve as its deputy minister. He also served, as we shall see later, as secretary to the Treasury Board and associate secretary to the Privy Council. His memoirs were published some two years after he died in 2010.[35]

Manion's recollections should be required reading for all students of public administration and public servants. He tells how the Canadian government managed the Hungarian refugee crisis in the mid-1950s. The minister, not the prime minister or his office, ran the policy and the program. Manion and his peers would not have tolerated ministerial partisan staff "actually writing" the citizenship guide. In addition, the minister himself would likely not have accepted that his political staff would write the guidelines. The minister always turned to public servants for policy advice, not to his political staff. He challenged them, Manion explained, but the relationship worked very well in managing "one of the greatest refugee programs in Canada's history."[36] Manion managed a "small" policy unit well into the 1960s and his mandate was always clear. Central agencies, interdepartmental committees, and outside policy networks were not much of a factor in his work and there were no lobbyists to deal with. Central agency officials knew their place and recognized that departments were not only a storehouse of knowledge about their sectors but also knew what worked in the field and what did not.

Things are vastly different today. Michael Hatfield, a recently retired senior economist with Human Resources and Skills Development Canada, writes, "Making sure that the director of every possible unit with the remotest interest in the policy area has signed off on policy advice often becomes more important than subjecting that advice to real scrutiny by people with the knowledge and capacity for careful vetting."[37] Flipping documents between policy shops in Ottawa, always with an eye on what the prime minister and his courtiers are interested in, often ignores a key ingredient in shaping sound policy – how it can be best implemented. The Ottawa-centric consultation process may resonate in the "Ottawa bubble" but much less so elsewhere. The government is good or at least better than it once was at managing the blame game and at extending the consultation process within the machinery of government, but at a cost – implementation.

The Trudeau years also brought a different era, and the trust between politicians and senior line department public servants began to wane. Manion writes about this transition. He reveals that he wrote a detailed letter to the secretary to the Treasury Board with a list of complaints about the growing intrusion of central agencies in the work of line departments, especially his. Before he received a reply, he was moved to the Treasury Board as the new secretary. Shortly after he arrived, he was presented with a draft letter to his successor in his old department referring to "the letter your predecessor had written to my predecessor" with a "bland reply to all his complaints."[38] His minister at the Treasury Board gave him the collection of the *Yes Minister* series, a not-so-subtle sign that things were changing.[39]

The relationship between politicians and public servants deteriorated further in the Mulroney years. Manion writes that "most (not all) of the Mulroney ministers were hostile" to the public service, and only in time did they realize that they needed "the professional support of the Public Service."[40] He explains that "unfortunately, the new Government had set up a network of 'Chiefs of Staff' to Ministers which was a real nightmare. Many of them believed they were the DMs' alter egos, with equal powers. In fact some believed they had the power to control access of the DM to his Minister. Moreover, they had a network and met weekly to plan strategy."[41] Things improved after Mulroney, at the urging of the Privy Council Office, told his ministers that their chiefs of staff were there to provide political support and "not to harass departments." Manion reports, however, that "ill feelings continued."[42]

There were other developments. Until the Martin years, ministers were not allowed to bring their partisan political staff with them into Cabinet committee meetings. Participation was strictly restricted to ministers and their senior line-departmental officials. Paul Martin would change this, with partisan political advisors attending Cabinet committees with their ministers and departmental officials. This approach remains in place to this day: ministers can turn to both their partisan political advisors and public servants for advice before their Cabinet colleagues. The change is both symbolic and substantive, demonstrating, as it does, the weakened position of the public service with regard to policy-making.

The relationship between ministers, their offices, and deputy ministers and their department has not returned to the pre-Mulroney days. Of course, the relationships vary a great deal, depending on the individuals involved. Some are better than others at making it work. However, the chief of staff and now the new positions of director of policy and director of communications in ministerial offices have changed the dynamic. Jacques Bourgault writes about a "ménage à trois" that involves the minister, his or her staff, and the deputy minister.[43] There is plenty of evidence to suggest that ministerial staffers are involved, in some cases directly, in the day-to-day operations of the department, particularly when an issue becomes fuel for the blame game.[44] The important point is that ministerial offices are more present and have a greater say in the running of government departments than in years past. They are – particularly the chief of staff – in constant communication with the Prime Minister's Office to ensure that the centre is fully briefed on issues that may create a political problem for the government.

WHAT ABOUT SOCIETY'S NEUTRAL SERVANTS?

When Manion wrote that the prime minister and ministers needed the professional support of the public service, he had the traditional model in mind. His point was that professional and politically neutral public servants have a strong loyalty to society in general, to public values, to evidence-based policy advice, and to seeing themselves as serving the public interest. They also see themselves as loyal to the government of the day, ready to serve whomever citizens elect. However, when the prime minister and ministers envisage something that is not in the public interest, their role is to warn them of the consequences. But they remain loyal to the prime minister and ministers and recognize that, providing they do not contemplate something that is illegal, politicians decide and public servants implement.[45] Max Weber explained why: "To take a stand, to be passionate ... is the politician's element ... indeed, exactly the opposite ... from that of the civil servant. The honor of the civil servant is vested in his ability to execute conscientiously the order of the superior authorities ... Without this moral discipline and self-denial, in the highest sense, the whole apparatus would fall to pieces."[46]

In the traditional model, the personnel of government are hired through a merit system, which is designed to secure the best policy advice possible and to prevent partisan political interference in implementing programs and delivering services. B. Guy Peters outlined the characteristics of a professional non-partisan public service: "(1) an apolitical civil service; (2) hierarchy and rules; (3) permanence and stability; (4) an institutional civil service; (5) internal regulation; (6) equality (internally and externally to the organization)."[47] This, all in the interest of having an independent public service able to provide frank and fearless policy advice and having non-partisan professionals – rather than partisan toadies – deliver programs. It is generally recognized that it is in the public interest to have a permanent, professional, and non-partisan public service. The traditional model makes government good at ensuring a level of fairness and uniformity in delivering government programs and shaping policy.

The danger in moving away from the traditional model is that the public sector is opened to a kind of free-for-all and there is risk that the public interest will be marginalized. A free-for-all in shaping policies makes it easier for special interests or well-resourced interest groups to crowd out the broader public interest.[48]

If the term *public interest* has any meaning at all when shaping public policy, the public service should most likely represent and pursue it.[49] The point is that the public service stands or should stand in sharp contrast to partisan political advisors, lobbyists, policy consultants, and special interest groups who are concerned with either short-term political interests, a sectional interest, or a future contract. While it is not the role of public servants to define the public interest, their task is to challenge. And while ministers will bridle, the tension between politicians and public servants is the point. Together, the politician and the administrator act as the platonic guardians of the public interest.[50]

The United Nations sought to deal with this by adopting a code of conduct in 1996 for public servants. It reads:

A public office, as defined by national law, is a position of trust, implying a duty to act in the public interest. Therefore, the ulti-mate loyalty of public officials shall be to the public interests of their country as expressed through the democratic institutions of government. Public officials shall be attentive, fair and impartial in the performance of their functions and, in particular, in their relations with the public. They shall at no time afford any undue preferential treatment to any group or individual or improperly discriminate against any group or individual, or otherwise abuse the power and authority vested in them.[51]

The government of Canada also decided to hold a values and ethics exercise for the public service in the mid-1990s. John Tait, a former deputy minister of Justice, led a task force and tabled a report in 1997. The report stressed the importance of democratic values and described the public service "as an important national institution in the service of democracy."[52] It was quite explicit on this point: "The concept of a professional public service does not include or require a guarantee of lifetime employment," adding, because it felt a need to do so, that "a government is quite within its democratic rights to determine the size of the public service or its role."[53]

Tying the public service to the public interest has been made more difficult in recent years, which may well explain why the United Nations and the government of Canada both saw a need to table a code and a report on the conduct and values of public officials. For reasons outlined earlier, the terms public interest, the common good, the collective interest, and the common understanding have lost some of their meaning in the global economy and in an increasingly plu-ralist society. Citizens look to different bodies and to different policy actors to sort out conflicts. The postwar consensus came to a close and with it the notion that the government could speak for all, or the great majority of members of society. In brief, as Canada's pluralistic society matured, governments came to recognize that it was virtually impossible to cover all interests and to find a common understanding that would link, among others, Aboriginals, environmentalists, farmers, entrepreneurs in the natural resources sector, minority-language groups, and feminists.

Ultimately, however, political leaders have to arbitrate between sectional interests. In doing so, they have to allocate resources and establish priorities. Some politicians have shifted to a narrow view of the public interest, insisting that government should only focus on the interests of taxpayers, promote low taxes, and avoid favouring sectional interests to the extent possible. The point, once again, is that in a democratic society, establishing the public interest is a highly political process that calls for negotiation between conflicting interests.[54] Politicians need to be good at doing this.

What about the public service? Apart from ensuring that the constitution and statutes are respected, there is a limit to how far they can go in defining the public interest. To be sure, they can claim a greater affinity with the public interest than can lobbyists, organized sectional interests, or politically partisan actors. That said, public servants have to defer to their political masters, unless the actions violate the constitution or statutes.

The role of the public service is under attack throughout the Western world. It has become more difficult for public servants to serve the public interest and to provide fearless advice. Public servants are expected to be loyal to their political masters, their institution, their colleagues, their departments, various oversight bodies, and the general public. They are also still expected to treat all citizens impartially, fairly, and equally. They are now being asked to take a back seat on policy and to focus more on management, though even here they are receiving mixed messages.[55] Marcel Massé, a former clerk of the Privy Council and later a senior minister in the Chrétien government, warned that "governments are paying too much attention to special interest groups and risk losing touch with ordinary Canadians in shaping policies and services ... public servants must find new ways to 'define' the public interest rather than letting powerful special-interest groups dominate the policy-making agenda."[56]

Because of collective bargaining and other developments, the public service also has its own sectional interests to promote. More is said on this point later. Sustained efforts, or at least sustained rhetoric, to make the public sector look like the private sector have had a profound impact on the public service. Managerialism has given rise to a new breed of public servants, one that makes it more difficult to shape policies and deliver programs and services in the public interest.

MANAGERIALISM

The private sector managerial revolution introduced by Margaret Thatcher that later made its way to all Anglo-American countries was designed to encourage or, failing that, force senior public servants to focus on managing operations and delivering better public services. The underlying idea was to give government managers greater discretion by freeing them from traditional bureaucratic constraints. The thinking or the hope was that government managers would focus on performance and outcomes rather than on processes and procedures.

The management revolution had a number of objectives. It was hoped that it would deal with the government overload problems by introducing private sector management techniques to government, by privatizing a number of activities, or by creating agencies with operational responsibilities. It was also hoped that it would force public servants to focus on results and introduce better management practices, which would, as an added bonus, reduce government spending.

The rise of New Public Management has been well documented by a multitude of authors, and there is no need to review it in any detail once again.[57] Suffice to note that very few voices still claim that the managerial revolution was a success or even that it had the desired impact. However, many make the case that it has fallen far short of expectations.[58] Rod Rhodes put it well recently when he wrote, "For my entire academic career, I have been watching the reform of government. It has been an ever-present relentless tide of change masquerading as improvement. Few will remember all these initiatives. Fewer lasted."[59]

NPM could never duplicate private sector conditions in government. More to the point, no government has been able to reconcile the need to hold government agencies and their bureaucrats accountable, requiring them to be subordinate to politicians while requiring them to be strong, decisive, and efficient, as NPM called for.[60] Efforts to reconcile the irreconcilable have only made government bureaucracies less decisive, more bureaucratic, and less certain about their role. They have become not as good as they once were, operating under the traditional model, and uncertain about how to function under the new management model.

Governments have been busy ever since the early 1980s trying to invent a bottom line and somehow create market forces within the public sector. The result has been a shift to performance-based account-ability, new oversight bodies, and new program evaluation efforts. Con-sequently, the Canadian bureaucracy today is more top-heavy, has more staff units as opposed to line units actually delivering programs and ser- vices, and produces far more reports than in years past. Today, 43 per cent of the Canadian public service is located in head offices in Ottawa. Thirty years ago, the figure was 27 per cent.[61] Public servants in field and regional offices deliver services and interact frequently with citizens, while public servants in Ottawa, much more often than not, work in policy, evaluation, and overhead functions and interact with one another. They are kept busy trying somehow to fabricate a bottom line.

Central agencies now recognize that they have gone too far in such attempts. The Treasury Board Secretariat and the Public Service Commission have recently unveiled plans to eliminate "ineffective and unnecessary rules and streamlining reporting requirements." Both agencies are committed to reducing the reporting burden by 25 to 50 per cent,[62] But it is not clear whether the two central agencies are meeting their targets. Without acknowledging that it was at least partly to blame, the Office of the Auditor General found that the reporting burden was unduly demanding for small government agencies.[63]

Public servants are valued today by politicians on the government side, not for their private sector–inspired management talents but for their ability to manage the blame game in Ottawa. Management has taken a back seat to crisis management, communications, spin, blame-avoidance, and to interdepartmental processes, or to the big picture, as defined by the centre of government. However, emphasis on management has brought benefits to senior public servants, enabling them to do things that would have been impossible thirty years ago: they now have greater discretion on staffing, easy or easier reclassification of subordinates, hiring of consultants, and, for a period, the transferring of funds that Parliament had earmarked for programs to operations and overhead costs, including salaries. The benefits (if one can call them benefits) for the senior managers include adding more and more staff at head office to produce more and more evaluations and performance reports to deal with never-ending requests for information from central agencies and officers of Parliament and to manage the blame game.

Today, there are an estimated 3,824 spin specialists or communications staffers in the federal government, including nearly 100 in the Prime Minister's Office and the Privy Council Office. Growth in their numbers began in earnest in the early 1980s and has shot up in recent years, with an increase of over 700 positions in the last six years alone.[64] Scott Reid, former director of communications to Prime Minister Martin, explains, "At the political level, there really were no formal positions known as director of communications in the early '90s. By 2003, every minister had both a communications director and a press secretary ... you saw changes of that kind happen, all of which are clear indications that the emphasis on communications was increasing at both the political and bureaucratic level."[65] It is revealing to note that, while the number of communications staffers has declined in recent years in regional offices, their ranks have grown by 13 per cent in Ottawa.[66] Clearly, the focus of communications staffers in government centres on those operating above the fault line.

No issue is too trivial for senior government officials to ignore in managing the blame game. Some observers, including Ralph Heintzman, have pointed to the "growing involvement of public servants in communications," suggesting that they are crossing the line at the highest level, putting "loyalty to the government of the day above loyalty to the public interest, and far above loyalty to the values of the very institution they were charged with leading."[67] No one knows for certain if they are crossing the line, because there is no sure way of knowing.

Are government operations better managed today than thirty years ago? Very little evidence suggests that they are. Spending is reduced only when prime ministers (circa Chrétien 1994–97 and Harper 2012–14) decide to implement ambitious program reviews or when the centre declares a one- or two-year spending freeze in government operations. Cuts are still imposed from the top down and, for the most part, still decided by across-the-board targets. There has been no marked difference in how non-performers are dealt with – when they cannot contribute, they continue to be parked in obscure offices performing obscure functions. The percentage of federal public servants terminated for incompetence or misconduct remains minuscule, fewer than 100 a year from a total staff complement of about 257,000, narrowly defined.[68]

Notwithstanding the implementation of NPM practices in government, incompetence or mismanagement will not result in termination, but bringing negative attention to your department may well do so. Three Health Canada employees were fired in June 2004 for speaking out against departmental policies. They had publicly expressed their concern over the use of bovine growth hormone to enhance milk production in cows.[69] One can only conclude that, from the perspective of the government, it is in the public interest to avoid dealing with non-performers, but that to terminate scientists who speak out publicly on health issues is a dismissible offence.

LOOKING BACK

The dominant view in government, going back to the Glassco and Fulton reports of the 1960s and taking on a new life and greater energy in the early 1980s, is that private-sector management practices are far superior to those found in government. The challenge was how to apply the slogan "Business is best" to government operations. How to turn the more ambitious senior public servants, well versed in policy, into strong managers? Governments are still searching for answers. It is no exaggeration that government management and implementation remain the preserve of the less gifted and the less ambitious. After more than thirty years of New Public Management efforts, we have learned that government is not as good as private sector firms, at least those that remain in business, in managing operations.

In addition, no one has been able to reconcile accountability requirements traditionally found in government with management practices inspired by the private sector. Accountability remains the preoccupation of everyone in and out of government, or, as Ralph Heintzman once observed, it is "the hole in the doughnut."[70] A senior British civil servant summed up the situation when he confided, "I would say that clarifying the role of ministers and officials is the major unresolved constitutional question. It is a question that has been deliberately left untouched – the Pandora's Box that now needs opening."[71] Private-sector management practices may have their own inherent logic, but Parliament, and in particular the media, will continue to hold everyone accountable as they see fit and on their own terms.

There are now a far greater number of performance-based accountability reports and fewer rule-based accountability requirements. This is not to suggest, however, that accountability has been strengthened by the reforms. If anything, government is less good today at holding people to account than it was in years past. The next chapter explores why.

6

I Could Never Find the Culprit

Elmer MacKay, who served as a member of Parliament from 1971 to 1993 and was a minister in both Joe Clark's and Brian Mulroney's Cabinets for some ten years, observed that one thing government is not particularly good at is holding people to account. He said that he found it very frustrating while in opposition and in government that, no matter how hard he tried, he could "never find the culprit."[1]

He is not alone. A debate raged in Ottawa throughout the period during which Paul Martin was prime minister over who was responsible for dividing the Department of Foreign Affairs and International Trade. The decision was widely condemned, with officials in both departments spending considerable time fighting over turf and who would get what in the divorce. The change required the approval of Parliament, but Parliament vetoed it. The government decided to go ahead with the divorce just the same, all the while saying nothing about cost. The media and retired diplomats were highly critical of the decision and the waste it entailed. Suddenly, no one in government would accept responsibility for having proposed the change. As Andrew Cohen explains, "Some say it came from the Clerk of the Privy Council, Alex Himelfarb. Some say it was Rob Fonberg, the deputy trade minister, who wanted a promotion ... Whoever its father may be, the reorganization is now an orphan. No wonder. Rarely has an idea been denounced so widely." Active and former diplomats see it as another blow to the ebbing power of Foreign Affairs, once the aristocracy of the bureaucracy. As Raymond Chrétien, Canada's former ambassador to Washington and Paris, says, "If the Prime Minister can find the culprit who recommended dismembering our foreign service, he should fire him!"[2] Neither the prime minister nor anyone else was able to find the one responsible, and no one was dismissed. If no one could find the culprit in such a high-profile issue, one can only imagine what it must be like for a minister, let alone an MP, trying to determine why things go wrong in government and who is responsible.

There have been any number of costly administrative mistakes by public servants that were completely free of political involvement. For example, Canadian public servants set out to overhaul the job classification system that had 840 pay rates. For twelve years, from 1990 to 2002, tens of thousands of employees from some sixty departments and agencies spent countless hours, and the government committed millions of dollars to consulting contracts, but to little avail.[3] No evidence suggests that those responsible for the initiative suffered any negative consequences. No one could find the culprit, or if they did, no one was held to account.

Politicians are complicit in this state of affairs, more so in recent years. Gone are the days when a minister or a prime minister would stand up in the Commons and take full responsibility for things that had gone wrong. It will be recalled that former prime minister Jean Chrétien told the Gomery Commission, which was looking into the sponsorship scandal, that he took responsibility, although he insisted that he was not to blame.[4] The implication was that one person was to blame, but another was responsible. Try that for size in the private sector.

Stephen Harper likewise took responsibility for the Duffy-Wallin Senate scandal but said that he was not to blame and pointed the finger at his chief of staff, Nigel Wright, along with the two senators. Unlike in the private sector, responsibility and blame are two very different things in government. In the private sector, anyone responsible is to blame when things go wrong; when they work out as planned, credit is duly given. The blame game is very different between the two sectors.

This chapter explores the changing face of accountability in government. It suggests that accountability explains why it is not possible to apply private-sector management practices to government. It also makes the case that numerous recent efforts to improve accountability in government, including the 2006 Accountability Act, have only muddied the waters and made it still more difficult to find the culprit. This, in turn, has made government less adroit than it once was at delivering programs and services and also less accountable.

MORE TURBULENCE IN GOVERNMENT

J.L. Perry and H.G. Rainey discuss the turbulence in managing government operations today and the difficulty in holding people to account, compared to the private sector, which has a smoother decision-making process.[5] The differences between the two are many, stark, and in many ways irreconcilable. Yet public sector reforms of the past thirty years have never stopped trying to reconcile the irreconcilable. They have not only made government less efficient and less accountable, they have also further damaged the credibility of the public sector.

Long-serving career public servants and students of public administration could have told politicians as much when they set out in the early 1980s to import private-sector management practices to governments. However, politicians then and since have been in no mood to listen.

Things can never be simple in government. Consider the following: private sector firms have a clear purpose: they produce and sell products or services to consumers to create economic benefits to the owners or shareholders. Government agencies, on the other hand, provide services to citizens under the watchful eye of politicians. They are constrained by a number of forces and have neither a market to provide revenues nor an unbending bottom line. They also do not compete for customers. The opposite is true on all fronts for private sector firms.[6] Indeed, both sectors deal with clients in very different ways, which influence how decisions are made.[7]

What to do? At least two things were thought to be necessary if the public sector was to emulate the private sector. First, public sector organizations should be instilled with a bias for action. Second, there should be a new accountability mindset, one focused on performance rather than on rules, processes, and procedures.

The objective was for public sector managers to promote an entrepreneurial spirit and then to figure out a way to hold them to account. Again, Margaret Thatcher led the way. Her reforms were far more ambitious and had a far greater impact in Britain than those of Mulroney, Chrétien, Martin, and Harper combined had in Canada.

That said, her reforms did and still have a profound influence on Canadian policy-makers.

Much has been written about the Thatcher reforms and about New Public Management. I have published extensively in these areas, and there is no need to go over the same territory here.[8] However, we need to revisit some of the reform measures to assist in answering the question of what government is good at.

The premise of the Thatcher reforms was that the work of public servants is to respond to the demands of ministers and Parliament. Too little attention was being paid to results and to clients, and too much to expenditures and activities. Unlike in the private sector, there were too few external pressures that would lead to improvement in performance.

The way ahead was to borrow from lessons learned in the private sector – give substantial freedom to government managers to manage their operations and programs as they saw fit. In return, managers would be held to a new, higher level of accountability, one that would hold them "rigorously to account for results achieved." The new approach would generate a "release of managerial energy." The goal was nothing short of a redefinition of the way the "business of government" was conducted.[9] The initiative, it was believed, would unleash an entrepreneurial spirit among government managers and then establish benchmarks to determine their performance.

It was felt, initially at least, that the approach would require a new accountability regime, one that could well compromise the doctrine of ministerial responsibility. At the last minute Thatcher had a change of mind on accountability. On the day that a report designed to overhaul government operations by creating program delivery agencies was released, she told the Commons that "there will be no change in the arrangements for accountability." Officials interpreted her statement to mean that there would be little difference between agencies and departments – indeed, Sir Robin Butler, head of the Home Civil Service, did not even think that "it would be necessary to revise the rules on civil servants giving evidence to select committees of Parliament."[10] He wrote, "No doubt this is because ministers ... made it clear that any constitutional changes to redefine ministerial responsibility were out of the question as were any suggestions to end Treasury controls over budgets, manpower and national pay bargaining."[11] Thatcher wanted new wine, but in the same wineskin. It is well

known, however, that senior civil servants were and remain very reluctant to tamper with the traditional accountability requirements.

The new wine called on the public service to overhaul its approach
to delivering services and managing operations. In short, Thatcher
served notice that it was no longer sufficient for government bureaucracy to be good at being a government bureaucracy, as traditionally
understood. Bureaucracy, with its reliance on the doctrine of ministerial responsibility, hierarchy, and traditional accountability requirements, had passed its best-by date. The goal was to make government
as good in managing operations as the private sector.

Thatcher and her advisors saw government managers as having to
deal with too many centrally prescribed rules. They identified five
critical issues confronting management in government: "First, a lack
of clear and accountable management responsibility, and the self-confidence that goes with it, particularly among the higher ranks in
departments. Second, the need for greater precision about the results
expected of people and of organizations. Third, a need to focus attention on outputs as well as inputs. Fourth, the handicap of imposing a
uniform system in an organization of the size and diversity of the present Civil Service. Fifth, a need for a sustained pressure for improvement."[12] The argument was that the private sector would never operate under these conditions, and nor should government. The solution:
establish executive agencies to deliver programs within a broad policy
and resources framework and provide managers "substantial freedom
to manage," much as they do in the private sector.[13]

The government of Canada tried to emulate the Thatcher reforms, but
it failed. It generated a new management vocabulary but little else. Mulroney and Paul Tellier, the clerk of the Privy Council, pledged to introduce a fundamental change in government operations. Inspired by the
Thatcher reforms, the Mulroney-Tellier reforms defined a new culture
and compared it with the one they wanted to discard (see table 3).

The contrast between the two is striking and instructive. It probably
came as a surprise for retired career officials of the golden era to discover that their culture was "rigid" and gave rise to "suspicious" and "secre-
tive" behaviour, which in turn served to "stifle creativity," which led them
to "communicate poorly." Still, the message could not be clearer, coming
as it did from the clerk of the Privy Council. The traditional values of
public administration were not only dated, they were counterproduc-
tive. Again, the message to public servants could not be clearer: being

Table 3
Changing terms

Old culture	New culture
Controlling	Empowering
Rigid	Flexible
Suspicious	Trusting
Administrative	Managerial
Secret	Open
Power based	Task based
Input/process oriented	Results oriented
Pre-programmed and repetitive	Capable of purposeful action
Risk averse	Willing to take intelligent risks
Mandatory	Optional
Communicating poorly	Communicating well
Centralized	Decentralized
Uniform	Diverse
Stifling creativity	Encouraging innovation
Reactive	Proactive

Source: Public Service 2000 Secretariat, Ottawa

good managers under the old culture was no longer on; rather, they now needed to be good managers like their private sector counterparts.

As I reported in my earlier work, the Mulroney-Tellier reforms required a change from a culture "centred on prudence and probity, to one which recognizes the primacy of service to clients while accepting the need for reasonable prudence and probity."[14] The efforts were based on more than 300 recommendations for "delayering," diminishing central controls, reducing the number of job classifications from seventy-two to twenty-three, and making it easier to staff positions. A number of broad strategies would support the change: decentralization of decision-making; empowerment; trust and confidence in a non-partisan, objective, and professional public service; reduction in controls over managers; more flexible organizational structures; upgraded skills of government managers; and a stronger sense of service to the public. Departments were also encouraged to launch their own reviews to identify "useless" red tape and to "delayer" management levels.[15]

The Mulroney-Tellier reforms did introduce special operating agencies (SOAs), which were modelled on the executive agency model developed in Britain. However, SOAs are only a pale imitation of the British version. In Canada, the agencies remain subordinate to their parent departments, and their heads report to the deputy minister of their department, rather than directly to the minister, as in Britain. The agencies cannot be said to have created a culture or promoted values different from the public service as a whole. Their leaders and personnel are selected much as are those of a regular government department, and their accountability requirements remain essentially intact, other than giving government managers more freedom to classify and staff positions and reallocate financial resources. Suffice to note that SOAs have met with little success. The lines of accountability were never properly defined, and it quickly became apparent that deputy ministers were "far too busy with their own jobs to give much time to SOAs."[16] In any event, as is the case for many public sector organizations, it is unclear how to evaluate them.[17] We do not know if programs under SOAs are better managed, and there is no way of knowing for certain.[18]

The SOA experiment was short-lived and no one in Ottawa speaks of it, though it may have led to substantial management reform at the Canada Customs and Revenue and the Canadian Food Inspection agencies. National unity concerns, the program review exercise of the mid-1990s, and other high-profile political issues shifted the focus of the prime minister and the clerk. Shortly after the Chrétien government came to power, it quickly appointed a new clerk. Chrétien had other priorities and had no interest to pursue further an initiative from the previous government. Shortly after it won power, the Harper government also appointed a new clerk and served notice that it would introduce policy changes in a number of areas with or without the help of the public service and that it would strengthen still more accountability requirements.

Harper introduced the "accounting officer" concept to Canada as part of his 2006 legislative package designed to strengthen accountability. Jean Chrétien had pledged to introduce the idea in 2003, but nothing came of it.[19] Harper's version of the accounting officer that came into law in 2006 is considerably watered down from the proposal he put forward during the election campaign. As it stands, it is quite different from the British version and operates "within the framework of ministerial responsibility."[20] Ralph Heintzman has labelled the Canadian version as "the flawed implementation of the British concept."[21] Heintzman is correct, and one would be hard pressed to identify just one example where it has had an appreciable impact on the accountability relationship between departments and Parliaments.

THIRTY YEARS LATER

The public-sector management revolution has been a failure. If any-thing, it has only made matters worse. The public service is demoralized and uncertain about its policy advisory role, and few, even inside bureaucracy, now claim that government managers are as good as their private sector counterparts in managing operations. Many would argue that government managers have actually lost ground when compared with their private sector counterparts in recent years, and there is evi-dence to support this view.[22] If anything, it is now more difficult to find the culprit.

In Canada, the NPM reform measures made the case that public ser-vants excel at giving the appearance of change while in fact standing still. Some thirty years after the Treasury Board introduced the Increased Ministerial Authority and Accountability initiative and the establish-ment of SOAs, twenty years after the high-profile PS 2000 initiative designed to empower government managers and sharpen their account-ability requirements was unveiled, and nearly ten years after the intro-duction of the Federal Accountability Act, which promised to stand up "for accountability and change the way government works," the clerk of the Privy Council launched yet another "vision" exercise in the summer of 2013. He felt the need to remind public servants that they "work in the public interest" and that every effort should be made to "ensure effi-cient and effective use of public resources in a way that is accountable."[23] Again, same wine, different wineskin.

If history is a guide, the clerk's vision exercise will lead to countless meetings, numerous position papers and reviews, and lucrative con-tracts for some consultants, but, in the end, its impact will be hardly visible. The clerk never bothered to explain why the vision and review exercises undertaken by previous clerks (circa 1990, 1996, and 2007), all designed to strengthen management and accountability require-ments, had failed or at least had not lived up to expectations, while his would. No one had been held accountable for the three previous exer-cises that had failed to deliver on their promise. The latest clerk's vision exercise, like the earlier ones, harks back to the traditional bureaucratic model where a fiat from above is believed to be enough to reinvent how government departments and agencies go about their work. This applies to deputy ministers in large departments, right down to lower-level frontline public servants who are in daily contact with the public.

Clerks since the 1980s have felt the need to fix the public service, to improve management, and to strengthen accountability. They invariably leave before the review is fully implemented. Wayne Wouters, the clerk who launched the 2013 revision exercise, announced his retirement in the summer of 2014. One former senior federal public servant wrote to say that the efforts are always only about "one-third complete" by the time the clerks who launched them take their leave.[24] Since 1992, the government of Canada has had seven clerks serving on average for about three years. By contrast, Ed Clark was CEO of the Toronto-Dominion Bank for some thirteen years, Gordon Nixon was CEO of the Royal Bank of Canada (RBC) for fourteen years, William Downe has been CEO at the Bank of Montreal (BMO) since 2007 and he is still at the post. Rick Waugh was CEO of Scotiabank from 2003 to 2012. Gerald McCaughey was appointed CEO at the Canadian Imperial Bank of Commerce (CIBC) in 2005.

PERFORMANCE OVER PROCEDURE

In the private sector, performance and the meeting and exceeding of goals matter more than procedures. You perform or you falter, and unless you turn things around, you die. If government managers were to be more entrepreneurial, and if the public sector was to be made to look like the private sector, it followed that its accountability requirements had to change. The shift away from rules and procedures to consumer choice and outcomes meant a new focus on assessing performance. Citizens would now be able to hold government to account, not only through elections but also by acting as consumers. The objective was to have government managers become increasingly accountable to performance measures and less to their superiors, procedures, or political masters.[25] If for no other reason, the need to manage the blame game made this impossible.

Leaving the blame game aside, how does government invent a bottom line? How does it introduce incentives to ensure that its managers focus on effectiveness and efficiency? How does government change an entrenched bureaucratic culture? To be sure, it is no easy task, given that government departments and agencies are monopolies or quasi-monopolies insulated from competitive pressures.[26]

Government managers in all departments, and not simply in special operating agencies, have been "empowered" to run their operations as NPM envisaged. As already noted, they now have a freer hand to staff and to classify positions, to hire consultants, and to manage their budgets than was the case forty years ago. Departmental managers have been empowered by pushing some decisions down to line departments.

In 1983, for example, the Treasury Board issued 6,000 decisions; in 1987 the number had dropped to 3,500; by 1997 it had fallen still further, to 1,100; today it is fewer than 1,000.[27] The Public Service Commission, for example, has been turned into an "audit" agency, with little say in staffing positions.

Prime ministers are quite happy to see line departments manage continuing programs that generate little controversy. They do not want departments and agencies to create political problems for the government by becoming embroiled in controversies, especially if the media get wind of it. When it comes to the blame game and permanent election campaigns, the ability to run a tight ship will always trump performance, however measured. For politicians on the government side, it is more important for senior public servants to be good at managing the blame game than being good at managing government operations.

Prime ministers are happy to have no one with substantial power in the policy-making process deal with issues that do not matter to them. It is much easier for them to manage a process where the location of its power is unclear, other than in their own offices, if only because it avoids bold moves or decisions. Bold moves require political power to see them come to fruition. In addition, bold moves initiated by anyone other than the prime minister or without the prime minister's blessing can create political problems. The process controlled by the centre of government enables it to keep potential rogue politicians and bureaucrats under watch.

When managing government operations and programs, prime ministers are also happy to empower managers, provided that they run on their tracks. Oversight bodies and an abundance of performance and evaluation reports, however inadequate, become the bottom line in government. But rather than constituting a bottom line, oversight bodies and performance reports have made government operations thicker. In other words, attempts to create a true bottom line in government have failed. Layers of bureaucracy have been added to head offices in departments and agencies, giving rise to numerous performance and evaluation reports that say very little, for fear of creating political problems. What they have achieved is to provide plenty of work for Ottawa-based consulting firms and, in the end, made decision-making far more complex than in years past and further muddied accountability in government.

The current accountability regime and the management environment illustrate the vast differences between the public and the private sectors. In the private sector, accountability is straightforward. A line runs unencumbered from employee to supervisor to manager to vice-president to chief executive officer to board of directors to shareholders. Performance expectations are equally straightforward: to outperform the projections of financial analysts and investors, to capture a larger share of the market, and to produce a higher return on investment. The chief executive officer knows to whom he or she is accountable and how performance will be determined.

Now consider the deputy minister. The lines of accountability are not clear, nor are performance measurements.[28] How do you measure the value of a defence program or a diplomatic initiative, let alone the role of the deputy minister in charge? How can government departments and agencies know if they are doing a good job? How can Parliament possibly decide whether departments and deputy ministers are doing a good job? How can one isolate a particular deputy minister's contribution in a government-wide initiative?

Potential measurements of performance are difficult to identify, difficult to quantify, and even more difficult to link directly to the deputy minister. Deputy ministers are the heads of their departments, and one could attempt to assess their performance on the basis of how well a department performs. The criteria for establishing performance are many and varied. But even then one has to address other issues: what about the role of the minister, what level of resources was the department able to secure, given the interdepartmental nature of policy and decision-making, and what role did the deputy minister play in that process? The list of questions goes on.

Deputy ministers also have an accountability relationship with a host of actors and presumably have to answer to all of them. They include:

• The prime minister, who appoints them and can remove them. One can assume that they will put the prime minister at the very top of their list;

• The clerk of the Privy Council and secretary to the Cabinet, head of the public service, and deputy minister to the prime minister (all one person). Deputy ministers emphasize this relationship: the clerk's advice probably helped get them their job, and the clerk prepares the annual performance review of deputy ministers;
• The minister, who is consulted in the deputy minister's annual performance review;
• The Treasury Board and the Financial Administration Act;
• The Public Service Commission and the Public Service Employment Act;
• Departmental clients, if NPM is to be taken seriously;
• The interdepartmental policy-making process;
• And, if the accounting-officer concept introduced as part of the Harper government Federal Accountability Act in 2006 is accepted, deputy ministers are also accountable, or at the very least answerable, to Parliament.

It is widely believed that deputy ministers must frequently report to their ministers. To be sure, ministers and their deputies often meet several times a week.[29] However, Jacques Bourgault maintains that the accountability requirement that truly matters for deputy ministers is to the prime minister and his office. He reports that a PMO staffer told an assistant deputy minister with responsibility for the government's economic recovery program, "We don't want your advice; we want you to do as you're told." Bourgault quotes media reports that the PMO was responsible for the retirement of Clerk of the Privy Council Kevin Lynch and of Deputy Minister of Infrastructure Louis Ranger.[30] Both Lynch and Ranger were highly respected, non-partisan public servants. Lynch had served as deputy minister of industry and finance. In June 2009, Ranger wrote an email to Transport Canada employees to report that the prime minister had announced his resignation.[31]

All this makes the point that performance is often in the eye of the beholder. Deputy ministers have complained of insufficient feedback on performance. Their evaluations or appraisals, as well as those of senior career officials, are "qualitative" and "personal in nature and place particular emphasis on management style."[32] This factor and many others allow them to take limited interest in "general management." Best to look to the prime minister's court for direction and pick "one or two really big difficult policy issues" to work on. But this is not what NPM had in store for reforming the public sector.

The auditor general has long championed performance evaluations in government. As the Office of the Auditor General tabled in its report in 2001, "We expected that by then [2001] most managers would be trying to manage for results and that many would have good systems in place. We found some progress in a few areas, but managing for results was clearly not yet the norm in the departments we audited ... The main problem is less a technical than a cultural problem. Public servants are not inclined to produce information that could embarrass their ministers. The accountability battery never gets charged up."[33]

No matter, new resources continue to be committed to program evaluation. When I published *The Politics of Public Spending in Canada* over two decades ago, program evaluations were supported by about $28.5 million and employed 168 persons. Today the government spends about $80 million every year and employs about 500 full-time equivalents. In addition, all departments hire outside consultants to carry out their evaluations. In 2009–10, for example, about 93 per cent of evaluations involved outside consultants to do at least part of the work.[34]

The OAG once again rendered its verdict on the government's program evaluations in 2008, and it was not complimentary. It argued that the government was ill prepared to evaluate all of its programs over a five-year period as the 2006 Federal Accountability Act (and later the 2009 government policy) required. The office was not impressed with the quality of the evaluations, pointing out that "often departments had not gathered the performance information needed to evaluate whether programs are effective." It added that of the 23 evaluation reports the office reviewed, "17 noted that the analysis was hampered by inadequate data, limiting the assessment of program effectiveness." The OAG criticized the TBS, claiming that "it did not provide sustained support for effectiveness evaluation – it made little progress on developing tools to assist departments with the longstanding problem of a lack of sufficient data for evaluating program effectiveness."[35] Precious few program evaluations generated program termination or reform.[36] Program performance units are fully staffed, but public servants are often kept busy turning a crank not attached to anything. In short, the record of program evaluation has been dismal.

One might pause to note that an assistant auditor general, a principal, a lead director, two directors, five other OAG officials, and some outside consultants all worked on the OAG report, *Evaluating the Effec-*

tiveness of Programs. It would have been interesting if someone had similarly evaluated the cost and value of the thirty-nine-page report, which became chapter 1 of the 2009 *Fall Report of the Auditor General.*

There is little political advantage for anyone to take on the OAG. Opposition parties are invariably the OAG's biggest allies until one is elected to power. The OAG is a large Ottawa contributor to the blame game, and opposition parties constantly draw from its findings. The government, meanwhile, does not wish to take on the OAG for fear of being accused by the media and opposition parties of trying to muzzle criticism.

This has enabled the OAG to roam essentially where it wants. Accountants, with some help from social science graduates, now audit almost anything and practise what Paul Thomas calls the "quasi-mystical art of value forming."[37] Officials in the Department of National Defence (DND) were likely taken aback when they saw former auditor general Sheila Fraser in full battle gear in a "photo op" in Kandahar, Afghanistan. The purpose of her visit was "to gain an understanding of what was going on in Kandahar, in both military and development terms, rather than audit."[38]

No one is satisfied with the government's program evaluations, but no one is prepared to deal with the problem either. It would be much more sensible if the government would focus on programs that in fact lend themselves to evaluation, as much of the literature now recommends.[39] While this makes sense from an effective public administration perspective, it does not from a political and blame game perspective and consequently it is not done. The OAG has become an important actor in the blame game. That is not how the private sector operates, where the blame game, to the extent that it exists, is played away from the media.

No matter their lack of success, governments have pressed ahead with performance accountability. Procedural accountability is regarded as dated and out of step with efforts to dress the public sector like the private sector.

By relying on centrally prescribed rules, procedural or administrative accountability had a greater capacity to find the culprit and provide redress in cases of maladministration.[40] Hierarchy enables one to go up and down the organization to see who does what, and centrally prescribed procedures enable one to determine if they have been respected. One can fudge performance and evaluation reports, but it is much more difficult to fudge adherence to rules.

Old-fashioned financial audits remain the most effective way to identify culprits. Though they rarely point to individual public servants,
they can establish if rules and procedures were followed and if standard
accounting practices were respected. In October 2013, for example,
auditors found significant accounting errors worth an estimated $1.5
billion during a financial audit at the Defence Department.[41]

Financial auditors also produced a scathing audit revealing a long
list of wasteful spending at Transport Canada in 2014. They found that
many rules had been broken. The department gave contracts to outside
consultants, while public servants were available to do the work at half
the price, had 25 per cent of its workstations vacant (try that for size in
the private sector), and awarded a contract to a moving company on an
"as needed basis" that proved very costly. The audit reported that four
movers were actually paid full-time for four years, paid for 8-hour days
rather than the 7.5 stated in the contract, and the $200,000 contract
grew to $1.1 million, following thirteen amendments.[42] Ministers and
MPs understood these findings far better than sanitized evaluation
reports. Still, no one was able to find the culprit or culprits.

Performance accountability is more easily pursued in a competitive
market, where success is more easily established. Government departments lack a proper pricing mechanism, profit levels, and competitive
market to properly establish performance. In procedural or administrative accountability, the public servant or the individual in a private
firm who relies on this form of accountability has to deal with the
shame and guilt with the failure to comply.[43]

Government by network, governing from the centre, and public
policies and program decisions make it still more difficult to establish
performance accountability in the public sector. Performance, to the
extent that it can be measured, is now the product of many hands,
while administrative accountability applies evenly to all.

If the objective is to hold individuals to account for the spending of
public money, there is plenty of evidence that administrative accountability and the prospect that spending will be made public will keep
things in check. High-end restaurants in Ottawa saw business slow
down and a few actually closed after federal public servants were directed to post their hospitality and other expenses on their departmental
websites.[44] As well, senators substantially cut their spending on travel,
food, and other expenses in the immediate aftermath of the 2013 Senate spending scandal. Hospitality spending alone among senators
dropped by 42 per cent over a twelve-month period.[45]

DO AS I SAY, NOT AS I DO

To shift a culture from traditional public administration to one inspired by the private sector is not without challenges. The New Public Management, which endorsed public-private partnerships, meant a shift to private sector notions of competition and consumer choice.

As Barry J. O'Toole argues, we have witnessed "recent trends" away from the ideal public service.[46] He writes, "Within the civil service the prevailing ethos has moved from one of public service towards one of private gain. The collegiate way of making decisions has been replaced by an emphasis on personal accountability. There has been a shift from uniform pay and promotion systems towards reward for individual performance. Competition not co-operation is the watchword. All fit in with the prevailing attitude amongst ministers that business methods are best ... Personal gain and private profit will have replaced public service. What will be the point of government?"[47]

The concern among some senior public servants was that promoting a business culture and a private sector ethos would erode the values long associated with the government and public administration. They set out to square the circle, somehow. Exercises from above to strengthen values and ethics became highly fashionable in government, starting in the mid-1990s, and they remain in vogue. We saw earlier that John Tait, a highly respected deputy minister, was asked to chair a task force on values and ethics in government. He tabled the report in 1997.

The Tait report concentrated its message on "four overlapping families of core public service values," the first of which was "democratic values." The report made the case that public service anonymity protects not only the neutrality of civil servants but also the authority of ministers, thus becoming a key democratic principle. It praised the doctrine of ministerial responsibility, insisting that it, too, protects the authority of ministers. It considered the impact of new organizational forms on the doctrine, concluding, like others in promoting management reform, that they need not involve fundamental change in ministerial responsibility.[48] That said, it also reported concerns among public servants the task force consulted, most notably that the doctrine had become "unclear, outdated, just unreal or meaningless," and called for "clarifying" the responsibility of ministers as essential to promoting values and ethics in government. However, it did not point the way ahead. It simply stated that a number of public servants felt that the doctrine was outdated.

Undaunted, the Tait report went on to contrast old values associated with traditional public administration with those associated with NPM practices. It reminded public servants that citizens are not customers, but rather the "bearers of rights and duties in a framework of community."[49] It spoke about the difference in "managing up" – the need to respond to the wishes of ministers – and "managing down" – looking down to employees and the quality of the organization and its performance. It went on to stress the challenge of demonstrating leadership in "a time of change," the need to promote decency, humanity, fairness, and ethical values, including integrity, honesty, probity, prudence, and equity – traditional values long associated with traditional public administration.

The several values initiatives, however, have not been without their critics, both outside and inside government. Some outside government have argued that the government should be very careful in replacing a "rules approach" with a "values approach,"[50] making the point that, if the role of the public service is limited to supporting and serving the government of the day, then a shift away from a rules-based approach could have significant implications. Values, the argument goes, operate on a higher level of abstraction than do rules and regulations. Accountability requirements are more certain under rules and regulations than under a values-based approach.[51]

Senior civil servants have given their full support to the values exercises. First Jocelyne Bourgon, then Mel Cappe, and later Alex Himelfarb – all three former clerks of the Privy Council – wrote about the importance of the initiatives in their annual reports to the prime minister on the state of the public service. Bourgon, for example, described the Tait report as an "honest dialogue" that employed an "inductive approach" that gave it a "quality of authenticity."[52] Mel Cappe wrote that "as public servants, we rely on the four sets of values [as outlined by Tait] to inform and guide us"[53] and added that "it may be more important to put our values into action than into words."[54] For his part, Alex Himelfarb wrote that "values and ethics are the immutable core of the Public Service. Our dedication to values and ethics must be unassailable and unwavering. We must exemplify these values, we must practice them at the highest possible level."[55] Cappe reminded senior managers that everything they do "is judged by their employees. If senior managers want to lead effectively, they have to start with promoting values."[56]

It is more than ironic that, as task force members were meeting to discuss values and ethics in government, as consultants were being hired to assist them in their work, as deputy ministers were being appointed to promote values, as clerks were stressing the importance of values, as the word spread that the "misconduct of some politicians … had damaged the image of public servants," and as his own department launched an ambitious values exercise of its own, Chuck Guité, a career official, was, in the words of the auditor general, "breaking every rule in the book." Yet his job description, approved by his deputy minister in 1997, called for a capacity "for quick action and cutting red tape."[57] In the NPM world, Guité was expected to become an entrepreneur. He received high praise from his superiors in his annual performance reviews and rose through the ranks to become a director general.[58] Guité is hardly the only public servant who broke rules. There have been many other well-documented cases of fraud and highly questionable behaviour inside the federal government bureaucracy in recent years.[59]

Yet there has been no let-up in trying to square the circle or somehow to adapt private-sector management techniques to public administration. Clerks have appointed deputy ministers as "champions" to lead the values and ethics exercise throughout government. A values and ethics code for the public service has been tabled and updated. An ethics counsellor has been appointed, and a values and ethics unit was established in the Treasury Board Secretariat. Line departments now have an ethics and values office that oversees developments in departments and prepares an annual report.[60]

While clerks have led the charge from the centre, they have looked the other way when it came to their own interests. One was appointed to head a Crown corporation – Canadian National Railway – that was subsequently privatized. Three of the last five clerks of the Privy Council were able to secure Canada's best and most sought-after ambassadorial appointments – Paris, Rome, and London. The three posts came with palatial residences. As the *Globe and Mail* described the official residence of the Canadian ambassador in Rome, "The villa, built in 1934 on ancient property near the start of the Appian Way, the Roman empire's most important strategic road, was the envy of most of his fellow ambassadors. The elegant house itself, covering 13,000 square feet, was not actually the main draw. It was the property, on four acres of meticulously groomed and lush rolling land within the 3rd Century Aurelian walls. The landscape featured part of the Appian Way and the tennis court was built over the ruins of a Roman house."[61] The government recently sold Canada's High Commission in London – One Grosvenor Square, described as one of "the most fashionable homes in London" – to a developer for the pricey sum of $530 million.[62]

None of the three clerks had previous foreign affairs experience. They simply struck a deal with the prime minister as they left the Privy Council Office.[63] The message could not have been lost on long-serving officials in Foreign Affairs. There is no intrinsic value to their work experience or their department, and clerks or heads of the public service will look after their own interests before those of government departments, institutions, and other public servants, no matter their traditions and standing in government, such as Foreign Affairs. The ambassadorial appointments served notice to all public servants that looking after one's own personal interest matters more than all the values and ethics exercises combined.

LOOKING BACK

This chapter makes the point that it was not possible to square the circle, to embrace a private sector ethos, or to retain the core values of the public service. An oversupply of performance reports and evaluation, and values and ethics exercises, have made government decision-making more complex and less accessible to members of Parliament. They also required new resources. The political and economic elites and large businesses have been able to cope because, again, they either have the knowledge or the resources to access the decision-making process.

Contrary to the private sector, much of what government does is not measureable. Government is better at managing administrative accountability than performance accountability. How can democratic values and human dignity be measured? Yet governments persist in calculating the immeasurable, happily keeping many public servants turning cranks not attached to anything. In short, government is not very good at imitating the private sector or at importing private-sector management practices.

Government was better at holding people to account and at finding the culprit when it relied on administrative accountability or clearly defined rules and procedures. Recent history has shown that government is not good at holding people to account through performance. Performance in government is all too often augmentable and overlooks the reality that most government departments deal with multiple goals.[64]

When Thatcher decided – and the Mulroney government followed – that reform measures would leave the doctrine of ministerial responsibility untouched, it sent a message to everyone that the status quo would prevail. All public servants had to do was wait for the storm to pass, which public servants are very good at doing whenever the need arises. The one change that suited public servants well was to do away with a number of centrally prescribed rules.

Government departments and agencies, in contrast to private sector firms, are defined by their "publicness."[65] Every voter, every citizen has an "ownership stake" in government organizations. Public servants operate in a fishbowl, which enables the media and hostile interest groups to raise questions about their direction. This makes creativity difficult and innovation risky in an environment where the blame game is always at play.[66]

Management reform has not made things better. How else can one explain that after thirty-five years of New Public Management, an Ottawa-based think tank could still declare that "perceptions of the public sector as slow, bloated, and ineffective persist"?[67] The March 2014 study was based on 130 interviews, many with current and former senior public servants.

In the next chapter, I discuss two government initiatives with which I have been closely identified. The chapter avers that NPM measures have had little impact on the behaviour of public servants. The tendency of public servants to exploit all opportunities to expand their organizations remains, while further making the case that accountability requirements are less certain today than in years past.

7

Apologia Pro Vita Sua

In November 1985 the Canadian prime minister asked me to consult political and business leaders from Atlantic Canada and prepare a report on the establishment of a regional economic development agency for the region. In October 1986 the secretary of the Treasury Board asked me to prepare a report on the creation of a new management development centre for senior federal public servants. One initiative was driven by a politician, the other by a senior public servant.

I refer to these two plans because of lessons learned for the public sector and also to shed more light on what government is good at. One stems from a government's political interest and the other from bureaucratic interest. One (the regional agency) was announced months before a general election, while the other came a few months after the 1987 election. Every effort was made to give the new regional economic development agency a high profile in the media. Politicians on the government side criss-crossed the region, singing its praises, while the other received much less attention. Apart from having a senior Cabinet minister announce the new management development centre, politicians have scarcely mentioned it since its establishment. There is, however, one common element – the size of both agencies has grown considerably over the years, much more than initially envisaged in either case.

My purpose is not to single out these two agencies for criticism. The two play by the same rules as the other departments and agencies, and they are home to the same bureaucratic culture found in government. Their expenditure budgets are squeezed whenever the prime minister decides that the time has come for an ambitious program review. And, like other departments, they will line up for new resources whenever the prime minister and his most senior courtiers decide to address other priorities or when the latest program review has run its course. This chapter once again makes the point that implementation remains the poor cousin in government, no match for the ability to generate whiz-bang ideas and managing the blame game.

ACOA: THE PROMISE OF A NEW BEGINNING
THAT WILL SUCCEED WHERE OTHERS HAVE FAILED

Prime Minister Brian Mulroney went to Saint John's, Newfoundland, on 6 June 1987 to unveil a new agency for Atlantic Canada. Never one to understate a case, he boldly declared that the Atlantic Canada Opportunities Agency (ACOA) represented a new beginning, with new money and a new mission. He was certain that it would succeed where all past federal development departments and agencies had failed and that it would "inflict prosperity" on Atlantic Canada.[1]

The federal government's approach to regional economic development had come under heavy criticism from the four Atlantic provinces by the mid-1980s, at the same time that the federal Department of Finance saw a new economic reality emerging in the country. The economic recession of that period had hit central Canada's manufacturing sector particularly hard. The federal government tabled a document titled *Economic Development for Canada in the 1980s*, which maintained that the regional economic balance was changing as a result of buoyancy in the West, optimism in the East, and unprecedented softness in key economic sectors in central Canada. Underpinning this view were the economic prospects associated with resource-based megaprojects.

The Atlantic region, in contrast to historical economic trends, was expected to enjoy a decade of solid growth, largely as a result of off-shore resources. The West was expected to capture over half of the investment in major projects. Ontario and Quebec, meanwhile, would face serious problems of industrial adjustment, brought about by increased international competition.[2]

The Department of Finance had it wrong. The economic recession of the early 1980s in central Canada did not last long, nor did it give rise to a new economy elsewhere. The Atlantic region never enjoyed a decade of solid growth in the 1980s, while Ontario and Quebec did. No matter, the government decided to put in place a new structure to promote regional economic development, one that clearly favoured central Canada. It established a new department – the Department of Regional Industrial Expansion (DRIE), with a regional incentive program that applied everywhere.

The DRIE minister, Ed Lumley, explained, "Combatting regional disparities is difficult even in good economic times ... It is much more difficult in a period when, because of a worldwide downturn, Canada's traditional industries are suffering from soft markets, stiff international competition, rapid technological change and rising protectionism from the countries that make up our market." A new program to meet these circumstances would have to be one that he could clearly recommend to the business community, to the Canadian public, and to members of Parliament. DRIE, Lumley reported, had come up with such a program. It was "a regionally sensitized, multifaceted programme of industrial assistance in all parts of Canada ... This is not a programme to be available only in certain designated regions. Whatever riding any Member of this House represents, his or her constituents will be eligible for assistance."[3] Mulroney inherited the approach and left it intact when he first came to power.

However, the new structure did not sit well with either Western or Atlantic Canada. In addition, contrary to what the Department of Finance's officials had predicted, by the mid-1980s some observers were suggesting that the economies of Southern Ontario and Quebec would overheat. Meanwhile, the economy of the four Atlantic provinces was still in the doldrums. To make matters worse, the four Atlantic provincial governments became highly critical of Ottawa's regional development efforts, even though three of the four were politically partisan allies of Mulroney's Progressive Conservative Party.[4]

The media were reporting that the bulk of spending under DRIE was being directed to Ontario and Quebec. For example, over 70 per cent of its spending under the Industrial and Regional Development Program (IRDP) was going to those provinces. By contrast, at least 40 per cent of the budget of the Department of Regional Economic Expansion (DREE) – the department that DRIE replaced – had been consistently allocated to Atlantic Canada.[5] In addition, some provincial government officials in Atlantic Canada began to report that, on occasions, firms that were thinking of establishing a plant in either their region or Southern Ontario, received more generous offers from DRIE to locate in Southern Ontario. They made the point that if the federal government was not prepared to overhaul the structure, then it would be best to abolish DRIE, because it was accelerating regional disparities rather than attenuating them.[6]

In late August 1986, New Brunswick Premier Richard Hatfield invited me to lunch in Fredericton. He had been in Toronto the week before, where he had met with Ontario's minister of industry, who had urged him to read my book on regional development. Hatfield told me, "When a minister from Ontario recommends that I read a book on regional development in Canada, I worry. What did you say in the book?"[7]

He asked if I thought that DRIE was doing good work in our region. I said, "Absolutely not." He responded, "What should we do?" I told him that the last thing Atlantic Canada needed was more government programs and more government money. We had plenty of both, I said, and we should have them work better, focus on local entrepreneurs, review federal policies and programs that discriminate against Atlantic Canada, assist small businesses with their marketing and their research and development, and have an agency dedicated solely to Atlantic Canada's economic development. Above all, we needed an agency with a "bias for action," rather than top-down bureaucratic programs, one with a clear mandate to advocate for the interests of Atlantic Canada. I told Hatfield that we needed to be innovative in resolving issues when establishing the administrative and bureaucratic structure of the agency.

Hatfield agreed, as far as I could tell, with most of my analysis and asked if I would prepare a "five-pager of speaking notes" on the matter for him. Hatfield told me that he needed the speaking notes quickly because he was meeting with the prime minister the following week, who was to make a brief visit to New Brunswick on his way to chair a Cabinet committee meeting in Saint John's, Newfoundland. I was later told that Hatfield simply handed my five-pager as is to Mulroney and urged him to read it. The prime minister returned to Atlantic Canada a few weeks later to meet the four Atlantic premiers and inform them that he understood that DRIE was not the answer and that he would be asking me to prepare a report on establishing a new economic development agency for the region. He also told the premiers that I would be consulting them, as well as other Atlantic Canadians, in preparing the report.[8]

I submitted my report in February 1987, and the prime minister did adopt most of my recommendations. The agency's headquarters were to be in Atlantic Canada. A deputy minister would head the agency, which would have a distinct status to ensure that it had somewhat more autonomy than a typical government department, while still not being a Crown corporation. Finally, its main focus would be the promotion of entrepreneurial development, but it would have three additional mandates: to play an advocacy role for the region in Ottawa, to coordinate the activities of other federal departments and agencies in Atlantic Canada, and to promote federal-provincial cooperation. The government accepted these proposals.

However, it rejected three other important recommendations. I had urged the government not to create new cash-grant programs, but rather to rely on existing government programs. I argued that there was no shortage of government programs handing out grants. I also suggested that the government limit the size of ACOA to 100 top-flight officials. Given that the agency would rely on other government programs, I saw no need to create a large bureaucracy. I envisaged an agency that could influence other federal departments and agencies to strengthen their role, presence, and activities in Atlantic Canada.

I imagined an agency with a limited number of high-profile officials, some borrowed from the private sector who would, in concert with the business community, identify economic opportunities. I concluded that the agency should be a catalyst, not only identify opportunities but also make them happen. I insisted that it did not need a large bureaucracy to do this. I recommended the establishment of a $250-million fund to be drawn from existing government departments and agencies, notably DRIE, which was being disbanded. I saw no need for "new" money. The government, however, was far more generous. It decided to give the agency $1 billion of "new money" and also transfer part of DRIE's old budget to it.

I also recommended that Atlantic Canadians be allowed to accumulate capital, tax free, to start new businesses rather than to rely on cash grants – a kind of RRSP for aspiring entrepreneurs wishing to invest in our region. The government did not introduce the tax scheme and decided that the agency should have its own cash-grant programs. As for the rest, it looked a great deal like what I had proposed in my report.

I was asked to go to Saint John's, Newfoundland, to meet with the prime minister to answer any questions that he may have about my report before he met with the media. Mulroney decided on Saint John's and 6 June 1987 for the announcement, because a by-election was being held in the city a fortnight later.[9] Mulroney knew what he wanted to say to the media about the new agency, and he asked precious few questions about my report. However, he did ask for my views on his government's proposed amendments to the constitution known as the Meech Lake Accord that he had negotiated with the ten provincial premiers. In hindsight, I can well appreciate that his proposed Meech Lake Accord had far more crucial political consequences for him and his government than the establishment of an economic development agency for Atlantic Canada.

It is easy to speculate why Mulroney accepted only parts of my report. For one thing, the Department of Finance would have strongly objected to my recommendation that a RRSP-type tax incentive be adopted rather than cash grants. Finance officials are constantly on the lookout to protect the integrity of the tax system, and they very carefully guard that responsibility. Their advice against my recommendation would also square nicely with the government's political interest. Cash grants tied to announcements enjoy a high profile in the local media and with local members of Parliament. Tax incentives do not.

Mulroney and his political advisors made an adroit political calculation in reviewing my report. Politicians of all stripes seek visibility above all else – they are good at this – and tax incentives are no match for grants. Cash grants, a billion dollars of new money (1987 dollars), and a federal physical presence with its head office in the region provide strong visibility and convey the message that the government is attaching high priority to the region, especially when there is a general election within the year, which was the case in 1987.

Mulroney's announcement was greeted with enthusiasm everywhere in Atlantic Canada. The local media gave it two thumbs up. The *Fredericton Daily Gleaner*, for example, ran a highly positive article with the headline "Atlantic Gets Big Boost."[10] The announcement was praised even by Liberal politicians from the region. In New Brunswick, for example, opposition leader Frank McKenna warmly welcomed the announcement and observed, "I believe with the composition of the Agency and terms of reference, there is reason to be optimistic."[11] Nova Scotia Liberal leader Vince MacLean echoed McKenna's sentiments.[12] That was likely enough for Mulroney to declare the ACOA initiative a success, and he was on to other things.

A POLITICAL SUCCESS IS WORTH REPEATING

One of the most powerful regional ministers in the Mulroney Cabinet was Don Mazankowski, the deputy prime minister, and one of his most important goals was to do for Western Canada what Trudeau, Marchand, and Pelletier had done for Quebec. He was determined to place the "Western" agenda front and centre on the national political agenda. His agenda was economic; he sought to put in place measures to diversify the Western economy. He, like other Westerners, was convinced that the West needed to develop sectors other than agriculture, oil, and gas.

In addition, by early 1987, the Mulroney government was in serious political difficulty in the West.[13] Public-opinion polls showed that the government was struggling to maintain a narrow lead and that, at one point, it trailed the New Democratic Party. In 1986, the government nearly lost a by-election in Pembina, Alberta, hitherto regarded as one of its safest seats in the country. Worse still, that same year, the government had awarded the CF-18 maintenance contract to a Quebec firm, although a Winnipeg firm had submitted the lowest bid. The public outcry in Western Canada against this decision resonates in the region to this day. A general election was expected in 1988, and it was important for Mulroney to solidify his Western base quickly, if he was to have any hope of winning a second mandate.

Mulroney went to Edmonton to announce the details of the new Western Economic Diversification initiative (WD).[14] He said that the agency would administer a $1.2 billion fund of new money, and that, like its sister agency, ACOA, WD would assume responsibility for DRIE's A-base or its current budget in Western Canada, thus adding still more financial resources to the announcement. The prime minister explained that his government's regional policy was designed to provide "federal leadership for each region, tailored to its unique potential and needs. At the same time, we want to ensure that regional perspectives are front and centre in the development of national priorities, and that regional economic development is backed by strong national centres of industrial and technological expertise."[15]

Mazankowski explained that WD would be similar in many ways to ACOA, and that it represented in reality the second phase of a multi-step redefinition of Ottawa's regional development policy. "We think it is

very important," he said, "to develop economic programs that fit a particular region and for the decision-making to take place in that region.
We believe that to establish a uniform policy across the country, admin-
istered out of Ottawa, is not the answer. Clearly, the approach we've had
in the past, in terms of addressing regional economic expansion, has not
worked."[16]

On 15 July 1987, the federal government unveiled yet another special agency to promote economic development, this time in Northern
Ontario. In announcing the Federal Economic Development Initiative for Northern Ontario (FEDNOR), the federal minister for the
region, James Kelleher, pointed out that the government had consulted the business community and the provincial government to determine what was needed. Although the reaction to the announcement
was positive, it was much less so than that following the decisions to
establish ACOA and WD. The Ontario government, for example, made
it clear that it had not been involved in the consultations; indeed, a
deputy minister declared, "There haven't been any senior level discussions yet, and it is not clear what FEDNOR is for."[17]

In time, Quebec and, more recently Southern Ontario and Canada's
North, would also secure their own federal regional economic development agency. At the moment, every postal code in Canada, even the
ones on Bay Street in the heart of Canada's financial district, has
access to a federal regional development agency.

This is a far cry from when Jean Marchand, the first minister of
DREE, declared in 1968 that if the federal government allocated less
than 80 per cent of its regional development budget east of Trois-
Rivières, then it should be viewed as a failure.[18] The point is that
political logic can be adjusted to accommodate the partisan political requirements of the day, and that political considerations matter
far more to party leaders than contemplating what government is
good at.

Mulroney went on to win a majority in the 1988 election, winning
twelve seats out of thirty-two in Atlantic Canada and forty-eight seats
out of eighty-six in Western Canada in essentially a three-party race.
Politicians, including Mulroney, knew how to measure political success, and establishing ACOA and WD was a success, at least a political
success. For senior politicians, their partisan advisors and many officials operating above the fault line, being good at generating political
success is what truly matters.

BUREAUCRACY MEASURES SUCCESS DIFFERENTLY

More than one senior ACOA official has told me over the years that I had it wrong when I recommended limiting its staff to 100, reallocating existing money to create a $250 million fund rather than allocating new money, and relying on existing federal and provincial programs to deliver initiatives rather than creating new ones.

They claimed that I was being politically naive in not recommending new money and new programs. They viewed the fact that the federal government was dealing with a $32 billion deficit as a separate issue, requiring a different debate and solutions. It was somebody else's problem. It will be recalled that the finance minister of the day, Michael Wilson, stressed the need to deal with the deficit in his budget papers that he tabled in Parliament on 18 February 1987.[19]

With regard to my recommending an agency with only 100 officials, they were convinced that I also had that all wrong. How could they, they asked, possibly compete or deal with other larger federal departments and agencies? How could they deal with the demands of central agencies and those of ministerial offices? How could they possibly give the kind of visibility to regional programs that the prime minister and ministers expected? How could they possibly define and pursue a new economic development strategy? And how could they defend the federal interest in their dealings with provincial governments with only 100 public servants? They made it clear from day one, to everyone from their minister to central agencies, that the 100 person-year figure was simply a non-starter.

To be sure, from a political perspective, the prime minister and the ACOA minister had more pressing issues to deal with than the number of public servants working at the agency. There was a general election only months away, and their goal was to have ACOA highly visible and to be seen delivering initiatives. ACOA and central agency officials could sort out how many person-years or full-time equivalents (FTES) ACOA would need. For a brief period at least, the political and bureaucratic interests merged and public servants took full advantage to grow the agency.

The pressure on ACOA in the early days to be seen making a difference in Atlantic Canada was intense – a general election was only months away.[20] Within several months they had in place a new program, together with a communication strategy to promote it. The

Action Program was formally introduced on 15 February 1988, and the response was overwhelming – no doubt in part because so many types of economic activities became eligible, but also because of the high-profile publicity campaign heralding its introduction. It was also one of the most generous regional development programs ever introduced in Canada. For whatever reason, the Action Program was quick off the mark. After a little more than a year, ACOA had reviewed over 34,000 inquiries, processed 6,800 applications, and approved 2,700 projects.[21] Applications, initially at least, came in at ten times the rate of any predecessor programs. By the fiscal year 1988–89, ACOA had received 9,634 applications and approved nearly 5,000 under its Action Program.[22] The general election was held on 21 November 1988.

ACOA was given 320 person-years when it was first established. Within months, senior ACOA officials made the case before its minister and central agencies in Ottawa that it still did not have sufficient staff to pursue fully its mandate. ACOA later reported that it had to add some fifty people on contract to deal with the backlog of applications under its Action Program.[23]

ACOA officials never relented in asking for more staff. They insisted that they could not deliver the Action Program, even begin to coordinate the activities of other federal government departments and develop a plan advocate role on behalf of the region before central agencies and other federal departments and agencies unless they had more staff.[24] No one asked if an agency with its head office over 1,000 kilometres away from the national capital could possibly have much of an impact in coordinating the activities of much larger federal departments and agencies. They should have, because history has revealed that the approach has not met with much success on this front.[25]

ACOA officials succeeded in adding staff to the agency, despite the impact of the ambitious Chrétien-Martin 1994–97 program review, which eliminated 45,000 public service positions and cut departmental spending by $17 billion over the three-year period.[26] At the end of the review, ACOA still had 309 person-years.[27]

ACOA nevertheless kept up the pressure to add more staff, even though the review had cut its expenditure budget by 25 per cent, including the Action Program. To comply with the cuts, ACOA ended all cash grants to private business, as did other federal government departments. ACOA also stopped funding economic development agreements with the four Atlantic provinces.²⁸

Once the necessary spending cuts were secured, Prime Minister Chrétien and his senior advisors turned to new priority issues. Chrétien successfully fought a general election in 1997 and later put in place measures to secure national unity, including the controversial clarity act.²⁹ Chrétien also focussed on initiatives that were personally important to him, including, among others, the Millennium Scholarship Foundation, efforts to promote national unity in Quebec, the Canadian Foundation for Innovation and demanding foreign affairs issues, including the war on terrorism. Chrétien also had to focus on Paul Martin, his minister of finance, who had designs on the leadership of the Liberal Party. In brief, for Chrétien, attacking the deficit was job done, and he was on to other pressing matters. The level of person-years in ACOA or other departments was not high on his agenda.

Senior ACOA officials did not take a back seat while other departments demanded new resources in the aftermath of the program review. They too sought to define new programs and grow their organization. And they did. They had the help of government MPs in the Atlantic region who became concerned that budget measures following the program review provided for new spending and new economic development – but that none seemed destined for the Atlantic provinces. The 1999 budget, for example, added $200 million to the Canada Foundation for Innovation, $75 million to the Natural Sciences and Engineering Research Council of Canada, $16 million to the National Research Council, $55 million to biotechnology research and development, $50 million to Networks of Excellence, $150 million to Technology Partnerships Canada, and $430 million to the Canadian Space Agency. But there was very little here that would benefit Atlantic Canada. Technology Partnerships Canada was viewed for what it was, a program designed for the economic circumstances of Ontario and Quebec, which were always able to secure the bulk of the program's budget, while the Canadian Space Agency was seen as mostly benefiting Ottawa and Montreal.³⁰

The 2000 federal budget held no greater promise for the Atlantic region, much to the dismay of Atlantic MPs who had made commitments in the general election campaign. The budget established a $60 million Foundation for Climate and Atmospheric Sciences but located its head office in Ottawa, provided $46 million for national pollution enforcement and the Great Lakes Action Plan, and added $900 million to the Canada Foundation for Innovation. It also gave the Montreal-based Business Development Bank of Canada an $80 million injection of new money to support its financing activities.[31]

The Atlantic government caucus met with Finance Minister Paul Martin in late 1998 and early 1999. MPs outlined their concerns about the political fortunes of the Liberal Party in their region and the difficult economic circumstances of their constituencies. Martin responded by asking, "Do you want another billion for the unemployment program?"[32] He challenged them to come forward with innovative ideas to grow the Atlantic economy.

Atlantic MPs hired a consultant and worked closely with ACOA officials to come up with a new program. Prime Minister Chrétien went to Halifax on 29 June 2000 to announce what he described as a "fresh approach to regional economic development." He explained, "The Atlantic Investment Partnership is a bold plan designed to ensure not only that Atlantic Canadians can take their rightful place in the new economy, but that they can make their place at home – in Atlantic Canada." He announced that $700 million would be committed to the region over a five-year period to strengthen its ability to compete in the global economy.[33] The $700 million was not all new money. Some $400 million was simply allocated from the existing ACOA budget to do different things.[34]

Still, ACOA officials saw new opportunities to grow the organization. They never talked about reallocating staff from the Action Program, which had been terminated. Government departments and agencies do not think like that, and ACOA is no different. They consider existing human resources as money in the bank and, whenever they are asked to take on new responsibilities, they simply ask for more staff. Cutting or reallocating staff is on their agenda only when the government holds a program review. There are no incentives to reallocate human resources, for a host of reasons, including having to negotiate with public sector unions. Senior government officials argue that they do not have the time, the inclination, or the resources to deal with unions. More to the point, there is simply no advantage and no benefit for them to do so. Best to avoid them whenever possible. In addition, in all my years interviewing public servants or working in government, I have never heard a single senior federal government manager tell me that he or she had too much staff or even enough to do what needed to be done. They also have little interest in dealing with non-performers. The system does not encourage it, and it is also simply not in the DNA of government officials to deal with the long drawn-out process required to deal with non-performers.

Senior government managers are good at making the case for more staff and, again, ACOA officials are no different. Chrétien's Halifax announcement opened the door for ACOA to go to central agencies for more person-years or FTES.

As early as 2005–6, ACOA could boast of having 678 person-years, up from 320 in its first year of operation and a far cry from the 100 I had recommended. The agency added new staff in all categories. By 2010–11 the number had grown once again, to 711. After securing a majority mandate, Stephen Harper focused on the expenditure budget, much as Chrétien had done in the aftermath of his 1993 majority victory, and launched an ambitious program review. ACOA came under scrutiny and its person-years allocation dropped to 566 for 2014–15,[35] which is 466 more than what I had recommended and nearly double what ACOA was allocated when it was established. If history is a guide, ACOA will join all the other departments and agencies lining up for new resources the moment there is an opening or when the prime minister decides to turn to other more pressing issues than the latest program review.

Over the years, ACOA has added new positions to all activities. In 2012–13 it allocated 82 person-years to policy, advocacy, and coordination and 271 person-years to internal services (such as financial management services, material services and other administrative services) and 188 person-years to enterprise and business development.[36] It is revealing to note that the activity that requires the most resources is to manage the overhead of the agency. One can hardly imagine that this would be the case in the private sector.

The Treasury Board Secretariat has consistently given ACOA a solid report card under its Management Accountability Framework (MAF). MAF speaks to process and to management, not to the agency's impact on the Atlantic economy. ACOA, in its 2011–12 MAF, ranked strong or acceptable under all headings (e.g., among others, internal audit, values and ethics, financial, management control, management of security, and people management). It had only one "opportunity for improvement" under the integrated risk-management heading.[37]

ACOA's impact on the Atlantic regional economy is another matter. It is hardly possible for anyone to provide a definitive answer. There is precious little evidence that Mulroney had it right when he observed that ACOA would succeed where others had failed and that it would "inflict prosperity" on Atlantic Canada. There is also little evidence that Chrétien had it right when he claimed a new ACOA investment program to be "a bold plan designed to ensure ... that Atlantic Canadians can take their rightful place in the new economy." Atlantic Canadians are still waiting to take their rightful place in the new economy. While it may not be clear what government is good at, we know that politicians excel at overstating a promise for better days.

It is simply not possible to assess the success of ACOA or its predecessors on the Atlantic Canada economy. Far too many factors determine the pace and location of economic activities. Federal regional development efforts are no match for the value of the US dollar, interest rates, employment insurance policy, and the like. ACOA spending has had an impact in Atlantic Canada, as have other federal economic development agencies in their respective regions, but how much of an impact we do not know and never will. Dan Usher summed it up well when he observed that trying to determine how many jobs were actually created under Ottawa's regional incentive programs is like trying to discover how many children would have been born in Canada in the absence of the government's family allowance program.[38]

What about senior public servants in Ottawa? They view regional economic development as important to all politicians and thus to be tolerated. It will be recalled that Stephen Harper, a right-of-centre politician who had been critical of ACOA while in opposition, established a federal regional economic development agency for Southern Ontario and another one for Canada's North. Few senior career officials in Ottawa, meanwhile, believe that regional development funding is money well spent. It is to be tolerated because politicians want it, and they are powerless to do anything about it. Tom Kent went to the heart of the issue when he said, "From the point of view of almost all conventional wisdom in Ottawa, the idea of regional development was a rather improper one that some otherwise quite reasonable politician brought in like a baby on a doorstep from an election campaign."[39] What it does, however, is provide opportunities to grow the machinery of government, establish new agencies, and add still more resources to central agencies and oversight bodies to keep an eye on the agencies to make sure that they run on their tracks. It also contributes to making government thicker and government operations less efficient.

ESTABLISHING THE CANADIAN CENTRE
FOR MANAGEMENT DEVELOPMENT

Gérard Veilleux, secretary to the Treasury Board, had cut his teeth in
the federal public service in the early 1970s as a junior Treasury Board
official under the watchful eye of Al Johnson. Johnson, a widely
respected public servant, had sought to establish a training and development centre for government managers, and Veilleux was asked to
give him a hand in developing the proposal.

The proposal went nowhere. Michael Pitfield, a senior Privy Council Office official and a close advisor to Prime Minister Trudeau, was
strongly opposed to the proposal, and that in itself was enough to kill
it. Pitfield felt that the federal government had no business in the
training or education sector; best to leave that to the provinces and
universities.

However, Pitfield left government as the Trudeau years were coming
to a close. When Trudeau appointed Pitfield to the Senate in December
1982, Veilleux decided that the time was ripe to strike again. He asked
me to prepare a proposal that he could submit to Paul Tellier, the clerk
of the Privy Council Office; the prime minister; and Don Mazankowski, deputy prime minister, arguably the most powerful member of
Mulroney's Cabinet. At the time, Mazankowski was president of the
Treasury Board and Veilleux's minister. Veilleux knew that if he could
sell the proposal to them, it would be a done deal.

I produced a nineteen-page document – "The Canadian Centre for
Management Studies" (CCMS). I argued that the centre was necessary
for several reasons. First, the federal public service required a "strong,
unifying and confident corporate culture," and the provinces and universities could not provide it. I quoted from the most recent annual
report of the Public Service Commission (PSC): "The sense of pride in
service that was the glory of the Public Service not all that long ago is
being eroded."[40]

Second, I argued that university-based programs were concentrat-
ing on public policy, not on public-sector management issues. I pointed out that fewer than 9 per cent of the papers published in *Canadian Public Administration* dealt with management. The government
needed to manage human and financial resources better, and an in-
house development and training capacity was needed.

Third, the government already had a training facility at Touraine,

Quebec, but it had problems. It was essentially an "orientation" centre for newly appointed managers, had no research capacity, and did not "enjoy the reputation and prestige of a nationally recognized centre of excellence either in teaching or research."[41]

The solution – to establish a dedicated centre for teaching and research in public sector management. In doing so, I stressed a number of caveats. First, I argued that it should stand alone, apart from any government department, and enjoy an "independent" status. I argued that "it must have the capacity to bring together practitioners and leading academics in a centre known for its rigorous standards, especially in teaching, but also in its efforts to push back the frontier of knowledge in public sector management. It must be seen to operate at arm's length from the pressures, both political and bureaucratic, of the federal government."[42]

I also argued that the new centre "need not be costly." I reminded readers that for Canadians to appreciate the work of the public service, it had to be known for its "objectivity, its frugality and its value to society as a whole." I made the following case: "Experience tells us that the key element in establishing a centre of excellence is getting the right people. There is no correlation between the money made available to a new centre of excellence and its chances of success." I added, "Every effort should be made to limit spending, at least in the initial stages, to no more than what is now available at Touraine (i.e., 44 person-years and $4.3 million annually)."[43]

I concluded with a series of recommendations on the curriculum (a combination of courses in management, communications, history, economics, political science, and constitutional and administrative law). The ideal faculty member, I argued, would be "a mix of two people – a top flight, broadly experienced university professor and a top flight broadly experienced practitioner. There are a few such people and, if they can be found and attracted year by year, then the problem of finding faculty members will have been solved." I urged that every effort be made to "attract experienced academics, on contract, who could develop courses" in collaboration with experienced practitioners.[44] I stressed, however, that the centre had to be given a degree of independence from government if it was to attract leading academics and promote rigorous research.

Senior Treasury Board Secretariat officials accepted the paper but made significant revisions. The centre was renamed the Canadian Centre for Management Development, the words "independent" and "able to operate at arm's length" were removed, and the section on funding was adjusted to read "not much more than what is now available" from "no more."[45] An important distinction, as time would reveal.

Veilleux took the proposal to Paul Tellier, clerk of the Privy Council Office, and Jack Manion, associate clerk, for their approval and for them to brief the prime minister. Both Tellier and Manion had little difficulty with the proposal.

Veilleux next went to his minister, Don Mazankowski. I accompanied Veilleux in one of his regularly briefings with the minister when the proposed centre was on the agenda. My sense was that Mazankowski was, at best, lukewarm to the idea. He knew, however, that Tellier, Manion, and his own deputy minister strongly supported the proposal and that Mulroney was on side. In the end, Mazankowski signed on – again, I suspect, with little enthusiasm. He wrote to the prime minister on 3 September 1987, attached the proposal, and said that he "fully supported the proposal." He explained that "most western industrialized countries have well established and highly credible teaching centres for public sector managers." He added, "The proposal recommends that every effort be made to limit spending to not much more than what is currently available for Touraine."

I was asked to accompany Mazankowski to Toronto for the announcement (he flew on the government jet while I flew commercial). I helped write the minister's speech, which he delivered as drafted. The occasion – a public policy dinner held on 14 April 1988 to honour four Canadians who had contributed to public service: Ted Newall, Allen Lambert, Bob Bryce, and Paul Tellier.

Mazankowski's speech read, "It is a great pleasure to announce the establishment of the Canadian Centre for Management Development ... Our vision is a credible, nationally and, perhaps in time internationally, recognized centre of excellence in teaching and research in public sector management."[46] Mazankowski also introduced the centre's first principal, Jack Manion, a long-serving, highly respected deputy minister in Ottawa, whom he called "an individual whose managerial skills are among the most highly respected in Ottawa."[47] He then announced that Paul Tellier had agreed to act as chairman of the centre's advisory board.[48] The fact that the centre was guided by an advisory board rather than a board of directors revealed that it would not enjoy independence from the government of the kind that I had envisaged.

The prime minister was not willing to let Manion leave the Privy Council Office until a number of major issues had been resolved. I did not know what the issues were, but Manion asked if I could go to the centre as deputy principal for one year and serve as acting principal. I agreed.

From the moment I stepped into CCMD, I felt pressure from central agencies and senior departmental officials to take on some of their senior staff. Essentially, their argument was that the public servants in question had served the system well, were loyal, and had a wealth of management experience that they could share with aspiring senior managers. They also often said that the individual in question did not fit in the reorganization or that he or she could not adapt to new ways of doing things. In many cases, the central agency or department offered to carry the salary for a year or so. The argument in brief – the individuals had been very loyal to the system and it was time for the system to be loyal to them. The idea of building "a credible, nationally and perhaps in time internationally, recognized centre of excellence" was not on their agenda. They needed to move someone out of the department that had gone by his or her best-by date, and the new centre provided a convenient out.

I resisted, but when the clerk, associate clerk, or secretary to the Treasury Board calls, it is not always possible to say no, especially when there is an offer to carry the individual's salary for at least one year. But it is a slippery slope. When you say yes once, it becomes difficult to say no the next time.

Jack Manion looked after the legislation establishing the centre. It breezed through the House of Commons without problems or even questions, but the Senate was a different matter. Michael Pitfield, now a senator, had the same concerns that he had had some fifteen years earlier. As Manion explains, "In Committee, it became clear that Pitfield opposed the very idea of the Centre and was just talking to obstruct. He kept asking the same questions of me over and over again. Finally he objected to the Chair that I was repeating the same answers. Unwisely, I blurted out 'when you stop repeating the same question, I will stop giving the same answer!' All hell broke loose. My staff hid their faces and the Senators went on about disrespect to the Senate. Ultimately I left, but it took two years to get the bill through the Senate."[49] Pitfield, as Manion explains in his autobiography, could never accept that the federal government would undertake activities that he felt more properly belonged to the universities.[50]

Initially, at least, the centre was able to operate with little more funding than what was allocated to the Touraine training centre. I also made it a priority to invite leading academics to come to the centre both to meet with practitioners and to produce original research. In the early years, the centre attracted internationally acclaimed scholars like B. Guy Peters, Christopher Hood, Christopher Pollitt, and Henry Mintzberg, among many others. We produced three peer-reviewed books published by McGill-Queen's University Press on public administration and public sector management that received positive reviews in learned journals.[51] In the centre's early years, Ralph Heintzman and John Tait also produced a seminal report on values and ethics in government that has been widely quoted both inside and outside government.[52]

I returned to my university shortly after Jack Manion came to the centre as full-time principal. I stayed on as a part-time research fellow for several years, but by design I had no management responsibility. Manion also retired in 1990, after only a few years as principal.

I saw the centre take on a new orientation. It moved away from fundamental research to what its officials labelled "action research." I have never understood what action research means. Perhaps it is the academic in me, but I saw action research as the kind of research that could not get accepted in peer-reviewed publications. To be sure, action research generates a lot of meetings and a lot of discussions, but few publications. It also has little lasting value to the literature and the classroom.

I have since seen the centre grow and grow. Physically, it sits in a beautiful heritage building opposite the National Gallery on Sussex Drive in downtown Ottawa. Its orientation course is mandatory and the other courses, we are told, "are grounded in the realities of the public service." The school offers courses in financial-management control, budgeting, evaluation, accountability, and the "essentials of managing in the public service." It also offers one-on-one coaching sessions.[53]

The school lists twenty-three faculty members but does not explain how it classifies or separates faculty members from other staff. None of the twenty-three are known for their publications or research. I have been in public administration for some forty years and I do not recognize any of the faculty members or their contributions to the field.[54] I am not aware of any substantive publication produced by the centre in recent years.

The government decided in 2004 to change the name from the Canadian Centre for Management Development to the Canada School of Public Service. It was not made clear why the name was changed, though the school was given the added responsibility for language training that was part of the Public Service Commission. In addition, the word "school" brands the organization as more of a learning institution than does the word "centre." The school now has a board of governors rather than an advisory board, and here again "board of governors" is commonly associated more with universities than a government agency or centre. Notwithstanding the name change, the board remains in essence an advisory board, and the school has all the trappings of a typical government department.

And despite rebranding the organization as a "school," very little research is now carried out other than perhaps of the "action research" variety. The school's website offers little in research activities or publications. Its 2012–13 report on plans and priorities also has little to say about research.[55]

It is not, however, for lack of resources. The school's budget for 2012–13 was over $110 million and had a staff complement of 744 full-time equivalents, down from a high of nearly $140 million in 2008–9, following cuts after the government's 2012 program review. The school transferred all direct delivery of language training to the private sector, retaining a capacity to develop new methodologies and to ensure that outside providers meet requirements. Still, the transfer and other decisions flowing from the program review eliminated 196 FTEs at the school between 2008–9 and 2012–13.[56] I note that there are now also FTEs in the private sector responsible for language training and they invoice the federal government for their work.

The school's resources are a far cry from the day it was established and the commitments Mazankowski made to the prime minister. Recall that he wrote the prime minister in September 1987, "Every effort [will] be made to limit spending to not much more than what is currently available at Touraine" (i.e., forty-four person-years and $4.3 million) and that "the objective is to develop a nationally and over time an internationally recognized centre of excellence in teaching and research in public sector management."[57] Recall also that the attached document read, "It is important to stress that establishing a new centre for management studies need not be costly. Experience tells us that the key element in establishing a centre of excellence is getting the right people. There is no correlation between the money made available to a new centre of excellence and its chance of success."[58]

Prime Minister Mulroney is no longer there to ask questions, nor is Mazankowski to provide answers. Mazankowski served only for six months as Treasury Board president. In any event, one can easily speculate that the new management centre quickly fell off their radar screens after Mazankowski announced its establishment. The centre had no political importance to either man, and both had bigger issues to deal with: the introduction of the HST, the implementation of the Canada-US Free Trade agreement, national unity, and the list goes on. Mazankowski would have paid much closer attention to the work of the newly established Western Diversification Agency than to a management centre for public servants in downtown Ottawa. It has been left to senior public servants to manage the centre-cum-school with very limited intervention from politicians.

I hear no one suggesting that the Canada School of Public Service is a nationally recognized centre of excellence, let alone an international one. It is not. I can write several 300-page books on Canadian public administration, as I have done, and – leaving aside the Tait and Heintzman work on values and ethics published in 1996 – not draw a single quote from the research carried out at the school in recent years. It is difficult to determine if it is a good teaching facility. I do have doubts, and anecdotal evidence leans the same way.[59]

And yet the school is considerably more expensive to operate than was first envisaged. It has not attracted leading scholars for the past ten years or so and instead has relied on career public servants. The practice of senior deputy ministers sending managers who have passed their best-by date to the school has only intensified.

I have watched over the years with interest as senior Treasury Board Secretariat or department officials were moved over to the school. They had never entered a classroom to teach or undertaken substantial research. The school has simply become a convenient place to park senior public servants while waiting for their retirement. But this is not without cost to taxpayers or to the school's success.

The school's current annual budget is allocated to four programs: foundation learning ($61 million and 300 FTEs), organizational leadership development ($15 million and 55 FTEs), public-sector management innovation ($11 million and 7,769 FTEs), and internal services ($23 million and 222 FTEs).[60] I note that internal services alone employ far more people than did the Touraine centre.

The school, like other federal government departments and agencies, must annually produce a report on plans and priorities as well as a departmental performance report, and must also deal with accountability requirements. The NPM vocabulary permeates these documents, as do attempts to emulate the private sector. One document, for example, reports on the school's desire to "grow its market share."[61] One can only assume that it wants to build a strong, distinct, corporate culture for the public service by looking to the private sector for inspiration. Whether or not the school is able to grow its "market share" has little bearing on the school's staff or their salaries.

The accountability reports, as is so often the case with federal government departments and agencies, essentially note that all is well. Evaluation reports also invariably reveal that the school is on the right track. How they arrive at this assessment is unclear. More to the point, how can one properly evaluate the school's performance? Given that it does little research, one has to focus on its teaching and management-development programs. How one can possibly evaluate its strategic goals that "public servants have the common knowledge and the leadership and management competences they require to fulfill their responsibilities in serving Canadians" or "effectively manage efforts to bring transformative change and renewal to the Public Service"?[62] How can one possibly determine if the objectives have been met and, even if one could, how could one discover which or even what agency was responsible for the success?

The Treasury Board Secretariat assessed the school's performance under its MAF in 2011–12. It gave the school relatively high marks, including an "acceptable" grade for values and ethics, leadership, governance, financial control, management, and management of projects of security, integrated risk management, people management, procurement, information management, asset management, and investment planning, and an "opportunity for improvement" grade for internal audit, as well as a strong grade for "evaluation."[63] It is not at all clear who benefits from the production of these documents, and if anyone needed proof that public servants working in evaluation units or on MAFs are kept busy turning cranks not attached to anything, one need look no further than this document.

No assortment of business terms and no metaphors borrowed from other sectors can obscure the fact that the school has never lived up to expectations. The goal established by the deputy prime minister on 14 April 1988 to "develop a credible, national, world-class centre of excellence in teaching and research known for its rigorous standards, most particularly in teaching, but also in the commitment to push back the frontiers of knowledge in public sector management" has never been met and it is very unlikely that it ever will.[64]

Again, it has not been for a lack of resources. The school's budget and human resources equal those of a mid-size Canadian university. Mid-size universities have about 250 professors in all disciplines with the necessary background to teach, and many carry out peer-reviewed research.

The head of the school wrote to all deputy ministers on 3 June 2014 to outline a new approach to learning that was based on six months of research and consultations with leading private firms, such as BMO, Deloitte, GE, KPMG, and other governments. She added that the school has "a solid track record," without providing evidence. She reported, however, that the school did not lack for resources, housing "a faculty of experts and top practicing public servants: 23 full-time practitioners and a cadre of more than 230 public servants (including many deputy minsters) from 40 departments and agencies teaching part-time."[65] The reader will note that this does not account for all staff at the school.

The new approach speaks to government-wide learning requirements, new online resources, and the establishment of committees to identify emerging priorities. The more substantial change, however, is how the school is funded. By the year 2016–17 the school will be financially supported through reallocations from departments and agencies. It is envisaged that departments will be taxed $230 per capita to support the school.

The school will enjoy a captive market, with all departments having no choice but to contribute.[66] It is difficult to see how the private sector could have inspired this funding model. Yet the school continues to employ the vocabulary from the private sector, insisting that the new approach "means a new business model." It is quick to add, however, that no "learning organization … can match" one of the school's attributes – which is "specific to the public service."[67]

Not only has the school not lived up to expectations and, despite demands from the Treasury Board Secretariat for accountability requirements and performance reports that all departments and agencies must address, the school has had its share of controversies. Some involve values and ethics, precisely the areas in which the Treasury Board gave the school an acceptable grade.

The *Globe and Mail* called the school a "classic government boondoggle" in 2013. It is worth quoting at length from the article:

> The school hires retired, pensioned civil servants to teach other civil servants such things as "Writing Targeted Briefing Reports" and "Managing a Meeting." There are hundreds of courses available; some are online and cost nothing, while others, such as "How Ottawa Works," are taught in the classroom and have tuition fees as high as $1,650. The problem is that the retired civil servants teaching the courses are earning eye-catching fees. Records show one is making $82,500 a year for working a half week (22.5 hours). A former associate deputy minister gets $38,000 for 50 days work. Faculty members get as much as $760 per day to prepare and teach a class. They are also high fees compared to the average annual salaries of university professors in Canada. A full-time professor at the University of Toronto earns about $136,000 per year. One school faculty member earns $154,300 annually for not quite full-time work. The federal procurement ombudsman, Frank Brunetta, reported last month that he found evidence the school directed contracts to favoured clients and violated its own procurement policies in doing so. This came after Treasury Board President Tony Clement wrote in a letter to the school last year that he is concerned about the possibility of "inappropriate contracting with former public servants in receipt of pensions, either because contractors are being chosen preferentially or because contractors are being hired to provide work of dubious value."[68]

The *Globe and Mail* could have added that retired public servants also benefit from an extremely generous pension plan. I suspect that if Mulroney and Mazankowski had known this turn of events, they would not have signed on to the proposal.

How could a *Globe and Mail* journalist uncover these lacunae while several senior public servants at the school and the Treasury Board Secretariat with expertise in evaluating performance make the case that all is well on the values and ethics front? Officials at these two agencies, more so than those in line departments, should be at the leading edge of new management thinking in government and how to make it work. If these officials are not up to the challenge, one can hardly imagine what it is like for others.

The school also speaks to political and bureaucratic elites looking after the economic interest of other bureaucratic elites. How else can one explain how retired senior public servants, all enjoying generous pensions and other advantages, are able to enjoy $80,000 plus contracts for half-time work?

At my own university and at most other universities, a retired professor invited to teach a course to accommodate the department because of a sabbatical leave or other unforeseen development, is paid $5,000 for the course. The $5,000 includes preparation and teaching time. I note that my university, unlike the federal public service, never launched an elaborate values and ethics exercise.

Other than officials at the school and apparently the Treasury Board Secretariat, precious few voices sing the school's praises. Writing some twenty years after the school was established, a former deputy minister and head of the Public Service Commission maintains that senior public servants "don't have the training to handle the tough policy and management issues facing government today."[69] She adds that "the state of mind of executives has come to be tainted by a multitude of bad habits ... rewarding failure, punishing success, failure to confront."[70]

LESSONS LEARNED

What lessons can be learned about what government is good at from this chapter? I was wrong in 1987 to think that a government agency could become a national or international centre of excellence in teaching or research. Government is not good at this, and the Canada School of Public Service speaks to this fact.

The school is hardly the only case that makes the point. A recent survey of scientists with the federal government reveals that not all is well with the government's scientific community. Ninety per cent of respondents said that they are not allowed to speak freely about their research to the public or to the media, nor are they permitted to publish in scientific journals; 86 per cent said that, if faced with a political decision putting health, safety, or the environment at risk, they do not believe that they could speak out without repercussions. Some 71 per cent felt that policy had been compromised in the past by political interference.[71]

Above all, scientists require the freedom to inquire, to collaborate with other scientists, and to test their findings with peers. Scientists want occasions to discuss their research and science, not government policy. They cannot succeed in their work if they have a shadow on their shoulders. In short, scientific imperatives simply do not square with political and bureaucratic imperatives. Surely government scientists and senior government managers can make a distinction between scientists discussing their research and discussing the merits of government policy decisions. If not, we should conclude that government is not good at letting scientists do research.

Thomas Homer-Dixon and Heather Douglas, both holders of chairs at the University of Waterloo, teamed up with a former federal public servant to make the case that "the connection between science and public policy within the federal government is broken." They add, "Whenever science seems likely to generate knowledge that could create difficulties for their political agenda, they try to bury the knowledge and destroy the government's capacity to generate it" and explain that "federal ministers have created rules that require government scientists – especially those working on resource and environmental topics – to get approval from senior bureaucrats before publishing their research."[72] No one and no issue is immune to the blame game.

In my report to the Treasury Board Secretariat, I said that to build a credible centre of excellence, it "must be independent ... it must be seen to operate at arm's length from the pressure, both political and bureaucratic, of the federal government ... A new culture must be free to surface that encourages original studies, including possible controversial issues."[73] That recommendation fell on deaf ears.

Politicians do not tolerate public servants generating controversies, whether or not they have a scientific basis. This has become even more important in recent years for reasons outlined earlier. Senior public servants know this better than anyone. They will happily discuss the importance of centres of excellence but establishing the conditions for them to prosper inside government is quite another matter. The pressures of the day will invariably outweigh other considerations. Senior public servants have joined their political masters in focusing on the immediate, on the short term, and on managing the blame game.

A newly appointed secretary to the Treasury Board, for example, decides that one of his or her most senior officials no longer meets requirements. He or she knows that one does not easily dismiss senior public servants. A phone call to the head of the Canada School of Public Service can quietly solve the problem. The Treasury Board secretary can persuasively claim that the senior official has a wealth of experience in human resources management and can be a solid asset to the school. No matter that the individual is ill-equipped to make a contribution in either teaching or research. The secretary of the Treasury Board has solved an immediate problem, and the head of the school is owed a favour by a senior member of the deputy ministers club.

In hindsight, it would have been much better to leave well enough alone. A simple low-cost orientation centre for newly appointed government managers is what government is good at. Anything more ambitious will not work unless it is given the independence to pursue initiatives that matter to the organization and its goals. That is unlikely, given political and bureaucratic requirements. In brief, governments are not good at giving independence to their departments or agencies or to adjust the level of independence so as to achieve the goals at hand.

The regional economic development field, meanwhile, is ideal for scoring political points. Politicians are good at that – it is their bread and butter. Assessing what government can do well in this sector is not what matters. What matters is being seen doing something, anything, for a region. Visibility is key and matters more than policy substance. A genuine regional perspective and a complete review of what government can do well in promoting regional economic development have little currency in Ottawa. What is important is announcing a billion dollars of new money for a region, a new regional agency and a new program. How else can one explain that every postal code in Canada now has access to a federal regional development agency? How else can you explain that a Progressive Conservative prime minister, a Liberal prime minister, and a Conservative prime minister have all gone down that same road?

Lowell Murray, ACOA's first minister and one of the agency's biggest supporters in its early years, summed it up well when he observed in June 2014 that "ACOA has lost its way."[74] Murray makes the point that what politicians are keenly interested in is packaging and selling new initiatives, and what public servants above the fault line are good at is helping politicians plan, develop, and sell new policies and new measures. Those who hold power and influence in government either have limited interest in implementation or, in particular in the case of the prime minister and his most senior advisors, cannot find time in their busy agenda to think about implementation. They all too often assume that the machinery of government will do as it is told.

Public servants below the fault line are left to pick up the pieces. They are no longer able to cope, as they are expected to deal with dozens of oversight bodies, numerous accountability requirements of questionable value, at least to front-line workers, the blame game, an outdated approach to human resources tied to the work of public sector unions, the always present possibility that interest groups will take matters before the court, and the widely held view that, no matter how hard they try, they can never measure up to their private sector counterparts.

We also know that public servants will invariably ask for more human resources whenever a prime minister unveils a new initiative. The notion that one can reallocate existing staff or free human resources from a program that has been terminated holds no currency with the public service. More to the point, governments are not good at doing that. This chapter makes the point that bureaucracy has an inherent tendency to expand, even when there is no good reason to do so.[75] Over the years I have had numerous discussions with senior ACOA officials about the growth in the agency's human resources. To a person, they make the point that "feeding" the system eats far more of their own time and that of their staff than is believed, even in Ottawa, and far more than it should.

The chapter underlines several important points. First, very little thought is given to the challenges of implementing new initiatives when they are being developed. Yet implementation is the key to success to any initiative. However, the best and the brightest do not join the public service to work in implementation. They want to work in central agencies; failing that, in policy units in line departments. The ambitious know full well that the road to the top is through policy, generating ideas, managing the blame game, being visible in Ottawa circles, and central agencies, not through program management.

Program managers, meanwhile, are left with the more difficult task of making ideas work in a complex political-administrative environment. In the case of ACOA, enormous pressure was put on Don Mc-

Phail, the agency's first deputy minister. He and his staff had to reconcile political pressure to launch new programs and to spend money before the election against financial management rules. He was later fired from his position, with Dalton Camp, a senior PCO-PMO official, pointing his finger at central agencies for McPhail's demise.[76]

Both ACOA and the Canada School of Public Service speak eloquently to the principal-agent theory. The goals and interests of elected officials (the principals) did not square with those of the agents (public servants).[77] In both cases, but in particular the Canada School, the agents disregarded the directives of the principals (recall the commitment made by central agency officials to the president of the Treasury Board and the prime minister that the cost would not be "much more than what is now available"), knowing that they could get away with it. Granting greater autonomy to agents in the hope of emulating the private sector has clearly favoured the agents.

This chapter also raises fundamental questions about the role of the public service in pursuit of the common good. How is the public interest served if public service scientists are not free to share their findings on public health and safety with the public?[78]

More to the point, I was wrong to assume that developing the concept, the idea, was the more important part in policy-making, hence the title of this chapter. As is so often the case in government, policy-makers simply assume that the machinery of government as presently constituted will deliver what it is told, and then off they go to hatch other proposals. To be sure, to many in government, that is the fun part.

Government is good at generating ideas. In the case of the government of Canada, it has thousands and thousands of political appointees and senior public servants operating above the fault line concerned primarily with begetting ideas and managing the political blame game. How to implement new initiatives is better left to others, to another day, and to government bureaucracies.

Lastly, it is worth repeating that the two agencies are in no way different from other departments. They are always ready to jump, on all occasions, to expand operations. Notwithstanding years of New Public Management measures, there is still no incentive for departments and agencies to re-allocate resources from within whenever they are asked to take on new responsibilities. For example, in the immediate aftermath of the 22 October 2014 Parliament Hill shooting, the government asked the RCMP to add "dozens" of officers to deal with threats to national unity.[79] The RCMP quickly served notice that it required new resources. This, even though the RCMP has an annual budget of nearly $3 billion and some 29,000 full-time equivalents, and coming on the heels of a report making the case that the number of staff at the head office in Ottawa had doubled over a ten-year period.[80]

All this makes the point that government bureaucracies have their own culture, their own ways of operating, and their own ways of defining success. The next chapter looks inside government bureaucracy to see what makes it tick. A close look at how government bureaucracy functions is necessary to answer the question, what is government good at?

8

Inside Government

In late 2009, Darrell Dexter, newly elected premier of Nova Scotia, asked me to prepare a report on how to promote economic development in his province. I consulted a wide range of private sector representatives, academics, and federal and provincial government officials and produced the report *Invest More, Innovate More, Trade More, Learn More: The Way Ahead for Nova Scotia*.[1] Entrepreneurs and aspiring entrepreneurs told me that they had a difficult time sorting out which government programs applied to their business and with whom they should communicate. One senior government official even made the point that the business community "should spend less time navigating through government departments and programs and more time navigating world trade opportunities."[2]

I asked to meet with some of the federal and provincial government officials in economic development to solicit their ideas and test my own thinking with them. Some twenty-two officials attended the meeting. We discussed the issue raised by the entrepreneurs at some length, and officials from both orders of government told me that they attached a high priority to "streamlining economic development programs" in the province. Meetings were being held, business plans were being formulated, and concrete steps were being identified to streamline federal-provincial programs. One federal official was actually working full-time on the initiative.

They had a clear objective in mind: "to become the most business-friendly jurisdiction in Canada in terms of accessing government programs and services."[3] They also had a name for it: the Integrated Service Delivery Project. The project had in fact been launched four years earlier, and several federal and provincial government departments had signed on to it. However, public servants told me that the project's implementation had been slow, for reasons that were not made clear, but things were changing, as both governments now attached a high priority to the project.[4]

In early 2014, two officials preparing an economic development plan for the newly elected Nova Scotia government of Stephen McNeil sent me a draft of their report for comment. I was surprised to read that one recommendation was to promote a "no wrong door" approach to entrepreneurs, as they navigate government economic development programs. Their plan called on both the federal and provincial governments to make their economic development programs "available seamlessly" to entrepreneurs. The plan once again called on governments to become the most business-friendly jurisdiction in Canada. They made reference to my earlier report and added that there had been "some progress but not nearly enough."[5] Progress, if any at all, is barely visible.

Contrast this with the private sector. In 1997, McCain Foods, a leading Canadian business in the frozen food market, bought out one of its main US rivals – Ore-Ida Food Division from H.J. Heinz. Purchasing Ore-Ida was a bold move that required an implementation strategy. At the time, McCain Foods had annual sales of $325 million in the United States, while Ore-Ida had $550 million. Thus, McCain Foods–United States had to absorb a business larger than itself and extricate the business from an ingrained Heinz corporate culture.

McCain Foods brought a number of Ore-Ida senior managers from the United States to its head office in tiny Florenceville, New Brunswick, for a briefing. Harrison McCain spoke to the assembled managers and essentially told them the purchase was critical to the success of McCain Foods, and jobs depended on it. He wanted to see them in a year, to discover if they were able to make the transition work. The transition required merging different human resources, financial, IT, and distribution systems, and forging a new corporate culture. One senior manager described it as "an around the clock fight for four to five months." Implementing the deal was no less important than negotiating the deal itself, and McCain Foods committed its most senior executives to ensure its success. Harrison McCain was able to report to all staff a year or so later, "Job done."[6]

How does government bureaucracy operate? Why is no one held accountable for the apparent inability of government officials, in at least some instances, to go beyond holding meetings to identify why progress is slow and then do something about it? Why is performance-based accountability unable to monitor and ensure performance? This chapter looks inside government bureaucracy to see how it operates, what matters, and how one measures success.

THE WORLD IS NOT ONE

Those outside government, and many politicians and aspiring politicians, tend to view government bureaucracy as a monolith. We owe this view to Max Weber, who saw government bureaucracy as such, designed to ensure predictability of government action by applying the same rules to specific cases.[7] Weber's bureaucracy was for an era when the government's role was largely administrative and limited, with no developmental responsibility. This view no longer holds.

To be sure, there are still units in government that deliver programs and services by applying the same rules designed to treat all citizens and employees equally. But government bureaucracy is today far more complex and far more diverse than when Weber surveyed the work of government bureaucracies some hundred years ago. Government units, in the case of the government of Canada at least, that actually deliver programs and services directly to Canadians are now in the minority.

Government departments and agencies today have complex mandates, house different organizational cultures, and have staff members with different educational background and skills. The Department of Finance is home to economists who do not deliver programs and services. They work on preparing the budget, providing advice to their minister and the prime minister, and monitoring government policies and federal-provincial fiscal arrangements. The Canada Revenue Agency is home to accountants and auditors and often deals directly with Canadians. The Department of Canadian Heritage, meanwhile, has staff with various backgrounds and deals mostly with groups and associations to promote the arts, culture, and official languages programs. Nearly all departments now have a developmental mandate.

Departments are different, and bureaucratic units serve different purposes. One would be hard-pressed to identify common characteristics. It is no exaggeration to suggest that Max Weber would not recognize the government bureaucracy that he once described, if he were to visit Ottawa today. Government departments are no longer staffed mostly by clerks carrying out routine work. Weber's generalizations remain useful but, as James Q. Wilson argues, "Beyond that point, distinctions are more important than generalizations."[8]

Government bureaucracies today are all about distinctions. Some departments have clients, others do not. Some deal directly with Canadians, others with associations, and still others with other government departments. Some agencies, like the passport office, try to serve clients much as private sector firms do, others like Corrections Canada have clients who require a very different approach.

It is hardly possible to understand what government is good at, without understanding the diversity of organizations, purpose, and activities of government departments. The mandate of some departments can be in direct conflict with that of other departments (for example, Natural Resources and Environment), and somehow the contradictions have to be sorted out. One does not often see this in the private sector.

The nature of organizations matters. The diversity in goals, purpose, staff, and ties to the centre of government can and very often do make one government organization vastly different from another. It also explains why no one has been able to define a general theory of bureaucracy and make it stick. I see none on the horizon. James G. March and Herbert A. Simon summed it up well when they wrote, "Not a great deal of a theoretical nature has been said about organizations, but it has been said over and over in a variety of languages."[9] James Q. Wilson was more blunt: "I have come to have grave doubts that anything worth calling organization theory will ever exist. Theories will exist but they will usually be so abstract or general as to explain rather little."[10]

Given the diversity of government organizations, it is hardly conceivable that one could develop a comprehensive, systematic, and tested theory to explain even in general terms the behaviour of all government organizations. What is possible, however, is to review government organizations and their behaviour to assess better what they are good at. That is the purpose of this chapter.

A FAULT LINE

In one of my earlier books, *Thatcher, Reagan, and Mulroney: In Search of a New Bureaucracy*, published in 1994, I wrote about a growing "fault line" separating public servants typically in regional or local offices and focused mostly on serving the general public, from those in Ottawa, who serve the system, the prime minister, and ministers. Those units actually delivering programs and services have one eye on hierarchy and the other on clients. Those in Ottawa, meanwhile, are preoccupied with managing up, and they, more often than not, have both eyes on the prime minister, the clerk of the Privy Council, ministers, deputy ministers, their careers, the national media, the blame game, and how they themselves fit in.

The fault-line theory appears to resonate with practitioners. The Tait report on values and ethics later picked on the theme and reported on the differences between managing up, with its emphasis on Parliament, Cabinet, or the policy-making process, and managing down, with its emphasis on clients.[11] The report adds, "Many senior public servants have made their careers because of their skills in managing up. They have been valued and promoted because they were adept at providing superiors with what they needed in a timely fashion, to serve ministers and the political process." On managing down, the Tait report explains that after fifteen years of New Public Management, some people view managing down as "little more than empty words, the public service slipping easily back as through a natural reflex, into its natural mode of managing up."[12] Tait's point was that bureaucracy was better at managing up than managing down, the very situation that NPM was designed to correct, but failed.

The Canadian public service is largely about managing up. The decision to concentrate more and more public servants in the National Capital Region (from 27 per cent thirty years ago to 43 per cent today) speaks to the importance of managing up. The tendency to concentrate more public servants in the National Capital Region to work above the fault line has continued under Harper's watch. The 2011–12 Harper program review eliminated 19,200 positions over three years. Statistics Canada reported in August 2014 that the number of federal public servants in the Ottawa-Gatineau region had increased by 6.1 per cent over the past twelve months, while the total dropped by 7.3 per cent elsewhere.[13]

A government survey was carried out in the 1980s to identify all jobs that had at least some responsibility for dealing with the general public, even if that "some" amounted to 10 per cent of their work. The survey found that only about 40 per cent of public servants dealt with the public as one of their responsibilities, again even if it amounted to only 10 per cent of their work. That percentage has very likely gone down in light of the trend to a greater concentration of public servants in the National Capital Region.[14] Thus we have reached the point where over 60 per cent of federal public servants work in policy advisory, coordination, oversight, and back-office functions. I know of no private sector firm that would tolerate such a ratio. If it did, it would not be in business for long.

However, whenever senior public servants in central agencies in Ottawa speak about their institution, they talk about public servants serving Canadians. They rarely, if ever, speak of the countless liaison and coordination units, policy, oversight bodies, or the work of central agencies. Rather, they refer to public servants working at border crossings, delivering old age cheques, coastguard employees, and front-line immigration officials. One only has to read annual reports of the clerk of the Privy Council to the prime minister (available on the Privy Council Office website) to see evidence.[15]

Above the fault line, what matters is the prime minister's agenda, the views of the clerk of the Privy Council, how to keep bouncing Cabinet ministers under control, the work of central agencies, and the blame game. In other words, best management practices do not rank very high above the fault line, only the rhetoric.

The prime minister's agenda allows no time to focus on issues below the fault line unless they cause serious political problems for the government. The prime minister meets staff from his office and from the Privy Council Office most mornings. At these meetings, press briefings often dominate the agenda. Lawrence Martin writes that the briefings start with the most-watched television programs and then proceed in descending order of importance. When Parliament sits, the prime minister will spend a great deal of time preparing himself and his ministers for the daily Question Period. Martin explains, "All the prepping is not intended to produce candid answers to opposition queries. The strategy is not to reveal information but to shield it and counterattack."[16]

There is never a shortage of issues that require the prime minister's attention. He needs to remain accessible to world leaders, provincial premiers, senior ministers, his staff, and key business leaders. He must attend to party affairs. He signs off on all major government decisions, and some small ones as well, and needs to pay attention to pressing matters, from budget issues, to possible trade agreements, and the blame game.

The prime minister, the clerk of the Privy Council, and senior ministers do not have the time or the inclination to be concerned about management issues unless, again, they become visible to the blame game played out in Parliament or to the media.

A management issue that makes it on the front pages of national newspapers will also make it on the radar screen of both the prime minister and the clerk. They and their advisors will monitor and, if necessary, manage the file until the media lose interest. Controversy surrounding the temporary foreign worker program in April 2014 is a case in point. The PMO-PCO got involved, and Jason Kenney, the minister responsible, decided to impose a moratorium on foreign workers' permits for fast food restaurants. In Parliament, Kenney blamed the Liberals for creating the program, the Liberals insisted that it was a Conservative mess because Kenney had been responsible for the program for six years, and the leader of the opposition called on the auditor general to investigate.[17] The blame game was played out for everyone to see on the evening news and political talk shows. The art of coping and survival is key to success inside government.

MPs take their cue from the media on questions to ask. They do not have the knowledge or the resources to explore management issues in any detail. Many MPs do not know if they should even be asking questions about management issues, or indeed even how government spending is managed, let alone what questions to ask. To be sure, elected politicians may well meddle in administrative matters inside a government department in order to keep a local office open or to nudge government jobs to certain constituencies, but again they will see little merit in concerning themselves with management issues unless they provide fodder to score partisan political points. This is often tied to whether or not rules were violated.[18]

Reg Alcock, former Treasury Board president, claimed that his Cabinet colleagues thought that he "was nuts for taking a strong interest in management issues."[19] The result is that the public service in Canada, particularly above the fault line, has become largely a self-governing institution that sees accountability in terms not of assigning blame when things go wrong but of applying lessons learned at some vague point in the future.

When Jean Chrétien came to power, he decided to streamline the Cabinet committee system. Both Trudeau and Mulroney had elaborate systems that soaked up a lot of ministerial time. Chrétien decided to have only five Cabinet committees, including the Treasury Board, down from fifteen at times under Mulroney and Trudeau.[20]

The Privy Council Office is organized to serve the prime minister, Cabinet, and Cabinet committees. Secretariats correspond to the mandates of the Cabinet committees. When Chrétien abolished several Cabinet committees in 1993, a number of PCO secretariats were left without a committee to work with. No matter, the secretariats reinvented themselves and came up with new mandates, which include all developments falling under their broad areas of responsibility, monitoring controversial issues, and preparing briefing notes for the prime minister. Without Cabinet committees to service and support, one can only assume that the PCO's workload would have fallen dramatically, and one could have questioned whether some secretariats should have been abolished or at least had a substantial reduction in PCO staff numbers. But it did not happen. Leaving aside the prime minister and the clerk of the Privy Council, no one was in a position to see to it, and prime ministers always have far too many issues on their plates to be concerned about the continuing viability of several policy secretariats. Prime ministers, unlike CEOs of private firms, are not motivated by the end game of profitability.

The heads of the PCO secretariats could have gone to the clerk to report that they and their staff had become redundant. But why would they do that? Best to reinvent their work to remain at the centre of government, enjoying a high-profile position. There was simply no incentive and no interest for them to admit to a reduced workload. The clerk could have asked for answers, but there was no advantage in doing so. Extra staff can deal with a potential crisis in the making, of which there is rarely a shortage. Unless the clerk is told by a program review exercise to cut into PCO operations, he or she will always have more important issues to address. If the high-profile Privy Council Office circles the wagons whenever change threatens its staff, then one ought not be surprised if other departments and agencies do the same. Government departments and agencies may not be immortal, but most government units are.[21]

FALLING ON HAND GRENADES

I once asked Jack Stagg, a senior PCO official, to describe his responsibilities in a few words. His response: "My job is to fall on hand grenades." The potential for errors, controversies, and what is called invisible errors – invisible because people outside of government, particularly in the media, have not uncovered them – is always high. This has become even more important in the era of permanent election campaigns. The ambitious public servant above the fault line needs to excel at managing controversies in order to advance to the next level. These skills are highly valued by the prime minister and his courtiers, including the clerk. Ambitious public servants know that they need to be good at managing controversies and generating whiz-bang ideas to climb the organizational ladder.

Such skills are highly valued because they are essential in assisting the prime minister and his court in managing the blame game. The blame game has become central to management in government, and it explains why evaluation reports are bland and add very little knowledge, why government scientists feel handcuffed in their work, and why government management-reform measures very rarely, if ever, meet expectations.

A June 2014 speech by Foreign Affairs Minister John Baird on the proposed Keystone pipeline speaks to the blame game and the ability of senior government officials to fall on hand grenades. Baird set off alarm bells in the prime minister's court when he said, "So if there's one message I'm going to be promoting on this trip, it's this: the time for Keystone is now. I'll go further – the time for a decision on Keystone is now, even if it's not the right one." Supporters of the pipeline and their lobbyists zeroed in on the "headline-grabbing remark."[22]

The Canadian Press obtained a revealing series of emails on the issue that point to "a sense of panic at the highest level of government: the Privy Council Office." It is worth quoting at some length how the media reported how officials above the fault line saw the event unfold:

In a series of emails marked "urgent," one official requested documented evidence that Baird had actually said what he was reported to have said. "I need that quote – need to know when he said it," said one message from a senior analyst in the PCO's communications department. "Need it by 8:30 (a.m.) please." The 17 people involved in the email chain came from various federal departments both in Ottawa and at the Canadian embassy in Washington. The hunt for Baird's remarks apparently lasted into the next day, even though his speech was carried live on Canadian network television. "Please forward to me ASAP, as requested yesterday," said another email from PCO, the morning after the speech. "Need it as quickly as you can get it." The email chain from June suggests the civil service deployed considerable effort to assist PCO. "Multiple people working on your request," one Foreign Affairs employee replied. "Regrettably this is taking more time than it should." For reasons not entirely clear in the email chain, the panic eventually abated. "We're still interested in seeing it but at this point you can dial down the urgency," said the PCO official. "Later in the day is fine, no one needs to skip a coffee break over this."[23]

The political world matters a great deal to those operating above the fault line, less so for those below the fault line and government scientists.

The government of Canada website lists some 350 different departments, agencies, Crown corporations, and entities of various types and organizations that submit their spending plans to Treasury Board every year. The machinery of government is thus a hodgepodge of organizations with a wide variety of mandates, all tied directly or indirectly to Parliament, the Cabinet or, more precisely, the prime minister and his courtiers, and to Ottawa's expenditure budget.[24]

There are by last count nearly 6,800 public servants working in central agencies and in five oversight bodies tied to Parliament.[25] I do not include officers of Parliament who have no or limited direct and continuing impact on the work of public servants in line departments (for example, among others, the Office of the Chief Electoral Officer or the Canadian Human Rights Commission).

These 6,800 public servants in central agencies and in oversight bodies and many more in line departments operate above the fault line. They do not deliver programs or services to Canadians. They perform oversight functions and, in the case of central agencies, they provide advice and coordinate the budget and expenditure management. They work with the ministerial offices, offices of deputy ministers and of associate and assistant deputy ministers responsible for policy planning, and with a growing number of units in departments working on briefing notes to ministers and their staff, and with communications units that have also been growing fast in recent years.[26]

Public servants operating above the fault line have the opportunity to contribute to new policy and to influence many program decisions. It is important to stress that how things work and what matters above the fault line are vastly different from what matters below the line. Above the fault line is where politicians and public servants work to define the public interest, to shape new policies, and to manage the blame game. They also decide who gets financial resources, the key to determine who has power and influence in the machinery of government.

Again, above the line, public servants are valued for their political skills, their ability to fall on hand grenades, to manage a political crisis and the blame game. Public servants operating above the line are rarely openly partisan, but they have good political judgment and they know how to diffuse a crisis that could put the government in a bad light.

The more senior officials above the line are members of the prime minister's court. Public servants wishing to move up the career ladder will take on the characteristics of those in more elevated positions and also reflect their values.[27]

It is above the line where one will find the ambitious, the upwardly mobile, and the more politically sensitive public servants. A good number of researchers have made the case that, as public servants move up the organizational hierarchy, the more goals become ambiguous and conflicting, and call for strong political skills.[28] Still, public servants above the line know that they do not possess the influence that generations of public servants before them had. The prime minister and senior ministers now have a multitude of advisors to turn to: chiefs of staff in ministerial offices, lobbyists, think tanks, consultants, and even Google searches.

Ministerial staff, notably chiefs of staff, have changed the political–public service landscape. They have far more influence than executive assistants to ministers had thirty or forty years ago. They work in a fuzzy world, in that they are neither elected nor appointed on merit. Their influence varies according to the minister they serve (it matters if the minister is a member of the prime minister's court) and their relationships with the Prime Minister's Office.

A former chief of staff to Prime Minister Mulroney observes, "They serve where public and political interests cross and collide" and believes that "more light, not less, needs to be shone on their activities." But, he argues, the trend is in the opposite direction. There was a time when "ministers answered for their staff and the opposition left staff alone," but this is no longer the case. He points out that the Harper government deleted an important section of the PCO's "Guide for Ministers." The most recent version of the guide has taken out the sentence "Ministers are personally responsible for the conduct and operation of their office."[29] Responsibility and the search for a culprit here, as in other situations, has become a moving target.

This may well encourage public servants to say what politicians want to hear, to feed ideology-based policy advice rather than evidence-based advice. If the prime minister, close advisors, and senior ministers cannot get the advice they are looking for, they can go elsewhere for it, and that is a point not lost on public servants.

Politicians now expect public servants to be enthusiastic about their political and policy agenda and in dealing with stakeholders. Neutral competence is not nearly as valued as it once was, at a time when public servants are more exposed to citizens, organized interests, the media, and Parliament because of access-to-information legislation and other developments.[30] This, Peter Aucoin maintained, has made public servants "promiscuously partisan to the government of the day."[31]

How, then, does one square the above with the charge from politicians in a Westminster-inspired parliamentary government that "bureaucracy is unresponsive and government departments have become unmanageable"?[32] The answer lies in the concentration of power in the Prime Minister's Office and the blame game.

Nothing of substance in the federal government happens without the prime minister's blessing, or that of his courtiers. But there are only so many hours in the day, only so many issues that are of interest to the prime minister. To be sure, political or bureaucratic crises do surface from time to time, and these, too, eat into the prime minister's agenda.

Keeping things running on their tracks will satisfy the prime minister, but not all ministers, some of whom do have a change agenda, but, unless they have the blessing of the centre, are very unlikely to succeed. In such cases, ministers much prefer blaming the bureaucrats rather than the prime minister and his closest advisors to explain their inability to move their change agenda forward. It is also safer for them if they wish to remain in Cabinet.

IF THE PRIME MINISTER HAD BEEN THERE

If the prime minister and premier had been present at the meeting I had with federal provincial officials in Nova Scotia in 2010 to discuss the need to streamline economic development programs and the Integrated Service Delivery Project, as mentioned at the start of this chapter, then there would have been no need four years later to raise the project again and to lament its slow progress. PMO-PCO courtiers would have insisted on progress. The distance between the prime minister and that group of public servants, however, needs to be measured in light years, not kilometres.

One may assume that public servants below the fault line are able to sort out how to bring the Integrated Service Delivery Project to fruition in Nova Scotia, but in that case one would be wrong. The project involves delicate political issues in which public servants tread carefully. It deals with federal-provincial relations, never an easy matter, it has an impact on visibility or who can claim credit for programs and services delivered, and it has a potential effect on financial and human resources. Only those operating high above the fault line have the authority to resolve these issues and move the project forward. Public servants below the line will continue to attend meetings, exchange documents, and prepare briefing notes in the hope that some day someone above the line takes an interest. Again, the goal, when the prime minister or his courtiers do not have their hands on the steering wheel, is to keep things running on their tracks, and to avoid giving ammunition to opposition parties or the media to embarrass the government.

Paul Tellier, former clerk of the Privy Council, told deputy ministers what the prime minister and the Privy Council Office expected them to provide – "error-free administration"[33] – which was no small challenge for a world encompassing some 350 organizations and coming on the heels of the government's intention to embrace New Public Management's dicta to empower managers. He also told them on numerous occasions that he and the prime minister "did not like surprises."[34] Tellier became incensed when the Al-Mashat crisis blew up in the media, because he "was not able to alert the prime minister of what was coming."[35]

All this speaks to the challenges for those operating below the fault line. Keeping things running on their tracks was considerably easier when Max Weber wrote his treatise on bureaucracy in which public servants worked in machine-like organizations, following directions in robot-like fashion, performing routine functions.

Creativity and an ability to adjust to changing circumstances – particularly in a federal and provincial context – are keys to success. Federal and provincial government officials working on Nova Scotia's desire to become the most business-friendly jurisdiction in Canada required management discretion and a capacity to innovate and to change course, but it was not to be. This makes it very difficult for units operating below the fault line to be as good as they would like to be at what they do.

IT'S ABOUT SURVIVAL

Politicians and public servants who operate above the fault line are busy managing conflicting goals, a fast-paced political environment, a twenty-four-hour news media, developments in the social media, constant demands on the expenditure budget, and permanent election campaigns. It is, in the words of former prime minister Chrétien, "a survival game played under the glare of light. If you don't learn that, you're quickly finished."[36] Above the fault line, politicians and senior public servants are either good at managing conflicting goals and the blame game, or they do not survive. It is also a world foreign to the private sector and vastly different from the one below the fault line.

Yet far too many people still view bureaucracy as a monolith, even those who have knowledge of the machinery of government. The Office of the Auditor General (OAG) has led the charge on many management reform efforts that are well outside the ambit of financial audits. It all too often views bureaucracy as a monolithic body with all parts having to deal with its accountability requirements.

Amendments to the Financial Administration Act in 2006 require departments to assess all continuing programs of grants and contributions every five years. The Treasury Board issued a policy in 2009 requiring all departments to evaluate all direct program spending for relevance and performance every five years. The OAG supports this initiative. In its review of the government's program evaluations, for example, it called on "Agriculture and Agri-Food Canada and Human

Resources and Skills Development to evaluate all of their ongoing grant and contribution programs every five years," adding that the two "departments may have funded programs that were not as effective or efficient as planned."[37]

It takes only a moment's reflection to appreciate that evaluating much of the activities carried out above the fault line holds little promise. How can one possibly evaluate all the work of a department like Canadian Heritage, for example, as it tries to manage conflicting goals, too many demands on resources, and the blame game? Government simply cannot be good at evaluating these activities, but it spends an inordinate amount of time and resources trying to do so.

The very nature of the blame game allows no politician or public servant to challenge the OAG on the matter. Central agencies and many units in line departments in Ottawa must know that a good number of program evaluations are of little value to anyone, yet at a cost to taxpayers. As already noted, the media and opposition political parties are not about to challenge the work of the OAG, because it is not in their interest to do so. Best to keep spending public money on measures that contribute precious little, other than providing fuel for the blame game by challenging the work of the OAG.

BELOW THE FAULT LINE

The fact once again is that politicians, the media, consultants, and public servants operating above the fault line spend inordinate time on ideas, political strategies, shaping new policies, and the blame game, while leaving implementation or management to the less-gifted administrative class. The key to climbing the bureaucratic ladder is to be visible to key decision-makers operating above the fault line in the National Capital Region.[38]

Delivering programs and services and operating in front-line offices offer no such prospects. It is rare indeed to see a deputy minister rise through the program ranks in a local, regional office, and then move on to head office to become deputy minister. The fact is that deputy ministers and associate deputy ministers typically spend the bulk of their careers operating above the fault line.

At the risk of being repetitive, operating below the fault line is vastly different from operating above it. Those below doubt very much that they dominate their deputy minister's agenda to the same extent they did some thirty years ago or, ironically, before the arrival of New Public Management. There is also a growing body of literature to support their claim.[39] In their detailed study of service in the field, Barbara Carroll and David Siegel quote a federal government official's claim that people working in regional offices "value the ability to work one-on-one with clients. That starts to break down immediately when you get into layers in Ottawa."[40] Another front-line program manager reported that he "tries to avoid involving head office or central agencies," as much as possible. He said that it is important

in a line operation to keep your head down, keep things under control here, and don't involve Ottawa people unless you absolutely have to. They will leave you alone if you don't give them a reason to call you. My measure of success is how often that phone rings and someone in Ottawa is on the line. If it rings often, we are doing something wrong. If it doesn't ring, we are doing fine. From time to time, you get head office people introducing a new approach. You know they have to keep busy so they come around with a new Treasury Board approach in this or that area. We just go along filling their forms while we deliver the programs.[41]

Public servants below the line need to be good at performing two key functions: feeding the beast and delivering programs and services. The first requires them to look up to the organization and move information to head office to enable it to feed ministerial offices, central agencies, and oversight bodies. The second requires them to look down to citizens and associations.

FEEDING THE BEAST

In some of my previous work, I have written about the need for public servants to – as more than one line departmental officials labels it – "feed the beast," and there is no need to go over the same territory here.[42] Suffice to note that regularly producing documents tabled in Parliament, responding to requests for information from officers of Parliament, the budget process, and performance and accountability requirements generated by central agencies and information to assist ministers and their staff to manage the blame game eat up a lot of time and resources from program managers in line departments. Front-line public sector workers, no matter their background or their responsibilities, share one common frustration: responding to the constant demand for information from central agencies and departmental headquarters.

Public servants report that the demand for information on policy and administrative issues has increased "exponentially" in recent years and now "eats up a lot of resources."[43] Central agencies have not only grown, but people who work in them also have more senior classifications and higher pay than those occupying similar positions in line departments. They also decide in large measure who makes it to the deputy minister and associate deputy levels. In addition, many in the Privy Council Office enjoy a deputy-minister-level classification, though they do not have the responsibility of managing a government department or a major government program. It simply comes with being in the Privy Council Office. It is one of many signs that the work of central agencies is more highly valued than that of line departments.

Given that central agency officials have no programs to manage and deliver, they can spend all their time on policy issues, working on briefing material, micromanaging specific files whenever a crisis flares up, coming up with new ideas with little concern about how they should be implemented, and demanding more and more information from front-line managers and their employees in order to monitor their programs and performance.[44] To be sure, central agencies also have a much stronger policy capacity than they had forty years ago. They have strategic planning capacities, and, if need be, they can have a direct hand in the day-to-day work of departments. At times, they can be heavily involved in transactions on specific departmental files, and at other times, not at all. It depends. If it involves the prime minister's interest or if the government's political standing may be in jeopardy, central agency officials will be present – even, if necessary, physically in the department, directing things.[45] If they require new money to deal with the issue, it will quickly be found.

Still, officials in central agencies need to rely on data provided by line departments, and that explains the constant stream of requests for information. It should surprise no one that once positions are added to central agencies, invariably they will give rise to more requests for information from line departments and agencies. This is their bread and butter. But that is not all. In addition to material for the blame game, ministers need to be briefed on proposed new initiatives. Just responding to access-to-information requests and any difficulties they create for the minister and the department can consume a great deal of ministerial and public servant time. New requirements, from access to information to whistle-blowing legislation, only add to briefing requirements. I also note that the government of Canada has more central agencies than in any other Anglo-American democracy, where access-to-information legislation has been in place for about thirty-five years, where federal-provincial relations generate a great many policy papers and briefing materials, and where there are also more oversight bodies than, for example, in Britain or Australia.

However, loyalty to one's department, its goals, and its clients appears stronger below the fault line than above. We know, for example, that staff turnover in regional and local offices is substantially lower than in Ottawa, though loyalty may not be the only or the most important factor.[46] Opportunities for advancement or transfers are more plentiful in Ottawa than in regional offices.

WHERE THE RUBBER MEETS THE ROAD

James Q. Wilson did the public administration a great service when he broke down government organizations into four classifications. Wilson based his classification system on the extent to which outputs can be measured and work observed. He refers to these as (1) production or machine-like organizations (controllable on the basis of outputs and processes readily observable), (2) procedural organizations (not controllable on the basis of outputs and processes readily observable), (3) craft organizations (controllable on the basis of outputs and processes not readily observable), and (4) coping organizations (not controllable on the basis of outputs and processes not readily observable). In the case of production organizations, he reports, the tasks are simple, stable, and specialized. Consequently, they are often centralized and formal, including examples such as the processing of tax returns and government printing bureaus. Examples of procedural organizations include peacetime armed forces, while examples of craft organizations include audit services and inspection and enforcement services, and examples of coping organizations include central government consulting services and some policy and advisory units.[47]

Meanwhile, Henry Mintzberg went further and identified seven organizational configurations, four of which – entrepreneurial, machine, professional, and innovative – can be quite useful in classifying public sector organizations. They vary in the primary means employed to coordinate work, which part of the organization dominates its work processes, and the extent and nature of decentralization.[48]

All this makes the point once again that the machinery of government is very complex and serves a multitude of goals, mainly conflicting ones, and that it is simplistic to think that one can reform the machinery by incorporating private-sector management measures to it. It is no less simplistic to think that one can view the federal government as a universe of policy and programs that can be evaluated or have their performance properly assessed.

To be sure, there are some organizations to which one can more easily incorporate private-sector management measures to its operation, though not as many as is generally believed. Production organizations are a case in point, where some private-sector management-inspired measures can apply and where performance can be evaluated. I recall that, in the mid-1980s, Revenue Canada could demonstrate that adding one tax auditor would generate $750,000 of new revenues for the government.[49] But one can hardly prove such concrete advantages when adding a new officer in the PCO or in a policy planning branch.

But even here there are limits. No program manager and no department will want to parade a negative evaluation report, unless senior departmental officials have grown tired of the program, and that is a very rare occurrence. I have read many program evaluations over the years, and negative evaluations are the rare exception. They report that there is often room for improvement but very seldom suggest that the program should be terminated or that it makes only a modest contribution. The blame game does not allow such frank assessments, which would give ammunition to opposition parties and the media. What about managing risks for production or procedural-type government organizations? Even with these operations, more akin to private sector organizations, they remain part of the public sector and its culture. James Q. Wilson's observation on public service culture is as valid in Canada as it is in the United States: "When a culture of forbearance and forgiveness descends on Washington, please alert the FBI at once for it will be evidence that somebody had kidnapped or anesthetized the entire legislative and judicial branches of government."[50]

In government culture, circumstances and organizational culture become critical, because goals are vague. Though a good number of them put in long hours, many public servants produce nothing that can be measured after the fact. Work incentives in government are far different from those found in business. Government managers cannot capture surplus revenues for themselves or often even for their own organizations. So why would anyone in government departments want to scrimp unless there is no choice?

Management and decision-making in government are tied to conditions and circumstances that differ substantially from those found in the private sector. Such conditions in the public sector often stress "procedural values" over "substance." Such values do not encourage efficiency. Indeed, they often run counter to it. Public servants must continually take their cue from politicians, whose work is always tied to a political function. While a chief executive officer of a large private firm may meet with the board of directors several times a year and nearly always get what he or she wants, the senior public official must navigate in a complex, conflict-ridden, and highly charged political environment. There is seldom an easy road to success in government. Simply getting things done "remains a wearisome and frustrating business."[51]

To many senior government officials, simply "coping" with the pressure of the day becomes important. The system is such that there are few rewards for competence, at least as those defined from a private sector perspective. Government officials in line departments know all of this intuitively. Indeed, they understand the organizational culture in government and know what is on, what can work, and what will not. What they may lack in management skills and in the ability to shape the activities of their organizations, they make up for in their ability to cope with an unpredictable political environment and with external forces. Protecting their organization becomes a key preoccupation; it is the true measure of success in government. Wilson spells out with great insight how officials often set out to ensure that their agencies will survive, if not expand. The do's and don'ts include fighting other government organizations that seek to perform similar tasks, avoiding tasks that will produce divided or hostile constituencies, and avoiding "learned vulnerabilities" or risks.[52]

Officials do not deny that fighting in one's corner is an important part of their work. But this, they insist, comes with the territory. Their purpose, after all, is not to fight for markets but rather to compete with others in government for a policy position, for jurisdiction, legitimacy, and resources in support of their political masters. This is what senior public servants and government departments are good at. No deputy minister wants to come back from a meeting with central agencies to report that the department has been earmarked for substantial cuts, deeper than those in other departments and agencies. For line departments, that is how success is measured, and it is also possible to measure it with relative ease.

Line-department officials working on "streaming economic development programs" and on the Integrated Service Delivery Project in Nova Scotia described at the start of this chapter had all the incentives at play to protect their departmental turf and to stop other departments from performing tasks similar to those of their own departments. That matters to public servants because their survival and that of their organizational units are tied to it.

A DEMORALIZED INSTITUTION

The desire to have an error-free administration and no surprises so as to better manage the blame game gives rise to a passive risk-avoidance approach of the kind seen in Nova Scotia. That approach stifles innovation and entrepreneurship as envisaged by NPM. And it has other consequences. It promotes a disbelief culture in government where the promise of public sector reforms is dismissed out of hand by public servants even before they are properly introduced. Public servants know intuitively that their work is not as valued as it once was, and that their focus is now less upon offering policy options and more on finding empirical evidence to justify what elected politicians have decided to do.[53]

Public servants expect more of their work than helping the prime minister and his court to deal with the political crisis of the day. They were once important architects of governance, but they "are now at best one among a host of equals and, at worst, seen by some as irrelevant to the real governance tasks at hand."[54] Jim Travers writes that the view among senior bureaucrats in Ottawa is that "instead of sous-chefs helping the government prepare the national menu, bureaucrats complain that they are being used as short-order cooks."[55]

We know that public servants are demoralized and that depression among senior officials has nearly doubled over the past five years. A recent survey reveals that managers "have become more stressed, unhappy, isolated and obese since the Association for Professional Executives of the Public Service of Canada began tracking health issues and the organizations they manage."[56]

The debate about the public service in recent years has not been about their policy advisory- or program-delivery role. Rather, it has been about the need to restore the equilibrium between public- and private sector workers, public service absenteeism, public servants claiming too many sick leaves, and the need to reduce benefits to current and retired public servants.[57] This is hardly the stuff to inspire an institution and public servants.

There is one thing common to all public sector organizations, independent of their mandates and whether they are production-like organizations or central agencies. Government departments, agencies, and public servants have to deal with a complex environment that is more conducive to inertia than to action. The next chapter addresses this issue.

9

Why Are Things So Complicated?

Consider the following difference between a private-sector and a government executive. The director of sales for a major Canadian frozen food firm will focus most attention on clients, given that clients and the quality of products and services are the key determinants of success. He or she will know the sales targets for the year, will be allocated a budget to operate from, and will have considerable flexibility to hire and dismiss staff. He or she will also be consulted when the firm prepares marketing plans and will be kept informed of the firm's production capacity. He or she will keep a watchful eye on the competition and on new trends in the frozen food market, make adjustments to the sales strategy when the need arises, and monitor developments in the government's regulations on the food industry.

In contrast, the director of enterprise development with ACOA is faced with quite different challenges. His or her world is far more complex, and a satisfied client is only one of several measures of success. Indeed, it is also not at all clear that the client or the product is even the key determinant of success.

The director of enterprise development will want to ensure that his or her unit is not drawn into a public controversy, generates no negative media attention, and poses no political problem for the minister or for the government. If these goals are achieved, it is a sure sign of success for the director and all the supervisors going up the line. But private sector firms do not play defence for long if they want to survive. In contrast and given the importance of the blame game, government departments will often prefer to ice two goaltenders, three defencemen, and one forward to ensure that all things remain on their tracks at all times.

This chapter looks at the complex environment in which public servants must operate to get things done. It is no exaggeration to say that
director-level officials now deal with complexity wherever they look,
whether it is up to their superiors, down to their staff, outside to
clients, or sideways to other government departments.

A WORLD OF MIXED MESSAGES

No other employer would want to subject their managers to such a
world of mixed messages as the government of Canada does. Indeed,
it is hardly possible to imagine a more uncertain or complex work
environment in order to get things done or to be good at your craft.

The constant message from the government for the past thirty years
or more is one of "empowerment," "letting the manager manage," "cal-
culated risks," and the need to do away with "centralized rules and regulations." But even here the message is never certain or straightforward.
As recently as 15 January 2014, for example, the president of the Treasury Board was directed to reimburse his department $195 for gold-
embossed cards that he had ordered back in 2011. The rules do not
allow for gold-embossed cards.[1] The president of the Treasury Board
has wide responsibility, including a central agency with a staff of 1,837
and total expenditure of $5.6 billion, in addition to his government-
wide responsibilities for both financial and human resources. In government the word *empowerment* works better in speeches and in vision
exercises than in reality. One can hardly imagine a senior executive
with even a medium-size private firm being instructed to reimburse
the firm $195 for having ordered the wrong business cards.

The message could not have been lost on line-department managers.
Vision, rhetoric, and borrowing best-management practices from the
private sector are one thing. How things actually work, however, is quite
a different matter. They are shaped by politics, turf, risk avoidance,
incentives peculiar to government, and employer-employee relations
that are out of step with those found in the private sector.

In late 2011, for example, Canada's Foreign Affairs Department told
its officials not to go above and beyond the call of duty or what was
expected of them. The department feared that exceeding standards
would raise expectations and also lead to inconsistent service delivery
across missions.[2] The intent was to apply the traditional Weberian
bureaucratic model to a world that cries out for something better. It

is difficult to even imagine that a private sector executive would ever issue such a directive. When it comes to management, things are relatively simple and straightforward in most private sector firms, but not so in government.

LOOKING UP TO POLITICS

As noted, the space between the director level and where the political and bureaucratic power lies in government should be measured in light years. It is very unlikely that a director in a line department will ever have direct contact with the prime minister or even with the PMO, where effective power now resides. The deputy minister in a line department may have direct contact with PMO officials from time to time, but very rarely with the prime minister.

The director of sales in the large frozen food enterprise can, when necessary, have direct access to the chief executive officer, albeit through his or her superior. The potential loss of a major client or the need to adjust a proposal to secure another important client may well be a good enough reason to talk directly with the CEO. A fault line, to the extent that it exists in large private firms between the CEO and the sales director, is quite porous and easily tossed aside whenever the need arises.

When a director in a line department looks up for direction or support for an initiative, there are a multitude of management layers, far more today than thirty years ago. Typically, a line department has a deputy minister and an associate deputy, a senior assistant deputy minister, several assistant deputy ministers, a few associate assistant deputy ministers, a number of directors general, and, at times, associate directors general. The deputy minister's office also has an executive assistant and on occasion one or two policy advisors. The minister's office, meanwhile, has a chief of staff, a director of policy, and a director of communications.

Tom Peters, a leading private-sector management guru, is convinced that too many management layers are action destroyers. Peters recommends five management layers from top to bottom, as in the Roman Catholic Church, for complex organizations, and only three for all others.[3]

The director of a line department will rarely, if ever, initiate direct contact with the minister's office. The risk is much too high. However, in more recent years, ministerial staffers have been in regular contact with officials down the departmental line to the director level, if not lower on occasion. Access to information, twenty-four hour news channels, the social media, the blame game, and the era of permanent election campaigns have forced ministers and their staff to respond quickly to questions from the media and elsewhere. Getting at the right information requires them to go to its source without always respecting levels in the organization. Front-line directors of programs will provide answers, but then make certain that their immediate supervisor is kept in the information loop so that they can in turn do the same, going up the organization to the deputy minister and sometimes to the Privy Council Office if the deputy minister considers it necessary.

Management layers have made the machinery of government and decision-making thicker and more complex than it needs to be. In consequence, these complications, together with the need to manage the blame game, have made the machinery even more risk-averse. Multiple management layers, the horizontal or interdepartmental nature of policy- and decision-making processes, the large number of oversight bodies, and the growing influence of central agencies have made it difficult for front-line directors to know who is the boss. Luther Gulick warned against such a development when he wrote, "From the earliest times, it has been recognized that nothing but confusion arises under multiple command. 'A man cannot serve two masters ...' The rigid adherence to the principle of unity of command may have its absurdities; these are, however, unimportant in comparison with the certainty of confusion, inefficiency, and irresponsibility which arise from the violation of the principle."[4]

Government officials, especially those in central agencies, do recognize problems inherent in having too many management levels, though attempts to fix the problem have failed. The Treasury Board Secretariat announced with considerable fanfare over twenty years ago that it would "cut executive-level jobs in a bid to improve morale and operations." It expressed concern that the executive category had grown to 2,562 members and argued that "if you take a whole layer out of the management pyramid, then the managers below automatically gain greater control over their operations."[5] Nothing came of this initiative. Several years later this line of thinking was completely abandoned, as new management and associate positions emerged in every department. The executive category also grew by more than

1,200 members. This, after the federal government shifted some of its activities to the provinces between 1995 and 1997.

Today, there are nearly 7,000 positions in the executive category, despite the Harper-led program review in 2012. Once again, the government has declared its intention to review management levels and has hired consultants to lend a helping hand.[6] The executive category has grown at twice the pace of the public service and has increased by 70 per cent since the late 1970s. In part, the fact that senior departmental officials have been empowered to classify and re-classify positions with a minimum of control from central agencies explains this growth. But evaluation and performance reports – the fabricated bottom line in government – do not explain or justify it.

Looking up the organization, out to clients, and down to staff, a line-department director sees mostly constraints. Unlike his or her private sector counterpart, the director has to navigate through laws, oversight requirements, policies, and expectations that will in effect define his or her approach to management. The director needs to manage the shop, bearing in mind access-to-information and whistleblowing legislation, the Official Languages Act, the Office of the Auditor General, the department's external audit committee, the work of evaluation units, privacy laws, the Charter of Rights and Freedoms, affirmative action policy requirements, the work of the public sector integrity officer, departmental values and ethics offices, the departmental ombudsman, the Office of the Comptroller General, vision exercises that pop up from the centre from time to time, central agencies, the need to always keep an eye on politicians, and the political blame game. It is no small achievement for a director to excel in managing this hodgepodge of contradictions and complexity, and many actually do. No matter, the perception remains that a director in a line department can never be good enough when compared with a private sector counterpart. One can appreciate that there is less risk involved if a director and his or her unit just keep things running on their tracks.

Governing from the centre and managing the blame game have – in the words of Richard Dicerni, a long-serving senior deputy minister with the federal government – led public servants to promote "upward delegation" or to push decisions above the fault line.[7] What is urgent, what is important, at times what is not important, and what may be controversial is pushed up to the prime minister's courtiers, or at least above the fault line for resolution.

LOOKING DOWN TO STAFF

Harrison McCain often said that there was no shame in hiring the wrong person – mistakes are often made, he insisted – but there is shame in keeping them.[8]

Most private sector executives have a relatively free hand in turfing out or reassigning non-performers. The same is not true in government. In the great majority of cases, non-performers are isolated, placed outside the mainstream, so that they are out of the way and left to their own devices or to tasks that are of little importance.

Government executives have to learn to work with collective bargaining, public sector unions, and even the courts, an environment that is largely foreign to their private sector counterparts. The public sector in Canada remains highly unionized. From a dead start in the mid-1960s, most government workers now have a union to look after their interests. Over 71 per cent of public sector workers now belong to a union, compared with about 17 per cent of private sector workers.[9]

It will be recalled that, for the first time in its sixty-year history, the union representing Ontario's provincial police released two attack ads targeting the leader of Progressive Conservative Tim Hudak in the middle of the 2014 provincial campaign. The union accused Hudak of wishing to launch a direct attack on collective bargaining. It insisted that union members "just don't want this Conservative as premier," arguing that "we're here for you. Who's Hudak here for?"[10] If the broader public interest is to take a back seat to the demands of public sector unions, so be it. They will argue that defining the broader public interest is someone else's responsibility.

As we saw earlier, the courts have also been drawn into management issues. Public servants report that many government managers have simply given up trying to dismiss employees on the basis of non-performance, fearing either that dealing with the unions will take too long or that they will have to defend their action in court. As Jeffrey Simpson writes, rights are "fundamentally about me and responsibility is mostly about us."[11] Table 4 reveals that 451 public servants were released for "misconduct" over a six-year period and 453 for "incompetence or incapacity" (about 75 employees annually) from a total staff complement of over 210,000 in the core public service and about 260,000 when separate agencies are included.[12]

The pattern of employee dismissal for misconduct or incompetence has not changed in recent years. In 2007–8, forty-nine employees were

Table 4
Federal public servants terminated, Canada

Year	Discharge for misconduct	Release for incompetence and incapacity	Total
2000	63	67	130
2001	107	81	188
2002	93	104	197
2003	77	92	169
2004	90	89	179
2005	21	20	41
2011	36	45	81
TOTAL	487	498	985

Source: Data provided by the government of Canada to the Commission of Inquiry into the Sponsorship Program and Advertising Activities, Ottawa, 31 May 2005. See also http://www.pwgsc.gc.ca /compensation/ppi,/ppim-3-5-3-3.html (accessed May 2014), which provides for a general categorization of the reasons for Public Service of Canada employee departures.

terminated for misconduct and another eighty-four for incompetence, while in 2010–11 the numbers were fifty-four and ninety-nine, respectively.[13] This may explain why the great majority of front-line managers and workers do not take annual performance evaluations seriously. Carroll and Siegel write that "virtually everyone" laughed when they asked public servants in the field about the performance appraisal system, suggesting that performance appraisal is largely a matter of going through the motions and that neither supervisor nor subordinates take it very seriously. One front-line worker observed, "There hasn't been anyone in the last seven years come and tell me I've ever done anything wrong. Nobody ever comes to look … They don't tell you you've done something right; and they don't tell you you've done something wrong. There's no review of the operation."[14] An assessment of the Public Service Modernization Act also recently returned a negative verdict on the ability of government managers to deal with non-performers. Some 65 per cent of respondents recorded a "not at all" or "to a moderate extent" answer when asked about the capacity of managers to deal with their employees, including non-performers.[15]

Certainly, it has never been easy to deal with non-performers in government. It is even more difficult today, given collective bargaining and the possibility that employees and their union representatives will go to court if management initiates any action to remove anyone for non-performance. It requires documenting in minute detail the causes for dismissal and numerous meetings with superiors, human resources specialists, and legal advisors to see the process through completion. To avoid the hassles, managers focus on things over which they have more control. In any event, they have little incentive to engage in what would likely be at least a two-year process to terminate an employee for non-performance. Many managers do not remain in the same position for much more than two years, moving on to a promotion or a lateral position with better prospects for advancement. Best to leave the problem for the next manager to deal with, and on it goes.

Even if managers think they have a solid case, there is no guarantee of success. For example, an arbitrator instructed a government department to rehire six public servants in Ontario who had been fired for exchanging pornographic emails at work that included images of bestiality, nude, obese, and elderly women, and degrading and violent sexual activity. The arbitrator ruled that the government lacked cause to dismiss the men, and his decision made it to the front pages of Canada's national newspapers. To be sure, the message was not lost on government managers.[16]

It is also revealing that "no sponsorship-related discipline" came to the attention of the "major government unions," even after the scandal hit the front pages of newspapers and after a commission of inquiry was launched. Union representatives were quick to argue that the problem was at the political level, not with public servants.[17] Former Cabinet ministers who met with Justice Gomery at five roundtables, however, stressed the point that public servants lacked the ability to impose sanctions or to replace incompetent staff. They also spoke about what they labelled widespread "institutional inertia" in government departments.[18] Though staff are very rarely penalized for incompetence or mismanagement, public servants can still be dismissed if they bring negative attention to the department. As noted earlier, three Health Canada employees were fired in June 2004 for speaking out against departmental policies.[19]

There is also evidence to suggest that federal public servants are underemployed. A senior analyst in the Department of Citizenship and Immigration spent more than half his working day looking at news, sports, and porn websites from his desk while working at head office. The department took the unusual step of firing him for committing "time theft" by claiming that he was accepting pay while surfing the Internet. The employee appealed to the Public Service Labour Relations Board (PSLRB), arguing that he wasn't given enough work to keep him busy, and that in any case he had met every deadline and received positive performance appraisals. The PSLRB ruled in favour of the employee and ordered the department to reinstate him immediately. The board argued in its ruling that it was surprised "that an employee could spend the amount of time that he did on non-work-related activities for months without his supervisors noting a lack of production or engagement."[20] Again, this ruling was not lost on other public sector managers: why bother trying to discipline or fire an employee? It explains why the Treasury Board study on compensation concluded that "it is relatively rare for public servants to be fired, with the greatest number of involuntary departures resulting from dismissal while on probation." The study pointed out that of the 4,883 separations of indeterminate employees that took place in 2002–3, only 22 were released for incompetence.[21]

Public servants are handed golden handcuffs the moment they join the public service.[22] The benefits, from parental leave to sick days, to vacation days and a generous pension plan, make it difficult for public servants to leave government. The incentives to perform better in government bureaucracies or to leave government to pursue other opportunities are perverse. This outdated approach to human resources management has, in the words of a senior federal public servant, created – too many "takers" in government. She suggests that government is now home to three types of public servants: leaders, bureaucrats, and takers.[23]

She maintains that it is more difficult for public service leaders to lead and we went over the reasons earlier. Bureaucrats, meanwhile, are solid, conscientious performers doing what they are asked to do. They continue to perform and deliver what is being asked, often under trying circumstances.

Takers are the non-performers, and once in, they take advantage of whatever is made available by collective agreements.[24] They demoralize the bureaucrats, as it is virtually impossible to demote or fire non-performers and takers. Meanwhile, the government manager is left with asking for still more resources whenever there are new demands or changes. Line managers, as we have seen, find that feeding the "beast" or responding to demands from central agencies is increasingly eating up resources. Those who would be expected to starve the beast are precisely the ones whose work is tied to a well-resourced beast – central agencies and oversight bodies. This in turn often explains the difference between what is conceived, what is intended, and what is implemented.

LOOKING AT PRODUCTIVITY FROM THE INSIDE

Those who wield political power have an interest in squeezing more from government programs and operations and report the good news to taxpayers. But why would public servants seek to do more with less? What incentives would entice them to identify measures to cut spending?

As already noted on several occasions, the prime minister and his office hold effective political power. However, the prime minister and PMO have limited time, expertise, and human resources to focus on controlling bureaucracy's ongoing cost. That said, when the prime minister decides to make it a priority, government operations are subjected to intense scrutiny and review, and deep cuts are invariably made inside the bureaucracy. But the timing has to be ripe for the prime minister to attend to the size of bureaucracy.[25]

Indeed, it is no exaggeration that significant spending cuts to government operations are possible only when they are initiated by the prime minister and only in the immediate aftermath of winning a majority mandate. As already noted, the ambitious Chrétien-Martin 1994–97 program review and Harper's 2012–14 strategic and operational review both speak to this reality. The numerous program evaluation units housed in all government departments and agencies have had virtually no impact in reducing the government's expenditure budget.

Across-the-board cuts to line departments and agencies ranging from 5 per cent to 25 per cent drove the Chrétien-Martin program review.[26] Arthur Kroeger, at one time the dean of deputy ministers in Ottawa, studied the exercise and concluded that "it is universally acknowledged by those who participated that this process was utterly unscientific."[27]

The results of the Chrétien-Martin review are well known: 45,000 public service positions were eliminated and major spending cuts were implemented in numerous programs. Seventy-three boards, commissions, and advisory bodies were shut down. All in all, $29 billion in cuts were achieved. By 1996–7, program spending was reduced to 13.1 per cent of GDP, the lowest level since 1951.[28]

The Harper government, fresh with a majority mandate, decided, as Chrétien had done in 1993–4, to hold a comprehensive program review starting in 2011 but to run between 2012–14 and to find $5.2 billion in annual savings by 2014. Departments and agencies were asked to bring forward to Treasury Board ministers two possible expenditure reductions – one at 5 per cent and the other at 10 per cent. Later, the minister of finance declared that some departments and agencies would face cuts of more than 10 per cent. All in all, some seventy departments and agencies were required to submit scenarios for at least a 5- and 10-per cent reduction to their budgets. The cuts were to be implemented over a two-year timeline, well ahead of the next general election.[29]

The review was part of the government's decision to eliminate the more than $30 billion deficit by 2014 by – in the words of Prime Minister Harper – finding "billions in fat."[30] One then wonders how the fat got there in the first place. One can only assume that various New Public Management–inspired reforms and the many program evaluation units were of little help. I argue that they had the opposite effect: they contributed to the fat.

Under the Harper review, the departments were free to identify low-priority activities, but the Treasury Board suggested that the review should focus on both programs and operating expenses – notably, salaries, professional services, consultants, and grants and contributions programs.[31] The process, like that of earlier strategic reviews, was designed to produce recommendations for Treasury Board ministers to examine, and as before, the final say on spending cuts remained with the prime minister. Borrowing a page from the principal-agent theory, the Harper government called on a private sector consulting firm to provide an independent assessment of the work of departmental officials and of their recommendations.

The theory suggests that the principal and agent have different interests, as the principal delegates part of his or her responsibilities to an agent. The agents control information that is not readily available to the principal, and the less they reveal, the more power they have and the better they can maximize their budgets. In short, they control information so that they can promote their own interests and that of their units.[32]

To assist with the Harper review, the Treasury Board president and the minister of finance agreed to a $20 million contract with Deloitte

Touche to provide "private sector advice to find billions in government fat." Finance Minister Flaherty explained, "It isn't good quite frankly for a government to just look at itself."[33]

The 2012 budget included not only $5.2 billion in cuts but the elimination of 19,200 public servants from the payroll. Flaherty explained, "We will implement moderate restraint in government spending. The vast majority of savings will come from eliminating waste in the internal operations of government, making it leaner and more efficient."[34] The cuts were to be implemented over a two- to three-year period and at least 7,000 of the job losses were to be handled by attrition. It should be noted that the Harper government has added 30,000 positions to the public service since it took power. The one conclusion that stands out from the two program reviews is that government managers may well be good at something, but they are not good at eliminating waste in their organizations. Cuts in spending, it seems, are possible only when the prime minister decides that the time has come to take action and institutes a special review to get the job done.

In both the Chrétien and Harper reviews, the prime minister personally signed off on all spending cuts, large and small. The process produced the recommendations but the buck always stopped on the prime minister's desk – yet one more sign that in Canada the prime minister governs from the centre.

But no sooner does the prime minister take his eye off the ball than bureaucracy quickly reverts to its old ways. It will push and pull every opportunity to grow. When one department sees another secure more resources, it will line up for its share. Consider the following: the federal public service grew by 34 per cent over ten years to 283,966 from 211,915 (2001–11). The bulk of the growth was in Ottawa-based units designed to serve the bureaucracy and accountability requirements, to generate policy advice, and to manage communications and media relations. More revealing, the expansion of the federal bureaucracy outpaced population growth over the same decade at a rate of three to one.[35] It is also interesting to note that much of the substantial increases in health-care spending flowing from the 2004 federal-provincial health-care agreement has gone to salaries.[36]

Harper's strategic review was set up in part to deal with this growth. One wonders why, with all the ambitious public-sector management reforms of the past thirty years, were all these public servants hired in

the first place? It will also be recalled that the federal government transferred a number of labour-intensive activities to provincial governments and third parties in the 1990s (for example, airports and ports).
And this leads to a second question: why did the Harper government
see the need to spend $20 million on outside consultants to assist in
identifying spending cuts? And a third: why were all those new employees hired in policy evaluation and other head office units not up to the
task? Are we to conclude that efforts to introduce private-sector management practices to government have been a failure? One thing is
clear: left to their own devices, government bureaucracies are unable to
streamline their operations. In brief, this is one thing that they are not
good at.

As already noted, notwithstanding a multitude of management
reforms introduced since the 1980s, there is still little incentive inside
government to promote good management. A former deputy minister at Industry Canada reports that when he arrived in the department
he saw a few units whose work was no longer relevant and decided to
do away with them. But when the next wave of across-the-board cuts
was introduced, he received no credit for having abolished the units,
and his department had to produce the same level of cuts as other
departments.[37] Lessons learned for the deputy minister.

Leaving aside the rhetoric, not much has changed inside the public
service. To be sure, government managers have more discretion in
some areas, such as in reclassifying positions. But this is hardly the
way to introduce a market-type discipline inside bureaucracy. It does,
however, make government operations more expensive and more
complex. There is still no end game of profitability, and it is still who
is right or wrong that matters in government. However, by adding
various points in the decision-making and oversight processes, it has
both made government thicker and made it more difficult to find
the culprit.

As before the arrival of NPM, managers have every interest in acquir-
ing a bigger budget, more staff, and spending the budget before the
end of the current fiscal year for fear that it would be reduced for the
next fiscal year. The purpose of public sector unions, meanwhile, is to
push as hard as they can to protect the economic interest of their
members, not to help find ways to see government units operate more
efficiently. Typically, government managers and their units are adept
at maintaining the status quo and growing operations by stealth.

Some leading students of public administration have recently sought to identify ways to improve productivity in government. Patrick Dunleavy and Leandro Carrera have done precisely this, but very quickly point to the challenge: "The fundamental difficulty of measuring productivity in government service has been that we do not have anything equivalent to a price for most of the many different services and goods that government departments and agencies produce."[38] They argue that it is particularly difficult for a national government to measure productivity, given the nature of its activities, and that a national government usually only has one department of each type (i.e., a large department to look after customs, tax collection, and the like) so that there is no basis for comparing productivity.

Productivity improvements, according to Dunleavy and Carrera, have been tied to program reviews, and automatic across-the-board cuts imposed by central agencies.[39] They have little confidence that one can assess, let alone improve, policy effectiveness where effectiveness is all too often in the eye of the beholder. They insist, however, that innovation and new information technology can improve and indeed has improved productivity in government, at least in Britain – for example, by introducing electronic tax forms, thus reducing the number of employees to process them.[40]

But why could more not be done? Computers now handle routine or standardized tasks with great efficiency. Government is home to many routine manual tasks and office functions, notably record-keeping and processing of applications. New information technologies enable organizations to achieve extremely high levels of processing with high levels of productivity.[41] Why then do government bureaucracies grow and grow whenever the prime minister and his courtiers take their eyes off the ball, and why are senior public servants unable to prune their organizations without a firm directive to do so from above?

It remains that for successful private sector innovation and productivity, improvements have to be continuous. Governments, on the other hand, can remain inattentive to productivity gains for long periods, then indulge in short-lived bursts of deep cuts to inputs every fifteen years or so, or when a newly elected government has been able to secure a majority mandate.[42] All too often, cuts to input costs are made in government during program reviews, with little appreciation of the impact on outputs or, in private sector parlance, on performance, market share, and profits. No leading private sector firm would initiate such a process.

LOOKING OUTSIDE: IT'S ALL ABOUT RISKS

Bureaucracy tends to look inward to its own circumstances and challenges. It has often been accused of working from the perspective of the "bubble of cocooned Ottawa."[43] There is little risk for public servants working inside the bubble, where they know intuitively the culture and the rules within which they have to work.

Reaching out to individuals and groups outside entails risk. People outside bureaucracy do not play by the same rules, and there is always the danger that they will go to the media or to politicians with their concerns. How it plays back to them and at what level, either political or bureaucratic, is never certain. More to the point, the risks are high and the rewards are few when dealing with outside groups.

Public servants are all too aware that their standing in society has fallen sharply over the past thirty years. Politicians have told them as much, as have numerous public opinion surveys and the media. A major study, based in part on a public opinion survey of both Canadians and public servants and on focus groups sponsored by the federal government, delivered a harsh verdict on the state of the Canadian public service. It concluded that Canadians see public servants as "disconnected, lazy and overpaid."[44]

The glory days of the Canadian public service are gone, and few know it better than public servants themselves. We need not revisit the points made in earlier chapters. Suffice to note here there are many signs that not all is well inside the Canadian public service: it is plagued with continuing morale problems; sick leaves have shot up by 68 per cent in the last ten years; clerks of the Privy Council have launched at least three vision or major reform initiatives over the past twenty years or so; public servants have repeatedly been told to emulate the private sector with little success to show for their efforts; and it no longer holds the influence it once did in shaping public policy.[45]

As a former British senior civil servant summed up his evaluation of the British civil service, in an assessment that applies equally well to the Canadian public service, "There was nothing else to do in the 1950s, 60s, and 70s, if you were an economist then you wanted to work in government. We ended up with far more talented people in the Treasury than we could possibly find interesting things to do. Times have changed. Now we feel a great deal of hostility towards the civil service. You have the feeling that ministers look at economists in the civil service and think – if you are really smart, why don't you go work with McKinsey or the banks?"[46]

Public servants do not reach beyond the bureaucracy with the self-assurance and confidence in their institution that they once did. Politicians prefer it that way. Having public servants circle the wagons makes it easier to control the message and manage the blame game. It is also part of the Westminster culture to have politicians highly visible to the public, but not public servants.[47]

Front-line public servants have to be in constant contact with clients. As long as they stay within the parameters of their programs, they avoid being embroiled in a public controversy. That, as we have already seen, is a measure of success, and it is something that public servants have learned to be good at. It is rarely for good reasons, at least from their perspective, and rarely good news whenever a public servant becomes visible in the media or in any kind of public controversy. The three Health Canada officials dismissed from their positions for voicing their views publicly is a reminder to public servants that it is in their interests to avoid visibility in public. A case in point: Kathryn May, a veteran journalist with the *Ottawa Citizen*, reports that her telephone calls to senior public servants are not returned nearly as often as in years past.[48]

The middle of the Canadian public service or officials between the more senior levels and those actually delivering programs and services also prefer to stay within the "bubble of cocooned Ottawa." Here, too, there is no advantage and plenty of downside for them when reaching outside. In any event, much of what they do is limited to what matters inside the bureaucracy: back-office functions, evaluation, coordination, liaison, and planning.

Public servants are caught in the middle of the constant call by the public to "do something" but "don't let the government do it."[49] Some of the top students of public administration in the Anglo-American world, such as Derek Bok, Chris Pollitt, Chris Hood, and others, began to zero in on the problem: citizens' mistrust of government often has its roots in the failing performance of bureaucracy.[50]

It is easier to reach outside an organization when members have confidence in their institution, when they believe that they will be supported by their superiors if things go off-track, and when they have a coherent message that the organization is prepared to be associated with through thick and thin. Modern-day government, tied as it is to permanent election campaigns, does not lend itself to that approach.

Public servants know better than anyone – because they live it – that politicians have introduced a new interpretation of the doctrine of ministerial responsibility. Politicians now routinely take responsibility – but not the blame – when things go wrong. Joe Clark, Jean Chrétien, and Stephen Harper, among many other politicians, have made it clear that they were prepared to accept responsibility, as the doctrine of ministerial responsibility calls for, but they were also quite prepared to point the finger at public servants to assign blame. Tom Axworthy, former principal secretary to Pierre Trudeau, writes that increasingly "ministers publicly blame officials for mistakes and officials have had to learn public relation skills in order to survive."[51]

The doctrine of ministerial responsibility, many politicians now argue, all too often stands in the way of holding accountable those actually responsible for decisions.[52] As is well known, politicians also have little interest in performance or evaluation reports, preferring to focus on rules in holding someone to account. Politicians and the media understand rules and regulations, but not fuzzy evaluation reports. Because of the nature of their work, politicians and the media attach great importance to catching the culprit.

However, the more senior public servants do reach outside the public service. For one thing, lobbyists are constantly trying to influence them. Lobbyists know full well that effective decision-making has been centralized in Ottawa, and the higher point of entry works best for them.

High-profile CEOs from Canada's leading financial and manufacturing firms will always get their phone calls returned. There are many advantages for senior public servants to keep lines of communications discreetly open to the country's leading business elites. It enables them to have a sense of where the private sector thinks the economy is going, to tell their political masters that they have been in contact with the country's leading CEOs, and the contacts may well come in handy later when looking for economic opportunities once they leave public service. Medium or small business owners, however, will not get their calls returned – those are delegated down the line. In short, economic elites have, one way or another, access to the prime minister's court where decisions that matter are made. Others have no such access.

The idea that governments can bring private sector executives into government to turn things around has met with precious little success. Indeed, a clash in culture and outlook is unavoidable when business executives are given a mandate to turn government operations around. By temperament, business executives will want to cut through the nonsense, jump to solutions, and make sweeping decisions on what is required. They are likely to give short shrift to the interdependence of functions in government, to vague and conflicting goals, to the built-in administrative constraints, the demands of political accountability, the media spotlight, and the sundry requirements of the political world. Public servants – well-versed in the ways of their institution and capable of sniffing out the most subtle of messages emanating from any part of the government machinery – are likely to become exasperated with business executives who briefly invade their turf and sell simple solutions to what they view as complex management problems.[53] Indeed, many public servants disdain such exercises, aware that the functions to be performed in government differ in so many respects from those involved in running a business.

However, senior public servants do take note of salaries in the private sector to assess their own remuneration. And why not, given that political leaders have been telling them for some thirty years that they should emulate their private sector counterparts? They are invariably disappointed: the CEOs of Canada's five big banks make about $12 million each per year.[54] By contrast, the highest ranking deputy ministers earn between $272,000 and $319,000, in addition to a performance award of up to 39 per cent, which works out to a potential earning of $443,410.[55] However, deputy ministers have a particularly generous pension plan – those who serve ten years as deputy have a pension equal to 90 per cent of their five best years of service, indexed for life. They can retire on full pension after thirty-five years of service and age fifty-five. They can also move on to other employment in the private and public sectors, and many do.

LOOKING BACK

Government agencies can embrace the status quo with far greater ease than can the private sector, for many reasons. The competitive nature of the global economy has devastated private sector unions but left public sector ones nearly intact. The government manager has to accommodate a variety of requirements imposed by central agencies and deal with ever more oversight bodies. But for the most part, the private sector is free of such constraints.

Large private sector firms can look to globalization to restructure their operations. They can shift manufacturing plants to countries with low labour costs, the marketing function to where the talent is, call centres to the highest bidder, and so on. Governments can hardly move any of their operations to another jurisdiction. This, and the absence of market forces, gives public sector unions a strong hand in their dealings with governments.

In government, the most important event that shapes behaviour occurred before most new recruits to the public service were born. In the immediate postwar period and given the success of government in mounting the war effort, a desire emerged for government to show the way for other employers, by becoming a model employer. In 1967, the Canadian Parliament agreed to collective bargaining and to give public servants the right to strike.[56] The right to strike had proven effective in the private sector to settle disputes. However, in government the right to strike was introduced in a sector where, by definition, there is no market to discipline either party's behaviour.[57] That decision still shapes the behaviour of both managers and employees in the government of Canada far more than all the private-sector management-inspired measures combined introduced over the past thirty years or so.

In addition, in spite of attempts to dress the public sector to look like the private sector, government departments remain monopolies or quasi-monopolies, insulated from competitive pressure. The absence of market pressure means that the "self-interest of public officials does not include the efficient delivery of services."[58] It also instils inertia in government operations. There are still precious few incentives for government managers to go head-to-head with public sector unions.

Left to its own devices, the public service will grow and grow. The post-Chrétien-Martin program review period reveals that when the prime minister and his senior advisors take their eyes off the ball, bureaucracy adds management layers and new positions. Again, only when the prime minister launches a program review does the public service see a reduction in its numbers and in its operating budgets. Financial audits or the threat of one also have an impact on government operations, as recent history has shown.[59] A freeze on departmental spending and centrally prescribed rules governing human and financial resources (e.g., classification of positions) or keeping government operations on a tight leash also work if the goal is to keep a close eye on the spending pattern of government operations.[60]

Governments are not very good at evaluation and assessing performance of many policies, programs, and some government operations. Yet they keep at it, thinking that somehow the efforts can make the public sector look like the private sector. It is also because the Office of the Auditor General tells them to do it, though the office keeps reporting that the efforts fall far short of the mark. Those in a position to say that this road leads nowhere are reluctant to do so. Politicians are in no mood to admit that government operations can never be made to work as well as the private sector and, in any event, always have more important political battles to fight than taking on the auditor general. Government managers, meanwhile, have every interest in making the case that, if they are to be efficient, then they need the latitude to act as would any competent manager in the private sector. Having subordinates in their organizations who produce relatively bland and harmless evaluation reports is a small price to pay. The current accountability requirements can be fudged and all too often be made to protect both ministers and public servants by enabling them to hide behind one another.

Line departments and agencies have lost their place under the sun. The policy and decision-making processes have become too complex, too interwoven at the interdepartmental level for a single-line department to take charge of an issue, let alone a policy, as it once did. Yet, as Nobel laureate Herbert Simon argues, "Organizational identification is a powerful motivator, rooted both in people's values and in their need to build a simplified model of the world that focuses upon their particular responsibilities and work environment. It is distinct from the self-interest which, of course, also plays an important part in organizational behavior."[61]

There is, however, a government responsibility that operates at arm's length from politicians and for which the responsible agencies have a relatively free hand to call a spade a spade. This is regulation, and it is an important responsibility for promoting the public interest. Regulating agencies have mandates to ensure food safety, appropriate financial transactions, and to preserve the quality of the natural environment. The next chapter looks at how government assumes this responsibility and how good it is at it.

Regulations:
You Can Feed the Animals

"If you go to the zoo," advised Forrest Gump, "always take something to feed the animals, even if the signs say 'Do Not Feed the Animals.' It wasn't the animals that put these signs up." Regulations are meant to be obeyed. But here, too, things have changed. As in other areas of government activities, there is an international trend towards greater economic deregulation in order to get government out of the way of the private sector so as to make national economies more globally competitive.

Government regulations have never enjoyed much currency, at least in some quarters, and have often been the butt of jokes. The *Economist* reports, for example, that a Florida state regulation requires vending machine labels to urge the public to file a report if the label is missing, and federal regulations insist that all trains must be painted with an *F* at the front in order to tell which end is which.[1] It took a journalist sixty-five days to get official permission to open a lemonade stand in New York.[2] The provincial government of New Brunswick decided in 2014 to lessen the regulatory burden on its businesses and declared that it would remove the rule that prohibited swearing at horses at county fairs.[3]

The merit or, much more often, the seeming straitjacket of government regulations is a matter that is now high on the political agenda. Governments throughout the Western world and no matter where they sit on the political spectrum, including both the federal and provincial governments in Canada, have been engaged in an ongoing debate on establishing the right regulatory regime. They have all launched one reform measure after another designed to reduce red tape, in the name of promoting competitiveness in the global economy and unleashing the creativity of the private sector. Government regulations and red tape are now regularly described, even by governments, as "job killers," hardly an endorsement for government regulation, which Prime Minister Stephen Harper once described as "a silent killer of jobs."[4]

Hardly a month goes by when the president of the Treasury Board does not announce with great fanfare that another important step has been taken to reduce regulations: in late 2012 we were told that Canada was among "world leaders in cutting red tape"; in November 2013 that "small business calls for less red tape" and that the government had heard the call and would react; in April 2013 that the government would "effectively cap the amount of red tape applied to business"; and in July 2013, he pledged to work harder still to reduce red tape.[5]

Eliminating government regulations and red tape, however, is never as straightforward as one might assume. The regulation of institutional and individual behaviour is one of the most important functions of government – failing to have a well-functioning regulatory regime at work can well put lives at risk and inhibit the development and continued viability of the business community.

For every regulation that exists, someone or some association insists that it is needed to promote the public interest. As well, new demands to protect the environment and to promote health, safety, and security require new regulations. Thus, some observers and organizations view government regulations not as a "burden" but, rather, as a necessary tool to keep in check private interests that "threaten the public good."[6] Regulations are required to protect citizens from unqualified medical doctors, bad drugs, bad medical equipment, bad or absent automobile safety requirements, and the list goes on. In short, there are plenty of vested interests in the regulatory and risk business.

There are core things that governments must do, and establishing regulations is one. Government has an umpire role to ensure that people play by the same rules. Citizens need regulations to protect the environment and their health and safety, while businesses need rules to sustain, among other things, an antitrust policy and a level playing field.

In brief, government is the one legitimate actor that can manage regulations, and if the government is not good at developing them and making certain that they are respected, then it can hardly be good at many other things. While one can argue about the role of government in promoting the broader public interest when it intervenes with programs in socio-economic sectors, few would argue against a minimum of government regulations in such key areas as the economy, the environment, and health and safety, to promote the common good.[7] If government has a set of core responsibilities that it must attend to, then managing regulation is one of them. ·

As economist and former senior federal public servant Paul Boothe points out, Canadians and their politicians have a "love-hate" relationship with government regulations. Politicians, he adds, hate the burden of regulations, but many also dislike the alternative – taxes and subsidies. No matter, he argues, regulations are here to stay, and the challenge is to figure out how to make them work well.[8] Whatever the state of the love-hate relationship with government regulations, it remains that an effective regulatory regime is necessary, not simply to protect consumers but also for market economies to function properly.

This chapter looks at how government manages regulations and how the approach has evolved in recent years. Government regulations matter to both businesses and individuals; they have the power to put firms out of business, but also to create new economic opportunities. Lack of regulations can expose the public to harm, but too many regulations can be a drag on the economy and make it less competitive. The *Wall Street Journal* maintains that US households pay nearly $15,000 every year "in regulatory hidden tax."[9] Governments everywhere strive to strike the right balance, like never before. The rise of neo-liberalism and the global economy forces governments to refine their approach to regulations in the interest or hope of unlocking greater national competitiveness. The question this chapter seeks to answer is whether government improved its capacity to manage regulations and how good it is at managing its regulatory regime.

G. Bruce Doern, Michael Prince, and Richard Schultz recently published a comprehensive and insightful review of Canada's regulatory regime. While it is not possible to provide a full appreciation of the study here, the authors point to the special challenges confronting Canada, given its "huge geographical-spatial terrain that extends further internationally in other complex ways."[10] The authors provide a historical perspective on Canada's regulatory policies (circa 1968 to 2014) and conclude that the country's regulatory regime "has operated in the middle and lower ranked realms of politically expressed priorities."[11]

The authors survey the ebbs and flows of regulatory reforms under four prime ministers, recognizing that prime ministerial power now shapes the government's agenda. Few prime ministers provided an overall view of regulatory change. When they did, they were pursuing another agenda, notably Trudeau and his Charter of Rights and Freedoms, and Mulroney and his free-trade agreement with the United States.[12] Harper adopted an aggressive reform strategy on deregulation, including a decision to sack the head of the Canadian Nuclear Safety Commission on flimsy grounds, a message that was not lost on regulatory agencies or on those who were in favour of energy development.[13]

CONTROL THEORY IN REGULATORY REGIMES

The theory of regulatory control hinges on three requirements that are linked to one another: standard-setting, information-gathering or observation, and behaviour modification. One can hardly operate effectively in isolation from the other two.[14] But here again government regulatory regimes are complex, and it is virtually impossible to satisfy all those with vested interests. As Chris Hood writes, "No one has ever seen a risk regulation regime and a lawyer, an economist, a political scientist and a practitioner will look at regimes from different perspectives."[15]

Information-gathering is a vital component of any regulatory regime, and controversy can quickly surface over any number of issues, from the quality of data to how scientific information is interpreted and by whom. In addition, how the information is collected can also be controversial – we have in recent years, in some ways, turned away from having regulators gather the information to impose legal requirements on participants, to using spot-checking and paying others to gather the information.[16]

Standard-setting is no less controversial. There are ways to establish standards, and businesses and their lobbyists will wish to monitor and seek to influence outcomes. It is also an area where different standards may apply in different countries, which can leave an impact on a firm's competitiveness.[17] As Chris Hood, Henry Rothstein, and Robert Baldwin argue, "Deterrence measures rely on the credibility of penalties and punishment expressed in the expected cost of non-compliance to violators, to prevent those regulated from breaking rules."[18]

REFORMING GOVERNMENT REGULATIONS

No politician wants to run an election campaign pledging to increase regulation and red tape, and no government wants to tell voters that they were able to fulfil that pledge. Increasing red tape, much like a commitment to increase taxes, is a sure way to lose public support, even to lose an election. Consumers are always anxious to gain access to new products, while businesses, large and small, often point to government regulations as a barrier to competitiveness, innovation, pursuit of new economic opportunities, and job creation. Global firms and their lobbyists are also able to threaten national governments, whenever they are contemplating new regulations, that they can always move to less regulated countries.

However, there are limits to deregulation. John Mack, former chief executive officer at Morgan Stanley, put it succinctly when he said, "We cannot control ourselves. You have to step in and control Wall Street."[19] While the goal is always to strike the right balance, many argue that balance has shifted too far away from regulation. They claim that the shift has placed governments in more of a reactive mode than is wise, and citizens have been on the losing end of the change. The shift away from direct enforcement to spot audits, in the opinion of some observers, is more akin to Forrest Gump's approach: the rules are there, but one can choose to ignore them.

THE TIMES THEY ARE A-CHANGIN'

One can trace changes in thinking about regulatory agencies by consulting publications. The public administration literature, for example, in the 1980s and even the 1990s stressed basic requirements to ensure a rigorous regulatory regime, founded on standard-setting and enforcement. I am referring to the work of James Mallory, G. Bruce Doern, and Richard Schultz, among others.[20] Their focus was on regulatory bodies as institutions and what was required to make them effective. They underlined the need for independence from political control and on their role as quasi-judicial bodies. They drew a distinction between regulatory agencies that had a business-friendly framework (i.e. intellectual property) and those that served the broader public interest as sectoral regulators. Doern, for example, reviewed in considerable detail the work of the Canadian Radio–television and Telecommunications Commission (CRTC) to assess how it went about balancing "the interests of consumers, the creative community and distribution industries."[21] He had little to report on the operating costs of the CRTC and on how its work could be adjusted to promote the competitive capacity of private sector firms in the global economy.

Beginning in the 1980s, with the arrival of right-of-centre politicians (Reagan, Thatcher, and Mulroney) and as the global economy took root, we saw a move towards what was labelled "smart regulation." The goal was to shift focus away from enforcement to compliance.[22] The thinking was that individuals and private sector firms are rational economic actors and would not wish to jeopardize their own economic interests. Moving away from direct enforcement would also entail fewer public servants, less cost to the Treasury, and a diminished burden on private firms.

To be sure, enforcing regulations entails substantial costs for both the public and private sectors. Every time regulatory agencies adjust rules or add new ones, the private sector has to absorb new financial burdens for the changing policies, revised manuals, and new practices. Meanwhile, resources allocated to regulatory agencies would, in the opinion of some politicians, be better allocated to deliver government programs and services or to lower taxes if government could move to smart regulation. The thinking again was that a new approach to regulation could both help the private sector and reduce government spending. Attacking red tape, eliminating some regulations, and shifting to smart regulation also became an important part of the agenda to withdraw the state as much as possible from the economy in order to promote a more competitive and innovative economy.[23]

Mulroney's Nielsen task force, which brought together private- and public-sector executives to review the government's expenditure budget, first served notice that Canada's regulatory regime needed an overhaul. It insisted that the regime was too costly for both taxpayers and the private sector. The task force estimated that in fiscal year 1985–6 the regulatory regime employed 34,500 public servants and cost taxpayers some $2.7 billion to cover compliance, monitoring, and inspection. It added that the regime's hidden costs for businesses amounted to more than $30 billion, too heavy a burden for the private sector.[24] Something had to be done, it argued, if the Canadian economy was to remain competitive.

The government responded by introducing new procedures that called for rigorous assessment of any proposed new regulations to make certain that benefits would clearly exceed costs. It also committed to undertake a thorough review of the effectiveness of its regulatory regime. To ensure follow-up, it created a new bureaucratic agency, a regulatory affairs branch in the Office of Privatization and Regulatory Affairs.[25]

The Office of the Auditor General reviewed the government's regulatory regime in 1989, three years after the Nielsen task force reported, and it was critical of the government's efforts. It argued that impact assessments had to be strengthened and that insufficient efforts were committed to identifying alternatives to regulation. The office was also highly critical of the government's efforts at evaluating the effectiveness of its regulatory regime and asked for a stronger commitment to program evaluation. However, there is no evidence to suggest that the auditor general's report had much impact on the government's management of its regulatory regime.[26]

But other things did, notably the government's desire to promote a pro-business agenda, the Chrétien-Martin program review, and the election of the Harper government. The Chrétien-Martin review eliminated a number of positions in regulatory agencies and sought to simplify some of the regulatory processes.[27]

It will be recalled that in 2010 the Harper government set up a Red Tape Reduction Commission, whose purpose was to "identify irritants to business" that stemmed from the "federal government's regulatory requirements" and to review the administration so as to "reduce the compliance burden on business." The government directed the commission to come forward with recommendations to enable businesses to "invest in growth and jobs, not in process."[28]

The commission did precisely that and the government of Canada has been aggressively reviewing its regulatory regime for the past several years. It published a document with a telling title: *Cutting Red Tape and Freeing Business to Grow.*[29] The government now provides regular updates on progress made in reforming its regulatory regime by publishing scorecards, and the reports, including the annual scorecards, are easily accessible on the Treasury Board website.[30]

The scorecard is designed to ensure progress, a message not lost on the public service that it could not be fully trusted to deliver what the government wanted. More to the point, the government felt that, left to its own devices, the bureaucracy would go through the motions, as it had in the past, and in the end accomplish very little. In addition, the government announced in 2012 that it would henceforth apply a "one for one rule," designed to put a "permanent control on the size and cost of administrative burden on business."[31] The rule requires that when a new or amended regulation is introduced that increases the burden on businesses, regulators are required to offset the burden by removing an old regulation.

The government also established a regulatory advisory committee with a mandate "to hold the government to account" on reforming its regulatory regime. The committee has five members, four from the business community and one representing consumers.[32] The committee's membership speaks to the standing the business community now enjoys in shaping new public policy. While the Mulroney government had a new bureaucratic unit to ensure follow-up on its commitment, the Harper government opted for an outside group of advisors, again making the point that the public service could not be trusted to do as it was told.

The government published its first scorecard report in January 2014, which enabled it to highlight the progress it had made. It reported that during fiscal year 2012–13, 86 per cent of all regulatory changes during the year either reduced or did not impose any new administrative burden on businesses.[33] The government also forced the departments and agencies to outline future regulatory initiatives and to make them public. It simply decided, without explaining on what basis it made the decision, that it was in the public interest to limit the regulatory burden on the business community to its present level, no matter any number of developments that may call for new regulations.

HARDLY ALONE

The Harper government is hardly the first government in Canada or in the Western world to attempt to lessen the regulatory burden on both the private and public sectors. In addition, governments now have to meet the requirements of free-trade agreements and international obligations in such areas as health and safety, security, and broader international trade obligations. This, if nothing else, has forced governments to review their regulatory regimes, but it also has made regimes more complicated.

Canadians' love-hate relationship with the country's regulatory regime was put to the test in the aftermath of the 2008 financial crisis. Many Canadians believe that the country's financial institutions were able to survive the crisis because of the country's regulatory regime. No banks failed and the government was not forced to buy shares in them to keep them alive.[34]

Though there is not universal agreement, many also believe that the United States' weak regulatory regime failed to ensure stable financial institutions during the financial meltdown. It will be recalled that the Glass-Steagall Act of 1933 was passed to stop a wave of bank failures during the Great Depression. The act, apart from establishing the Federal Open Market Committee, also split conventional banking from investment banking. Accordingly, regulations required that taking deposits and making loans were to be kept separate from trading stocks and other securities.[35]

The push to deregulate in the 1980s and 1990s led the US Congress to repeal the Glass-Steagall Act and replace it with the Gramm-Leach-Bliley Act. This struck many regulations off the books and allowed commercial and investment banks, security firms, and insurance companies to merge. Many observers believe that the act, at least in part, caused the 2007–8 subprime mortgage financial crisis, and more is said about this below.[36] The push to deregulate came not only from the business community but also from regulators themselves. Alan Greenspan, the Federal Reserve chairman, believed that the instinct for self-preservation would result in sufficient self-regulation to ensure viable financial institutions. He later admitted that he had overestimated the business community's ability to regulate itself.[37]

Hank Paulson, who had a front-row seat as the 2008 financial crisis unfolded as US Treasury secretary, maintains that the crisis was caused by a major flaw in the system: "weak regulation." He writes, "Congress in its wisdom, or in this case lack thereof, had deprived the regulator of the same broad powers that a banking regulator had to make judgements."[38]

In the immediate aftermath of the crisis, governments around the world sought to respond as best they could, with one stimulus package after another. Moreover, a series of new regulations were introduced, ranging from restrictions on short-selling of financial stocks, together with new rules requiring banks to hold enough capital to cover at least 3 per cent of their total assets.[39]

To be sure, efforts were made to understand the cause of the crisis and to identify ways to avoid a similar one in the future. In many cases, governments turned to the private sector for solutions, and it had little appetite for more red tape or government regulation, other than in the financial sector.

The US inquiry report on the financial crisis maintains that key government agencies were "behind the curve" and have a lot to answer for. The inquiry determined that the agencies, including the regulatory agencies, were hampered because they simply did not have a clear grasp of the financial system they were charged with overseeing, particularly as it had evolved in the years leading up to the crisis. It went on to make the point that "more than 30 years of deregulation ... supported by successive administrations and Congresses and actively pushed by the financial industry at every turn, had stripped away key safeguards. In addition, the government permitted financial firms to pick their preferred regulators in what became a race to the weakest supervisor."[40]

There is a consensus emerging that events leading up to the crisis were far too complex for government agencies and regulators to understand, let alone to regulate.[41] The global nature of financial markets, new technology, and complex financial firms operated beyond their grasp. Governments were left reacting to events as best they could – essentially shutting the barn door after the horse had bolted.

Governments are often very good at responding after the fact, or when they are expected to deal with a crisis with alacrity. Public opinion demands it, and for a period, however brief, governments are able to focus on a clear objective. It will be recalled that the United States enacted a new law – the Dodd-Frank Wall Street Reform and Consumer Protection Act – in 2010, bringing significant changes to the country's financial regulatory regime. The objective was to prevent another financial crisis and to ensure that taxpayers are not left on the hook to bail out banks that are too big to fail.[42] A multitude of new regulations suggest that the pendulum has swung sharply in the direction of regulation, if only temporarily.

The act is a very complex piece of legislation. It established 243 rules, carried out sixty-seven studies, issued twenty-two periodic reports, and created two new regulators. The regulatory agencies are no longer concerned simply with regulating financial institutions. They are also required, among many other things, to establish an office to promote the participation of minority-owned and women-owned businesses in the agencies' programs and control.[43] The Glass-Steagall Act ran to 37 pages but the Dodd-Frank Act runs to 848 pages and required close to 400 pieces of detailed rulemaking by regulatory agencies.[44] There were also some efforts to regulate financial institutions at the international level after the 2008 financial crisis. However, all of this makes the point that government is good at closing the barn doors after the horses have bolted.

LAC-MÉGANTIC

The 2008 financial crisis is not the only one that saw regulators rush to close the barn door after the horse had bolted. It will be recalled that a derailment of dangerous goods at Lac-Mégantic, Quebec, in the summer of 2013 devastated the town's centre and killed forty-seven people. Transport Canada quickly moved in with a series of new regulations immediately after the incident. It too stood accused of being ill-equipped to assess risks and of failing to impose a strong regulatory regime in the transportation of dangerous goods.

The Office of the Auditor General was quick off the mark with "I told you so": "Fourteen years ago, Transport Canada recognized the need to shift from an inspection-based oversight approach to one that integrates the oversight of a safety management system ... the transition is taking too long." It added that Transport Canada completed only 26 per cent of its planned audits of federal railways over a "three-year period," which was not good enough.[45] To add to Transport Canada's woes, the media reported that one month before the Lac-Mégantic disaster, a private firm – Irving Oil – had raised concerns about a lack of proper testing on the crude oil that was being shipped by rail.[46] The point – a private firm was ahead of the curve and the government agency responsible for rail safety was not. The events forced the agency into a reactive mode.

Within days of the Lac-Mégantic disaster, the government issued an emergency directive ending the practice of moving dangerous goods with only a one-person crew and also served notice that it would shortly bring forward legislation to establish new regulations for the industry. The emergency directive called on the industry to ensure that no locomotive attached to one or more loaded tank cars transporting dangerous goods is left unattended on a main track and that directional controls are removed from any unattended train, thus preventing them from moving forward or backward on a main track. It is important to note that the emergency directive was announced by a career public servant rather than by the minister.[47] The Transportation Safety Board of Canada also announced that it would conduct a full investigation into the Lac-Mégantic derailment.[48]

In January 2014, Transport Canada unveiled yet another set of new regulations to guide the transportation of dangerous goods, introducing greater requirements for pressure-relief valves and other safety features on tank cars carrying dangerous goods.[49]

There have been still more changes to the regulatory regime since the Lac-Mégantic accident, which include new testing requirements of crude oil being shipped, stronger reporting stipulations to Transport Canada, and a requirement to inform municipalities on the nature and volume of dangerous goods transported by rail through their communities. Transport Canada now requires that the automatic brake on locomotives is set in full-service position, and operators have to comply fully with their company's instructions on hand brakes. The minister also announced that the department would increase the number of inspectors and auditors on rail safety.[50] Later still – in April 2014 – the government banned the use of some 5,000 of the least crash-resistant cars hauling dangerous good, called for new emergency protocols for all shipments of crude oil by rail and required that older-model tank cars be phased out over a three-year period.[51]

All of the regulations were introduced after the incident. This prompted Transport Canada to issue a news release to clarify its role in promoting the safe transportation of dangerous goods. The release sought to shift or at least to share the blame with others. The department said, "Transport Canada does not advise railway operators in advance of inspections for equipment and operations …Transport Canada's oversight role includes monitoring railway companies for compliance with rules, regulations and standards, as well as the overall safety of railway operations through audits, inspections and investigations. Rail companies are inspected regularly as part of Transport Canada's risk based inspection program." It added, "Transport Canada has already taken steps to increase rail safety in Canada and will continue to do more."[52]

THE BLAME GAME

The 2008 financial crisis and that of Lac-Mégantic, like many crises that involve public sector oversight, share several things in common. The blame game kicks into gear the moment the crisis becomes public, and regulators are left scrambling to define new regulations. Politicians are quick to grab the media spotlight to pledge that new measures will be put in place to ensure that such a crisis will not happen again. They also happily point the finger at others, often bureaucrats, in managing the blame game.

The official American inquiry into the 2008 financial crisis in the end blamed everyone: bankers, regulators, government officials, and some homeowners. It reported widespread failure in financial regulations, was highly critical of the Federal Reserve's failure to put an end to toxic mortgages, pointed to irresponsible risks by Wall Street bankers, and reported a breakdown in corporate governance. The inquiry insisted that government officials lacked proper understanding of the "financial system they oversaw." It was also particularly critical of the government's regulatory regime, especially as it responded to the drive for greater deregulation, arguing, "What else could one expect on a highway where there were neither speed limits nor painted lines?"[53]

In the case of the Lac-Mégantic incident, the Transportation Safety Board of Canada announced it would hold a "full investigation." It explained that it would find out "what happened, why it happened and what needs to be done to prevent it from happening again."[54]

Politicians, meanwhile, do not wait for reports before naming culprits. Thomas Mulcair, the leader of the opposition, was quick off the mark to pin the blame on the government. Within hours of the incident, he said, "We've got to get beyond this new system that they seem to be wanting to put in place of self-regulation. Governments have to regulate in the public interest. Nothing is more important in what governments do than taking care of the safety of the public."[55] He later argued that "pro deregulation governments" in recent years, in particular the Harper government, have "gutted" regulations in "health, safety and environmental protection as a path to prosperity."[56]

The auditor general also "found significant weaknesses" in Transport Canada's oversight of regulated railways. He argued that Transport Canada officials lacked the "necessary knowledge, had too few safety auditors, had poorly trained inspectors and there was an absence of follow-up sanctions to their work."[57] Liberal Party transportation critic David McGuinty was no less damning of the government's regulatory regime, pointing out that the Harper government spends more on advertising than on rail safety.[58] Even the transport minister, Lisa Raitt, got into the act and singled out her bureaucrats, saying, "I've told Transport Canada officials that the public expects better of them."[59] Yet one more sign that the doctrine of ministerial responsibility has taken new meanings in recent years. The bureaucrats, meanwhile, stayed silent, pointing fingers at no one, at least publicly.

The Transportation Safety Board of Canada tabled its final report on the accident on 19 August 2014 and pointed out that its purpose was not "to lay blame."[60] The board's chair insisted that "accidents never come down to a single individual, a single action or a single factor."[61] However, the report did find enough blame to assign to the Montreal, Maine and Atlantic (MMA) railway and to the regulators at Transport Canada.

The report pointed out that MMA did not have a "functioning safety management system to manage risk." It identified eighteen factors that "played a role in the accident" and argued that "take any one of them out of the equation and this accident may not have happened." Among other things, the board pointed to MMA's "management acceptance of rail wear on the main track that was well beyond industry norm" and its "tolerance of non-standard repairs."[62]

The report was also critical of the government, making the case that Transport Canada contributed to a climate allowing the accident to happen. It argued that Transport Canada had some regulations in place, but its oversight was lacking. Regulations are one thing, the report pointed out, but "they have to be audited with sufficient depth and with sufficient frequency" to be effective. They were not. It concluded, "Without sufficient national monitoring, Transport Canada does not have adequate assurance that its regions are providing effective oversight of regional railways to ensure that the risks to the public are being properly managed."[63] The report also made the case that Transport Canada lacked the inspectors and the necessary expertise and training to ensure a well-functioning regulatory regime.[64] The Transportation Safety Board, a federal Canadian agency, essentially made the case that there is not much merit in having a regulatory regime without the necessary enforcement and oversight capacity to make it work.

The department responded with a pledge to review the report's findings and respond "within 90 days." The minister also pointed out that, since the accident, the department had introduced new safety standards for certain tanker cars and required railways to slow down trains and prepare emergency response plans for trains carrying dangerous goods.[65]

HOW GOOD IS THE GOVERNMENT'S REGULATORY REGIME?

In the absence of a market and a price mechanism to establish success in government, for reasons outlined earlier, it is hardly possible to provide a definitive answer. What possible objective criteria could one employ to establish a clear answer? Monopolies are monopolies, with all their benefits and drawbacks. To be sure, the fact that a flurry of new regulatory measures are unveiled immediately after a major incident occurs suggests that there was room for improvement. But how can one possibly know if a crisis was a direct result of a weak regulatory regime?

We can review what prompted recent reforms and consider whether, in fact, they strengthened the regulatory regime. The trend for the past twenty years or so has been to lessen the financial burden on both the public and private sectors and to encourage private sector firms to be more competitive. For example, the government designated crude oil as a dangerous substance only after the Lac-Mégantic accident, though the minister explained that the department "intuitively ... knows that crude is a dangerous good and should be treated as such."[66] Intuition, it seems, is always sharper in government departments in retrospect and after the blame game has kicked into high gear.

In Canada, as elsewhere, the business community has applied pressure on the government to lessen the regulatory load, and continues to do so. The day after Lisa Raitt was appointed minister of transport and no less than a week after the Lac-Mégantic derailment, lobbyists for the Canadian National Railway (CN) met with her. A few days later, she met with Canadian Pacific (CP). The media submitted access-to-information requests to learn what was discussed at the two meetings. They were informed that in both cases, "no information was found that contained the information" they were seeking. One has to assume that no briefing material was prepared for the minister before the meetings; if so, it was a highly unusual development.[67]

Again, as already noted, the private sector often makes the case that the global economy and free-trade agreements require a level playing field if it is to prosper. Governments, not simply the business community, now recognize that it is no longer possible to think of regulatory levels in Canada simply in terms of the federal-provincial orders of government. It is now much broader. How can a firm compete in the era of free-trade agreements, the business community will persuasively argue, if it is asked to deal with a far more demanding regulatory regime than a competing firm in a neighbouring country with much more modest requirements?

It is a message that is increasingly being heard, with some even calling for greater global regulatory convergence. The International Federation of Accountants, for example, insists that "global regulatory convergence would provide numerous public interest benefits," yet another sign that debate over the public interest has gone global. The federation explains that it would reduce information costs, help emerging economies, provide an underpinning for a global regulatory system, and improve the comparability of financial information.[68]

A number of governments have turned to self-inspection to lessen the regulatory burden on their businesses. This enables firms to carry out an internal enforcement of externally defined standards and regulations.[69] It allows the government to establish regulations and to promote a combination of self-inspection with unscheduled audit inspections. It also enables the government to establish rules of behaviour, combined with state sanctions, while reducing costs to both the public and private sectors. But spot-audits can never be as rigorous as an onsite regular enforcement presence.

However, the government of Canada plans to accomplish two overarching objectives in reforming its regulatory regime. It insists that a greater reliance on self-inspection does not inhibit its capacity to "protect and advance the public interest in health, safety and security, the quality of the environment, and social and economic well-being of Canadians as expressed by Parliament in legislation and ... promote a fair and competitive market economy that encourages entrepreneurship, investment, and innovation."[70]

No matter the new policy, no matter the nature of a new approach, whether or not it involves self-regulation, governments (from Chrétien's "smart regulation" to Harper's "one for one rule") will invariably maintain that they are strengthening their regulatory regimes. Governments will also insist that they have no choice but to move away from the traditional bureaucratic model of command-and-control – the approach in place from the immediate postwar period to the late 1980s. That model, they explain, required too many financial and human resources to operate and entailed far too many detailed input or process-oriented regulations. In brief, it was too costly and too cumbersome. It was also geared, they argue, to a one-size-fits-all world that could no longer work in light of pressure from the business community and budget cutbacks.[71] This raises the question, would the Lac Mégantic incident or the September 2013 bus crash with a Via Rail train in an Ottawa suburb that cost six lives likely have happened thirty or forty years ago when a command-and-control traditional bureaucratic model was in place? Probably not. But we will never know for certain, and that enables governments to claim that they are strengthening the regulatory regime, no matter the revisions.

Transport Canada has been working on new rail safety regulations since 2011 and is still at it. The government now has an elaborate process to develop regulations that takes at least two years to produce results. It includes central agency oversight, interdepartmental consultations, risks assessment, stakeholder consultations, a cost-benefit analysis, and legal drafting. Lobbyists and industry representatives will invariably want to be consulted and, if they do not agree with the revisions, then at least will try to slow the process down. Politicians will also wish to pick the right time to unveil the regulations, which can slow the process further.[72]

In the case of the Lac-Mégantic derailment, the oil industry could not wait for the decision-making process to run its course. It needed to move oil gushing out of land-locked North Dakota. There were simply not enough pipelines to move the oil, and trains became the obvious solution, since tracks were already laid. As late as 2008, not a single barrel of oil left North Dakota by train. The required infrastructure – loading facilities – was quickly put in place and, within a few years, mile-long trainloads of oil were moving.

The government regulation-making process proved incapable of keeping up with the industry's requirements. Canadian and US regulations did not, for example, differentiate between moving a single car filled with oil from a train carrying one hundred oil-loaded cars. In the case of Lac-Mégantic, seventy-two carloads of crude oil exploded in the heart of the city. The regulations also failed to ensure that the rail cars had sufficiently thick shells to carry dangerous goods, a lacuna that was later fixed.[73]

Either because the regulation-making process was too complex and slow or because government preferred it that way, the railways were essentially left in "charge of themselves" when shipping oil. It is worth quoting Grant Robertson and Jacquie McNish at length on this point:

> There were no rules determining how much crude could be placed on one load, or how many tankers could be strung together without creating the risk of large explosions. There were no regulations requiring railways to place buffer cars periodically through these hazardous loads to help minimize the danger of an explosion. The number of inspectors designed to oversee the industry, meanwhile, had dropped from one for every 14 tanker cars on the rails to just one for every 4,000. In this specific instance, the paperwork relating to the cargo was wrong, underestimating the volatility of the oil, and there are serious concerns about whether the contents were properly tested prior to shipment.[74]

In other words, the regulatory regime in place failed the residents of Lac-Mégantic.

There are retired public servants who remember when things were different. Wayne Benedict recalls, when working in the industry in the 1980s, seeing "federal regulators prowling the tracks, trains and yards." He explains that regulators "would actually ride trains to ensure compliance," but when he left the industry in 2003 "you very rarely if ever saw the regulators on the railroad property."[75]

Ian Bron, former chief of marine transportation security regulatory affairs, reports "a lack of oversight," and a "system of regulation that is effectively a rubber stamp checklist. Paperwork is being examined but [there are] no inspectors on the ground doing proper tests of the systems to make sure they work." He adds, "Transport Canada is first and foremost a reactive agency and so will only address issues when they become a public scandal."[76]

What Benedict and Bron witnessed was a shift beginning in the late 1980s that saw regulators moving from an independent enforcement role to one of self-inspection and auditing. It was and remains part of a broader public policy agenda for government to move away from an enforcer role to one of greater cooperation between the public and private sectors and a stronger reliance on the private sector to police itself. In the case of the railway industry, as in many other sectors, it was a shift from the traditional bureaucratic model of command-and-control to one that recognizes the industry's obligation for safety and a view that it is in the economic interest of firms to establish and abide by demanding regulatory requirements. This does not always work, particularly when firms do not have the resources or the willingness to police themselves properly.

The 1996 revisions to the Canada Transportation Act gave rise to a number of "short-line" railway companies or "feeder railways." There are now fifty short-line operators in Canada. The 1996 revisions allowed both CN and CP to sell less-profitable and low-density lines to short-line operators. The two large railway companies could not operate these lines at a solid enough profit, because their wages and operating costs are higher than those of short-line operations. Short-line operators, however, are treated much as are large operators. They are all required to develop a safety plan, leaving regulators to rely on irregular audits rather than prescriptive and detailed technical inspections.[77]

While the command-and-control model may be less necessary for large firms with the resources to police themselves, they may well be needed for smaller firms. But the model has lost some of its currency. As Doern, Prince, and Schultz conclude in their exhaustive study of Canada's regulatory regime, the "command-and-control regulation is ... in decline in economic and marketplace" sectors.[78]

Though the shift to self-regulation holds advantages – cost savings for government and more responsive rules for the private sector – it comes at a cost to the public interest, as this chapter maintains. Others have also made a similar case. The C.D. Howe Institute, for example, reviewed the move to "self-regulated organizations" for the professions and its impact on the public interest. The study quoted Margot Priest, an observer of regulatory regimes, to make the case that there was "sufficient evidence of regulatory failure to indicate that government cannot completely abdicate its responsibilities to self-regulation." The institute's study concluded, "Industries should not be granted self-regulatory powers without some constraints against self-interested and anti-competitive behaviour."[79]

The shift to self-regulation also calls for reams of reports to be submitted regularly to regulatory agencies. A senior executive with Corus Entertainment, a publicly traded media conglomerate, reports that the number of reports the firm has to produce has increased greatly in recent years. She adds that no one knows if these reports are taken seriously or if they are even read, since no feedback is usually provided. She also makes the point that relevant regulatory agencies simply can no longer keep pace with changes in the industry. She explains that the Internet and firms like Google and Netflix are having a profound impact on the sector but that they are able to operate under the radar of regulatory agencies.[80] The government regulatory regime, she insists, is simply too slow and ill-equipped to deal with the pace of change in the global economy, in society, and in her industry. Doern, Prince, and Schultz agree. They write that in the telecommunications sector, both the complexity of the sector and the regulatory mandates "were unworkable and often ignored in the face of changing economic and social realities."[81]

LOOKING BACK

The reforms to the government's regulatory regime of recent years have attenuated considerably the strength of the three components of the theory of regulatory control – one of the core responsibilities of government and one area in which government should be good at. The goal to cut government spending, the role of lobbyists, the desire to unleash the private sector to compete in the global economy, and the incapacity of government and its regulators to keep abreast of fast-paced changes in the economy have all combined to weaken the Canadian regulatory regime to gather data, to set standards, and to change behaviour – the three components that make up the theory of regulatory control. Government continues to collect data, but it is not always clear to what end. Government no longer has the capacity that it once had to set standards, monitor compliance, and change behaviour. Government is good at jumping into action with promises of tighter regulation after a crisis hits the media or at rushing in to close the barn doors after the horses have bolted.

One can hardly debate the merits of smart regulation or of deregulation in isolation from the broader public policy agenda. One can make the case that if we are to embrace globalization and free-trade agreements, we should also embrace the level-playing-field argument increasingly being heard from the business community. Indeed, in time we may well be pushing responsibility for establishing and monitoring regulations up to regional and even international bodies.[82]

In the last thirty years or so, governments have moved further and further away from the traditional bureaucratic model in most of their activities and from their traditional guardian role, including the management of their regulatory regimes. Those with economic power are now free to roam the corridors of government and knock on the doors of politicians, notably ministers and the Prime Minister's Office, to press their case. They can also attempt to influence regulators by marshalling resources and arguments to support their positions. Those with economic power who do not have the inclination, the ability, or the knowledge to do so can always retain hired hands to do it for them. Many do. Those with economic power have access, or can buy it; ordinary citizens cannot. Billionaire Edgar Bronfman was once asked why he had relatively easy access to world leaders and to key decision-makers in government. His answer? "Position and money."[83]

The line dividing the public and private sectors, so clearly visible thirty to forty years ago, has become increasingly blurred. Senior government officials have traditionally benefitted from very generous pension plans with the thinking that they would commit to public service for a long time and to the public interest during their careers and even in retirement. Generous pension plans are still in place, and career public servants continue to benefit from them. Now, however, they easily move to the private sector and to lobby firms where their knowledge of government, the policy and decision processes, and the working of the government's regulatory regime are important assets. They sell their services to the highest bidder – the economic elites.

Senior public servants are very able at reading political tea leaves. They live cheek-by-jowl with politicians. To get the message, they need to be told only a few times by their political masters from either the left or right that the private sector is superior and is the key to economic success in the global economy. The result is that private sector values can migrate to the public sector, even to regulatory regimes, as the past thirty years or so have shown.

Others have followed to differentiate public sector values from private sector ones. Jane Jacobs, for example, wrote that the private sector values attach importance to profit, initiative, and enterprise, that it spends to enhance productivity and is open to inventiveness. The public sector values obedience and rules, respects hierarchy, and is inclusive.[84] The two are not easily reconcilable, but that has not stopped governments from trying to make them so.

The message that government should get out of the way of the private sector and let it create jobs is also not lost on regulators. Prime Minister Harper's view that government regulations are silent job killers speaks directly to the thousands of public servants working in regulatory agencies. It raises the question, who wants to work in agencies that silently kill jobs?

I stress, however, that this is hardly a Canada-only phenomenon. The desire to rely more and more on businesses to regulate themselves is the clarion call of those wishing to unleash the private sector to do what it does best – innovate, create wealth, compete in the global setting, and create jobs. One think tank in the United Kingdom went so far as to call on the government to simply reduce the number of its regulators to enable the economy to "experience a burst of innovation and growth."[85] The message to governments – just do it, and growth and jobs will follow.

In the 1980s there were signs that senior public servants accepted the argument that they had too much influence over policy and decided to turn the policy-making steering wheel over to politicians and say, "Now, you drive." It will be recalled that the clerk of the Privy Council deliberately offered little policy advice in preparing briefing books for the incoming Mulroney government in 1984.[86] There is now evidence that government has also decided to turn over part of the regulatory regime to the private sector and say, "Now, you drive." This is not simply because governments in the Western world have decided that the most promising way to reduce spending and to promote economic growth is to look after the basics only and to permit the private sector to innovate to lessen the regulatory burden to the extent deemed appropriate by politicians and their advisory committees, which are made up largely of private sector representatives.

In any event, the public sector as structured simply cannot react quickly enough to change its regulatory regime to accommodate fast-changing economic circumstances. The regulatory process, with its requirement to consult widely and to take its lead from the prime minister and his courtiers, competing as it has to with a wide array of other pressing public policy issues in the era of permanent election campaigns, is too slow to be the important player that it once was. In addition, even sectoral issues, whether in the financial or railway industries, have become extremely complex – far too complex for a regulatory agency operating in a national setting to master.

We are often reminded that government is not as good as it once was in properly regulating all the key sectors of the economy and of society. Lac-Mégantic is hardly an isolated case. One can identify cases in virtually every sector where the regulatory regime did not perform in recent years. We know, for example, that Health Canada came under "criticism for its handling of 'off-label drugs.'" The media reported that the regulator did not have the analytical ability to track the consequences of off-label prescribing. We also know that Health Canada has not been able to provide any evidence that "it has ever investigated, prosecuted or fined a single drug company for off-label promotions." Yet Joel Lexchin, a drug safety expert, maintains that off-label drugs entail "significant public safety implications. This is a major problem for doctors and patients alike."[87]

Governments live in hope that somehow disasters or crises tied to a weaker regulatory regime, or one that reduces onsite inspection, can be avoided, because it is in the interest of private firms to avoid them. When they cannot, politicians are left to manage the blame game and to call for new regulations the day after the incident. The authors of a recently published comprehensive review of Canada's regulatory regime concluded that the country's "regulatory system is rife with unruliness … related to regulatory agencies, unruliness related to regulatory regime complexity, and unruliness to regulatory agenda setting."[88]

Changes in the government's capacity to manage a regulatory regime speak to a broader agenda. Government is no longer the credible actor that it once was, for a number of reasons: senior politicians all too often reject evidence-based advice; the rise of well-funded interests and lobby groups conjure up facts as they would like them to be; a far more interventionist judiciary than in years past challenges government policies and decisions; a machinery of government too slow to keep up with a global economy in which economic circumstances change rapidly with little warning; political and administrative institutions trying to cope as best they can with incessant demands from oversight bodies; and a political-media environment pushing decisions of any significance up to the prime minister and his courtiers. It is in this context that one now answers the question, what is government good at?

PART THREE

Answering the Question

Good at What?

What is government good at? It depends. The preceding chapters suggest that politicians and public servants operating above the fault line are good at generating blame, avoiding blame, blaming others, playing to a segment of the population to win the next election, avoiding risks, embracing and defending the status quo, adding management layers and staff, keeping ministers out of trouble in the media, responding to the demands from the prime minister and his office, and managing a complex, multi-objective prime ministerial–centric large organization operating a politically volatile environment. Conversely, they are not as good at defining the broader public interest, providing and recognizing evidence-based policy advice, implementing policy, managing human and financial resources with efficiency and frugality, innovating and reforming themselves, making expenditure reductions unless the prime minister in a majority government decides that the time has come, being accountable to Parliament and to citizens, dealing with non-performers, paying sufficient attention to service delivery and frontline workers, and evaluating the impact of policies and programs.[1]

It is important to stress that the prime minister, ministers, and many senior public servants see considerable merit in the ability of government to be good on all these points. It comes with the territory and it is their territory. They set the rules. They insist that contemporary politics and all its requirements place a premium on having the right political strategies and tactics to win elections and deal with a never-ending parade of political controversies, political scandals, and bureaucratic miscues. It is the most important measure of success, and for them government has to be good at these things if it is to be good at anything else.

It is worth repeating that contemporary politics places a premium on managing perceptions. Though Canadians may attach considerable importance to an efficient delivery of government programs and services and management of financial and human resources, what matters to ministers and senior public servants is if the prime minister and his most trusted advisors think that government is good at keeping things running on their tracks and out of political trouble. The first order of business for the prime minister and his courtiers is political survival, and those elected to political power have the most important say on what government should be good at. Government, like other large organizations, cannot be good at everything, and again managing a politically volatile environment is what matters to those who hold effective power and want to keep it.

Is government good at achieving what it sets out to accomplish in specific policy sectors? Here too it depends on the sector and on the socio-economic circumstances of the day. To answer the question, one would have to assess the impact of various policy interventions, which is beyond the scope of this book. That said, the two major policy initiatives reviewed earlier – regional economic development and human resources development within the government – suggest that recent efforts, at least in these two areas, have fallen short of expectation.[2] We also saw that program evaluation units in departments have limited ability to assess the success of policies and programs.[3]

In some cases, asking what is government good at is beside the point. There are things that governments do and must continue to do, whether or not they are good at it. No national government will turn over responsibility for the country's armed forces to the private sector. Notwithstanding the arrival of Bitcoin, monetary policy will remain a state responsibility. The state will not give up its monopoly on controlling violence in society, nor should it. If it ever did, anarchy would soon follow. One only has to look at the chaos that engulfed Argentina following a police strike in December 2013 or the ungoverned space in Nigeria and Syria to see evidence of this.[4]

Foreign affairs and negotiating trade agreements are state responsibilities and will remain so. The courts have moved in on the responsibility to define the public interest, but only up to a point, and government still retains the power to raise taxes and spend public money. No government will want to renounce fully its role in establishing a regulatory regime. On its own, the market could never establish, arbitrate, and apply many of the rules of the game to the marketplace. The business community itself knows full well that regulation-free capitalism is not possible.[5] Although there is plenty of room for disagreement on the extent to which a government should intervene, no modern government will agree to walk away completely from key socio-economic sectors, including education, health, social services, transportation, and public works. National governments will want to control who becomes a citizen of their countries and will continue to keep a close eye on their borders. We can push governments to be more efficient and more transparent in delivering these programs, but the state will not wish to transfer these responsibilities to someone else.

THE PURSUIT OF THE PUBLIC INTEREST

It seems that only when government pursues an all-encompassing, easily understood goal that has wide public appeal can it pursue the public interest. Planning and pursuing the war effort during the Second World War remains a prime example. The goal was to defeat the enemy – one can hardly be more straightforward than this. Everyone could easily relate to the overriding objective, and citizens understood that it was in the national interest to defeat the enemy. It was easy or easier to keep narrow sectoral interests in check.

There was also no need to push many issues up to the prime minister's court, and few had any desire to engage in the blame game. Government units and Crown corporations knew the task at hand, and tolerance for administrative miscues was high. The media also supported the war effort. But wars and other crises that generate an all-encompassing goal that enjoy wide support are thankfully rare.

There has to be a consensus that the country is facing a crisis, but when a consensus emerges, the government is at its best. A recent example was the ability of national governments to deal with the immediate aftermath of the 2008 financial meltdown, although the regulatory regime, at least in the United States, was not able to prevent it. Andrew Coyne, hardly known for advocating a stronger role for government in society, had this to say: "It is hard to overstate how narrowly we escaped a total collapse of world finance. That it did not collapse, I have no hesitation in saying, was entirely due to massive government interventions."[6] Each succeeding crisis, however, leaves the government larger than it was before and a new status quo to protect.[7]

To be sure, it has never been easy for the government of Canada to articulate and pursue the national interest, given the country's wide regional differences, both culturally and economically. But contemporary politics has made it even more difficult. For one thing, the pursuit of the national interest is no match for the pursuit of political power. This has wide-ranging implications for what and how government is good at in the era of permanent election campaigns.

The modern state still requires an ability to define the public interest and a level of obedience and trust in processes, rules, and taxation. Political leaders call on the rest of us to trust them by relying on their integrity, competence, and good intentions. Political parties for decades served to "generate and sustain" a level of trust and shared interest between citizens, groups of citizens, the party itself, and political institutions. Politicians now "take on a market where trust is more elusive and the grounds for distrust easier than ever to disseminate."[8]

The all-important objective for a party leader is to win power. Nothing new here, one would argue. The difference is that party leaders are now equipped with sophisticated tools to develop marketing strategies to capture enough votes to win elections. However, these tools are often better suited to dispel trust than generate it.[9] The tactic is increasingly to appeal to narrow interests. A leading Canadian journalist summed it up well when he wrote, "Remember the central truth about contemporary Canadian politics. Policy is not about the broad public interest or the 60 percent of voters who will never vote Conservative. It is about the Conservative base and perhaps the voters who have abandoned the party for the moment. They must be lured back for the Conservatives to win another majority."[10] With a collapse in membership and the requirements of permanent election campaigns, political parties have turned to party elites to run things, and that has made parties more disconnected from the population at large.

All major political parties – not just the Conservative party – with the help of their favourite pollsters, are now good at gauging public opinion, identifying who benefits from what policy, and assessing what can be sold politically. Cherry-picking from the common good so as to target a particular group of voters can now be easily done to suit a partisan political agenda. However, the price to pay is the broader public interest. But in the eyes of party leaders and their courtiers, that price is well worth paying if it enables them to win power and to keep it once in office.

Cherry-picking from the common good to secure the support of a slice of the population leaves the general population on the outside. The public interest is increasingly defined by highly organized activists, interest groups, lobbyists, and the courts. Access-to-information legislation and other sustained efforts to promote transparency have strengthened the hand of organized interest groups. They have the resources and the knowledge to employ the information and identify the key government officials to help them grapple with complex public policy issues. Meanwhile, the great majority of citizens do not have the time, the background, or the resources to do the same. Political institutions and political parties no longer have the capacity to encourage the "emergence of political outcomes representing the interests of as large a part of the population as possible."[11]

Elections are still fought over leadership, policy, and political commitments. Party leaders now have their courtiers to help them fight election campaigns and come up with "whiz-bang" ideas. Their focus is invariably on what they will do, should they win, not on how they will do it once they have won. Thus begins the culture now ingrained in government: governing is 90 per cent ideas and 10 per cent implementation. It is a culture that is also found in the judiciary, among lobbyists, and with the political, economic, and bureaucratic elites. The thinking is to get the right policy answer, and the machinery of government, the implementation arm of government, will do as it is told. However, it is hardly possible to get the right policy answer without giving equal weight to implementation.

GOVERNMENT AND WICKED PROBLEMS

Notwithstanding the challenges confronting present-day politicians and the public sector, government needs to be good at dealing with society's "wicked problems" and at developing big ideas, if only because no one else is good at it or has the capacity, the resources, and the interest to do it. For example, the government will want to play a role in such areas as contending with climate change, promoting development in Aboriginal communities, dealing with natural disasters, and building basic infrastructure. The pressure to do something comes from bureaucracy, the media, interest groups, the international community, the courts, and politicians from all sides. The pressure to intervene often has very little to do with political ideology and everything to do with the pursuit and retention of political power and for government to be seen attacking wicked problems.

There is a growing body of literature on society's wicked problems and on the role of government in addressing them.[12] Wicked problems are highly complex, require a range of perspectives to address them, and defy definitive solutions.[13] They also require committing resources and paying proper attention to implementation, with little assurance that the proposed solutions will have the desired impact. But they cannot be ignored. The private sector has little interest or patience in dealing with such problems, viewing them as akin to lost causes, better left to government or even unattended.[14]

History also reveals that governments do intervene to attack wicked problems. Government will all too often look to new funds to deal with such problems rather than reallocate resources from the existing budget. No government will ignore a national disaster, be indifferent to an Aboriginal community facing a political or economic crisis, or avoid debate that rages on about the impact of climate change. Wicked problems have no visible beginning or end. They often require changing the behaviour of individuals through government programs, education, fines, taxes, or other sanctions. They require investing resources, again with no assurance that the desired benefits will be achieved, and often without the tools to assess the impact.

GOVERNMENT AND VISIONARY INVESTMENTS

Governments can come up with big ideas and successfully put together visionary investments, which it does not often get credit for. The government of Canada had a direct hand in building the railways, Air Canada, the infrastructure for air service, the country's automobile industry, and the list goes on.

Many Canadians applauded Chris Hadfield when he became the first Canadian to walk in space and when he was chosen to be the commander of the International Space Station. Without government, Hadfield would not have gone into space. Canada's space agency has since decided to play a lead role in pushing back the frontiers of knowledge and investing in leading-edge innovations, including a major contribution to the development of a space telescope.[15] If the government had not stepped in, none of this would have happened.

We recently learned that US scientists are a step closer to developing fusion energy. If they are successful, we will have access to virtually an inexhaustible supply of energy. They have been working on the initiative for years and are still in no position to put a specific date on when they will reach the final step. One thing is certain: without government, the development of fusion energy would be many generations away, or never happen.[16]

Government also had a direct hand in developing the Internet, GPS positioning, and nuclear power. In Canada, the government can claim to have played a pioneer role in developing the country's aerospace industry and a number of pharmaceutical products.[17] To be sure, high-performing national economies have a strong entrepreneurial private sector, but they also have a public sector heavily involved in research and development funding and in putting together visionary funding, which would otherwise not be provided.

Governments were crucial in development of such high-profile firms as Apple, Google, and BlackBerry. The US government provided pivotal funding to Apple in its early stages with a $500,000 loan before it went public. However, that was only the tip of the iceberg. Batteries developed by the US Department of Energy power the iPod, iPhone, and iPad. Liquid-crystal display was developed by the National Institute of Health, the National Science Foundation, and the Department of Defense, and the intelligent personal assistant employed in Apple's operating system was developed by the US Defense Advanced Research Projects Agency.[18]

The National Science Foundation provided a grant that produced the algorithm that led to Google's search engine. BlackBerry benefitted from assistance and procurement contracts from the government of Canada in its early years. It still does with federal public servants equipped with a BlackBerry, rather than the iPhone. A partial list of commercial products that flowed out of the space program include freeze-dried food, Dustbusters, Speedo swimsuits, hand-held high-density LED units, scratch-resistant lenses, improved radial tires, and solar cells.[19]

McCain Foods today dominates the world's frozen french fry market, but it is highly unlikely that it would have been able to do so without generous government funding in its formative years.[20] Donald Young, a plant biologist working in a regional research centre with the federal Department of Agriculture, developed the Shepody potato, which transformed the frozen french fry business in Canada, then in Europe. The Shepody is now grown around the world and is one of the three most grown varieties in North America. Leading private sector executives in the frozen food business readily admit that no private sector firm would have developed the Shepody, at least in the 1960s, because it lacked the incentives to undertake the required fundamental research.[21]

They also argue, however, that it is highly unlikely that a government biologist would develop the Shepody today. They make the point that "federal public servants are more risk-averse today" and preoccupied with writing "reports about the state of the agriculture sector than undertak-[ing] practical research."[22]

Firms have little interest in admitting that their success is a result of a helping hand from government, either through direct financial assistance, a timely procurement contract in their formative years, or products flowing out of government-sponsored research and development. In Canada, the government's war effort in the 1940s laid the foundation for a significant part of the country's manufacturing sector, through the establishment of thirty-two Crown corporations to produce, among other things, aircraft, synthetic rubber, and advanced technologies.[23] Many of these Crown corporations were later privatized, and some of them are still in operation. Governments developed the Saint Lawrence Seaway, which enables ocean-going vessels to navigate from the Atlantic Ocean to the Great Lakes, thus allowing Canadian businesses to export their products.

Government investment in research and development has also led to a wide number of commercially viable products. One can find them in the medical field, information technology, the transportation sector, and the energy field. It is likely more than a coincidence that countries that suffered the most from the 2008 financial crisis were those that had the lowest levels of government-led R&D investment.[24]

This is not to suggest that all visionary investments have been successful, but some have. To be sure, visionary investments are very expensive, uncertainty is high, and it is virtually impossible to see a profit, at least for the immediate future. In brief, government is good at defining big "public good" initiatives and doing things that would otherwise "not get done at all" because the markets lack the incentives to provide public goods.[25] They are classic "public goods," in that investment in fundamental research sponsored by governments is designed to advance knowledge and have a long-term horizon, making it difficult for private firms to appropriate returns, thus the public good argument.[26] These investments can bring a number of benefits to society – notably training and employment – and, in time, turn out commercially viable products and new economic opportunities. Many economic analysts now keep a close watch on R&D investments, publications in peer-reviewed journals, and the share of patent applications to assess a country's economic strength and prospects.[27]

In brief, government is good at looking to the long term, dealing with wicked problems, and making visionary investments. This allows it to play a pivotal role in creating the economy of the future, and countries that have governments that are good at it will have stronger economies. This makes the point once again that government should do things that no one else is doing, wishes to do, or is able to do.[28] In short, governments are better at establishing circumstances for success than at managing success. They are good at this or better than anyone else, if only because no one else is willing to step up to the plate.

In a representative democracy, it is the visionary investments, the attempts to deal with wicked problems, transparent and corrupt-free political and administrative institutions, and a capacity to deal with all citizens with integrity and fairness that are key to a country's economic prosperity and political stability. Canada has seen political stability and solid economic growth for the past seventy years. It has always been at the forefront in defending human liberties. It has also remained relatively corruption-free where the rule of law applies, and the press is free to roam essentially where it wants. Canada has become a respected member of G8 and G20 countries. Bloomberg ranks Canada second in the world as a country to do business.[29]

Governments can claim some of the credit for this state of affairs. Where things break down for government is more in the "how" and less in the "what," or, in the implementation stages, in dealing with the deficient processes of public administration and in isolating better the requirements of contemporary politics from management.

It is important to stress that visionary investments, leaving aside some notable exceptions, do not require government to manage operations or deliver the products. Though sponsored by government, the work is carried out in arm's-length organizations or in the private sector. Put differently, government does not manage economic success, leaving that to others. While government funds the investments, outside researchers are asked to turn the investments into concrete products. They are free to operate on the periphery of the requirements of contemporary politics, away from the blame game, the immediate concerns of those operating above the fault line, and having to deal with the deficiencies in public administration – all critical factors in being able to operate efficiently. These are factors that many outside government do not appreciate.

CONTEMPORARY POLITICS:
IT EXPLAINS MANY SHORTCOMINGS
IN GOVERNMENT OPERATIONS

Politics has never been for the faint of heart. Not only have the arts of the possible and of compromise been made more difficult today, politicians do not enjoy the standing in society that they once did, as has been well documented elsewhere.[30] Part of it is their own doing. However, politicians also have to deal with a better informed and more educated population, numerous transparency requirements, and the social media, which have all made life more difficult for them and made governing more demanding. This in turn has an impact on what government does well and less well.

Former deputy prime minister Sheila Copps describes politics "as a dirty game."[31] Michael Ignatieff, who left the world of academe for the political arena, described politics as a game with no referee in which players make up the rules as they go along. "Anything goes," he writes. And he adds, "Of the three elections that I fought, none was a debate on the country's future. All were vicious battles over standing. It is striking that in five and a half years in politics, none of my opponents ever bothered to attack what I was saying, what my platform said, or what I wanted to do for the country. They were too busy attacking me."[32] Despite the cruel fate that politics served him, he still maintained that "politicians are the custodians of democracy, of a relationship of trust with the people, but also of the institutions of your country."[33] The fact is we have no backup plan: politicians, political institutions, and public servants are what we have to make our system of governance work and to make our society function coherently.

Politics, with all its partisanships, conflicts, power struggles, imperfections, and obsession with managing media spin still remains the only tested alternative to government by coercion.[34] If the imperfections have not become more numerous in recent years, they certainly have become more visible. They have also made it much more difficult for those willing to serve, and this should be of concern to all citizens.

Ignatieff did not shy away from expressing his deep concern about the state of Canadian politics. He said, "Canadians are staring at a hollowed-out democracy, in which solitary politicians hurl abuse at each other in an empty chamber, and power accrues ever more steadily to the prime minister, to the Supreme Court, to the bureaucracy and to the press. And all of them regard the people elected to represent the people with contempt and derision. That would be terrible and that's close to where we are."[35]

It would indeed be terrible, and there is a direct link between the health of political institutions and what government can be good at. Only politicians can heal political institutions; they are their institutions to fix. They need to start by looking at the state of how they play adversarial politics. I cannot do better than quote Nevil Johnson:

> The danger of adversary politics ... is that it encourages persistent irresponsible competition and too much oversimplification ... Where conflict does not exist, adversary politics manufactures it; where genuine conflict is present, adversary politics exacerbates it, and yet may frustrate its resolution; and where the clash of opinions and interests is many-sided and complex, adversary politics offers little hope of creating that basis of consensus which is indispensable if there is to be effective political authority. These are the difficulties to which a particular style of politics has given rise. They are likely to be overcome only through changes in the ground rules of political life, which would change the adversary mould itself.[36]

Tom Flanagan, described by the media as an architect of what partisan politics has become, acknowledges that in the current political culture one does whatever it takes to win. More to the point, "people and principles are expendable. Dissent is not tolerated. Policies are props that are fashioned to appeal to voters. Everything is evaluated through the prism of whether it will help or hurt the leader."[37]

Political institutions pay a heavy price when political "ruthlessness" sets in. While it may well be important for politicians on the government side to see government good at managing the requirements of contemporary politics, including the blame game, it appears that many voters do not share this view. One only has to look at declining voter turnout for evidence. Voters do not always understand how the

machinery of government operates and decides, but they do understand personal attacks in the era of permanent election campaigns.
MPs "trashing" one another and their institutions is akin to trashing
the idea of politics and public service.[38] This makes it exceedingly difficult for both political institutions and government to be good at
many things.

For one thing, it is becoming increasingly difficult for people to
serve. There are few successful business persons, academics, or individuals in other professions who are willing to enter the political arena
with its constant media scrutiny, ruthlessness of partisan politics, and
demands of the day. There are too many disincentives to induce them
to serve in politics. The hyper-partisanship, having to parrot the talk-
ing-points dictated by party leaders and their advisors, and having to
deal with a plethora of oversight bodies is not to everyone's taste. Journalists also report that social media and emails make it very difficult
for the mainstream media to avoid stories about the private lives of
public figures.[39]

The requirements of contemporary politics may well explain why
our political class is increasingly dominated by career politicians.
They start younger and rise to the top a lot faster. Though they bring
a narrow skill set to their work, they excel at partisan politics and at
surviving the gruelling twenty-four-hour news cycle and social media.
However, they lack the ability to test policy prescriptions against experiences gained outside of politics. Yet when dealing with the advice
from public servants, they often "know better" because they too have
made politics and government their life. This, among other factors,
has put public servants on the defensive.[40]

Public servants openly talk about the serious morale problem that
plagues their institution. As already noted, evidence-based policy
advice, once the terrain of the public service, is no longer as valued as
it once was. Too many senior public servants are kept busy managing
the blame game, serving the prime minister's court, and overseeing
the production of performance and evaluation reports to ensure that
they are properly sanitized so as to cause minimum damage to their
political masters and their departments. They are good at doing this,
but it comes at the expense of being good at other things, notably
addressing a broader agenda that speaks to the public interest and at
ensuring that the implementation side of government is as good as it
needs to be.

Unlike the private sector, where the bottom line is an unrelenting measure of success and failure, things are never that straightforward inside government. Citizens may not value the ability to generate or manage blame, to sidestep accountability requirements by producing bland performance reports, and to promote whiz-bang ideas. However, politicians on the government side do, and they value colleagues and public servants with these abilities.

Citizens meanwhile may well conclude that leader-centric, media-driven, permanent election campaigns, the growing influence of single-issue interest groups, public sector unions, and an overloaded machinery of government have degraded the ability of government to be good at formulating, and especially at implementing politics that are in the broader public interest. Senior politicians on the government side and senior public servants likely regard contemporary politics as the reality within which they have to work, a reality from which they cannot escape. We thus need to nuance our assessment of what government is good at and recognize that things look different inside government.

GOVERNING COMPLEXITY

Governing has become more complex because societies have become more complex, while businesses and citizens have become hesitant about the role of government in the economy.[41] Government is no longer the repository of knowledge in all key sectors. Specialized knowledge is now available to any who know their way around a computer, who have access to think tanks, research institutes, data on government departmental websites in Canada and abroad, including statistical agencies. Single-issue groups or associations know how to find and make use of this information to press their case before government, the judicial courts, and the court of public opinion.

The private sector now also has a larger presence in the public policy arena than in years past, thus adding more voices and more hands to the shaping of public policy, and that makes governing more complex and implementation more difficult. The National Energy Program (NEP) was a seminal moment in Canada's public policy-making and had a profound and lasting impact on how the private sector deals with governments.

The program was widely condemned, particularly in Western Canada.[42] As we well know, bumper stickers appeared: "Let the Eastern Bas-

tards Freeze in the Dark." The business community became highly critical of the program, and particularly of the fact that it was taken by surprise. The NEP was introduced without warning, as part of the 1981 federal budget. No less worrisome for the private sector, business-friendly
ministers in Cabinet were also taken by surprise.[43] The budget closed
a number of tax advantages for the business community at a time
when economic growth had come to a stop. Many business people
decided that action was urgently needed to ensure that they would
never again be taken by another surprise like the NEP. They decided
then that government was not good at assessing the health of the economy and at avoiding measures that could put it into a recession.

The fallout sent a shockwave throughout Ottawa. Ian Stewart, a
widely respected career public servant, resigned as deputy minister of
finance, and the minister of finance, Allan J. MacEachen, was shuffled
out of the department. The Alberta premier, Peter Lougheed, was able
to secure a promise from Brian Mulroney that, if Mulroney were to
become prime minister, he would immediately fire Ed Clark, the
architect of the NEP.[44] He kept his promise, and Clark went on to a
highly successful career in banking, culminating as president and CEO
of the Toronto Dominion Canada Trust.[45]

From that moment on, the business community turned increasingly to lobbyists and organized groups to protect its interest before governments. It provided funding to think tanks, associations, and organizations with mandates to promote a business-friendly perspective
in shaping new policies. A small group of business leaders based in
Toronto and Ottawa got together in 1987, for example, to launch such
a new group, the Public Policy Forum, whose purpose was to encourage the private sector to "seek ways of using its knowledge and experience more directly in charting national policies."[46] To encourage this
emphasis, the forum seeks to foster strong two-way communication
between senior government representatives and the business community. To secure the necessary funding to operate, the group enlisted
eighteen corporate sponsors, including some of Canada's largest firms,
such as Gulf Canada, IBM Canada, Imperial Oil, and the Royal Bank of
Canada. It also obtained the support of three federal departments.[47]

Other business groups were similarly created to influence governments. One, the Canadian Council of Chief Executives, labels itself
"the senior voice of Canada's business community, representing 150
chief executives ... responsible for most of Canada's private sector

investments, exports …"[48] A former senior minister in the Chrétien government is the organization's CEO and it too sponsors a host of studies and produces recommendations on public policy.

In January 2014, for example, it tabled a report claiming that public satisfaction with Canada's public school system was low. The report offered a series of recommendations on how to improve the school system, including hiring teachers on the basis of merit, not seniority, and suggesting that teachers' performance should be evaluated more rigorously and conducted more often. Making recommendations was the easy part. The more difficult part is how to implement them. How best to evaluate the performance of teachers? Who should evaluate them? How to bring public sector unions onside?[49] How can one develop an evaluation system that punishes the incompetent teacher without crippling the competent one?[50] The devil in public policy does not come forward in the recommendations but rather in their implementation.

The report raises several important points. First, the perception, if not the reality, is that government is not as good as it once was in developing policy. Second, in public policy, everyone knows more about the subject than the ones actually delivering the program, or, in this case, everyone knows more about teaching than the teachers.[51] Third, organized groups and even senior public servants, as we shall see below, tend to focus far too much effort on shaping new policy and far too little on its implementation, the phase without which the initiative cannot succeed. Fourth, there are now many organized groups in society from the business community to single-issue groups, whose sole purpose is to have a say in creating a public policy while offering very little on how best to implement it. Emphasis is often exclusively on what should be done and on policy prescriptions, rarely on how it should be done. Fifth, the business community never hesitates to tell government that it is failing in many areas of public policy, but few in the public sector are any longer prepared to criticize the private sector. Governments have lowered corporate taxes, streamlined their regulatory regimes, and signed free-trade agreements. Yet one rarely sees a government official tell the business community to step up to the plate and create more jobs or do something about income disparities. Governments simply no longer have the credibility to do so, and public sector institutions do not have the self-confidence to speak out. It will be recalled, for example, that in the immediate aftermath of the 2008 economic crisis, governments turned to senior private sector executives for ideas to stimulate the economy. Sixth, those with the resources or access to resources will go to great lengths to influence policy, leaving those without the resources on the outside looking in.

Last, there is a disconnect between stated government goals and what is actually accomplished. This disjunction triggers a serious legitimation problem for government. The goal of establishing a "nationally and in time an internationally recognized centre of excellence" with the Canadian Centre for Management Development (CCMD), later renamed the Canada School of Public Service, has fallen far shy of the mark. Mulroney's commitment to "inflict prosperity on Atlantic Canada" when he established the Atlantic Canada Opportunities Agency (ACOA) has also similarly gone adrift, as has Chrétien's pledge that his "bold plan" would ensure that Atlantic Canadians can take their "rightful place in the new economy."

Governments are largely responsible for the growing pressure on their finances. The public sector is still not good at reallocating resources to reflect changing circumstances and priorities. The machinery of government relies far too much on the prime minister's decision to launch and pursue a program review and essentially to across-the-board cuts to reduce expenditures. Such exercises, much more than other reforms, account for the bulk of productivity improvements. Government operations remain too expensive, and government now generates too many reports and sponsors too many activities inside government that are of limited value to those outside of government and, often, to those inside. The point is that government is good at generating sharp squeezes on spending but much less good at producing and sticking with long-range financial plans.

The result is that government is not good at starving low-priority activities in order to fund high-priority ones, all too often relying on new money to support high-profile initiatives. Core responsibilities or responsibilities that government should be good at, such as a well-functioning regulatory regime, are treated the same as all other activities and subjected to across-the-board cuts whenever the prime minister puts his mind to it.

FOR THE REST, IT'S THE PRIME MINISTER

There is only one policy actor in government – the prime minister – who can establish a clear goal and see to it that departments pursue it. All political and policy roads lead to his office. Governing from the centre is now firmly entrenched, and it is how things work in Ottawa. When I published *Governing from the Centre* in 1999, some questioned whether I had overstated the case.[52] I hear no such voices now, and governing from the centre is taken as a given by public servants and many politicians, including Cabinet ministers. Cabinet is now no more than a focus group – how else can it be explained that two key decisions on Canada's deployment in Afghanistan, one by a Liberal government and the other by a Conservative government, were made by prime ministers and their courtiers when the relevant ministers (National Defence and Foreign Affairs) were not even in the room.[53] It is one thing to strike major political decisions without consulting Cabinet. It is quite another to not even involve the responsible ministers. Cabinet government, it seems, now belongs to the history books.

There was also a time, not long ago, when regional ministers played an important role in Ottawa's decision-making.[54] This is no longer the case.[55] Regional ministers have no profile in Ottawa and very little even in their home provinces. They have been replaced by courtiers in the PMO and favourite pollsters in the prime minister's court. It is important to underline the point that the more political power is disseminated, the less likely it will be captured by political and economic elites and vested interests.

However, there are limits to how many goals the prime minister can give life to and ensure that they are pursued as directed. And even the prime minister has to contend with public opinion, a powerful force that can never be ignored, particularly when an election is on the horizon. Prime ministers lead very busy lives, much more than the busiest private-sector chief executive officer. The rarest of commodities in Ottawa is time with the prime minister. Everyone, it seems, wants it, from his chief of staff, the clerk of the Privy Council, thirty-nine Cabinet ministers, members of the government caucus, ten provincial premiers, foreign heads of government, some heads of international organizations, leading members of the business community, a handful of lobbyists who are known supporters, some journalists, and the more senior members of his political party.

All prime ministers have a political and policy agenda and pet projects to pursue. They and their staff will keep their eyes on the ball to see them through.[56] Policies, programs, and issues that do not enjoy priority with the prime minister are expected to run on their tracks and not create problems for the government. This matters inside government and to those operating above the fault line, far more than is assumed by those outside government. If there is one theme that emerges from the political memoirs of former Canadian politicians, it is that small mistakes will do you in, not large policy issues.[57]

All this explains a great deal about how government functions and why government operations are not run as efficiently as they once were. As Francis Fukuyama maintains, creativity and innovation require a high level of autonomy and risk-taking.[58] To delegate authority to front-line program managers, allowing them to improvise and to adjust programs so as to accommodate changing circumstances is much too risky in the era of permanent election campaigns. It also explains why government scientists are not free to share their findings or to voice concerns, for fear of creating problems for those working above the fault line. Consequently, they are expected to play by the same rules as all other public servants operating below the fault line. Blame avoidance pervades government organizations at all levels and shapes the working of government to a far greater extent than is generally believed.

The bulk of government departments, agencies, and programs are expected to avoid providing fodder for the media, while the prime minister and his court focus on priorities that matter to them and the government. But when goals are vague, circumstances and events of the day dominate.[59] In this climate, management discretion is the byword. However, management discretion does not easily square with managing permanent election campaigns from the centre, knowing that it is the small mistakes that will do you in, not large policy issues. The risk for the prime minister and his courtiers is too high. This explains why talk of empowerment is always central to every new wave of public service reform, but invariably falls out of fashion.[60] Government is as good as the private sector in stressing the importance of empowerment to managers in line departments, but it seldom goes further than talk. This in turn explains the tendency in government to delegate decisions upward for resolution rather than down, even decisions that should normally be taken by front-line managers. It is a safer route for managers.

Dealing with circumstances and events of the day, as best one can without management discretion, does not, however, make for effective or efficient organizations. This is felt particularly down the line in departments and agencies where, without a clear mandate for change from the prime minister, they are simply expected not to rock the boat. It explains why some are convinced that if the government was running Ford Motors, it would still be producing the Edsel.[61] It also explains why the main problem with government expenditure is not so much what it spends on new initiatives but what it continues to spend on old ones that have outlived their usefulness. In short, government is good at generating new ideas and often at managing political controversies. It is not so good at scrutinizing existing expenditures, implementing ideas, and delegating authority.

Governing from the centre and the importance attached to managing the blame game stifles creativity and promotes a stale and risk-averse bureaucracy, at a time when the political and economic environment cries out for creativity and innovation.

MEA CULPA

Public servants may well be tempted to tell politicians and political institutions, "Heal thyself." However, public servants also have a lot to answer for. Government is no longer as good as it once was in delivering programs and services. Though some of the reasons for this state of affairs are beyond their control, public servants need to take ownership for a number of others and accept a good part of the responsibility. Public sector unions also need to ask themselves whether their approach harks back to an irrelevant era and whether they have become part of what ails government operations.

Senior public servants cannot blame politicians for the creation of the numerous management levels in line departments and agencies. There is little to prevent senior public servants from reducing the number of management layers between top and bottom to no more than six. This would strengthen government operations and improve morale among rank-and-file public servants. Public servants also need to accept responsibility for the loss of a parsimonious culture in government, for how else can one explain that the only time that spending is reduced and public service positions are eliminated is when the prime minister launches a program review and then keeps an eye on it to ensure its success? It is the public servants, not the politicians, who created the multitude of "associate" positions in management levels. Government managers and public sector unions, not politicians, need to explain why they are unable to deal with non-performers.

Notwithstanding numerous measures to make the public sector look like the private sector, there are still no or little consequences in government for a job done poorly, and public servants themselves must accept a good part of the blame. Public servants also remain more concerned about protecting or expanding their budgets than in the efficient performance of their units or departments.[62]

The requirements of the global economy have imposed discipline on the private sector, but not on government operations. We saw earlier that 71 per cent of public sector employees belong to a union, compared to only about 17 per cent for the private sector. It is revealing to note that there were several strikes in my province in late 2013 and early 2014 – all in the public sector, none in the private. Non-government employees have every right to ask why public sector employees can remain isolated from the requirements of the global economy. Public sector unions have become a very conservative force, making change to government operations and management practices very difficult at a time when change is buffeting everyone else.

Wayne Wouters, a former clerk of the Privy Council, referring to the government's sick-leave policy, went public with his views that "our system is not conducive to a modern workforce."[63] In the absence of market forces and the pressure of the marketplace, there is no incentive to change or to innovate. On average, Canadians miss 9 work days a year for illness, disability, and other personal reasons, but when one isolates the public sector, the number jumps to 12.5 days.[64] Public sector unions have demonstrated a knee-jerk reaction against change. They have, for example, recently challenged the government's efforts to sharpen its employee performance regime, opposed government attempts to claw back sick leave and disability benefits, and resisted the government's decision to eliminate severance pay.[65] These are hardly isolated cases.

Study after study also points to the lack of productivity in government, compared with the private sector, this after some thirty-five years of NPM measures. A recent study, for example, revealed that even dentists in government are substantially less productive than their private sector counterparts.[66] There are many other similar examples.[67] The public sector priced itself out of many activities, now gone to the private sector and to volunteer associations, and public servants and public sector unions need to explain why.[68] If one compares government and private sector provision of similar services, the private sector almost always performs more cost-effectively.[69]

Public servants, not just politicians, are responsible for the public sector's loss of standing in society and for the perception, if not the reality, that government is not as good as it once was in shaping policy and delivering programs and services. The socio-economic conditions that gave licence to government in the 1960s and 1970s to expand operations, become the model employer, and show other employers how to deal with employees are gone. Unless public servants and public sector unions come to terms with this reality, they will not be able to regain the confidence of Canadians.

WE ARE ALSO TO BLAME

We voters also need to share responsibility for this state of affairs. An example speaks eloquently to that reality. In the mid-1970s, the large Canadian retailer Eaton's closed its catalogue operations in Moncton, New Brunswick, throwing 1,000 people out of work. Monctonians essentially looked on the matter as a business decision, and there was little protest by the local media and community leaders. Governments were asked to intervene with special job-creation measures, but there were no demonstrations against Eaton's itself, and the company was not asked to keep its catalogue operations open.

In contrast, however, when CN decided in the 1980s that it no longer required its repair and maintenance shops in Moncton, Roméo LeBlanc, a powerful minister in the Trudeau Cabinet representing the riding adjoining Moncton and at a time when regional ministers had some political clout, made it clear to CN that closing "the Moncton shops would not be acceptable – period."[70] CN knew full well that it would not be any easier to close the Winnipeg or the Montreal shops, because both cities were represented by powerful Cabinet ministers – Lloyd Axworthy (Winnipeg) and Marc Lalonde (Montreal). CN simply had to carry on with the status quo, no matter the cost to taxpayers.

With the election of the Mulroney government, CN again sought to close the Moncton shops, and this time there was no senior Cabinet minister to fight for Moncton. With only one junior minister representing New Brunswick, CN was finally able to close the Moncton shops. The reaction in Moncton was swift, highly vocal, and determined. The local member of Parliament was asked to resign, a "Save Our Shop" committee consisting of leading community spokespersons was established, several widely reported demonstrations took place, and the matter dominated the local media for three years. Municipal, provincial, and some federal politicians insisted that the "federal government" was treating Moncton unfairly. In short, Monctonians had one set of expectations for government – even for Crown corporations operating in a competitive environment and at arm's length from the government – and another for the private sector. When a leading member of the Moncton community was asked to comment on this discrepancy, he responded that "business must make business decisions. Otherwise the business will not survive long. Eaton's is a business and it must compete. In government, especially in the federal government, there is a great deal of waste. Moncton is not getting its share of the waste. In losing the CN shops, we are now getting even less of our share."[71]

Politicians were responding to voters' wishes when they decided to privatize a number of Crown corporations. Precious few voices are being heard calling for these businesses to be renationalized. Among other former Crowns, CN is today a private sector firm with a much freer hand to shut down activities. It decided in early 2014 to discontinue operations on a seventy-kilometre stretch of its line, thus jeopardizing passenger-rail service between the Maritime provinces and the rest of Canada. This time, public pressure to save the line was directed at the government, not at CN. In the end, the government did come to the rescue with funding to save and repair the line.[72] This is but one of many examples of public sector organizations being unable to manage as efficiently as their private sector counterparts, because voters will not easily let them do so. It makes the case once again that government is better at establishing the circumstances for economic success than at managing economic success.

This is hardly an isolated story. Ontarians know a great deal about government inability to compete in the marketplace. A debate has raged in the media for the past few years about the failings of Ontario Power Generation (OPG), which, despite having made a number of misguided and costly decisions, keeps rolling on. It prompted one observer to write, "OPG seems to have adopted the same grading scale as an elementary school: Nobody fails. Two-thirds of executives and top managers have received 'high scores' on their performance evaluations since 2010, entitling them to bonuses of up to 150 percent of their base salaries. Senior management grew to 238 people last year from 152 in 2005, despite a 20-per-cent drop in the amount of electricity the utility generates. Vice-presidents and directors with 'no specific titles or job descriptions' more than tripled to 40 people, 'with each earning healthy six-figure salaries.'"[73]

LOOKING BACK

Government is at its best when establishing circumstances for economic success, dealing with society's wicked problems, and pursuing an all-encompassing goal that enjoys broad public support. Government also remains the best-suited actor in society to ensure equality, fairness, and justice in delivering certain public services. Government is the only actor that should enjoy a monopoly on the legitimate use of violence in society. It is also the single actor that can establish a regulatory regime to promote the public interest.

However, government is no match for the private sector in managing economic success. Government has not been able to instil an entrepreneurial culture and a bias for action in departmental organizations or below the fault line. Politicians continue to point to the same problem and essentially come up with the same solutions as Margaret Thatcher and her contemporaries in Anglo-American democracies did thirty-five years ago. Yet government is actually moving away from a private-sector management culture in government.

The numerous measures, starting with the Thatcher reforms of the early 1980s to recent New Public Management initiatives, were and are all designed to fix government below the fault line. In Canada, and even in Britain where they got their start, such efforts have fallen short of expectations. How else can one explain a lead editorial in the *Times* in the summer of 2013, some thirty years after the Thatcher revolution, that argued, "The virtues of the central Civil Service have not changed in more than a century, but neither have its vices," or a front page article in the *Financial Times* with the headline "Whitehall to Adopt Business Style in Unified Management Overhaul?"[74] B. Guy Peters maintains that if there is a consensus on past attempts to reform government operations, it is that most end in failure: "Reading evaluations of major government reform efforts from a number of national settings appears to indicate that a finding of no significant results is often the indicator of a reform success, while a failure often is characterized by serious negative side effects."[75] In Canada, all public service renewals have left the public service worse off, at least below the fault line.[76]

The rhetoric from thirty-five years ago remains the same, yet government managers still cannot prune their organizations, reallocate resources from within, or deal with non-performers. The tendency is for government operations and bureaucracy to grow and grow until the prime minister decides that the time is ripe for a program review. One is left with the conclusion that, left to its own devices, government bureaucracy would simply grow year after year. In brief, we continue to misdiagnose the patient.[77]

Why? The problem with bureaucracy below the fault line has everything to do with what happens above it. We citizens retain a double standard, imposing requirements on government operations that we do not impose on other sectors. Politicians and the media engage in a blame game that has no parallel in years past and has a profound impact on the work of program managers. We continue to add transparency requirements and expand the number and size of oversight bodies, thinking somehow that they will generate better management practices.

In summary, several powerful forces now inhibit the performance of government in defining the public interest, shaping public policy, and delivering programs and services. They range from a nearly dysfunctional Parliament, to a drop in social cohesion, an overloaded government, leader-centric political parties and their courtiers, the blame game, the rise of the new media, the shift to performance accountability and the inability to make it work, the growing fault line dividing the public service, the tendency for those operating above the fault line to view policy-making as 90 per cent ideas and 10 per cent implementation, the growing involvement of the courts in shaping public policies and even in laying down parameters on how they should be implemented, the focus on new initiatives and "whiz-bang" ideas, and citizens' double standard for the public and private sector.[78]

Other fundamental challenges confront our political and administrative institutions. Both need to resonate better with citizens and provide greater access to them to influence their policy and decision-making processes. It is in the citizens' interest that their voice be better heard and that the performance of government improves. The concluding chapter explores these issues.

12

Upstairs, Downstairs

The increasingly deficient processes of public administration outlined earlier hold wide implications, not only for the role of government in society but also for the capacity of citizens to influence their governments. Contemporary politics and the processes of public administration have created an upstairs-downstairs to governing. Interest groups and the economic elites, with the required resources to navigate the complex processes of government and the courts, can access the policy- and decision-makers who matter to the prime minister and his courtiers, while the average citizen is increasingly disconnected from the processes of government.

Implementation issues that matter to efficient public administration and to the average citizens are left to run on their tracks. Yet many implementation issues, given how the blame game works, can now be resolved only at the most senior levels. The distance between where difficult and even not so difficult issues surface and where effective decision-making now resides in government is such that, leaving aside those that matter to the prime minister and his courtiers, only the ones that grab the attention of the media in a negative light will be sent to the proper levels for resolution.

Yet good intentions expressed in policy pronouncements or even in law can and very often do run aground in the implementation phase or below the fault line.[1] Jeffrey L. Pressman and Aaron Wildavsky stressed the importance of implementation in *Implementation*, which was widely read at the time.[2] The book inspired studies on the gap between policy formulation and program implementation. Andrew Graham described Pressman and Wildavsky's book as a "wake-up call, a shock of cold water."[3] However, the wake-up call was not heard inside governments. The gap between policy formulation and implementation has not narrowed over the past forty years; if anything, it is now much wider.

As the public-policy environment becomes more complex, policy-making also becomes more porous and as various reform efforts, such as New Public Management measures, never live up to expectations, implementation becomes still more uncertain. Governing from the centre has established even more distance between the key policy makers and front-line program managers. If one includes associate positions in the mix, there are now anywhere between eight and thirteen levels between a front-line manager in a line department and the prime minister. As already noted, in contrast, the Roman Catholic Church has five levels between the parish priest and the pope. All key decisions and what truly matters in government, at least to those who hold effective power, take place above the fault line, but what often truly matters to the average citizen often takes place below it.

Average citizens tend to assess how good government is by how long it takes to secure a decision on their applications, by wait times before talking to a public servant on a designated 1-800 number, by real or perceived waste in program delivery, and by comparison of their wages and benefits with those of public servants. Western governments are now dominated by the centre, by prime ministers and presidents, together with thousands of highly educated public servants. All are far removed from implementation. Thousands of ambitious, upwardly mobile, and well-connected public servants are very good at generating ideas, falling on hand grenades, devising solutions to political problems, selling new government measures, and better at bringing a broader perspective on politics, policy issues, and the machinery of government than are public servants operating below the fault line. That is why many join the public service: to be part of the action, to be in the thick of things, and to contribute to policy-making. There is also always a ready market for their work. The prime minister and courtiers are constantly on the lookout for fresh thinking to old problems that they have an interest in: how to deal with a difficult issue, how to get a minister out of a political quagmire, how to make a government initiative look good in the media. These public servants look up to see how well they are doing, not down to line departments. Looking up holds important rewards, looking down, precious few.

This is but one of many signs of the tendency to adopt an upstairs-downstairs approach to governing. The upstairs of government has also grown in recent years at the expense of the downstairs – recall that some forty years ago 28 per cent of federal public servants worked in the National Capital Region (NCR). Today, the number is over 43 per cent. The two most recent major program review exercises also hit the regional and field offices harder than those in the NCR.[4]

Public servants operating at the centre, or consultants and lobbyists operating close to the centre, dominate the idea-generating function of government. These are people with strong political skills – not necessarily partisan ones – and again they are highly valued. It explains why they also populate central agencies and why they are now increasingly found in line departments and agencies at the more senior levels and in various policy, liaison, or coordination shops.

A provincial minister of finance once explained the importance of the idea-generators to government: "The only way we feel we can get elected is to invent something new – to come up with some whiz-bang idea that's going to capture votes."[5] Once in power, the prime minister and senior ministers and their advisors are in no mood to be told that what they want is impossible because it is not administratively feasible.[6] The goal is to announce the "whiz-bang" idea, not to become captured in the details of implementation. Public servants above the fault line are expected to come up with the whiz-bang ideas or, failing that, to package the ideas, to see them through, and to ensure that they are made public in the most positive light. One can assume that they are good at doing that.

All governments, wherever they may sit on the political spectrum, always need someone safe at the centre to plan, package, and announce whiz-bang ideas. The Harper government has often talked about the need to shrink government and to eliminate programs. But even with a majority mandate, it does not hesitate to play "retail politics" and come up with new spending plans. In the summer of 2013 and in the immediate aftermath of his program review, Harper himself, and several of his ministers, criss-crossed the country to announce a host of new spending commitments in several sectors. Harper unveiled new expenditures for harbours in several communities, while his ministers did the same for the canola industry, infrastructure, aerospace, defence, measures to promote Canadian exports, regional development, and the list goes on.[7] Government spending has increased by about 23 per cent since Harper came to power.[8]

Senior public servants operating above the fault line are also highly valued because hardly a day goes by without a need to defuse a

political controversy, the kind of controversy that rarely, if ever, sur-
faces in the private sector. The need for quick thinking, the ability to
come up with a suggestion to make the prime minister and ministers
appear in control and decisive in the twenty-four hour news cycle and
in the social media, has come to matter a great deal to the prime minister and his courtiers. Paul Tellier's dictum to the deputy minister's
community – "No surprises" – speaks to this reality. In just one of the
weeks I was working on this book – a typical week in the life of a government – the minister of veterans affairs got in political hot water for
closing local offices, the prime minister had to respond once again to
developments in the Senate scandal, the minister of employment was
urged by the provinces to rethink the government's job grants program, the government had to respond to charges that it was short-
changing Aboriginal communities on policing services, and some
ministers were called on to explain the inclusion of data on digital
communications by Canadian citizens in its national security efforts.[9]

No wonder the trend towards higher numbers of partisan appointments at the centre of government.[10] These advisors again are also
bright, often young, zealous, highly partisan, and out to make the government look good or competent in the media. They work hand-in-
hand with ambitious public servants eager to show their loyalty to the
government of the day, not only to implement the government's agenda, but also to promote it.[11]

A senior finance official, in a mass e-mail, urged public servants to
"retweet messages" to promote the Harper government's new tax measures, using the slogan "Strong Families."[12] The tax proposal included
provisions to allow income splitting for families with children under
eighteen. The proposal had not received parliamentary approval when
the assistant deputy minister sent out his email to all departments in
November 2014. It was also highly controversial with both the New
Democratic Party and the Liberal Party critical of the proposed tax measure.[13] Senior public servants above the fault line are now in the habit
of "demonstrating enthusiasm for the government's agenda, either as a
tactic to advance their careers or in the mistaken notion that neutral
public servants should be, as one British scholar put it, "'promiscuously partisan' – that is, partisan to the government of the day but willing
to change when a different party takes over."[14]

In addition, media attention can, on very short notice, now turn an
issue, however trivial, into an important file that has to be handled by

the centre. The theory, if not the practice, is that a stronger centre allows the top decision-makers to respond quickly to criticism and the blame game, to focus on new policy challenges and on specific issues that matter to the prime minister and his courtiers. The flip side of the theory is that it does not allow the centre to follow many policy issues with tenacity, or for any long stretch of time, to enable the principal to keep tabs on how well the agents are doing at pursuing his or her priorities.[15] It also pushes too many decisions upstairs rather than down the organization, where many properly belong. Only those with the resources or ability to hire the necessary resources have access to those sitting at the top of government organizations.

Idea-generating partisan advisors and public servants in central agencies with no program responsibilities are in an ideal position to assist their political masters to thrive in what Jean Chrétien described as a survival game played under the glare of light.[16] Government units operating upstairs or above the fault line are good at managing public affairs, permanent election campaigns, and navigating a wide and growing array of accountability and transparency requirements. They have also become proficient at dealing with interest groups and associations and lobbyists. Indeed, the majority of lobbyists and Ottawa-based consultants are former politicians, partisan political advisors, and senior public servants.[17] The ability to thread a way through complex policy-making and accountability requirements may not seem important to people outside government, but it is to those inside.

ELITES TALKING TO ELITES

With Parliament losing relevance, with political parties becoming empty vessels in shaping public policy, and with the rise of court government, governing has become a process of economic elites talking to political and bureaucratic elites. The public interest is formed less by evidence-based policy advice and more by elites talking to one another and by party pollsters able to pinpoint a policy initiative that would appeal to a slice of the population whose vote could deliver victory to the party leader. When evidence-based policy loses currency, the door is opened to interest groups, to the loudest voice, and to those with the resources to influence decision-makers.[18] The larger public interest is all too often lost.

One traditional role of MPs is to act as an antidote to the permanent government. But MPs have been pushed aside. As we saw earlier, MPs matter at election time but – and this they readily admit – they too are expected to run on their tracks and not create problems for their party leader. This has given way to a world in which the prime minister's courtiers talk to a handful of senior Cabinet ministers, a few carefully selected deputy ministers, lobbyists, former public servants turned consultants, heads of friendly associations, and some CEOs of larger private firms. This permeates all aspects of government – even regulation. As we saw, smart regulations have all too often given rise to report-writing rather than on-site inspection.

DOWNSTAIRS

As already noted, government is not as good as it once was or as good as it should be below the fault line. Here is where one can draw some parallels with the private sector. Many of the units below the fault line are "machine," "production," or "procedural" organizations.[19] They process applications and tax returns, and provide services to citizens much as private sector firms provide services to customers.

At one time, hard-nosed government managers could compare their work to that of hard-nosed private sector managers.[20] There was a time when decisions in machine- or production-like organizations were made by a single government department, at times within a single office, with the onus squarely on the program manager, but no longer.

We have seen that government is not as good as it needs to be in a fast-changing socio-economic environment when managing financial resources (e.g., it cannot prune programs and organizations unless the prime minister launches an ambitious review after securing a majority mandate), in managing human resources (e.g., it cannot deal with non-performers), and in delegating decision-making authority to managers. The need to empower managers is invariably front and centre in all "vision" exercises and public service reforms. However, it loses all meaning when political and bureaucratic elites have to cope with the political crisis of the day, of which there is never a shortage. Rather than deal with the problems head on, government elites have established a fault line where decisions of any significance are delegated up to them.

We have overloaded the machinery of government with responsibilities, obligations, and oversight requirements. The courts, rather than acting as a constraint on government, have become an instrument to expand its scope. We have set government off on too many new tasks and, in the process, lost sight of what government is good at and the need to resource its core responsibilities properly. But political, bureaucratic, and economic elites always have an agenda that matters to them, independent of what government may be good at.

The prime minister gets his way on matters that matter to him. The clerk of the Privy Council, the deputy minister of finance, the secretary to the Treasury Board, and a handful of senior deputy ministers can easily cope with whatever constraints come their way. They are members of the prime minister's court and, when in doubt, they can always clear things up very quickly with the prime minister or his office. The country's leading economic and political elites and lobbyists have access to key decision-makers and can exert influence.

But things are vastly different downstairs in departments and agencies. As noted earlier, the distance between a senior program manager and the prime minister's court needs to be measured in light years. The manager now has to deal with a growing number of contextual goals, a multitude of constraints, and, when looking up, a multitude of management layers. Nothing belongs to a department anymore, even less to a manager and his or her unit. By definition, government by network offers a host of potential loyalties. Again, one's unit and even one's home department can no longer constitute the full story. For example, to define Canada's climate-change strategy involved fourteen departments and all central agencies managing a complex series of 250 programs; these dealt with the international community, public education, transportation and industrial policies, together with a great variety of activities ranging from incentives to housing and regulations to ensure energy efficiency.[21] Unless the prime minister takes an interest in the issue or public opinion forces government to act, public servants will attend a countless number of meetings and still see limited progress. In brief, government is unable to vest discretion at the appropriate level in organizations to resolve issues as they surface. The more goals and constraints that have to be attended to, the less discretionary authority is delegated down the line. Virtually all decisions that require program managers to step outside their tracks are pushed upstairs to the very top.[22] This explains in part why government departments are not good at adjusting to changing circumstances, which is a much-valued capacity in a fast-changing political and economic world.

This has given rise to a disbelief culture below the fault line – the view that no reform from above will stick or work. Thus, when reforms are announced, public servants downstairs simply go through the motions of implementation, convinced that this is just another passing fad that will soon die out, and things will shortly get back to normal. The instinct is to batten down the hatches and wait out the passing storm, knowing that those above the fault line and the authors of the latest reform efforts will soon be pursuing other priorities.[23] The view that government is not good at reforming its operations is now widely held, even inside government.

Why? To be sure, no one likes to be reinvented from the top, from a vision coming out of the office of the clerk of the Privy Council or from a political campaign commitment. No politician is at risk of losing votes when attacking bureaucracy. Commitments to fix bureaucracy are often freely made during the heat of an election campaign but rarely well thought out. Constant attacks on bureaucracy, the widespread belief that the private sector is superior to the public sector, a bewildering array of accountability and transparency requirements, and the need for public servants to help manage the blame game have all made government less good than it once was at delivering programs and services and at dealing efficiently with the concerns of the average citizen.

Government is also coping, as best it can, with varying degrees of success with an old industrial model of labour relations. This matters more to public servants operating below the fault line, who actually manage programs and deliver services, than those working above the line. The majority of public servants operate below the fault line, and they have to deal with citizens and their urgencies of the day. Negotiations with unions are carried out by a central agency, and program managers are hardly involved. However, they have to adjust their operations and resources as best they can to accommodate whatever agreement has been reached with the unions.

We saw earlier that public sector unions will go to bat for their members whenever disciplinary action against them is contemplated. Government managers have little say in setting salaries, working conditions, and the process for declaring employees surplus. Even if collective bargaining does not inhibit a manager from making a tough decision, it becomes a convenient cover to avoid doing so. It has never been easy to deal with non-performers in the public sector, but it is even more difficult today, given that employees and their union representatives can go to court to counter removal for non-performance. No manager wants the ensuing hassle. Public servants upstairs always have more important things to deal with – at least from their perspective – than helping those below the fault line deal with human resource issues.

Governments would much rather talk about reform and vision exercises than actually bring implementation to the centre of government and make it a priority of the prime minister and his courtiers. Political requirements, the problem of government overload, the pressures of the day, the era of permanent election campaigns, and the apparent inability to fix its bureaucracy simply do not allow the prime minister to pay close attention to reforming operations below the fault line. This explains why the organizational culture below the fault line just keeps rolling on, whether or not Conservatives, Progressive Conservatives or Liberals hold the levers of political power.

A leading student of public administration put his finger on the problem when he wrote, "Politicians make bold statements but often are unsure about what changes they want. When they propose change they move on to other policy concerns all too quickly. They talk the talk but do not walk the walk."[24] Their focus is always above the fault line unless something below it causes problems for them. Christopher Pollitt and Geert Bouckaert maintain that politicians do not always respect the rules and responsibilities allocated to them by public service reforms, all too often interfering in administrative issues at the wrong moment or when it suits their agenda.[25]

President Obama likely decided that he had done all the required heavy lifting when he fought an election over Obamacare and, together with his staff, spent considerable time and effort planning the initiative and how best to make it public. Consideration about its implementation took a back seat, and he paid a heavy price.[26]

The Ontario government felt that it had come up with the right solution when it announced that it would issue gift cards to buy food to help those affected by the 2013 ice storm. Politicians got all the media attention they wanted on the day of the announcement. Gift cards, however, soon ran out, and chaos followed in grocery stores. A spokesperson for the minister of community safety declared that there was "no blame to be laid."[27] Inability to find the culprit appears to be a public sector phenomenon. However, it does once again bring to mind the 90 per cent / 10 per cent scenario: to those on the receiving end of public services, government should be 90 per cent about implementation, while those at the centre of government where effective decision-making power lies, view government as 90 per cent about ideas.

MANAGEMENT DISCRETION IS NEEDED

Notwithstanding a litany of management reforms, the machinery of government has not been adapted to the complexity of today's society and the requirements of the modern economy. The notion that we can have a risk-free public administration only inhibits government action at a time when front-line managers and their staff should be given more freedom, not just to manage their operations but, more importantly, to react quickly to emerging opportunities. Modern society and the fast-paced global economy require nothing less.

Ed Clark maintains that government is incapable of focusing properly on operations or on management. He explains that as president-CEO of TD Bank, he decided to establish a unit to focus on service to customers. He adds, "Just shaving a few seconds off the time it takes a customer to carry out a transaction at the bank means a great deal to both the customer and the bank."[28] He attached a great deal of importance to the initiative and kept a very close eye on its development, insisting on regular briefings. He maintains that this type of initiative could never enjoy a high priority in government, at least at the required level to ensure progress. He is right. The distance between a similar initiative in government and those with effective power to decide (i.e., the prime minister, the Prime Minister's Office, and senior officials in the Privy Council Office) makes the approach virtually impossible. Federal and provincial officials in Nova Scotia have not been able to make the Integrated Service Delivery Project work, not only because those with the power to decide are much too busy to take an interest in the proposal, but also because they are unwilling to move authority down the line to enable front-line program managers to do more than attend meetings.

Effective decision-making at times requires management discretion to allow individual problem-solving to make exceptions. Making rules and making certain that they are enforced evenly is what governments have been good at. But that belongs to a different era. That approach worked well when governments were staffed mostly by clerks processing applications from a limited number of programs. Recall that when Bob Bryce joined the Finance Department in 1938, he discovered that "some policy work" was being done by the deputy minister and a handful of clerks.

Once again we note that the bureaucratic world that Max Weber described is long gone. This world was simple, staffed largely by clerks whose loyalty was straightforward – public servants were neutral servants of their political masters. Now the media influence, transparency requirements, governing from the centre, managing the blame game, the horizontal nature of policy-making, the changing policy-advisory role of public servants, lobbyists, the work of the judiciary, and public-private partnerships all working in a volatile public-policy environment have made public servants less sure of their loyalties.[29] One ought not to be surprised, then, that at least some of them have decided to give their loyalty to their own personal economic interest.[30]

There is no need to go over the same material we discussed earlier – suffice to point once again to the work and requirements of central agencies and the evaluation industry that has penetrated every corner of government, while ignoring many things that government does that cannot be measured, which also have grown substantially in number and scope in recent years.[31] The growth in government spending on overhead functions that cannot be attributed to programs has also grown in tandem.

The constraints, number of oversight bodies, and heavy hand of central agencies and their incessant demands for performance reports have slowed decision-making to an unacceptable level and have made government operations too complex for meaningful accountability and out of touch with Canadians. All management reforms have been little more than shots in the dark, generating unintended consequences, undermining what they sought to accomplish, and giving birth to new problems.[32] They have enabled prime ministers and clerks of the Privy Council to announce "major" reforms from on high, but little else has come of them.

Anyone wishing to compare the constraints and the thickness of government that program managers have to deal with today, as opposed to forty years ago, needs only to read Jack Manion's *How*

Lucky I've Been and then look at today's public-administration literature. One could also consult an article recently written by two retired
senior deputy ministers who detail the constraints with which program managers must contend. They quote a "highly respected manager" who told them that having to respond to the accountability
framework, change management initiatives, and provide paperwork
to central agencies meant that he and the departmental staff "were
spending less than 45 percent of our time on actually delivering the
various programs for which we were responsible."[33] Ironically, in one
of its audits of the evaluation function in Environment Canada, the
OAG discovered that officials in the unit spent "about 40 percent" of
their time on tasks other than evaluation, without reporting what the
other tasks may have been.[34] Thus, those charged with actually delivering public services spent less than 45 per cent of their time doing
so, while those charged with evaluating programs spent 60 per cent of
their time doing something else.

Constraints and processes are known and safe and will never get anyone in political hot water. These and other encumbrances imposed by
public sector unions limit the ability of managers to deal with many
human resources issues. They speak to the old saying in government,
"Never do anything for the first time."[35] This and the fact that there are
precious few rewards in government for being known as a good manager go a long way in explaining that government is not as good as it
needs to be in implementing policy and programs.[36] Given the many
oversight bodies, the work of central agencies, and the demands of
those operating above the fault line, it is also becoming increasingly difficult to determine who is a good manager in government.

There is limited upward mobility for those operating below the
fault line delivering programs and services.[37] However, those who are
promoted above the line soon take on the characteristics, values, and
policy preferences of those upstairs, occupying more senior positions.
They soon realize that opposing the institutional status quo or en-
couraging the system to gain a better understanding of the challenges
below the fault line holds little promise for change or their own
career and economic interests. Rules of appropriateness have to be
respected if one is to prosper.[38] More to the point, the values and perspectives of public servants are not static, they adjust to accommodate
the organizational setting within which they operate.

RUNNING ON THEIR TRACKS
DOES NOT REQUIRE MANAGEMENT DISCRETION

Everyone above the fault line has an interest in program managers and their staff running on their tracks. Politicians on the government side prefer it that way, because it enables them to control the machinery of government better and to avoid fuelling the blame game. Recall that senior politicians insist that small mistakes are the problem in politics, not large and complex policy issues. Senior public servants also prefer it because it enables them to focus on policy and the prime minister's priorities. But this comes at a price: it makes the implementation side of government the poor cousin.

Politicians know that they have a short time frame in which to have an impact. The prime minister and his courtiers want to see change in selected areas, and they spend inordinate time deciding what to do and managing the politics of the day on the assumption that implementation will take care of the details of administration. But, as Pressman and Wildavsky observed, "The separation of policy design from implementation is fatal."[39]

Program managers and their staff increasingly also see program delivery, management, and political roles flowing into one another, barely distinguishable. They know full well that, given access-to-information legislation, the media, and the growing distrust politicians have towards them, it is best to keep their heads below the parapet. There is comfort down there, producing bland evaluation reports, feeding briefing material to central agencies, and responding to information requests from ministerial offices. Thicker government, public sector unions, and constraints in some perverse way hold advantages for program managers. They muddy the obligations that agents have to the principal.[40]

They also enable bureaucracy to grow by stealth. Both the Canada School of Public Service and the Atlantic Canada Opportunities Agency (ACOA) grew substantially beyond what the principals were told to expect. Shortly after they were born – no matter that they were initially designed to be small – they took on all the trappings of large departments. They grew and grew, and in that sense they are in no way different from other departments and agencies.

I had a hand in developing both the school and ACOA. The focus was on developing the concept, the broad contours of the organizations, and the legislation. We did not think nearly enough about implementation, and Canadian taxpayers have paid and continue to pay a heavy price for a system that is in serious need of repair. The goal was to launch the two initiatives, announce them with great fanfare and promise, then move on to other things. That is how things work upstairs, above the fault line.

MANAGING FINANCIAL AND HUMAN RESOURCES

It is worth repeating that meaningful expenditure reductions take place only when the prime minister decides and keeps a close watch on the process.[41] Prime ministers sign off on all spending cuts, large or small. Once the prime minister takes his eyes off the objective, spenders swing back into action. That is precisely what officials with ACOA and the Canada School of Public Service did, and again they are not different from all the other departments and agencies.

Nothing much has changed in managing financial resources, other than managers having a freer hand to spend in certain administrative matters. Across-the-board cuts, albeit with some modifications, still give rise to proposed spending cuts for prime ministers to consider. Prime Minister Harper did not rely solely on the machinery of government to come up with possible spending cuts; he turned for advice to Deloitte Touche consultants.[42] It appears that departments and agencies constantly try their hand at securing more resources and then simply sit and wait for the prime minister to launch an exercise to reduce spending. To be sure, as this study makes clear, they are not in the business of coming forward on their own for ways to reduce spending.

The government's inability to manage financial resources properly, to prune organizations continually, and to go beyond across-the-board cuts whenever the prime minister decides the time has come, has made it very difficult for government to be good at delivering programs and services. Thicker government and the tendency to grow organizations by stealth have made it difficult for government to make hard choices and to manage operations efficiently.

Across-the-board cuts – which have guided all spending reviews in Ottawa, including the Chrétien-Martin (1994–97) and the Harper (2012–14) program reviews, make it difficult for government to be good at delivering core responsibilities. We saw earlier that regulatory agencies do not have the capacity and resources to understand the increasingly complex world that they are trying to regulate or often to ensure compliance. We also saw that it takes more than two years to review a regulatory regime in a single sector. Private sector firms make the case that they cannot remain on the sidelines while regulatory agencies try, as best they can, to keep pace with a fast-changing global economy. The result is that firms in some sectors are often left in charge of themselves and public servants above the fault line to spin the new approach and label it "smart regulations" or whatever wording might be in fashion. Officials in regulatory agencies now spend a great deal of time reading reports prepared by those responding to smart regulations.

The choice facing modern government is clear: unless the government is able to rebalance the 90 per cent ideas to 10 per cent implementation and attack "thick government" head on by overhauling overhead requirements, it will be asked to withdraw from many public sector activities or turn over responsibility for implementation to other sectors. Talking about reform while focusing mainly on packaging new policies and managing the blame game will, as the past has made clear on many occasions, make government operations look inept. It has eroded and will continue to erode further the confidence public servants have in their institution and give reason to Canadians to believe that government is not good at managing their taxes.

As already noted, there is growing evidence that public servants are losing confidence in their institution and in their work. The well-documented morale problem that has plagued the public service over the past thirty years or so speaks to this problem.[43] There are reports, for example, that public servants are now "too timid" to pursue wealthy Canadians who hide money in overseas tax havens. A report by the Walker Consulting Group reveals that officials with the Canada Revenue Agency show little effort in "chasing wealthy tax cheats versus the resources it puts towards smaller players who claim a few too many dollars in charitable donations."[44] Wealthy Canadians have access to competent and high-priced tax lawyers and accountants that Canada Revenue officials are hesitant to take on. Smaller players or the average citizen do not.

The pressure to reduce the scope of government and to transfer activities to the private and voluntary sectors will only intensify, unless government bureaucracies improve their operations. In time, government will be left with managing responsibilities that, by definition, simply cannot be transferred to others, and politicians and voters will have to accept that these operations will be more costly and inefficient than they need to be. The problem is that the social and community infrastructures, which existed before governments decided to intervene in virtually every socio-economic sector, is no longer there to pick up the slack if or when governments vacate these fields. One can ask if government can enjoy much public support if it is seen to be capable only of dealing effectively with visionary investments and wicked problems.

Citizens know intuitively that government operations are not performing at acceptable levels. This explains why, in recent years, many politicians have been able to ride the anti-government wave to power. Few political leaders are still prepared to advocate new taxes or tax increases, or to expand the role of government. Left-of-centre and leader of the New Democratic Party (NDP) Thomas Mulcair recently pledged not to increase taxes if he were to become prime minister.[45] Similar commitments were made during the 2014 Ontario provincial election campaign. The leader of the NDP said that she would trim "$600 million in government waste," and the leader of the Progressive Conservative party vowed to cut 100,000 public sector jobs, if elected.[46] Not to be outdone, the Liberal leader and premier, Kathleen Wynne, pledged to balance the budget in two years by reducing spending.[47] Politicians are reluctant to talk about, let alone impose, new taxes, because voters will punish them if they do. This is a tacit admission that government is not efficient with taxpayers' money. Those who have increased taxes, like Nova Scotia's former premier Darrell Dexter, have gone down to defeat after only one mandate. Meanwhile, politicians have responded by carving out strategies to turn this disenchantment into votes, rather than address the fundamental question, why does government enjoy less support than it did forty years ago? What is it that government is no longer good at, and why?

Over the years, we have added one program after another, one unit after another to the machinery, one officer of Parliament after another, while substantially expanding central agencies, and made them responsible for a wide variety of activities. Taken in isolation, one may be able to justify every new program, new unit in line departments, new officer of Parliament, and new unit in central agencies. However, when they are taken together, we have created a machinery that can no longer operate efficiently, as it tries to deliver programs and services in the era of permanent election campaigns. In short, we have – in the words of a middle-level manager working in a line department – "created a big whale that can't swim."[48]

Leaving aside the prime minister and a handful of courtiers, the government now governs only at the margin. The government decision-making process is bogged down by too many oversight bodies, too many management levels, too many obligations to consult interest groups, and too many lobbyists pursuing the narrow interests of their clients. But that only explains part of the challenge. Citizens no longer vote as citizens. Fewer and fewer citizens now even bother to vote. Those who do will vote as environmentalists, members of public sector unions, doctors, business-owners, and members' groups pursuing narrow interests. Politicians are always more responsive to the wishes of those who vote, and that creates a vicious cycle of voters and non-voters. This makes it exceedingly difficult for politicians, once in power, to rally a public consensus or the national interest behind them.

If government is no longer able to pursue the national interest, broadly defined, then it is left to respond to crises, to narrow interests, and to the concerns of political and economic elites. This explains much of what is wrong with government. Leaving aside the prime minister, no one is in charge in government. Problems simply roll on through one consultative process after another, kept in check by one oversight body after another. The competitive and fast-paced nature of the global economy is pushing government to the sidelines but also leaving the public sector to pick up the pieces after things go wrong, as they did in the 2008 financial meltdown.

THE WHALE CAN SWIM FOR SOME

The whale can swim for some. The country's political and economic elites know how or, if not, have access to resources to speak to the country's political and bureaucratic elites and to navigate through the machinery and influence it. But it cannot swim nearly as well for others, and by extension, the broader public interest, thus leaving citizens dissatisfied with both the policy process and government operations.

It will be recalled that Canada's chief justice said, "We have a wonderful justice system for corporations and for the wealthy. But the middle class and the poor may not be able to access our justice system."[49] The same can be said about government. CEOs of leading corporations and the country's political and economic elites have access or can hire access to officials operating upstairs, above the fault line where policies and all-important decisions are struck. The average citizen does not.

Institutions designed to give voice to the broader public interest are no longer able to do so. Membership in political parties has dropped substantially and they have all become leader-centric. The work of Parliament is no longer respected by Canadians, and MPs themselves are increasingly publicly expressing their displeasure over the workings of their own institutions. There is an important message that cannot be ignored when the winning candidate in a June 2014 by-election in Fort McMurray was chosen by only 7 per cent of the electorate.[50]

Parliament and the public service below the fault line should be the traditional ally of the average citizen, but they no longer are. Unlike the economic elites, citizens view government as the big whale that can't swim. We saw earlier an Elections Canada survey that pointed to "negative attitudes towards the performance of government" as a significant reason for the trend towards lower voter turnout.[51] We also saw that only 27 per cent of Canadians think that the federal government deals with issues that are important to them.[52] We note that from 1965 to 1984 the number of people expressing trust in the federal government remained in the 56–60 per cent range but fell to 49 per cent by 1988 and to 34 per cent in 1993, and has remained below 40 per cent ever since.[53] The growing mistrust citizens have towards government is rooted, at least in part, in the poor performance of bureaucracy operating below the fault line.

Larry Diamond, one of the world's leading students of democratic development, makes the case that "ultimately, if democracy is to become stable and effective, the bulk of the democratic citizenry must develop a deep and resilient commitment to it."[54] We are moving away from this commitment, not getting closer.

The average citizen, who has had to adjust to the requirements of the global economy, sees a growing disconnect between his or her economic well-being and that of public servants. Public servants, university professors, teachers, and nurses, for the most part, belong to unions that can push and pull for better working conditions and gold-plated pension plans, and that will jump to the defence of non-performers, while few private sector employees have any such protection. The perception of the average voter is that government is good at serving prime ministers and their courtiers, at accommodating the wishes of the country's political, economic, and bureaucratic elites, and at looking after the interests of politicians and bureaucracy. Perception is not far from reality. To the average citizen, government above the fault line no longer belongs to them, while government below the fault line no longer meets expectations in delivering programs and services. Little attention is paid to implementation or to the growing strength of economic elites and single-issue groups and associations that focus above the fault line and on the courts.

This has wide implications for representative democracy. It flies in the face of Samuel Huntington's argument that democracy has an anti-elite bias or ethic.[55] Power is never static. It moves back and forth between complex actions, and within the machinery of government between political and bureaucratic actors. The shift is markedly away from the average citizen and towards the economic and political elites. This explains why membership and volunteers in political parties is on the decline, why support for political and administrative institutions is falling, and why, in nearly all representative democracies, Canada included, there has been a sharp increase in the number of people who report that government does not care about their opinions.[56] If government cannot be good at representing citizens and at balancing the interests of various forces in society, it cannot, over time, be good at much else.

Francis Fukuyama summed it up well when he wrote, "While democratic political systems theoretically have self-correcting mechanisms that allow them to reform, they also open themselves up to decay by legitimating the activities of powerful interest groups that can block needed change."[57] This is what is happening in Canada as our political and administrative institutions are becoming dysfunctional, enabling organized groups, together with Canada's political and economic elites, to shape the public policy agenda to align with their narrow interest.

If our political and administrative institutions cannot go beyond political and economic elites and connect with citizens to pursue the broader public interest, other than in times of crises, if government cannot reform its operations above the fault line and strengthen operations below the line, and if public servants cannot run government operations without always looking for ways to add new resources, government will not enjoy the support necessary to make things happen in the public interest and to pursue public goods.

In brief, if government cannot learn to row better, then it will not have the credibility to steer. As noted, there are things that properly belong to government, from managing a regulatory regime to delivering programs in certain sectors. Responsibility and the rowing for these sectors cannot be turned over to others.

Unless implementation is given equal weight, new policy and whiz-bang ideas will never fully prosper. Public servants below the fault line are struggling to cope with bolts of lightning from politicians and senior bureaucrats above the line, as well as from a growing number of oversight bodies and the media, all the while trying to make performance accountability work in a world where it simply has no footing. At the same time, they are aware that society no longer values their work or their performance as it once did.

Our political institutions and government bureaucracies face becoming increasingly irrelevant, unless action is taken. They can't do this on their own, and how it can be achieved should be a matter of national debate. Unless both are able to perform at a higher level, more and more activities will be hived off to the private and voluntary sectors, and even those matters that only government can handle because no one else has the mandate or capacity to take them on – the visionary investments, the promotion of innovation, the wicked problems, and management of a complex regulatory regime – may well be left without the resources to make a difference. The broader public interest and citizens will both be the poorer.

Notes

PREFACE

1 "Investment Wanted to Slip Public Sector Cuffs," *Financial Times*, 10 July 2013.
2 "Cable's Right Call on Royal Mail," *Financial Times*, 10 July 2013.
3 "Britain Cannot Afford the Royal Mail, Says Minister," *Telegraph*, 10 July 2013.
4 Herbert A. Simon, "Public Administration in Today's World of Organizations and Markets: John Gaus Lecture," *Political Science and Politics* (December 2000): 754.
5 Ibid.

CHAPTER ONE

1 Karen McCreadie, *Adam Smith's The Wealth of Nations: A Modern-Day Interpretation of an Economic Classic* (Oxford: Infinite Ideas, 2009).
2 Thomas Sowell, *On Classical Economics* (New Haven, CT: Yale University Press, 2006).
3 Paul Samuelson, *Economics*, 19th ed. (New York: McGraw-Hill, 2010).
4 Mark Moore, *Creating Public Value: Strategic Management in Government* (Cambridge, MA: Harvard University Press, 1995), 28.
5 Albert O. Hirschman, *Exit, Voice and Loyalty: Responses to Decline in Firms, Organizations and States* (Cambridge, MA: Harvard University Press, 1970).
6 See Donald J. Savoie, *Whatever Happened to the Music Teacher?: How Government Decides and Why* (Montreal and Kingston: McGill-Queen's University Press, 2013).

7   See, among many others, J. Perry and K. Kraemer, eds., *Public Management: Public and Private Perspectives* (Palo Alto, CA: Mayfield, 1983).

8   Statistics Canada, *Public Service Employee Survey PSES* (Ottawa: Statistics Canada, 2 February 2012).

9   "You Tell Us: Civil Service Morale," *Guardian*, 27 March 2013, http://www.theguardian.com/public-leaders-network/2013/mar/26/civil-service-morale-public-sector. See also "Joint Union Evidence to the Senior Salaries Review Body" (London: FDA, October 2012), 14.

10 Mariana Mazzucato, *The Entrepreneurial State* (London: Anthem, 2013).

11 Recall, for example, Lyndon B. Johnson's call for a Great Society through domestic programs and Pierre E. Trudeau's vision of a Just Society.

12 "David Cameron Promises Public Sector Revolution," *Telegraph*, 20 February 2011, http://www.telegraph.co.uk/news/politics/8337237/David-Cameron-promises-public-sector-revolution.html.

13 Quoted in "Modernizing Government," presented to the UK Parliament by the prime minister and the minister for the Cabinet Office, 1999, 11.

14 Elaine C. Kamarck makes this point in *The End of Government ... as We Know It: Making Public Policy Work* (Boulder, CO: Lynne Rienner, 2007), 8.

15 Donald J. Savoie, *Harrison McCain: Single-Minded Purpose* (Montreal and Kingston: McGill-Queen's University Press, 2014).

16 "Top 1000: Exclusive Rankings of Canada's Most Profitable Companies," *Globe and Mail*, 27 June 2013, http://www.theglobeandmail.com/report-on-business/rob-magazine/top-1000/top-1000/article12829649/.

17 EKOS Research, *Rethinking Government* (Ottawa: EKOS Research, March 2008), 4.

18 *Nanos Survey: What Canadians Think of the Federal Civil Servants* (Ottawa: Nik on the Numbers, 20 June 2013).

19 "Who's the Boss?" Samara Democracy Report 4, Ottawa, 3 December 2012, 1.

20 The articles and editorial are from the *Telegraph Journal* and the *Globe and Mail*, 7 January 2014.

21 Peter H. Schuck provides an excellent overview of these developments in his *Why Government Fails So Often and How It Can Do Better* (Princeton, NJ: Princeton University Press, 2014).

22 Ibid., 4.

23 Gavin Newsom, quoted in "Schumpeter: Fixing the Republic," *Economist*, 20 April 2013.

24 Savoie, *Whatever Happened to the Music Teacher?*, 131.

25 See Donald J. Savoie, *Breaking the Bargain: Public Servants, Ministers and Parliament* (Toronto: University of Toronto Press, 2003), 11.

26 Barry J. O'Toole, *The Ideal of Public Service: Reflections on the Higher Civil Service in Britain* (London: Routledge, 2006), 2.

27 See Savoie, *Breaking the Bargain*; and Jack Manion, *How Lucky I've Been* (Ottawa: Luhn, 2012).

28 "Schumpeter: Cronies and Capitals," *Economist*, 20 August 2013.

29 "Student Organization Has Become an Out-of-Touch, Money-Squandering Bureaucracy, University Groups Allege," *National Post*, 27 December 2013, http://news.nationalpost.com/2013/12/27/canadian-federation-of-students.

30 See, among others, Christopher Pollitt and Geert Bouckaert, *Public Management Reform: A Comparative Analysis – New Public Management, Governance, and the Neo-Weberian State*, 3rd ed. (Oxford: Oxford University Press, 2011), 219.

31 "David Cameron Promises Public Sector Revolution," *Telegraph*, 20 February 2011, http://www.telegraph.co.uk/news/politics/8337237/David-Cameron-promises-public-sector-revolution.html.

32 Donald J. Savoie, *Thatcher, Reagan, Mulroney: In Search of a New Bureaucracy* (Pittsburgh: University of Pittsburgh Press, 1994).

33 "Broken," *Economist*, 13 July 2013.

34 Schuck, *Why Government Fails so Often*.

35 See, among many others, David Sainsbury, *Progressive Capitalism: How to Achieve Economic Growth, Liberty and Social Justice* (London: Biteback, 2013).

36 Richard Saillant, *Au Bord du Gouffre: Agir dès maintenant pour éviter la faillite du Nouveau-Brunswick* (Moncton: Institut canadien de recherche en politiques et administration publiques, 2014), 42.

37 "NASA – Excerpt from the 'Special Message to the Congress on Urgent National Needs," John F. Kennedy, 25 May 1961, http://www.nasa.gov/vision/space/features/jfk_speech_text.html#.VMpoAy6ORmQ.

38 "The Obama Plan: Stability and Security for All Americans," n.d., http://www.whitehouse.gov/assets/documents/obama_plan_card.PDF.

39 "President Obama Apologizes to Americans Who Are Losing Health Coverage," *Washington Post*, 7 November 2013, http://www.washingtonpost.com/politics/president-obama-apologizes-to-americans-who-are-losing-their-health-insurance/2013/11/07/2306818e-4803-11e3-a196-3544a03c2351_story.html.

40 See, among others, Carl Dahlström, B. Guy Peters, and Jon Pierre, eds., *Steering from the Centre: Strengthening Political Control in Western Democracies* (Toronto: University of Toronto Press, 2011).

41 See, among others, Savoie, *Thatcher, Reagan, Mulroney*.

42 See, among others, Savoie, *Whatever Happened to the Music Teacher?*

43 See James L. Perry and Hal G. Rainey, "The Public-Private Distinction in

Organization Theory: A Critique and Research Strategy," *Academy of Management Review* 3, no. 2 (1988), 182–201.

44 See, among many others, O.P. Dwivedi, ed., *The Administrative State in Canada: Essays in Honour of J.E. Hodgetts* (Toronto: University of Toronto Press, 1982).

45 Ibid.

46 "Astounding," CN Tower, http://www.cntower.ca/en-ca/about-us/history /astounding.html.

47 See, for example, Alan Wolfe, *The Future of Liberalism* (New York: Vintage Books, 2010), 229.

48 See, among many others, Jean-Jacques Laffont and David Martimort, *The Theory of Incentives: The Principal-Agent Model* (Princeton, NJ: Princeton University Press, 2002).

49 See, among many others, Orville C. Walker and Robert W. Ruekert, "Marketing's Role in the Implementation of Business Strategies: A Critical Review and Conceptual Framework," *Journal of Marketing* 51, no. 3 (1987): 15–33.

50 Peter F. Drucker, "*Really* Reinventing Government," *Atlantic Online*, February 1995, www.theatlantic.com/past/politics/polibig/reallyre.htm.

51 Ibid.

52 Among others attending the conference were Professors Christopher Hood, Christopher Pollitt, Gwyn Bevan, and Martin Lodge.

53 George Jonas, "The Problem with Democracy? It's Biased toward the Incompetent," *National Post*, 13 July 2013, http://fullcomment.nationalpost.com /2013/01/30/george-jonas-the-problem-with-democracy-its-biased-toward-the-incompetent/.

54 Consultation with Francis McGuire, Moncton, July 2013.

55 Consultation with Jim Casey, Bradenton, Florida, 24 January 2014.

56 Consultation with Richard Saillant, a colleague at the Université de Moncton, October 2013.

57 See Savoie, *Harrison McCain: Single-Minded Purpose*.

58 Consultation with Jean Chrétien, Fox Harbour, Nova Scotia, 22 July 2013.

59 Consultation with Ed Clark, Fox Harbour, Nova Scotia, 22 July 2013.

CHAPTER TWO

1 See, for example, Paul Johnson, *A History of Christianity* (London: Weidenfeld and Nicolson, 1976), 343.

2 Jeffrey Callen of the Rotman School of Management at the University of Toronto, quoted in "Religious Communities Keep Companies from Sinning," *Globe and Mail*, 7 February 2014.

3 "Priest Sex Abuse Claimant Sues Moncton Diocese," CBC, 29 June 2012, http://www.cbc.ca/news/canada/new-brunswick/priest-sex-abuse-claimant-sues-moncton-diocese-1.1260460.

4 "Catholics in Crisis," 30 April 2010, Week, www.theweek.com/article/index/202388/catholicsincrisis.

5 Interview with Monsignor Daniel Jodoin, bishop of Bathurst, New Brunswick, Le Téléjournal Acadie, 27 November 2013, http://ici.radio-canada.ca/regions /atlantique/2013/11/26/007-eveque-eglises-nouveau-brunswick.shtml.

6 See, for example, "As Churches Crumble, Communities Fear Loss of Heritage," *Globe and Mail*, 13 December 2010, http://www.theglobeandmail.com /news/national/as-churches-crumble-communities-fear-loss-of-heritage/article 1836185/.

7 "Canada Marching from Religion to Secularization," *Globe and Mail*, 10 December 2010.

8 Margaret Wente, "The Inequality We Don't Talk About," *Globe and Mail*, 28 November 2013, http://www.theglobeandmail.com/globe-debate/the-inequality-we-dont-talk-about/article15636708/.

9 Neil Nevitte, *The Decline of Deference: Canadian Value Change in Cross-National Perspective* (Peterborough, ON: Broadview, 1996).

10 Robert D. Putnam, *Bowling Alone: The Collapse and Revival of American Community* (New York: Simon and Schuster, 2001), 338.

11 Ibid.

12 Niall Ferguson, *The Great Degeneration: How Institutions Decay and Economies Die* (New York: Penguin, 2013).

13 R. Johnstone, *Religion in Society. A Sociology of Religion*, 3rd ed. (Englewood Cliffs, NJ: Prentice Hall, 1988), 122.

14 Maurice Basque, quoted in Donald J. Savoie, *I'm from Bouctouche, Me: Roots Matter* (Montreal and Kingston: McGill-Queen's University Press, 2009).

15 Martin Normand, quoted in "Patrimoine canadien: les organismes auraient dû paniquer il y a longtemps," *Acadie Nouvelle*, 6 May 2014.

16 R. Freeman, "Working for Nothing: The Supply of Volunteer Labour," *Journal of Labour Economics* 15, no. 3 (1997): 140–65.

17 Alan Penn made this observation in a document that he forwarded to me on 9 May 2014. Mr Penn reports that he is in his "fifth decade of work of evaluating Aboriginal government structures in Canada."

18 See Daniel Bourgeois, *Canadian Bilingual Districts: From Cornerstone to Tombstone* (Montreal and Kingston: McGill-Queen's University Press, 2006).

19 Leslie A. Pal, *Interests of State: The Politics of Language, Multiculturalism, and Feminism in Canada* (Montreal and Kingston: McGill-Queen's University Press, 1993).

20 Lord Wilson of Dinton, "The Mandarin Myth," fourth lecture in a series on Tomorrow's Government, London, Royal Society for the Encouragement of Arts Manufacturers and Commerce, 1 March 2006, 4.

21 Canada, Department of Reconstruction and Supply, *Employment and Income*, with special reference to the *Initial Period of Reconstruction* (Ottawa: King's Printer, 1945), 21.

22 A.W. Johnson, *Social Policy in Canada: The Past as It Conditions the Present* (Halifax: Institute for Research on Public Policy, 1987).

23 See R.F. Harrod, *The Life of John Maynard Keynes* (New York: Harcourt, Brace, 1951), 241.

24 Robert B. Bryce, *Maturing in Hard Times: Canada's Department of Finance through the Great Depression* (Montreal and Kingston: McGill-Queen's University Press, 1986), 228.

25 J.L. Granatstein, *The Ottawa Men: The Civil Service Mandarins, 1935–1957* (Toronto: Oxford University Press, 1982), 279.

26 OECD, "OECD Outlook 91 Database," annex table 25 (Paris: OECD, n.d.).

27 R.M. Bird, rev. M. Smart, "Public Expenditure," *Canadian Encyclopedia*, n.d.

28 See, among others, David K. Foot, ed., *Public Employment and Compensation in Canada: Myths and Realities* (Ottawa: Institute for Research on Public Policy, 1978); and "Population of the Federal Public Service by Department," Treasury Board of Canada, 27 November 2014, http://www.tbs-sct.gc.ca/res/stats/ssa-pop-eng.asp. The 2011 figure includes RCMP and Canadian Forces members and Ministers' exempt staff.

29 George Post, *Conversations with Canadian Public Service Leaders* (Ottawa: Canadian Centre for Management Development, March 1996), 13.

30 Gordon Robertson, *Memoirs of a Very Civil Servant* (Toronto: University of Toronto Press, 2001), 38.

31 A.W. Johnson, "The Role of the Deputy Minister," *Canadian Public Administration* 4, no. 4 (1961): 363.

32 Quoted in Henry Parris, *Constitutional Bureaucracy* (London: George Allen & Unwin, 1969), 80.

33 Herman Finer, *The British Civil Service* (London: Allen and Unwin, 1937), 160.

34 "Most Don't Believe in Hell," CBN News, 28 March 2007, http://www.cbn.com/cbnnews/127721.aspx.

35 "Heaven Tops Hell in Canadian Belief Poll," *National Post*, 3 September 2010, http://news.nationalpost.com/2010/09/03/heaven-tops-hell-in-canadian-belief-poll/.

36 See, among many others, Pippa Norris and Ronald Inglehart, *Sacred and Sec-*

ular: Religion and Politics Worldwide (Cambridge: Cambridge University Press, 2004); Scott Atran, *In Gods We Trust: The Evolutionary Landscape of Religion* (New York: Oxford University Press, 2002).

37 Anthony Giddens, *Modernity and Self Identity* (Stanford, CA: Stanford University Press, 1991), 84.

38 See Charles Murray, *Coming Apart: The State of White America, 1960–2010* (New York: Random House, 2012).

39 Mark 10:25.

40 See Donald J. Savoie, *Power: Where Is It?* (Montreal and Kingston: McGill-Queen's University Press, 2010), 58.

41 I acknowledge that social capital, social cohesion, and a more cohesive society are concepts with a multitude of definitions. See, among many others, Jane Jenson, *Defining and Measuring Social Cohesion: Social Policies in Small States* (London: Commonwealth Secretariat and United Nations Research Institute for Social Development, 2010).

42 Gillian Tett, "Funding and the Patriotism Test," *Financial Times*, 7 January 2010, http://www.ft.com/intl/cms/s/0/0306069c-fbb4-11de-9c29-00144feab49a.html#axzz3RYdBRePs.

43 Lawrence Martin, "A Tip for the PM's New Image Fixer," *Globe and Mail*, 17 September 2013, www.theglobeandmail.com/globe-debate/a-tip-for-the-pms-new-image-fixer/article14347091.

44 George Perlin, "The Malaise of Canadian Democracy: What Is It? How Is It to Be Explained? What Can We Do about It?," in Hans J. Michelmann, Donald C. Story, and Jeffrey S. Steeves, eds., *Political Leadership and Representation in Canada: Essays in Honour of John C. Courtney*, 154–75 (Toronto: University of Toronto Press, 2007).

45 Kenneth Newton and Pippa Norris, "Confidence in Political Institutions: Faith, Culture, or Performance?," in *Disaffected Democracies: What's Troubling the Trilateral Countries?* ed. Susan J. Pharr and Robert D. Putnam (Princeton: Princeton University Press, 2000), 70.

46 Ralf Dahrendorf, "Afterword," in ibid., 313.

47 See, among many others, H. Bierhoff, *Prosocial Behaviour* (London: Psychology Press, 2002); B. Bozeman, *Public Values and Public Interest: Counterbalancing Economic Individualism* (Washington, DC: Georgetown University Press, 2007); and D. Kreps, "Intrinsic Motivation and Extrinsic Incentives," *American Economic Review* 87, no. 2 (1997): 359–64.

48 See, among others, Bozeman, *Public Values and Public Interest.*

49 Paul Martin made attacking the democratic deficit the centrepiece of his election strategy. See "Martin Urges Parliamentary Reform, End to 'Democ-

ratic Deficit," CBC News, 22 October 2002, http://www.cbc.ca/news/canada
/martin-urges-parliamentary-reform-end-to-democratic-deficit-1.328167.

50 Howard A. Doughty, review of *Participatory Democracy: Prospects for Democratizing Democracy*, by Dimitrios Roussopoulos and C. George Benello, *College
Quarterly* 9, no. 4 (2006), http://www.collegequarterly.ca/2006-vol09-num04-
fall/reviews/doughty3.html.

51 Mancur Olson, *The Logic of Collective Action: Public Goods and the Theory of
Groups* (Cambridge, MA: Harvard University Press, 1971).

52 See, among others, C.L.R. James, "Every Cook Can Govern: A Study of
Democracy in Ancient Greece Its Meaning for Today," in *Participatory
Democracy: Prospects for Democratizing Democracy*, ed. Dimitrios Roussopou-
los and C. George Benello, 315–37 (Montreal: Black Rose Books, 2005).

53 John R. Hibbing and Elizabeth Theiss-Morse, *Stealth Democracy: Americans'
Beliefs about How Government Should Work* (Cambridge: Cambridge University Press, 2002).

54 See Max J. Weber, "Politics as a Vocation," *Anthropological Research on the
Contemporary* (January 1919), http://anthropos-lab.net/wp/wp-content
/uploads/2011/12/Weber-Politics-as-a-Vocation.pdf. Joseph Schumpeter, *Capitalism, Socialism and Democracy* (New York: Harper, 1940).

55 Russell J. Dalton, "The Social Transformation of Trust in Government," *International Review of Sociology* 15, no. 1 (2006): 134.

56 Ibid., 137.

57 EKOS Research, *The Trust Deficit: What Does It Means?* (Ottawa: EKOS Research,
14 May 2013), 1.

58 Ibid., 2.

59 Jon H. Pammett and Lawrence LeDuc, *Explaining the Turnout Decline in
Canadian Federal Elections: A New Survey of Non-Voters* (Ottawa: Elections
Canada, 2003).

60 Elections Canada, "Voter Turnout at Federal Elections and Referendums,"
n.d., http://www.elections.ca/content.aspx?dir=turn&document=index
&lang=e&section=ele.

61 Pammett and LeDuc, *Explaining the Turnout Decline*.

62 Sharanjit Uppal and Sébastien LaRochelle-Côté, "Factors Associated with
Voting," Statistics Canada, 24 February 2012,
http://www.statcan.gc.ca/pub/75-001-x/2012001/article/11629-eng.htm.

63 John Ibbitson, "The Alarming Decline in Voter Turnout," *Globe and Mail*, 14
October 2011, http://www.theglobeandmail.com/news/politics/the-alarming-
decline-in-voter-turnout/article4247507/.

64 See, among others, Pammett and LeDuc, *Explaining the Turnout Decline*, 79.

65 See, for example, Keith Archer, "Increasing Youth Voter Registration: Best Practices in Targeting Young Electors," *Electoral Insight* 5, no. 2 (2003): 26–40.

66 Quoted in "The Wealth Paradox: What Growing Inequality Is Costing Future Generations," *Globe and Mail*, 8 November 2013.

67 Alan B. Krueger, "Land of Hope and Dreams: Rock and Roll, Economics and Rebuilding the Middle Class," presentation to the Rock and Roll Hall of Fame, 12 June 2013, Cleveland, Ohio.

68 See, among others, Conference Board of Canada, "Income Inequality," October 2013, http://www.conferenceboard.ca/hcp/details/society/income-inequality.aspx.

69 Tavia Grant, "Rich Earn 155 Times More Than Average Worker," *Globe and Mail*, 25 January 2011, http://www.theglobeandmail.com/report-on-business/economy/rich-earn-155-times-more-than-average-worker/article563399/.

70 See OECD, *OECD Tax Database* (Paris: OECD, 2013); and OECD, *Focus on Top Incomes and Taxation in OECD Countries: Was the Crisis a Game Changer?* (Paris: OECD, May 2014).

71 See "Some Thoughts on Canadian Unionization Rates," Law of Work, n.d., http://lawofwork.ca/?p=52; and Greg Keenan, "As Unions Lose Power, Canada Gets the Blue-Collar Blues," *Globe and Mail*, 16 November 2013, http://www.theglobeandmail.com/news/national/time-to-lead/as-unions-lose-power-canada-gets-the-blue-collar-blues/article15472784/?page=all.

72 Josh Boak, "Top 5 Reasons Why Your CEO Just Got a Big Fat Raise … and 5 Reasons Why You Didn't," *Financial Post*, 27 May 2014, http://business.financialpost.com/2014/05/27/the-ceo-of-your-company-just-got-a-huge-raise-you-didnt-heres-why/?__lsa=c3be-cd73.

73 Keith Banting and John Myles, "Canadian Social Future: Concluding Reflections," in *Inequality and the Fading of Redistributive Politics*, ed. Keith Banting and John Myles (Vancouver: UBC Press, 2013), 426.

74 "Should We Really Leave Inequality to the Policy Elites?" *Globe and Mail*, 10 May 2014.

75 Tavia Grant, "Five Myths about Canada's Middle Class," *Globe and Mail*, 19 November 2013, www.theglobeandmail.com/news/nationaltime-to-lead/five-myths-about-middle-class/article15515586/.

76 "Middle-Class Angst Bottom-Rung Vision," *Globe and Mail*, 17 October 2013.

77 "PM Harper's Speech at Conservative Convention in Calgary," 1 November 2013, http://looniepolitics.com/spotlights/pm-harpers-speech-conservative-convention-calgary/.

78 Thomas Piketty, *Capital in the Twenty-First Century* (Cambridge, MA: Belknap, 2014).

79 OECD, *Perspectives on Global Development 2012: Social Cohesion in a Shifting World* (Paris: OECD, 2012).

80 See, among many others, Daniel Dorling, *Injustice: Why Social Inequality Persists* (Bristol: Policy, 2010); and M.I. Midlarsky, ed., *Inequality, Democracy and Economic Development* (Cambridge: Cambridge University Press, 1998).

81 See, among others, Marc Musick and John Wilson, *Volunteers: A Social Profile* (Bloomington, IN: Indiana University Press, 2008).

82 Mark Carney, "Inclusive Capitalism: Creating a Sense of the Systemic" (speech to the Conference on Inclusive Capitalism, London, England, 27 May 2014).

83 David Lasby and Cathy Barr, *Talking about Charities: 2013* (Edmonton: Muttart Foundation, 2013).

84 *Research Bulletin – Trends in Individual Donations: 1984–2010* (Toronto: Imagine Canada, 15, no. 1, 1 December 2011).

85 Norah McClintock, *Understanding Canadian Volunteers* (Toronto: Centre for Philanthropy, 2004), 2.

86 "Ambulance New Brunswick Won't Replace St John Ambulance," CBC News, 28 August 2013, http://www.cbc.ca/news/canada/new-brunswick/ambulance-new-brunswick-won-t-replace-st-john-ambulance-1.1305339.

87 David Taras and Christopher Waddell, eds., *How Canadians Communicate IV: Media and Politics* (Edmonton: Athabasca, 2012), 111.

88 Daniel McHardie, "How the Media Influences Public Policy: A Case Study on the New Brunswick Government's Failed Attempt to Sell NB Power" (master's thesis, University of New Brunswick, 2014), 27.

89 Chris Waddell, "Final Thoughts: How Will Canadians Communicate about Politics and the Media in 2015?" in Taras and Waddell, *How Canadians Communicate IV*, 371.

90 See, among others, Tom Flanagan, "Political Communication and the Permanent Campaign" in Taras and Waddell, *How Canadians Communicate IV*, 129.

91 See, among others, Waddell, "Final Thoughts."

92 Elly Alboim, "On the Verge of Total Dysfunction: Government, Media and Communications," in Taras and Waddell, *How Canadians Communicate IV*, 47.

93 Ibid., 46–8.

94 Quoted in Howard Rosenberg and Charles S. Feldman, *No Time to Think: The Menace of Media Speed and the 24-Hour News Cycle* (New York: Continuum, 2008), 90.

95 Quoted, ibid., 1.

96 Michael Ignatieff, *Fire and Ashes: Success and Failure in Politics* (Toronto: Random House Canada, 2013), 141.

97 See, for example, L. Hlavach and W. Freivogel, "Ethical Implications of Anonymous Comments Posted to Online News Stories," *Journal of Mass Media Ethics* 26, no. 1 (2011): 21–37.

98 "Why Do We Have to Be Boring?: How Ottawa Spends Weeks Planning a Single Tweet Using a Rigorous 12-Step Protocol," *National Post*, 2 February 2014, http://news.nationalpost.com/2014/02/02/how-ottawa-spends-weeks-planning-a-single-tweet-using-a-rigorous-12-step-protocol/.

99 D. Lenihan, *It's More Than Talk: Listen, Learn and Act, a New Model for Public Engagement*, Report of the Public Engagement Initiative (Fredericton: Government of New Brunswick, 2008).

100 David Frum, "In Praise of the Prime Ministerial Control Freak," *National Post*, 6 December 2013.

101 Tom Quiggin, quoted in "The Implications of the Federal Government's Monitoring of Social Media," *Ottawa Citizen*, 30 November 2013.

102 See, for example, "PCO's New Gig, as Central Social Media," *Hill Times* (Ottawa), 20 January 2014, 16.

103 See, among others, Savoie, *Breaking the Bargain*.

104 J.L. Granatstein, *Canada's War: The Politics of the Mackenzie King Government* (Toronto: University of Toronto Press, 1990).

105 J.C. Abegglen, *Sea Change: Pacific Asia as the New World Industrial Centre* (New York: Free Press, 1994), 26.

106 George Will makes the same point in his "The Absurdity of Progressive Attacks on Corporate Taxes," *Telegraph-Journal* (Saint John), 18 August 2014.

107 See, among many others, K. Ohmae, *The End of the Nation State: The Rise of Regional Economies* (London: HarperCollins, 1995).

108 Deanne Julius, "Globalization and Stakeholder Conflicts: A Corporate Perspective," *International Affairs* 73, no. 3 (1997): 453.

109 Wade MacLauchlan, Georgetown Conference on Rural Development, Georgetown, Prince Edward Island, 3 October 2013.

110 See, for example, Paul Hird, "The Global Economy: Myths and Realities," *International Affairs* 63, no. 3 (1997): 409.

111 Nicolas Sarkozy made the observation at Fox Harbour, Nova Scotia, 22 July 2013.

112 Susan Delacourt, *Shopping for Votes: How Politicians Choose Us and We Choose Them* (Toronto: Douglas and McIntyre, 2013), 23.

113 Michael Ignatieff, *The Rights Revolution* (Toronto: House of Anansi, 2007).

114 Savoie, *Whatever Happened to the Music Teacher?*.

115 Mark Bevir, *Democratic Governance* (Princeton: Princeton University Press, 2010), 34.

116 See, among others, Delacourt, *Shopping for Votes*.

117 "Pain Caused by Sanctions on Russia for 'Greater National Interest,' Stephen Harper Tells Canadian Businesses," *Financial Post*, 24 March 2014.

118 Quoted in Kelly Pullen, "With Friends Like Harper: How Nigel Wright Went from Golden Boy to Fall Guy," *Toronto Life*, 25 March 2014, http://www.torontolife.com/informer/features/2014/03/25/nigel-wright-golden-boy-to-fall-guy/.

119 See Bozeman, *Public Values and Public Interest*.

CHAPTER THREE

1 S.E. Finer, *The History of Government from the Earliest Times*, 3 vols. (Oxford: Oxford University Press, 1997).

2 Donald J. Savoie, *Court Government and the Collapse of Accountability in Canada and the United Kingdom* (Toronto: University of Toronto Press, 2008), chap. 2.

3 Richard Mulgan, *Holding Power to Account: Accountability in Modern Democracies* (New York: Palgrave Macmillan, 2003), 12.

4 James Madison, *The Federalist Papers*, no. 10: *The Utility of the Union as a Safeguard against Domestic Faction and Insurrection* (New York: Daily Advertiser, 22 November 1967).

5 Cheryl Simrell King and Camilla Stivers, "Citizens and Administrators: Roles and Responsibilities," in *Public Administration and Society: Critical Issues in American Government*, ed. Richard C. Box (London: M.E. Sharpe, 2004), 272.

6 See, among others, Christopher Hitchens, "The Export of Democracy," *Wall Street Journal*, 12 July 2005.

7 John Dunn, *Setting the People Free: The Story of Democracy* (London: Atlantic Books, 2005), 15.

8 It explains why the Fathers of Confederation opted for an appointed Senate.

9 Dunn, *Setting the People Free*, 53–5.

10 Adam Tomkins, *Public Law* (Oxford: Oxford University Press, 2003), 42.

11 The Acts of Settlement 1701 established that Parliament could control the identity of the monarch by altering the line of succession.

12 See, among others, Jeffrey Goldsworthy, *The Sovereignty of Parliament: History and Philosophy* (Oxford: Oxford University Press, 2001), 16–18.

13 Quoted in Joyce Lee Malcolm, "Doing No Wrong: Law, Liberty, and the Constraint of Kings," *Journal of British Studies* 38 (April 1999): 161.

14 See, among others, G.L. Harris, *King, Parliament and Public Finance in Medieval England to 1369* (Oxford: Oxford University Press, 1975).

15 Ivor Jennings, *Cabinet Government*, 3rd ed. (Cambridge: Cambridge University Press, 1959), 14.

16 Things have, of course, changed in recent years in Great Britain in that Scotland, Wales, and Northern Ireland have all been granted their own spheres of jurisdiction.

17 See David E. Smith, *The Canadian Senate in Bicameral Perspective* (Toronto: University of Toronto Press, 2003).

18 Ibid.

19 "The Golden Age of the Commons," *Economist*, 8 January 1998, www.economist.com/node/110428.

20 Among many factors, access-to-information legislation and the new media make it more difficult for Parliament to function today than in years past.

21 See, for example, J.L. Granatstein, *Canada: 1957–1967 – The Years of Uncertainty and Innovation* (Toronto: McClelland and Stewart, 1986); and David MacKenzie, ed., *Canada and the First World War: Essays in Honour of Robert Craig Brown* (Toronto: University of Toronto Press, 2005).

22 Donald J. Savoie, *The Politics of Public Spending in Canada* (Toronto: University of Toronto Press, 1990).

23 Quoted in "House Committee Chairs Should be Elected by All MPs, Tory MP Trost Says," *Hill Times* (Ottawa), 29 October 2013, 4.

24 Sergio Marchi, "Time to Fix Canada's Political Culture," *Ottawa Citizen*, 28 August 2014, http://ottawacitizen.com/opinion/columnists/marchi-time-to-fix-canadas-political-culture·

25 Michael Chong, The Reform Act: 2013, www.michaelchong.ca, 3 December 2013; and "Michael Chong Points the Way Home to Westminster," *Globe and Mail*, 6 December 2013, http://www.theglobeandmail.com/globe-debate/editorials/michael-chong-points-the-way-home-to-westminster/article15805650/.

26 Based on documents Michael Chong sent to me on 11 September 2014, including a news release, and a "Backgrounder: Reform Act, 2014." The media also reported on the proposal. See, for example, Josh Wingrove, "Conservative Back Bencher Reins in Bill That Would Empower MPs," *Globe and Mail*, 11 September 2014, http://www.theglobeandmail.com/news/politics/conservative-backbencher-reins-in-bill-to-empower-mps/article20552486/.

27 Jennifer Ditchburn, "Stephen Harper Gives Stamp of Approval to Watered Down Reform Act: Sources," *National Post*, 17 September 2014,

http://news.nationalpost.com/2014/09/17/stephen-harper-gives-stamp-of-approval-to-watered-down-reform-act-sources/, 17 September 2014.

28 Laura Ryckewaert, "Hill Journalists Say There's Too Much Government Information Control and Parliament Has Lost Its Power," *Hill Times* (Ottawa), 1 March 2014, http://www.hilltimes.com/news/politics/2014/03/01/hill-journalists-say-theres-too-much-federal-government-information-control/37686.

29 I am thinking, among others, of the work of Ned Franks and Peter Aucoin.

30 C.E.S. Franks and David E. Smith, "The Canadian House of Commons under Stress: Reform and Adoption," in *From New Public Management to New Political Governance*, ed. Herman Bakvis and Mark Jarvis (Montreal and Kingston: McGill-Queen's University Press, 2012), 98.

31 "Celebrating Five Years," Samara, http://www.samaracanada.com/about-us/celebrating-five-years.

32 Samara, *It's My Party: Parliamentary Dysfunction Reconsidered* (Ottawa: Samara, 2011), 6.

33 Samara, *Lost in Translation or Just Lost? Canadian Priorities and the House of Commons* (Ottawa: Samara, 2013), 1.

34 Carolyn Bennett, Deborah Grey, and Yves Morin, *The Parliament We Want: Parliamentarians' Views on Parliamentary Reform* (Ottawa: Library of Parliament, 2003), 7.

35 Samara, "It's My Party," 6.

36 Ibid., ch. 2, 1.

37 Samara, *Welcome to Parliament: A Job with No Description* (Toronto: Samara, June 2010), 14.

38 "André Arthur: The MP Who Moonlights as a Bus Driver," *Globe and Mail*, March 2011.

39 See, for example, Savoie, *Whatever Happened to the Music Teacher?*

40 Both MPs quoted in "'You Learn to Be an MP by the Seat of Your Pants,' Say Former MPs," *Hill Times* (Ottawa), 30 November 2010.

41 Samara, *Welcome to Parliament*, 18.

42 The *Economist* makes this point in the case of Britain in "The Golden Age of the Commons," 8 January 1998, http://www.economist.com/node/110428.

43 Richard Mulgan, "Comparing Accountability in the Public and Private Sectors," *Australian Journal of Public Administration* 59, no. 1 (2000): 89.

44 David Docherty, *Mr Smith Goes to Ottawa: Life in the House of Commons* (Vancouver: UBC Press, 1997), 125.

45 Savoie, *Breaking the Bargain*, 183.

46 Quoted in Elizabeth Renzetti, "When MPs Hate Politics, It's Time for

Change," *Globe and Mail*, 14 April 2014, http://www.theglobeandmail.com
/globe-debate/when-mps-hate-politics-its-time-for-change/article17945286/.

47 John Meisel and Matthew Mendelsohn, "Meteor? Phoenix? Chameleon? The
Decline and Transformation of Policy in Canada," in *Party Politics in Canada*, ed.
Hugh G. Thorburn and Alan Whitehorn (Toronto: Prentice Hall, 2001), 176.

48 Hugh Segal, quoted in Vaughan Lyon, *Power Shift: From Party Elites to
Informed Citizens* (Bloomington, IN: iUniverse, 2011), 267.

49 "Political Parties Failing Canadians: Survey," 18 February 2014, *Ottawa Citizen*,
http://ottawacitizen.com/news/local-news/political-parties-failing-canadians-
survey.

50 Delacourt, *Shopping for Votes*, preface and 144.

51 Ibid., 13, 104, 144, 156, 209, and 213.

52 Graham Steele, *What I Learned about Politics: Inside the Rise – and Collapse –
of Nova Scotia's NDP Government* (Halifax: Nimbus, 2014), 167–8.

53 See, among others, David E. Smith, *Across the Aisle: Opposition in Canadian
Politics* (Toronto: University of Toronto Press, 2013).

54 "PMO's Enemies List Reveals Tight Management of Cabinet, Say Former
Conservative Staffers," *Hill Times* (Ottawa), 22 July 2013, 1 and 4.

55 John Ibbitson, "Enemies' List Memo Tells Us Fervour Often Trumps Pragma-
tism in Harper's Government," *Globe and Mail*, 18 July 2013,
http://www.theglobeandmail.com/news/politics/globe-politics-insider
/enemies-list-memo-tells-us-fervour-often-trumps-pragmatism-in-harpers-
government/article13295711; and Lawrence Martin, "PM's Enemies List?
Here Comes the Judge," *Globe and Mail*, 6 May 2014, http://www.theglobe
andmail.com/globe-debate/pms-enemies-list-here-comes-the-judge/article
18478032/.

56 "Behind the Curtain: Ontario Liberal Emails Offer Rare Glimpse into Back-
rooms of Power," *Globe and Mail*, 10 August 2013. See also Ignatieff, *Fire and
Ashes*.

57 Consultation with Dominic LeBlanc, Moncton, 6 August 2011.

58 Donald J. Savoie, "A Perfect Storm in Reverse: The 1994–97 Program Review
in Canada," in *When the Party's Over: the Politics of Fiscal Squeeze in Perspective*,
ed. Christopher Hood, David Heald, and Rozana Himaz, 207–27 (Oxford:
Oxford University Press, 2014).

59 Savoie, *Politics of Public Spending in Canada*.

60 Robert F. Adie and Paul G. Thomas, *Canadian Public Administration: Prob-
lematical Perspectives* (Scarborough, ON: Prentice Hall, 1982), 141.

61 Quoted from "Scrutinizing Spending Estimates," *Hill Times* (Ottawa), 20
June 2011, 8.

62 Lowell Murray, "Souper homage à Donald J. Savoie," speech, Bouctouche, NB, 8 June 2011.

63 Canada, House of Commons, *Debates*, 7 February 1994, 961.

64 Auditor General, *Government Decisions Limited Parliament's Control of Public Spending* (Ottawa: Office of the Auditor General, May 2006), 1.

65 Sharon Sutherland, *Current State of Research Activities on the Parliament of Canada*, submitted to the Library of Parliament, Ottawa, June 2009, 2.

66 Laura Ryckewaert, "Hill Journalist Says There's Too Much Government Information Control and Parliament Has Lost Its Power," *Hill Times* (Ottawa), 1 March 2014, http://www.hilltimes.com/news/politics/2014/03/01 /hill-journalists-say-theres-too-much-federal-government-information-control /37686.

67 John L. Manion to the author, 29 December 2001; and John L. Manion, *Information for Parliament on Government Finance*, prepared for the Office of the Auditor General, 18 April 1992, 23–4.

68 Bill Curry, "Nine Surprises Found in the Harper Government's Latest Omnibus Budget Bill," *Globe and Mail*, 5 November 2013, http://www.the globeandmail.com/news/politics/globe-politics-insider/nine-suprises-found-inside-the-harper-governments-latest-omnibus-budget-bill/article15262811.

69 Quoted in "Feds Bring Down Legislative Hammer on Massive Budget Implementation Bill," *Hill Times* (Ottawa), 4 November 2013, 19.

70 Quoted in Savoie, *Breaking the Bargain*, 203.

71 Quoted in Kevin Theakston, *The Civil Service since 1945* (Oxford: Blackwell, 1995), 169.

72 David McLaughlin, "In Canada's Damaged Democracy, Partisanship Has Taken the Place of Trust," *Globe and Mail*, 26 June 2013, http://www.theglobe andmail.com/globe-debate/in-canadas-damaged-democracy-partisanship-has-taken-the-place-of-trust/article12793131/.

73 "Parliament's Broke, MPs Should Fix It," *Hill Times* (Ottawa), 25 April 2011, 8.

74 "The Globe's Election Endorsement: Facing Up to Our Challenges," *Globe and Mail*, 27 April 2011, http://www.theglobeandmail.com/globe-debate/editorials/the-globes-election-endorsement-facing-up-to-our-chal-lenges/article585060/.

75 Louis Balthazar, "Is the Decline of Parliament Irreversible?" *Canadian Parliamentary Review* (Winter 2005): 17.

76 Robert Marleau, "Legislative Process," *Hill Times* (Ottawa), 18 February 2002.

77 Samara, *Who's the Boss?* (Ottawa, ON: Samara, 2012), 1 and 2.

78 Ulrich Beck and Elizabeth Beck-Gernsheim, *Individualization* (London: Sage, 2002), 26.

79 See, among others, "Oliver Stone Defends Edward Snowden over NSA Revelations," *Guardian*, 5 July 2013, http://www.theguardian.com/film/2013/jul/05/oliver-stone-edward-snowden-nsa.

80 David Hollenbach, "The Common Good Revisited," *Theological Studies* 50, no. 1 (1970): 77.

81 Bevir, *Democratic Governance*, 3.

82 Ibid., 33.

83 Rosanna Tamburri, "Long-Form Census Remains Hot Topic for Canadian Researchers," University Affairs, 4 June 2012, http://www.universityaffairs.ca/news/news-article/long-form-census-remains-hot-topic-for-canadian-researchers/.

84 Bevir, *Democratic Governance*, 3.

85 Ibid., 20.

CHAPTER FOUR

1 Donald J. Savoie, *Governing from the Centre: The Concentration of Power in Canadian Politics* (Toronto: University of Toronto Press, 1999).

2 See, among others, Tom Bentley, *Everyday Democracy: Why We Get the Politicians We Deserve* (London: Demos, 2005), 7; and "Generation Y Speaks: It's All Me, Me, Me," *Sunday Times*, 4 February 2007.

3 Herman Bakvis and Mark D. Jarvis, eds., *From the New Public Management to New Political Governance* (Montreal and Kingston: McGill-Queen's University Press, 2012).

4 Delacourt, *Shopping for Votes*, 14.

5 "The Chief Justice Gives Voice to Unwritten Principles," *Globe and Mail*, 15 May 2006.

6 See, among others, "Supreme Court Pick Favours 'Restraint,'" Canada.com, 28 February 2006, http://www.canada.com/story.html?id=2b739989-870d-4a41-8167-9ed1789faab2.

7 Christopher P. Manfredi, *Judicial Power and the Charter: Canada and the Paradox of Liberal Constitutionalism* (Toronto: McClelland and Stewart, 1993), 212.

8 Ibid., 212–15.

9 Donald R. Songer, *The Transformation of the Supreme Court of Canada: An Empirical Examination* (Toronto: University of Toronto Press, 2008), 253.

10 Allan C. Hutchinson on the judicial appointments process, "Process to Bring Judicial Politics into Public View," *Lawyers Weekly*, 23 September 2005, www.lawyersweekly.ca/index.php?section=article&articleid=155.

11 Quoted in Emmett Macfarlane, *Governing from the Bench: The Supreme Court of Canada and the Judicial Role* (Vancouver: UBC Press, 2013), 50.

12 Rainer Knopff and F.L. Morton, *Charter Politics* (Toronto: Nelson Canada, 1992), 7.

13 Christopher P. Manfredi and Antonia Maioni, "Courts and Health Policy: Judicial Policy Making and Publicly Funded Health Care in Canada," *Journal of Health Politics, Policy and Law* 27, no. 2 (2002): 213–40.

14 Ian Greene, Carl Baar, Peter McCormick, George Szablowski, and Martin Thomas, *Final Appeal: Decision-Making in Canadian Courts of Appeal* (Toronto: James Lorimer, 1998).

15 Macfarlane, *Governing from the Bench*, 12.

16 Ibid., ch. 1. See also Bob Tarantino, "Court Politics," *Literary Review of Canada*, January–February 2014, 8.

17 Remarks of Beverley McLachlin, Chief Justice of Canada, University of Western Ontario, Faculty of Law, London, Ontario, 6 November 2002, 4 and 5.

18 Mark S. Harding and Rainer Knopff, "Charter Values vs Charter Dialogue," *National Journal of Constitutional Law* 31, no. 2 (2013): 161–81.

19 "Constitutionalizing Everything: The Role of Charter Values," *Review of Constitutional Studies* 18, no. 2 (2013): 143.

20 Jeff Gray, "Female Players Say Fake Soccer Turf Violates Charter, Threaten Legal Action," *Globe and Mail*, 5 August 2014, http://www.theglobeandmail .com/report-on-business/industry-news/the-law-page/elite-law-firms-say-fake-soccer-turf-violates-charter-for-women-athletes/article19915686/.

21 Raymond Bazowski, "The Judicialization of Canadian Politics," in *Canadian Politics*, ed. James Bickerton and Alain-G. Gagnon (Peterborough, ON: Broadview, 2004), 203.

22 See, among others, F.L. Morton and Rainer Knopff, *The Charter Revolution and the Court Party* (Peterborough, ON: Broadview, 2000).

23 Chris Morris, "NB Holds More Talks on Early French Immersion after Losing Court Case," Canadian Press, 12 June 2008, http://hamlit2008.blogspot .ca/2008/06/wow-lots-to-report-from-press-in-nb.html.

24 "Michel Bastarache reprend du service," *L'Acadie Nouvelle*, 23 August 2008, 3.

25 D.F. Philpott and C.A.M. Fiedorowicz, *The Supreme Court of Canada Ruling on Learning Disabilities* (Ottawa: Learning Disabilities Association of Canada, 2012), 2.

26 Quoted in Steve Mertl, "Supreme Court Decision in Favour of Dyslexic B.C. Students Has Wide Implications for School Boards across Canada," Yahoo News, 10 November 2012, https://ca.news.yahoo.com/blogs/dailybrew /supreme-court-decision-favour-dyslexic-b-c-student-224858176.html.

27 Quoted in "Top Court Strikes Down Quebec Private Health-Care Ban," CBC
News, 9 June 2005, http://www.cbc.ca/news/canada/top-court-strikes-down-
quebec-private-health-care-ban-1.547692.

28 Richard Saillant, *Over the Cliff? Acting Now to Avoid New Brunswick's Bankruptcy* (Moncton: Canadian Institute for Research on Public Policy and Public Administration, 2014).

29 Marilyn L. Pilkington, "Enforcing the Charter: The Supervisory Role of Superior Courts and the Responsibility of Legislatures for Remedial Systems,"
Supreme Court Law Review 25 (2004): 77–99. See also full text of the Supreme
Court of Canada decision at Lexum, http://scc-csc.lexum.com/scc-csc/scc-csc
/en/item/2096/index.do, and http://www.canlii.org/en/ca/scc/doc/2003/2003
scc62/2003scc62.html.

30 Justice Colin Westman quoted in "The New Face of Judicial Defiance," *Globe
and Mail*, 13 December 2013.

31 Sean Fine, "Ottawa's Refugee Health-Care Cuts 'Cruel and Unusual,' Court
Rules," *Globe and Mail*, 4 July 2014,
http://www.theglobeandmail.com/news/politics/ottawas-refugee-health-cuts-
cruel-and-unusual-court-rules/article19459837/.

32 Debra Black, "Court Strikes Down Conservatives' Cuts to Refugee Health-Care
Coverage," *Star*, 5 July 2014, http://www.thestar.com/news/canada/2014/07/04
/court_rules_against_conservative_governments_refugee_health_cuts.html.

33 Quoted in ibid.

34 Ignatieff, *Fire and Ashes*, 63–4.

35 Peter Russell, "The Political Purposes of the Canadian Charter of Rights and
Freedoms," *Canadian Bar Review* (Charter ed.) 61 (1983): 51–2.

36 Anne Gilbert and Joseph Yvon Thériault, "Vers l'institutionnalisation des
services à la petite enfance francophone : entre judiciarisation et compromis
politique," *Revue de l'Université de Moncton* 35, no. 2 (2004): 168.

37 Savoie, *Court Government and the Collapse of Accountability*, 52.

38 Ibid.

39 Ibid.

40 Ibid.

41 Department of Aboriginal Affairs and Northern Development, *Aboriginal
Consultation and Accommodation* (Ottawa: Minister of the Department of
Aboriginal Affairs and Northern Development, 2011), 1.

42 Ibid., 12.

43 Ibid., 1.

44 "Federal PS Unions Unite to Challenge Constitutionality of Omnibus Budget Bill," *Globe and Mail*, 10 December 2013.

45 "Cabinet Cannot Keep All Its Secrets," *National Post*, 12 July 2002. See also Savoie, *Court Government*, 215.

46 Canada, Supreme Court of Canada, "Statistics 2002 to 2012" (Ottawa: Supreme Court of Canada, 2013), 4.

47 Ibid.; and consultation with Roger Bilodeau, registrar, Supreme Court of Canada, 23 December 2013.

48 Commissioner for Federal Judicial Affairs, *Process for an Application for Appointment* (Ottawa: Office of the Commissioner for Federal Judicial Affairs, n.d.).

49 Songer, *Transformation of the Supreme Court of Canada*, 109–11. See also Adam M. Dodek, *Reforming the Supreme Court Appointment Process 2004–2014: A Ten-Year Democratic Audit* (Ottawa: University of Ottawa, Faculty of Law, May 2014).

50 Various consultations with Roméo LeBlanc, various dates between 1982 and 2004, Ottawa and Grande-Digue, NB.

51 See, for example, Joseph Fletcher and Paul Howe, "Public Opinion and the Courts," *Choice* 6, no. 3 (2000): 4–53.

52 See, for example, Tim Naumetz, "Majority Sides with Supreme Court Ruling on Senate Reform, Not Prime Minister's Office," *Hill Times* (Ottawa), 6 May 2014, http://www.hilltimes.com/news/politics/2014/05/05/majority-sides-with-supreme-court-ruling-on-senate-reform/38411.

53 See, for example, *Globe and Mail*, accessed 20 November 2013, www.globeandmail.com/report-on-business/industry.

54 Quoted in Kirk Makin, "Access to Justice Becoming a Privilege of the Rich, Judge Warns," *Globe and Mail*, 10 February 2011, http://www.theglobeandmail.com/news/national/access-to-justice-becoming-a-privilege-of-the-rich-judge-warns/article565873/.

55 "Ontario's Legal System Too Costly and Complicated, New Chief Justice Says," *Globe and Mail*, 9 September 2014.

56 "Issues & Associations Directory," Hillwatch.com, n.d., http://www.hillwatch.com/PPRC/Links_Directory/Issues_and_Associations/.

57 Bevir, *Democratic Governance*, 57.

58 Patrick Weller, "Introduction: The Institutions of Governance," in *Institutions on the Edge? Capacity for Governance*, ed. Michael Keating, John Wanna, and Patrick Weller (St Leonards, Australia: Allen and Unwin, 2000), 4.

59 See, for example, "Contracting Out Saves Public Money, Clement says," *Toronto Star*, 4 December 2013.

60 I do not have authority to release the name of the consultant. His email is dated 2 February 2014.

61 Atlantic Canada Opportunities Agency, *Section II: Analysis of Programs by Strategic Outcome – 2013–14 Report on Plans and Priorities* (Moncton: Atlantic Canada Opportunities Agency, 2014).

62 Gordon Robertson, "The Changing Role of the Privy Council Office," *Canadian Public Administration* 14, no. 4 (1975): 488 and 500.

63 Harvie André made this observation on a number of occasions, including on 19 October 2005 at the Edmonton roundtable of the Commission of Inquiry into the Sponsorship Program and Advertising Activities.

64 Lord Wilson of Dinton, "Mandarin Myth," 26.

65 Jeffrey Simpson, *The Friendly Dictatorship* (Toronto: McClelland and Stewart, 2002).

66 "House of Commons Most Lobbied Government Institution," *Hill Times* (Ottawa), 30 June 2014, 1 and 6.

67 See Savoie, *Power: Where Is It?*, 181.

68 See, among others, Savoie, *Governing from the Centre*.

69 John Kenneth Galbraith, *The Anatomy of Power* (Boston: Houghton Mifflin, 1983), 142.

70 "Minister of Finance Announces Formation of Economic Advisory Council," news release, Department of Finance, Ottawa, 18 December 2008.

71 Bill Curry, "Boardroom Confidential: What CEOs Are Asking of Jim Flaherty," *Globe and Mail*, 15 August 2012, http://www.theglobeandmail.com /news/politics/boardroom-confidential-what-ceos-are-asking-of-jim-flaherty /article4483479/.

72 Shawn McCarthy, "Oil Industry Successfully Lobbied Ottawa to Delay Climate Regulations, E-mails Show," *Globe and Mail*, 8 November 2013, http://www.theglobeandmail.com/report-on-business/industry-news/energy-and-resources/oil-industry-successfully-lobbied-ottawa-to-delay-climate-regu-lations-e-mails-show/article15346866/.

73 "The 10 Lobby Groups with the Most Contact with Federal Officials," *Maclean's*, 22 November 2012.

74 "Ritz, Moore Most Lobbied Ministers Last Year," *Hill Times* (Ottawa), 27 January 2014, 1 and 16.

75 "Who Meets with PMO and Why," *Hill Times* (Ottawa), 2 June 2014, 1 and 16.

76 Ibid.

77 "Industry, Foreign Affairs, Finance Rank as Top Lobbied Departments in 2013–14," *Hill Times* (Ottawa), 23 June 2014, 7.

78 See, for example, "Former Natural Resources Chief of Staff, PMO Adviser Joins Barrick Gold," *Hill Times* (Ottawa), 3 February 2014, 4.

79 "Accountability Act's Five-Year Lobbying Ban Sends Retiring PMOs Out Early: Moore," *Hill Times* (Ottawa), 16 July 2007, 1 and 7.

80 Veteran *Globe and Mail* columnist Hugh Winsor made this observation before Justice Gomery at the Toronto roundtable consultations, Commission of Inquiry into the Sponsorship Program and Advertising Activities, Ottawa, 5 October 2005, 18.

81 Bernard Crick, *In Defence of Politics* (Chicago: Chicago University Press, 2004), 67.

82 "Schumpeter: Cronies and Capitols," *Economist*, 10 August 2013.

CHAPTER FIVE

1 "No Ordinary Politician," *Economist*, 13 April 2013.

2 Ibid.

3 See Savoie, *Thatcher, Reagan, Mulroney*.

4 Ibid.; and see also Lord Wilson of Dinton, "Mandarin Myth."

5 Consultation with a former senior official in the British government, various dates. See also Savoie, *Thatcher, Reagan, Mulroney*.

6 See, among others, Savoie, *Breaking the Bargain*.

7 Richard Crossman, *The Diaries of a Cabinet Minister* (London: Hamilton and Cape, 1975), 1:90.

8 Shirley Williams, "The Decision Makers," in *Policy and Practice: The Experience of Government* (London: Royal Institute of Public Administration, 1980), 81.

9 See Savoie, *Thatcher, Reagan and Mulroney*, 82.

10 Ibid., 100.

11 See, among others, Savoie, *Thatcher, Reagan, Mulroney*, ch. 5.

12 Bevir, *Democratic Governance*, 36.

13 Ibid., 68.

14 See, among many others, Savoie, *Thatcher, Reagan, Mulroney*.

15 Quoted, ibid., 4.

16 Savoie, *Governing from the Centre*, 249.

17 John L. Manion and Cynthia Williams, "Transition Planning at the Federal Level in Canada," in *Taking Power: Managing Government Transitions*, ed. Donald J. Savoie (Toronto: Institute of Public Administration of Canada, 1993), 109.

18 Edward Bridges, "Portrait of a Profession," in *Style in Administration*, ed. K.A. Chapman and A. Dunsire (London: Allen and Unwin, 1950), 50.

19 Savoie, *Governing from the Centre*, 302.

20 Jacques Bourgault, "The Mintzberg Model and Some Empirical Evidence: Putting It to the Test," in *Managing Publicly*, ed. Henry Mintzberg and Jacques Bourgault (Toronto: Institute of Public Administration of Canada, 2000), 159.

21 Ibid., 166.

22 Public Policy Forum, *Managing Change: The Evolving Role of the Commonwealth's Top Public Servants* (Ottawa: Public Policy Forum, December 1998), 46.

23 Bourgault, "Mintzberg Model," 167.

24 "The Top 100 Most Influential People in Government and Politics in Ottawa," *Hill Times* (Ottawa), 22 December 2008, 19.

25 *Power and Influence: 100 Most Influential People in Government and Politics in 2012* (Ottawa: Hill Times Publishing, 2012), 4–17.

26 J. Geddes, P. Wells, J. Gatehouse, J. Smyth, A. Wherry, and M. Petrou, "The 25 Most Important People in Ottawa," *Maclean's*, 27 November 2012, http://www.macleans.ca/news/canada/25-most-important-people-in-ottawa/.

27 The point was made by the group in a letter to the minister responsible for Statistics Canada. "CRDCN Letter to Minister Clement: Census Long-Form Questionnaire," 9 July 2010, http://www.rdc-cdr.ca/article/crdcn-letter-minister-clement-census-long-form-questionnaire.

28 "From Census to Wireless: A Lesson in Intransigence," *Globe and Mail*, 14 September 2013.

29 Bill Curry, "Internal Memo Reveals Ottawa Cut Labour Market Data Spending," *Globe and Mail*, 11 June 2014, http://www.theglobeandmail.com/news/politics/memo-reveals-ottawa-cut-labour-data-spending/article19112612/.

30 Ibid.

31 Quoted in Susan Delacourt, "Tory Government Takes Aim at Bureaucracy," *Toronto Star*, 17 January 2008.

32 See Savoie, *Politics of Public Spending*, 81.

33 Andrew Griffith, "Resetting Citizenship and Multiculturalism," *Optimum Online* 43, no. 2 (June 2013), http://www.optimumonline.ca/print.phtml?lang=french&e=giprtpwarfgr&id=436.

34 "Former CIC Mandarin Says Public Policies Came from Minister's Anecdotes," *Hill Times* (Ottawa), 23 September 2013, 1 and 28.

35 Manion, *How Lucky I've Been*.

36 Ibid., 118.

37 Michael Hatfield, "Public Service Not Irrelevant," *Hill Times* Ottawa), 16 June 2014, 13.

38 Ibid., 164.

39 Ibid., 166.

40 Ibid., 182.

41 Ibid.

42 Ibid.

43 Jacques Bourgault, "Federal Deputy Ministers: Serial Servers Looking for Influence," in *Deputy Ministers in Canada: Comparative and Jurisdictional Perspectives*, ed. Jacques Bourgault and Christopher Dunn (Montreal and Kingston: McGill-Queen's University Press, 2014), 376.

44 Savoie, *Whatever Happened to the Music Teacher?*, ch. 8.

45 See, among others, Savoie, *Breaking the Bargain*; and J.D. Aberbach, R.D. Putnam, and B.A. Rockman, *Bureaucrats and Politicians in Western Democracies* (Cambridge, MA: Harvard University Press, 1981).

46 Max Weber, "Politics as a Vocation," in *From Max Weber*, ed. H.H. Gerth and C.W. Mills (New York: Oxford University Press, 1946), 95.

47 B. Guy Peters, *The Future of Governing* (Lawrence, KS: University Press of Kansas, 2001), 4.

48 Frederick Mosher expressed this concern is his *Democracy and the Public Service* (New York: Oxford University Press, 1982), 185–6.

49 Paul Light makes this point in his *The New Public Service* (Washington, DC: Brookings Institution, 1999), 127.

50 R.A.W. Rhodes, "Recovering the Craft of Public Administration in Network Governance" (paper presented to the International Political Science Association World Congress, Montreal, 19–24 July 2014), 6.

51 United Nations, International Code of Conduct for Public Officials (New York: United Nations, 1996).

52 John Tait, "A Strong Foundation: Report of the Task Force on Public Service Values and Ethics (the Summary," *Canadian Public Administration* 40, no. 1 (1997): 8.

53 Ibid., 11.

54 See, among others, Don Kettl, *The Transformation of Governance: Public Administration for Twenty-First Century America* (Baltimore: Johns Hopkins University Press, 2002).

55 See, among others, J.V. Denhardt and R.B. Denhardt, *The New Public Service: Serving, Not Steering* (Armonk, NY: M.E. Sharpe, 2003).

56 "Interest Groups Too Powerful," *Ottawa Citizen*, 29 May 1988.

57 See, among many others, Christopher Pollitt and Geert Bouckaert, *Public Management Reform: A Comparative Analysis* (Oxford: Oxford University Press, 2000).

58 See, among many others, Barry O'Toole, *The Ideal Public Service: Reflections*

on the Higher Civil Service in Britain (London: Routledge, 2006); and Savoie, *Breaking the Bargain.*

59 Rhodes, "Recovering the Craft of Public Administration," 2.

60 See Bevir, *Democratic Governance*, 68.

61 See Savoie, *Whatever Happened to the Music Teacher?*

62 "Tackling the Web of Rules," Treasury Board Secretariat, 12 June 2009, http://www.tbs-sct.gc.ca/reports-rapports/wr-lr/index-eng.asp.

63 "Governance of Small Federal Entities," ch. 2 of *Report of the Auditor General of Canada*, December 2008.

64 Based on information from the Treasury Board Secretariat, as reported in Steve Maher, "Stephen Harper's PR Obsession Fostering Paranoia and Paralysis in Public Service," 30 November 2011, *Province*, 2 December 2011, http://blogs.theprovince.com/2011/12/02/stephen-maher-stephen-harpers-pr-obsession-is-fostering-paranoia-and-paralysis-in-public-service/.

65 Quoted in "PM Harper Takes Communications Strategy to a Whole New Level," *Hill Times* (Ottawa), 21 November 2011, 33.

66 "Swelling of Feds' Communications Staff Reflects Growing Public Relations State," *Hill Times* (Ottawa), 11 August 2014, 1 and 4.

67 Ralph Heintzman, "Loyal to a Fault," *Optimum Online*, 40, no. 1 (March 2010), http://www.optimumonline.ca/print.phtml?e=igsifurriyunsrw&id=358.

68 See Savoie, *Whatever Happened to the Music Teacher?* Statistics Canada, however, reports that there are 276,463 people employed in federal public administration. See Bill Curry, "Federal Public Service Shed 31 Percent More Jobs Than Budgeted," *Globe and Mail*, 4 August 2014, http://www.theglobeand mail.com/news/politics/globe-politics-insider/federal-public-service-shed-31-per-cent-more-jobs-than-budgeted/article19893002.

69 "Whistleblower Scientists to Fight Government Firing," CBC News, 15 July 2004, http://www.cbc.ca/news/canada/whistleblower-scientists-to-fight-government-firing-1.497874.

70 Conversations with Ralph Heintzman, various dates.

71 Quoted in G. Lodge and B. Rogers, *Whitehall's Black Box: Accountability and Performance in the Senior Civil Service* (London: Institute for Public Policy Research, 2006), 63.

CHAPTER SIX

1 Based on several consultations with Elmer MacKay.

2 Andrew Cohen, "Double Foil and Trouble, Foreign Burn and Trade Bubble," *Globe and Mail*, 22 February 2005.

3 Fraser Institute, *Government Failure in Canada, 2005 Report*, Occasional Paper Series 86 (Vancouver: Fraser Institute, October 2005), 39.

4 Savoie, *Court Government and the Collapse of Accountability*, 323.

5 Perry and Rainey, "Public-Private Distinction in Organization Theory."

6 See, among others, Paul C. Nutt, "Comparing Public and Private Sector Decision-Making Practices," *Journal of Public Administration Research and Theory* 16, no. 2 (2006): 290.

7 See, among others, M. Hitt, R. Ireland, and R. Hoskisson, *Strategic Management: Competitiveness and Globalization – Concepts*, 3rd ed. (St Paul, MN: West, 2003).

8 See, among many others, Savoie, *Thatcher, Reagan and Mulroney*.

9 Kate Jenkins, Karen Caines, and Andrew Jackson, *Improving Management in Government: The Next Steps* (London: Her Majesty's Stationery Office, 1988), 9 and 15.

10 See Geoffrey Fry, Andrew Flynn, Andrew Gray, William Jenkins, and Brian Rutherford, "Symposium on Improving Management in Government," *Public Administration* 55, no. 4 (1988): 445.

11 Butler, cited in House of Commons, London, *Official Report*, 18 February 1988. See also Peter Hennessy, *Whitehall* (New York: Free Press, 1989), 621.

12 Christopher Pollitt, *Managerialism and the Public Service: The Anglo-American Experience* (Oxford: Basil Blackwell, 1998).

13 See, among others, Savoie, *Thatcher, Reagan, Mulroney*.

14 John Edwards, manager of PS 2000, "Revitalization of the Canadian Public Service," notes for a speaking engagement to the Association of Professional Executives, 11 March 1991, Ottawa, 131.

15 Paul Tellier, "Public Service 2000: The Renewal of the Public Service," *Canadian Public Administration* 33 no. 2 (1990): 131.

16 Savoie, *Thatcher, Reagan and Mulroney*, 240.

17 Alti Rodal, "Special Operating Agencies: Issues for Parent Departments and Central Agencies" (Ottawa: Canadian Centre for Management Development, 1996), 5.

18 See federal government officials, quoted in Savoie, *Breaking the Bargain*, 58, 59, and 293.

19 See Savoie, *Whatever Happened to the Music Teacher?*, 122.

20 Office of the Prime Minister, *Federal Accountability Action Plan: Turning a New Leaf* (Ottawa, 11 April 2006), 30.

21 Ralph Heintzman, "Establishing the Boundaries of the Public Service: Toward a New Moral Contract," in *Governing: Essays in Honour of Donald J.*

Savoie, ed. James Bickerton and B. Guy Peters (Montreal and Kingston: McGill-Queen's University Press, 2013), 92.

22 See, among many others, Savoie, *Whatever Happened to the Music Teacher?*.

23 Canada, *Blueprint 2020: Building Tomorrow's Public Service Together* (Ottawa: Privy Council Office, 2013), 6.

24 Louis Tenace, email to author, 31 December 2013.

25 Bevir, *Democratic Governance*, 75.

26 Ibid., 73.

27 Savoie, *Power: Where Is It?*, 169.

28 See, among many others, Carol Weiss, *Evaluation Research: Methods for Assessing Program Effectiveness* (Englewood Cliffs, NJ: Prentice-Hall, 1972); Aaron Wildavsky, "The Self-Evaluating Organizations," *Public Administration Review* 32, no. 5 (1972): 509–20; and James Wilson, *Bureaucracy: What Government Agencies Do and Why They Do It* (New York: Basic Books, 1991).

29 Bourgault, "Federal Deputy Ministers," 377.

30 Ibid.

31 Consultation with a former senior federal government employee, 2 September 2014. See also Bruce Campion-Smith, "Trouble at Transport: Clashes over Spending," *Star*, 20 June 2009, http://www.thestar.com/news/canada /2009/06/20/trouble_at_transport_clashes_over_spending.html.

32 Savoie, *Breaking the Bargain*, 164.

33 Auditor General, *Reflections on a Decade of Serving Parliament* (Ottawa: Office of the Auditor General, 2001), 35–6.

34 Treasury Board of Canada Secretariat, *2010 Annual Report on the Health of the Evaluation Function* (Ottawa: Treasury Board of Canada Secretariat, 2010), 3 and 4.

35 Canada, *Evaluating the Effectiveness of Programs*, 2009 Fall Report of the Auditor General of Canada (Ottawa: Office of the Auditor General of Canada, 2009), 3–5.

36 See Office of the Auditor General, *Annual Report* (Ottawa: Office of the Auditor General, 1986).

37 Paul G. Thomas, "Are There Enough Ethics in Government Yet? How Would We Know?" (speech to the Annual Meeting of the Conflict of Interest Commissioners of Canada, Winnipeg, 4 September 2014), 8.

38 "Auditor General Assesses Afghan Mission," *Star*, 23 January 2010, http://www.thestar.com/news/canada/2010/01/23/auditor_general_assesses_af ghan_mission.html.

39 See, among many others, Christopher Pollitt and Geert Bouckaert, *Public*

Management Reform: A Comparative Perspective (Oxford: Oxford University Press, 2004).

40 Bevir, *Democratic Governance*, 35.

41 Lee Berthiaume, "Federal Auditors Found $1.5 Billion in Significant Defence Department Accounting Errors," *Ottawa Citizen*, 9 October 2013, http://www2.canada.com/ottawacitizen/news/archives/story.html?id=4fe9634 e-b4af-4fb5-a613-f9e7ba081495&p=1.

42 "Audit takes Transport Canada to task on wasteful spending contracts," http://www.theglobeandmail.com/news/politics/audit-takes-transport-canada-to-task-on-wasteful-spending-contracts/article16222387/, 7 January 2014.

43 Bevir, *Democratic Governance*, 43.

44 See, among others, Savoie, *Court Government*, 134.

45 See, among others, Jordan Press, "Senators Cut Spending on Food, Travel and Other Expenses in Wake of Spending Scandal," *National Post*, 23 December 2013, http://news.nationalpost.com/2013/12/27/senators-cut-spending-on-food-travel-and-other-expenses-in-wake-of-spending-scandal/; "Senate Expense Puts a Chill on Senators' Spending, Expense Records Show," *Hill Times* (Ottawa), 1 and 24; and "Senators' Optional Travel Plunges after Wallin Audit," *Ottawa Citizen*, 30 September 2014.

46 O'Toole, "Ideal of Public Service," 2.

47 Ibid., 5.

48 Tait, "Strong Foundation."

49 Ibid., 11.

50 John Langford, "Acting on Values: An Ethical Dead End for Public Servants," *Canadian Public Administration* 47, no. 4 (2004): 432.

51 Ibid., 433.

52 Jocelyne Bourgon, "Dedication," in John C. Tait, "A Strong Foundation," *Report of the Task Force on Public Service Values and Ethics* (Ottawa: Canadian Centre for Management Development, January 2000), 4-5.

53 Privy Council Office, *Seventh Annual Report to the Prime Minister on the Public Service of Canada* (Ottawa: Privy Council Office, 31 March 2000), 2.

54 Privy Council Office, *Ninth Annual Report to the Prime Minister on the Public Service of Canada* (Ottawa: Privy Council Office, 29 March 2002), 11.

55 Privy Council Office, *Tenth Annual Report to the Prime Minister on the Public Service of Canada* (Ottawa: Privy Council Office, 31 March 2003), 14.

56 Office of the Auditor General, *Report of the Auditor General of Canada*, ch. 2, "Accountability and Ethics in Government" (Ottawa: Office of the Auditor General November 2003), 12-18.

57 Savoie, *Breaking the Bargain*, 117.

58 See ibid.
59 Savoie, *Court Government*, 132–5.
60 See, among many others, Savoie, *Whatever Happened to the Music Teacher?*
61 Eric Reguly, "By Selling Its Palace in Rome, Canada Harms Its Global Clout," *Globe and Mail*, 7 November 2013, http://www.theglobeandmail.com/news/world/world-insider/by-selling-its-palace-in-rome-canada-is-slashing-its-global-clout/article15308668.
62 "Indian Developer Buys Canadian High Commission in London for $530 Million," *Globe and Mail*, 28 November 2013.
63 See Savoie, *Power: Where Is It?*, 204.
64 Nutt, "Comparing Public and Private Sector," 289–318.
65 See, among others, Perry and Rainey, "Public-Private Distinction in Organization Theory."
66 W.M. Blumenthal, "Candid Reflections of a Businessman in Washington," in *Public Management: Public and Private Perceptions*, ed. J. Perry and K. Kraemer, 22–33 (Palo Alto, CA: Mayfield, 1983).
67 Public Policy Forum, "Flat, Flexible, and Forward-Thinking: Public Service Next" (Ottawa: Public Policy Forum, March 2014), 5.

CHAPTER SEVEN

1 Quoted in Donald J. Savoie, *Regional Economic Development: Canada's Search for Solutions* (Toronto: University of Toronto Press, 1997), 150.
2 Department of Finance, *Economic Development for Canada in the 1980s* (Ottawa: Department of Finance, November 1981).
3 Department of Regional Industrial Expansion, "Speaking Notes: The Honourable Ed Lumley to the House of Commons on the Industrial and Regional Development Program" (27 June 1983), 1, 2; and Office of the Prime Minister, "Reorganization for Economic Development," news release, 12 January 1982.
4 See, for example, Donald J. Savoie, *Visiting Grandchildren: Economic Development in the Maritimes* (Toronto: University of Toronto Press, 2006).
5 Ibid., 138.
6 See, among others, Savoie, *Regional Economic Development*.
7 Ibid., 139.
8 See "Announcing My Appointment," news release, Office of the Prime Minister, 28 October 1986.
9 Jack Harris was first elected to Parliament for the NDP in that by-election.
10 See, among many others, "PM Launches New Agency for Atlantic Canada,"

Halifax Sunday Herald, 7 June 1987; and "Atlantic Canada Gets Big Boost," *Fredericton Daily Gleaner*, 8 June 1987.

11 "Hatfield, McKenna Voice Support," *Fredericton Daily Gleaner*, 9 June 1987. See also "Regions Leaders' Reaction Positive," *Fredericton Daily Gleaner*, 8 June 1987.

12 CBC Radio News (Halifax), 8 June 1987, MIT Media Tapes and Transcripts.

13 See "Tories Seek to Regain Support with Western Diversification Plan," *Ottawa Citizen*, 9 August 1987.

14 "Western Diversification Initiative," news release, Office of the Prime Minister, 4 August 1987.

15 Canada, "Notes pour une allocution du Premier Ministre Brian Mulroney sur le développement régional devant les Chambres de Commerce d'Edmonton et de l'Alberta" Office of the Prime Minister, 4 August 1987, 3 (my translation).

16 "Aid Package Focus of PM's Trip," *Globe and Mail*, 1 August 1987.

17 "Tory Activists, Friends Fill New Board," *Globe and Mail*, 21 November 1987.

18 See Savoie, *Visiting Grandchildren*, 89.

19 Department of Finance, *Budget Papers: The Economic Outlook and Fiscal Plan* (Ottawa: Department of Finance, 18 February 1987).

20 See, among others, Savoie, *Visiting Grandchildren*, 150–5.

21 Canada, *Report of the Minister for the Fiscal Year 1988–9* (Moncton: Atlantic Canada Opportunities Agency, 31 August 1989), 31.

22 Ibid., 36.

23 Savoie, *Visiting Grandchildren*, 158.

24 Ibid., 159–60.

25 See Savoie, *Visiting Grandchildren*.

26 Savoie, "Perfect Storm in Reverse," 207–27.

27 Atlantic Canada Opportunities Agency, *Atlantic Canada Opportunities Agency 1997–98 Estimates: A Report on Plans and Priorities* (Moncton: Atlantic Canada Opportunities Agency, February 1997), 14.

28 Savoie, *Visiting Grandchildren*, 175.

29 "PQ Takes Clarity Bill Complaints to Ottawa," CBC News, 11 November 2000, http://www.cbc.ca/news/canada/pq-takes-clarity-bill-complaints-to-ottawa-1.238898.

30 Canada, Budget Document, *Budget Speech*, Department of Finance, 16 February 1999.

31 Canada, *Budget Documents: Making Canada's Economy More Innovative* (Ottawa: Department of Finance, 28 February 2000).

32 Savoie, *Visiting Grandchildren*, 179.

33 "Prime Minister Announces New Atlantic Investment Partnership," news release, Office of the Prime Minister, 29 June 2000.

34 Savoie, *Visiting Grandchildren*, 182.

35 This and the preceding information is drawn from Treasury Board of Canada Secretariat, *Atlantic Canada Opportunities Agency: Report on Plans and Priorities* (various years) (Ottawa: Treasury Board of Canada Secretariat).

36 Ibid.

37 Treasury Board Secretariat, *2011–12 MAF Results: Atlantic Canada Opportunities Agency* (Ottawa: Treasury Board Secretariat, n.d.).

38 Savoie, *Regional Economic Development*, 121

39 Canada, *Proceedings of the Standing Senate Committee on National Finance*, no. 12, 22 March 1973, 14–24.

40 Quoted in Donald J. Savoie, *The Canadian Centre for Management Studies* (Ottawa: Treasury Board Secretariat, July 1987), 8.

41 Ibid., 2–3.

42 Ibid., 6.

43 Ibid., 10.

44 Ibid., 12.

45 These comments were written in the margin of my paper, and the document was revised to reflect these concerns.

46 "A New Commitment to Public Sector Management," notes for an address by Don Mazankowski to the Public Policy Forum, Toronto, 14 April 1988, 16.

47 Savoie, *Canadian Centre for Management* Studies, 17.

48 Ibid., 18.

49 Manion, *How Lucky I've Been*, 205–6.

50 Ibid., 205.

51 The three books were coedited by B. Guy Peters and myself.

52 Task Force on Public Service Values and Ethics, *A Strong Foundation: Report of the Task Force on Public Service Values and Ethics* (Ottawa: Canadian Centre for Management Development, 1996).

53 "Required Training," Canada School of Public Service, n.d., http://www.csps-efpc.gc.ca/forlearners/requiredtraining/index-eng.aspx.

54 "Our Faculty," Canada School of Public Service, n.d., http://www.csps-efpc.gc.ca/faculty/index-eng.aspx.

55 Canada School of Public Service, *2012–13 Report on Plans and Priorities* (Ottawa: Canada School of Public Service, n.d.). The document is available on the school's and the Treasury Board's websites.

56 Ibid. See also the *Report on Plans and Priorities 2008–09*.

57 Don Mazankowski, president of the Treasury Board, to Brian Mulroney, prime minister, 3 September 1987, 1.

58 Ibid., attached document, "The Canadian Centre for Management Studies," 12.

59 I base this observation on conversations that I have had with federal government officials in recent years.

60 Canada School of Public Service, *2012–13 Report on Plans and Priorities* (Ottawa: Canada School of Public Service, n.d.). The document is available on the school's and the Treasury Board's websites.

61 Ibid., 8.

62 Ibid., 8 and 14.

63 Treasury Board Secretariat, "2011–12 MAF Results: Canada School of Public Service" (Ottawa: Treasury Board Secretariat, n.d.).

64 Mazankowski's to Mulroney, 8.

65 Linda Lizotte-MacPherson to all deputy heads, Canada School of Public Service, Ottawa, 3 June 2014.

66 Ibid. See also Canada School of Public Service, *Backgrounder: New Approach to Learning* (Ottawa: Canada School of Public Service, 2 June 2014).

67 Ibid.

68 "Ottawa's Civil Service School Is Teaching the Wrong Lessons," *Globe and Mail*, 2 April 2013, http://www.theglobeandmail.com/globe-debate/editorials/ottawas-civil-service-school-is-teaching-the-wrong-lessons/article10664421/.

69 Quoted in Kathryn May, "Federal Executives Lack Training, Flexibility, Expert Says," *Ottawa Citizen*, 17 June 2014, http://ottawacitizen.com/news/national/federal-executives-lack-training-flexibility-expert-says.

70 Ibid.

71 Alex Boutilier, "Canadian Government Scientists Can't Speak Freely Because of Meddling: Survey," *Star*, 21 October 2013, http://www.thestar.com/news/canada/2013/10/21/canadian_government_scientists_cant_speak_freely_survey.html.

72 Thomas Homer-Dixon, Heather Douglas, and Lucie Edwards, "Fix the Link Where Science and Policy Meet," *Globe and Mail*, 23 June 2014.

73 Savoie, *Canadian Centre for Management Studies*, 6.

74 Quoted in "Executive at Centre of Patronage Storm Joins Public Service," *Globe and Mail*, 24 June 2014.

75 Bevir, *Democratic Governance*, 31.

76 Savoie, *Visiting Grandchildren*, 160.

77 Terry M. Moe, "The New Economics of Organization," *American Journal of Political Science* 28, no. 4 (1984): 739–77.

78 See, among many others, Abbas Rana, "Cappe Agrees with Harper," *Hill Times*, 28 October 2013, http://www.hilltimes.com/civil-circles/hill-life-people /2013/10/28/cappe-agrees-with-harper-scientists-should-not-be-free-to/36425.

79 "RCMP Seek to Replace Officers Moved to National Security Case," *Globe and Mail*, 19 December 2014.

80 RCMP, *Royal Canadian Mounted Police 2013–2014 Department Performance Report* (Ottawa: RCMP, 2014), 8; and "RCMP Slims Ottawa Bureaucracy in Bid to Shift Focus Back to Policing," *Globe and Mail*, 7 June 2012.

CHAPTER EIGHT

1 Donald J. Savoie, *Invest More, Innovate More, Trade More, Learn More: The Way Ahead for Nova Scotia* (Halifax: Government of Nova Scotia, July 2010).

2 Ibid., 26.

3 Ibid.

4 Ibid., 26–7.

5 Commission on Building Our New Economy, "Draft: Summary Report" (Halifax: Commission on Building Our New Economy, n.d.), 7. See also, *Now or Never: An Urgent Call to Attention for Nova Scotians* (Halifax: OneNS.ca, 2014), 41.

6 Donald J. Savoie, *Harrison McCain: Single-Minded Purpose* (Montreal and Kingston: McGill-Queen's University Press, 2013), 211.

7 James Q. Wilson, *Bureaucracy* (New York: Basic Books, 1989), 14.

8 Ibid., x.

9 James G. March and Herbert A. Simon, *Organizations* (New York: John Wiley and Sons, 1958), 5.

10 Wilson, *Bureaucracy*, xi.

11 John C. Tait, *A Strong Foundation: Report on the Task Force on Public Service Values and Ethics* (Ottawa: Canadian Centre for Management Development, 2000), 29–37.

12 Ibid., 36.

13 James Bagnall, "Public Admin Jobs Rising in Ottawa Despite PS Cuts Elsewhere," *Ottawa Citizen*, 5 September 2014, http://ottawacitizen.com/news /public-admin-jobs-rising-in-national-capital-region.

14 See Savoie, *Politics of Public Spending in Canada*, 213.

15 There have been twenty such annual reports as of 31 March 2013. See Privy Council Office, *Twentieth Annual Report to the Prime Minister on the Public Service of Canada* (Ottawa: Privy Council Office, 30 March 2013).

16 Lawrence Martin, "A Day in the Life of Stephen Harper," *Globe and Mail*, 9 October 2010.

17 Campbell Clark, "What the Foreign Workers Program Really Needs: Transparency," *Globe and Mail*, 30 April 2014, http://www.theglobeandmail.com /news/politics/globe-politics-insider/transparency-is-the-best-start-to-fix-the-temporary-foreign-worker-program/article18335874/.

18 Jonathán Malloy, "The Standing Committee on Public Accounts," in Commission of Inquiry into the Sponsorship Scandal and Advertising Activities, *Restoring Accountability: Research Studies*, vol. 1, *Parliament, Ministers and Deputy Ministers* (Ottawa: Commission of Inquiry, 2006), 64–100.

19 Quoted in Savoie, *Court Government and the Collapse of Accountability*, 283.

20 For a list of Cabinet committees, Mackenzie King to Chrétien, see Savoie, *Governing from the Centre*, 43–5.

21 Herbert Kaufman, *Are Government Organizations Immortal?* (Washington, DC: Brookings, 1976).

22 Alexandra Panetta, "One Baird Speech, 17 Busy Civil Servants: How a D.C. Event Sowed Panic in Ottawa," *Globe and Mail*, 21 June 2014, http://www .theglobeandmail.com/news/politics/one-baird-speech-17-busy-civil-servants-how-a-dc-event-sowed-panic-in-ottawa/article19282158/#dashboard/follows/.

23 Ibid.

24 Savoie, *Whatever Happened to the Music Teacher?*, 16.

25 I secured the information from the government of Canada website, Treasury Board Secretariat. I included for fiscal year 2013–14 the following: PCO, PMO, PSC, TBS, Finance, Canada School of Public Service, OAG, Offices of the Commissioner of Lobbying, Information, Privacy, Official Languages, and Parliamentary Budget Offices.

26 See, among others, Savoie, *Whatever Happened to the Music Teacher?*

27 Kenneth Prewitt and William Nowlin make a similar observation about politicians in "Political Ambitions and the Behaviour of Incumbent Politicians," *Western Political Quarterly* 22, no. 2 (1969): 298–308.

28 See, among many others, Chris Hood and Martin Lodge, "From Sir Humphrey to Sir Nigel: What Future for the Public Service Bargain after Blairworld?," *Political Quarterly* 77, no. 3 (2000) 360–68. See also Stella Manzie and Jean Hartley, *Dancing on Ice: Leadership with Political Astuteness by Senior Public Servants in the U.K.* (Milton Keynes, UK: Open University, 2013).

29 David McLaughlin, "It's Time to Shine More Light on Canada's Political Staff," *Globe and Mail*, 26 November 2013.

30 Evert Lindquist and Ken Rasmussen, "Deputy Ministers and New Political

Governance: From Neutral Competence to Promiscuous Partisans to a New Balance?," in Bakvis and Jarvis, *From New Public Management*, 191.

31 Peter Aucoin, "The New Public Governance and the Public Service Commission," *Optimum Online* 36, no. 2 (2006): 33–49.

32 See, for example, Jonathan Boston and John Halligan, "Political Management and New Political Government: Reconciling Political Responsiveness and Neutral Competence," in Bakvis and Jarvis, *From New Public Management*, 208.

33 Savoie, *Governing from the Centre*.

34 Ibid., 330.

35 Quoted in ibid. See also Sharon Sutherland, "The Al-Mashat Affair: Administrative Accountability in Parliamentary Institutions," *Canadian Public Administration* 34, no. 4 (1991): 595.

36 Jean Chrétien, *Straight from the Heart* (Toronto: Key Porter Books, 1985), 18.

37 Office of the Auditor General, *2013 Spring Report of the Auditor General of Canada*, chapter 1, "Status Report on Evaluating the Effectiveness of Programs" (Ottawa: Office of the Auditor General, 2013), paras 1.17 and 1.18.

38 See, among others, Savoie, *Governing from the Centre*.

39 See, among many others, Barbara Carroll and David Siegel, *Service in the Field: The World of Front-Line Public Servants* (Montreal and Kingston: McGill-Queen's University Press, 1998).

40 Ibid., 147.

41 Quoted in Savoie, *Whatever Happened to the Music Teacher?*, 118.

42 See, for example, Savoie, *Governing from the Centre*; and Savoie, *Breaking the Bargain*.

43 Savoie, *Court Government*, 20.

44 See Savoie, *Governing from the Centre*.

45 Ibid., ch. 5.

46 Savoie, *Visiting Grandchildren*.

47 Wilson, *Bureaucracy*, chs 2, 7, 10, and 17.

48 See Henry Mintzberg, *Mintzberg on Management: Inside Our Strange World of Organizations* (New York: Free Press, 1989), 106–7, and chs 8 and 9.

49 This was discussed at meetings I attended when I served as assistant secretary planning at the Treasury Board Secretariat in Ottawa in 1986–1987.

50 James Q. Wilson, "The 1994 John Gaus Lecture: Reinventing Public Administration," *Political Science and Politics*, December 1994, 671.

51 Nevil Johnson, "Management in Government," in *Perspective on Management: A Multi-Disciplinary Analysis*, ed. Michael J. Earl (Oxford: Oxford University Press, 1983), 185.

52 Wilson, *Bureaucracy*, 217.

53 B. Guy Peters and Donald J. Savoie, "In Search of Good Governance," in Bakviş and Jarvis, *From New Public Management*, 29–45.
54 Ibid., 41.
55 James Travers, "Branding Team Harper, *Star*, 6 February 2007, http://www.thestar.com/opinion/editorialopinion/2007/02/06/branding_team_harper.
56 Kathryn May, "Depression among PS Executives Nearly Doubles, New Study Finds," National Newswatch, 24 September 2013, http://www.nationalnewswatch.com/2013/09/25/depression-among-ps-executives-nearly-doubles-new-study-finds/#.VBiz7hbkFm5.
57 See Howard Levitt, "Time to Restore the Equilibrium between Public and Private Sector Workers," *Financial Post*, 14 May 2013, http://business.financialpost.com/2013/05/14/time-to-restore-the-equalibrium-between-public-and-private-sector-workers/; Kathryn May, "Clément Puts Alarming Public Service Absenteeism at Top of Priority List," National Newswatch, 7 November 2013, www.nationalnewswatch.com/?s=Clément+puts+alarming+public+service+absenteeism+at+top+of+priority+list; and Kathryn May, "Sick Leave Gap between Public and Private Sectors Explained by Unionization Rates and Demographics: Statscan," National Newswatch, 21 September 2013, http://www.nationalnewswatch.com/2013/09/21/sick-leave-gap-between-public-and-private-sectors-explained-by-unionization-rates-and-demographics-statscan/#.VBi2fxbkFm4.

CHAPTER NINE

1 "Clement Pays Back Taxpayers for Cards," *Toronto Star*, 15 January 2014.
2 See, among others, Lee Berthiaume, "Don't Work so Hard, You're Showing Up Your Less Ambitious Colleagues, Canadian Diplomats Told," *National Post*, 11 November 2011, http://news.nationalpost.com/2011/11/11/dont-work-so-hard-youre-showing-up-your-less-ambitious-colleagues-canadian-diplomats-told/.
3 Tom Peters, *Thriving on Chaos: Handbook for a Management Revolution* (New York: Harper-Perennial, 1991), 426.
4 Luther Gulick and I. Urwick, eds., *Papers on the Science of Administration* (New York: Institute of Public Administration, 1937), 9.
5 "Treasury Hopes Senior Cuts Will Boost Employee Morale," *Citizen* (Ottawa), 18 April 1980.
6 "Review Targets Public Services Executives," *Citizen* (Ottawa), 13 January 2014.

7 Richard Dicerni, "A Letter to a New Deputy Minister," *Public Sector Management* 25, no. 1 (2014): 6 and 7.
8 Chris Griffiths made the same point in his "What's Worse Than Hiring the Wrong People? Keeping Them," *Globe and Mail*, 21 January 2014, http://www
   .theglobeandmail.com/report-on-business/small-business/sb-managing
   /human-resources/whats-worse-than-hiring-the-wrong-people-keeping-
   them/article16417809/.
9 "Unions on Decline in Private Sector," CBC News, 2 September 2012,
   http://www.cbc.ca/news/canada/unions-on-decline-in-private-sector-
   1.1150562; and Ed McHugh, "Paradoxical That Canadian Unions Healthiest
   in Public Sector," *ChronicleHerald*, 25 March 2012, http://thechronicleherald
   .ca/bcw/77537-paradoxical-canadian-unions-healthiest-public-sector.
10 Margaret Wente, "The Police Get Political," *Globe and Mail*, 3 June 2014,
   http://www.theglobeandmail.com/globe-debate/the-police-get-political
   /article18952122/; and Kaleigh Rogers and Adrian Morrow, "Union for
   Ontario Provincial Police Releases Attack Ads Targeting Hudak," *Globe and
   Mail*, 2 June 2014, http://www.theglobeandmail.com/news/politics/police-
   unions-shouldnt-engage-in-partisan-politics-during-election-tories-say/article
   18954315/.
11 Jeffrey Simpson, "In a World Full of Rights, We Ignore Our Responsibility,"
   Globe and Mail, 23 January 2009, http://www.theglobeandmail.com/globe-
   debate/in-a-world-full-of-rights-we-ignore-our-responsibilities/article1147299/.
12 To some observers, the size of the Canadian public service may well be a
   moving target. It depends whether one is looking at the core public service
   (over 210,000), the core plus separate agencies (about 260,000) and both
   combined with Crown corporations and all entities submitting plans and
   budgets to the Treasury Board (about 425,000).
13 This information was provided to me by Treasury Board Secretariat officials
   on 15 February 2012. They informed me that the data came from the
   "Regional Pay System."
14 Barbara Wake Carroll and David Siegel, *Service in the Field: The World of
   Front-Line Public Servants* (Montreal and Kingston: McGill-Queen's University Press, 1999), 119.
15 Treasury Board of Canada Secretariat, *Report of the Review of the Public Service Modernization Act*, 2003, ch 5, 22 December 2011,
   http://publications.gc.ca/site/fra/431799/publication.html.
16 "Politician Laments Reversal of Firings over Email Porn," *Globe and Mail*, 13
   July 2004.

17 "Civil Servants to Be Held Accountable for Ad Scam: Brison," accessed 11 October 2005, www.canada.com.

18 Jean-Jacques Blais made the case about the "bureaucratic inability to impose sanctions" at the Toronto roundtable (Commission of Inquiry into the Sponsorship Program and Advertising Activities, 5 October 2005). See also Simon Doyle, "NRCan's Institutional Inertia Impedes Renewable Energy Development in Canada: Advocates," *Hill Times* (Ottawa), 10 July 2006, http://www.hilltimes.com/feature/2006/07/10/nrcans-institutional-inertia-impedes-renewable-energy-development-in-canada/17033.

19 "Whistleblower Scientists to Fight Government Firing," CBC News, 15 July 2004, http://www.cbc.ca/news/canada/whistleblower-scientists-to-fight-government-firing-1.497874.

20 "But Was It Time Theft?" *Globe and Mail*, 9 September 2010.

21 Treasury Board Secretariat, *Expenditure Review of Federal Public Sector* (Ottawa: Treasury Board Secretariat, 2007), 1:11.10, and n166.

22 Consultations with Ailish Campbell in Moncton, 15 August 2014. Ms Campbell is a director general with Industry Canada on an exchange with the Canadian Council of Chief Executives.

23 Ibid.

24 Ibid.

25 This is true for political leaders. See, for example, James P. Pfiffner, "Can the President Manage the Government?," in *The Managerial Presidency*, ed. James P. Pfiffner, 3–20 (College Station, TX: Texas A&M University Press, 1999).

26 Savoie, "Perfect Storm in Reverse."

27 Arthur Kroeger, "The Central Agencies and Programs Review," in *Managing Strategic Change: Learning from Program Review*, ed. Peter Aucoin and Donald J. Savoie (Ottawa: Canadian Centre for Management Development, 1998), 14–15.

28 See, among many others, Armelita Armit and Jacques Bourgault, eds., *Hard Choices or No Choices: Assessing Program Review* (Toronto: Institute of Public Administration, 1996).

29 Jason Fekete, "Budget Could See Some Departments Cut by More Than 10%: Flaherty," *National Post*, 10 January 2012, http://news.nationalpost.com/2012/01/10/budget-could-see-some-departments-cut-by-more-than-10-jim-flaherty/.

30 Bruce Campion-Smith, "Harper Pledges to Cut "Fat," *Star*, 7 June 2011, http://www.thestar.com/news/canada/2011/06/07/harper_pledges_to_cut_fat.html. See also Treasury Board Secretariat, "Treasury Board President Reaf-

firms Commitment to Reduce Government Spending and Return to a Balanced Budget" (Ottawa: Treasury Board Secretariat, 4 August 2011).

31 "Address by Treasury Board President Tony Clement to Public Service Executives at APEX Symposium," 8 June 2011, Treasury Board of Canada Secretariat, http://www.tbs-sct.gc.ca/media/ps-dp/2011/0608-eng.asp.

32 See, among many others, Gareth D. Myles, *Public Economics* (Cambridge: Cambridge University Press, 1997).

33 Quoted in "Flaherty Defends Hiring Consultant," *Times and Transcript* (Moncton), 21 September 2011.

34 Quoted in Kathryn May, "Budget: Public Servants Hit with Job Cuts, Pension Changes," *Ottawa Citizen*, 28 March 2012, http://www.ottawacitizen .com/business/Budget+Public+servants+with+cuts+pension+changes/6380896 /story.html.

35 Savoie, *Whatever Happened to the Music Teacher?*, chap. 11.

36 Richard Saillant, *Over the Cliff? Acting Now to Avoid New Brunswick's Bankruptcy* (Moncton: Canadian Institute for Research on Public Policy and Public Administration, 2014).

37 Consultations with Richard Dicerni, deputy minister of Industry Canada from 2006 to 2012, various dates.

38 Patrick Dunleavy and Leandro Carrera, *Growing the Productivity of Government Services* (Cheltenham, UK: Edward Elgar, 2013), 2–3.

39 Ibid., 5.

40 Ibid., part 3.

41 A. Corsani, "Le capitalisme cognitif: Les impasses de l'économie politique," in *Sommes-Nous Sortis du Capitalisme Industriel?*, ed. C. Vercellone, 55–75 (Paris: La Dispute, 2003).

42 Aled ab Iorwerth, "Mastering Leviathan: A Review Article on Growing the Productivity of Government Services," n.d., mimeo, 8.

43 See, among others, Penny Collenette, "A School for Bureaucrats Is a Good Idea – But It Must Live Up to Its Principles," *Globe and Mail*, 4 April 2013, http://www.theglobeandmail.com/globe-debate/a-school-for-bureaucrats-is-a-good-idea-but-it-must-live-up-to-its-principles/article10763816/.

44 "Stop Talking about Fixing Government, Just Do It, Public Says," *Citizen* (Ottawa), 21 April 2006.

45 Bill Curry, "Government Spending 68% More on Sick Leave in Last Decade, Budget Watchdog Says," *Globe and Mail*, 6 February 2014, http://www.the globeandmail.com/news/politics/government-spending-on-sick-leave-grew-68-per-cent-in-a-decade-budget-watchdog-finds/article16724830/.

46 The former senior British civil servant made this observation at the conference.

47 See, for example, Savoie, *Court Government and the Collapse of Accountability*.

48 Various conversations with Kathryn May, *Ottawa Citizen*.

49 Kamarck, *End of Government*, 6.

50 Ibid.

51 Thomas S. Axworthy and Julie Burch, *Closing the Implementation Gap* (Kingston: Centre for the Study of Democracy, School of Policy Studies, Queen's University, 2010), 5.

52 Joe Clark summed it up when he observed, "A minister cannot be held responsible for matters that concern him if he was not informed," Canada, House of Commons, *Debates*, 6 June 1991, 1277.

53 See Savoie, *Thatcher, Reagan, and Mulroney*, ch. 7.

54 "Bank CEO Earnings: Here's What the Heads of Canada's Big 5 Banks Earned Last Year," Huffington Post, 25 January 2014, http://www.huffington post.ca/2012/03/15/canda-bank-ceo-earnings_n_1349031.html.

55 Bill Curry, "Top Government Brass Gain from Layoffs," *Globe and Mail*, 4 July 2013, http://www.theglobeandmail.com/news/politics/top-government-brass-gain-from-layoffs/article12978666/.

56 Ruth Hubbard, "Performance, Not Model Employer," *Optimum Online*, 43, no. 2 (June 2013), http://www.optimumonline.ca/article.phtml?e=jqlm rocl&id=438.

57 Treasury Board Secretariat, *Expenditure Review of Federal Public Sector Compensation* (Ottawa: Treasury Board Secretariat, 2007), 15–24.

58 Bevir, *Democratic Governance*, 73.

59 See, among others, "Regular AG Audits of MPs Expenses Would Prevent Spending Scandals," *Hill Times* (Ottawa), 16 December 2013, 1 and 25.

60 Kathryn May, "Public Service Unions Brace for Coming Showdown over Sick Leave," *Ottawa Citizen*, 1 January 2014, http://ajc-ajj.net/files/library/36_-_Press_Monitoring_December_16_2013_to_January_6,_20141.pdf.

61 Simon, "Public Administration in Today's World," 752.

CHAPTER TEN

1 "Over-Regulated America," *Economist*, 16 February 2012, www.economist.com/node/21547789.

2 Ferguson, *Great Degeneration*, 7.

3 "Tories Move to Reduce Red Tape for Small Businesses," *Telegraph Journal* (Saint John, NB), 28 January 2014.

4 Quoted in "Tony Clement Introduces Legislation Aimed at Removing Out-dated Regulations," Global News, 29 January 2014, http://globalnews.ca/news/1115845/tony-clement-introduces-legislation-aimed-at-removing-outdated-regulations/.

5 See various news releases: "Minister Clement Unveils Red Tape Reduction Action Plan," Treasury Board Secretariat, 1 October 2012, http://www.tbs-sct.gc.ca/media/nr-cp/2012/1001-eng.asp; "Minister Clement Highlights the Government of Canada's Efforts to Reduce Red Tape," Treasury Board Secretariat, 24 April 2013, http://www.tbs-sct.gc.ca/media/nr-cp/2013/0424-eng.asp

6 Allan Gregg, "Foreword," in G. Bruce Doern, Red Tape, Red Flags: Regulation for the Innovation Age (Ottawa: Conference Board, 2007), 10.

7 See, among others, Richard A. Posner, "Theories of Economic Regulation," Journal of Economic and Management Studies 5, no. 2 (1974): 335–58.

8 Paul Boothe, "Economists and Regulation Making" (paper presented at 2013 Policy Conference, Canadian Association for Business Economics, 5 April 2013, Ottawa), 6.

9 "Regulator without Peer," Wall Street Journal, 17 April 2014.

10 G. Bruce Doern, Michael J. Prince, and Robert J. Schultz, Rules and Unruli-ness: Canadian Regulatory Democracy, Governance, Capitalism, and Welfarism (Montreal and Kingston: McGill-Queen's University Press, 2013), 7.

11 Ibid., 55.

12 Ibid., 59.

13 Ibid., 63–5.

14 See Christopher Hood, Henry Rothstein, and Robert Baldwin, The Govern-ment of Risk: Understanding Risk Regulation Regimes (Oxford: Oxford University Press, 2001), 23.

15 Ibid., 12.

16 S. Jasanoff, The Fifth Branch: Science Advisors as Policymakers (Cambridge, MA: Harvard University Press, 1990).

17 C. Heiman, Acceptable Risks: Politics, Policy and Risky Technologies (Ann Arbor: University of Michigan Press, 1997).

18 Hood, Rothstein, and Baldwin, Government of Risk, 27.

19 Quoted in Ferguson, Great Degeneration, 59.

20 See, for example, G. Bruce Doern, "Regulating on the Run: The Transforma-tion of the CRTC as a Regulatory Institution," Canadian Public Administration 40, no. 3 (1997): 516–38.

21 See Canadian Radio-television and Telecommunications Commission, Syn-opsis (Ottawa: CRTC, 1995), 2, and 17.

22 See, among others, Kamarck, End of Government, 71.

23 Mazzucato, *Entrepreneurial State*, 1.

24 Canada, *Report of the Ministerial Task Force Report on Program Review*, vol. 16 (Ottawa: Department of Supply and Services, 1986).

25 Office of Privatization and Regulatory Affairs, *Federal Regulatory Plan* (Ottawa:. Office of Privatization and Regulatory Affairs, 1989).

26 Auditor General, *1989 Report of the Auditor General of Canada: Federal Regulatory Review Process* (Ottawa: Office of the Auditor General, 1989), ch. 17.

27 Savoie, "Perfect Storm in Reverse."

28 *"Cutting Red Tape… Freeing Business to Grow,"* Red Tape Reduction Commission, 2 October 2012, http://reduceredtape.gc.ca/index-eng.asp.

29 Ibid.

30 See, for example, Canada, *List of Regulations Associated with Treasury Board*; and Treasury Board of Canada Secretariat, *The 2012–2013 Scorecard Report: Implementing the Red Tape Reduction Action Plan*, January 2014, http://www .tbs-sct.gc.ca/rtrap-parfa/report-rapport/asr-fea-eng.pdf.

31 "Minister Clement Highlights the Government of Canada's Efforts to Reduce Red Tape," Treasury Board of Canada Secretariat, 24 April 2013, http://www.tbs-sct.gc.ca/media/nr-cp/2013/0424-eng.asp.

32 "Minister Clement Introduces Members of the New Regulatory Advising Committee," Treasury Board of Canada Secretariat, 25 September 2013, http://www.tbs-sct.gc.ca/media/nr-cp/2013/0925a-eng.asp.

33 Treasury Board, *2012–2013 Scorecard Report*.

34 See, among many others, "The Financial Crisis," *Globe and Mail*, 14 September 2013.

35 George Benston, *The Separation of Commercial and Investment Banking: The Glass-Steagall Act Revisited and Reconsidered* (New York: Oxford University Press, 1990).

36 See, among others, Kevin Carmichael, "Five Years Later," *Report on Business*, September 2013, 29–34.

37 US Government, *The Financial Crisis: Inquiry Report* (Washington: US Government Printing Office, 2011), xviii.

38 Hank Paulson, "This Is What It Was Like to Face the Financial Crisis," *Bloomberg Businessweek*, 12 September 2013, 18.

39 "Canadian Banks Unfazed by New Capital Rules," *Globe and Mail*, 13 January 2014.

40 US Government, *Financial Crisis*, xviii.

41 The Financial Inquiry makes this point. See ibid.

42 "Wall Street Reform: The Dodd-Frank Act," White House, n.d., http://www .whitehouse.gov/economy/middle-class/dodd-frank-wall-street-reform.

43 There are a number of other similar requirements. See US Government, *Financial Crisis*.

44 "Call to Arms," *Financial Times* (London), 4 September 2014.

45 Auditor General, "2013 Fall Report Press Conference: 26 November 2013."

46 "Irving Raised Oil Testing Concerns a Month before Lac-Mégantic Tragedy," *Globe and Mail*, 21 December 2013.

47 Scott Deveau, "Transport Canada Issues Emergency Rail Safety Directive after Lac-Mégantic Disaster," *National Post*, 23 July 2013, http://business .financialpost.com/2013/07/23/transport-canada-issues-emergency-rail-safety-directive-after-lac-megantic-disaster/.

48 Transportation Safety Board of Canada, "Lac Mégantic Update," 12 July 2013.

49 Transport Canada, "Regulatory Proposal under Development," 14 January 2014.

50 Transport Canada, "Transport Canada Announces Emergency Directives to Rail Safety," news release, 23 July 2013; and Transport Canada, "Minister Lahey Issues Statement on Rail Incident in Lac Mégantic, Québec," news release, 7 July 2013.

51 Kim Mackrael, "Railways Told to Create Emergency Plans for Crude Oil Shipments," *Globe and Mail*, 23 April 2014, http://www.theglobeandmail .com/news/politics/railways-told-to-create-emergency-plans-for-crude-oil-shipments/article18125191/.

52 Transport Canada, "Statement regarding Transport Canada's Railway Safety Regulations," news release, 14 September 2013.

53 *Financial Crisis*, 344.

54 Transportation Safety Board of Canada, "Lac-Megantic Update," news release, 12 July 2013.

55 Quoted in "Mulcair Slams Harper over Lac-Megantic," CTV News, 6 July 2013, http://montreal.ctvnews.ca/mulcair-slams-harper-over-lac-megantic-1.1356485.

56 Quoted in Tobi Cohen, "Thomas Mulcair Links Lac-Mégantic Disaster, 'Gutting' of Regulations by Conservatives," *National Post*, 13 August 2013, http://news.nationalpost.com/2013/08/13/thomas-mulcair-links-lac-megantic-disaster-gutting-of-regulations-by-conservatives/.

57 The Auditor General's Office did not tie their report specifically to the Lac Mégantic incident. See Bruce Cheadle, "'Significant Weaknesses' Found in Audit before Deadly Lac-Mégantic Crash," CTV News, 26 November 2013, http://www.ctvnews.ca/politics/significant-weaknesses-found-in-audit-before-deadly-lac-megantic-crash-1.1561010.

58 David McGuinty quoted in Jessica Hume, "Transportation Safety Board
    Calls for Tougher Standards on Rail Tank Cars," *Ottawa Sun*, 2 January 2014,
    http://www.ottawasun.com/2014/01/23/tsb-calls-for-tougher-standards-on-
    rail-tank-cars.

59 Quoted in Paul Chiasson, "Auditor General's Report: Federal Government
    Failing on Rail Oversight" *Star*, 26 November 2013, http://www.thestar.com
    /news/canada/2013/11/26/federal_government_failing_on_rail_oversight
    _auditor_general.html.

60 Kim Mackrael, "Lac-Mégantic Report Likely to Focus on Safety Protocols,
    Regulation," *Globe and Mail*, 18 August 2014, http://www.theglobeandmail
    .com/news/national/lac-megantic-report-likely-to-focus-on-safety-protocols-
    regulation/article20105551/.

61 Transportation Safety Board of Canada, "TSB Identifies Systematic Problems
    Leading to Lac-Mégantic Train Accident and Calls for Additional Safety
    Defences to Improve Rail Safety," 19 August 2014.

62 Transportation Safety Board of Canada, *Railway Investigation Report*,
    R13D0054 (Ottawa: Transportation Safety Board of Canada, August 2014),
    125-32.

63 Ibid., 131.

64 Ibid., 70-97.

65 Kim Mackrael and Grant Robertson, "Lac-Mégantic Report Blames Lax
    Oversight, Weak Safety Culture," *Globe and Mail*, 19 August 2014,
    http://www.theglobeandmail.com/news/national/tsb-releases-final-report-on-
    lac-megantic-rail-disaster/article20106828/?cmpid=rss1

66 "Ottawa to Designate Crude Oil as Highly Dangerous," *Globe and Mail*, 13
    December 2013.

67 "No Record from Transport Minister Raitt's Meeting with Rail Lobbyists,"
    Hill Times (Ottawa), 25 November 2013, 6.

68 International Federation of Accountants, "Global Regulatory Convergence
    and the Accountancy Profession," position paper no. 6 (New York: Interna-
    tional Federation of Accountants, September 2012), 1 and 2.

69 See, among others, Hood, Rothstein, and Baldwin, *Government of Risk*.

70 Treasury Board of Canada Secretariat, *Cabinet Directive on Streamlining Regu-
    lation* (Ottawa: Treasury Board of Canada Secretariat, 2007), 1.

71 G. Bruce Doern, *Red Tape, Red Flags: Regulation for the Innovation Age*
    (Ottawa: Conference Board of Canada, 2007), 45.

72 The process was outlined in a briefing book prepared for the minister of
    transport. See also "Critics Urge Feds to Release Draft Railway Safety Regu-
    lations," *Hill Times* (Ottawa), 30 September 2013, 1 and 18.

73 "Amid Lac-Mégantic Fallout, Irving Oil Pledges Rail-Safety Upgrade," *Globe and Mail*, 17 February 2014.

74 Grant Robertson and Jacquie McNish, "Inside the Oil-Shipping Free-for-All That Brought Disaster to Lac-Mégantic," *Globe and Mail*, 2 December 2013, http://www.theglobeandmail.com/report-on-business/industry-news/energy-and-resources/a-pipeline-on-wheels-how-a-changing-industry-brought-disaster-to-lac-megantic/article15711624/?page=all.

75 Quoted in Jessica McDiarmid, "Lac Megantic Train Explosion: A Regulatory Failure?," *Star*, 29 July 2013, http://www.thestar.com/news/canada/2013/07/29/lacmegantic_train_explosion_a_regulatory_failure.html.

76 Ian Bron quoted in "I Couldn't Just Sit By and Watch Things Happen," *Hill Times* (Ottawa), 23 June 2014, 15.

77 See, among others, Scott Deveau, "Short-Line Rail Operators, the 'Special Teams' of the Railway Industry, Defend Safety Record," *Financial Post*, 13 July 2013, http://business.financialpost.com/2013/07/13/short-line-rail-operators-the-special-teams-of-the-railway-industry-defend-safety-record/.

78 Doern, Prince, and Schultz, *Rules and Unruliness*, 306.

79 Robert Mysicka, "Who Watches the Watchmen? The Role of the Self-Regulator," Commentary No. 416 (Toronto: C.D. Howe Institute, October 2014), 22.

80 I consulted the senior executive with Corus on 2 February 2014. I do not have permission to reveal her identity.

81 Doern, Prince, and Schultz, *Rules and Unruliness*, 306.

82 See, for example, Les Whittington, "EU Trade Pact Could Weaken Ottawa's Power to Regulate Banks," *Star*, 7 September 2014, http://www.thestar.com/news/canada/2014/09/07/eu_trade_pact_could_weaken_ottawas_power_to_regulate_banks.html.

83 "Canadian Born Billionaire Edgar Bronfman Dies at 84," *Globe and Mail*, 22 December 2013, http://www.theglobeandmail.com/report-on-business/canadian-born-billionaire-edgar-bronfman-sr-dies-at-84/article16082824/.

84 See, among others, Jane Jacobs, *Systems of Survival* (New York: Random House, 1991).

85 T. Ambler and K. Boyfield, *Reforming the Regulators* (London: Adam Smith Institute, 2010), 4.

86 See, among others, Savoie, *Breaking the Bargain*.

87 David Bruser, Jesse McLean, and Andrew Bailey, "Dangers of Off-Label Drug Use Kept Secret," *Star*, 26 June 2014, http://www.thestar.com/news/canada/2014/06/26/dangers_of_offlabel_drug_use_kept_secret.html.

88 Doern, Prince, and Schultz, *Rules and Unruliness*, 304.

CHAPTER ELEVEN

1 I owe many of these observations to an anonymous reviewer of an earlier version of the manuscript.

2 I explore in detail why it is not possible to assess properly the impact of regional development programs (among many others, the value of the Canadian currency, interest rates, the state of the US economy) in Savoie, *Visiting Grandchildren*.

3 That said, many observers have commented on Canada's successful immigration policy. Among others, I am thinking of the work of Jeffrey Reitz. See, for example, Jeffrey G. Reitz, "Canada, New Initiatives and Approaches to Immigration and Nation-Building," in *Controlling Immigration: A Global Perspective*, ed. James F. Hollifield, Philip L. Martin, and Pia M. Orrenius, 88–116 (Palo Alto, CA: Stanford University Press, 2014).

4 "Argentinian Looting Spreads Amid Police Strike," *Guardian*, 10 December 2013, http://www.theguardian.com/world/2013/dec/10/argentinian-looting-spreads-police-strikes.

5 See, for example, Doern, Prince and Schultz, *Rules and Unruliness*.

6 Andrew Coyne, "Post-Economic Politics in Canada," *Literary Review of Canada*, 14 May 2012, http://reviewcanada.ca/magazine/2012/05/post-economic-politics-in-canada/.

7 James Q. Wilson, and John J. Dilulio Jr, *American Government: The Essentials – Institutions and Policies* (Boston: Wadsworth-Cengage, 2011), 467–8.

8 John Dunn, *Setting the People Free: The Story of Democracy* (London: Atlantic Books, 2005), 183.

9 Delacourt, *Shopping for Votes*.

10 Jeffrey Simpson, "Harper-Flaherty Tax Rift: A Chasm That Must Be Closed," *Globe and Mail*, 19 February 2014, http://www.theglobeandmail.com/globe-debate/harper-flaherty-tax-rift-a-chasm-that-must-be-closed/article16954531/.

11 Francis Fukuyama, "America in Decay: The Sources of Political Dysfunction," *Foreign Affairs* (September/October 2014): 20.

12 V. Schneider, "Government and Complexity," in *The Oxford Handbook of Governance*, ed. D. Levi-Faur, 129–42 (Oxford: Oxford University Press, 2012); and E.P. Weber and A.M. Khademian, "Wicked Problems, Knowledge Challenges, and Collaborative Capacity Builders in Network Settings," *Public Administration Review* 68, no. 3 (2008): 334–49.

13 Beryl A. Radin, *Challenging the Performance Movement: Accountability, Complexity and Democratic Values* (Washington, DC: Georgetown University Press, 2006).

14　For a classic essay on the topic, see C.W. Churchman, "Wicked Problems," *Management Science* 14, no. 4 (1967): 141–2.

15　Andrea Hill, "Government Unveils Plan, but No Money, for Canada's Space Agency," National Newswatch, 10 February 2014, http://www.nationalnews watch.com/2014/02/08/government-unveils-plan-but-no-new-money-for-canadas-space-agency/#.VBoDGhbkFm4.

16　See, for example, Will Dunham, "U.S. Scientists Achieve 'Turning Point' in Fusion Energy Quest," *Globe and Mail*, 13 February 2014, http://cached .newslookup.com/cached.php?ref_id=123&siteid=2115&id=4824799 &t=1392277944.

17　See Mazzucato, *Entrepreneurial State*; and F.L. Block and M.R. Keller, eds., *State of Innovation: The U.S. Government's Role in Technology Development* (Boulder, CO: Paradigm, 2011).

18　Eric Reguly, "A Bite of the Big Apple," *Report on Business* (Toronto), September 2014, 24.

19　National Aeronautics and Space Administration, *Nasa Spinoff* 2002 (Washington, DC: National Aeronautics and Space Administration – Commercial Technology Division, 2002).

20　Savoie, *Harrison McCain*.

21　Ibid., 83.

22　Ibid., 272.

23　Ibid., 31.

24　Mazzucato, *Entrepreneurial State*, 41.

25　J.M. Keynes, quoted in Kamarck, *End of Government*, 27. See also J.M. Keynes, *The End of Laissez-Faire* (London: L. & V. Woolf, 1926).

26　Ibid., 57.

27　OECD regularly produces studies in research and development from a comparative perspective. See, for example, *Innovation in Science, Technology and Industry: Research and Development Statistics* (Paris: OECD, 2013).

28　See, for example, Kamarck, *End of Government*.

29　"Best Countries for Business 2014," Bloomberg, 21 January 2014, www.bloomberg.com/slideshow/2014-01-21/best-countries-for-business-2014.html.

30　See, among others, Neil Nevitte, *The Decline of Deference: Canadian Value Change in Cross-National Perspective* (Toronto: University of Toronto Press, 1996).

31　Sheila Copps, "Elections Reform Bill Weakly Disguised as Effort to Handcuff Elections Canada CEO," *Hill Times* (Ottawa), 17 February 2014, 9.

32　Ignatieff, *Fire and Ashes*, 134 and 174.

33 Ibid., 180.

34 Ibid., 150.

35 Quoted in John Ibbitson, "Too Much Executive Power Is Harming Democracy," *Globe and Mail*, 2 February 2013.

36 Quoted in Vaughan Lyon, *Power Shift: From Party Elites to Informed Citizens* (Bloomington, IN: iUniverse, 2011), 157–8.

37 "The Conscience of a Conservative," *Globe and Mail*, 26 April 2014. See also Tom Flanagan, *Persona Non Grata: The Death of Free Speech in the Internet Age* (Toronto: McClelland and Stewart, 2014).

38 See, for example, "Politicians Should Reclaim Themselves, Say Authors of New Book *Tragedy in the Commons*," *Hill Times* (Ottawa), 5 May 2014, 22.

39 See, for example, Frances Bula, "Mayor Gregor Robertson's Separation from Wife Sparks Messy Media Brawl," *Globe and Mail*, 6 July 2014, http://www
.theglobeandmail.com/news/british-columbia/mayors-separation-from-wife-sparks-messy-media-brawl/article19485865/.

40 See, for example, Donald J. Savoie, "The Perils of the Career Politician," *Globe and Mail*, 6 October 2014.

41 Carl Dahlström, B. Guy Peters, and Jon Pierre, "Steering from the Centre: Strengthening Political Control in Western Democracies," in *Steering from the Centre: Strengthening Political Control in Western Democracies*, ed. Carl Dahlström, B. Guy Peters and Jon Pierre (Toronto: University of Toronto Press, 2011), 3.

42 John F. Helliwell, Mary E. MacGregor, and André Plourde, "The National Energy Program Meets Falling World Prices," *Canadian Public Policy* 9, no. 3 (1983), 284–96.

43 Donald Johnson, president of the Treasury Board and widely regarded as a friend of the business community, was not informed of NEP before it was announced in the budget. See also Manion, *How Lucky I've Been*, 144.

44 See ibid., 186–7.

45 Ibid., 174.

46 See Public Policy Forum, *The Forum Salutes Four Great Canadians* (Toronto: Public Policy Forum, 12 April 1988).

47 Ibid.

48 Canadian Council of Chief Executives, http://www.ceocouncil.ca/. The website outlines the organization's objectives and publications.

49 "Effective Management of Human Capital in Schools: Recommendations to Strengthen the Teaching Profession" (Ottawa: Canadian Council of Chief Executives, 2014).

50 John Micklethwait and Adrian Wooldridge, *The Fourth Revolution: The Global Race to Reinvent the State* (New York: Penguin, 2014), 197

51 Kelly McParland makes this point in his "I Was a Student Therefore I'm an Expert in Teaching," *National Post*, 28 January 2014, http://fullcomment .nationalpost.com/2014/01/28/kelly-mcparland-i-was-a-student-therefore-im-an-expert-in-teaching/.

52 I note, however, that only a handful of practitioners and no scholars challenged the book's thesis. See, for example, Eddie Goldenberg, *The Way It Works: Inside Ottawa* (Toronto: McClelland and Stewart, 2006). This book, perhaps unwittingly, provides plenty of evidence that governing from the centre is how things work in Ottawa.

53 Lowell Murray, "Power, Responsibility, and Agency in Canadian Government," in *Governing: Essays in Honour of Donald J. Savoie*, ed. James Bickerton and B. Guy Peters (Montreal: McGill-Queen's University Press, 2013), 27.

54 Herman Bakvis, *Regional Ministers: Power and Influence in the Canadian Cabinet* (Toronto: University of Toronto Press, 1991).

55 See, among others, Savoie, *Whatever Happened to the Music Teacher?*.

56 Savoie, *Governing from the Centre*.

57 See, among others, John C. Crosbie, *No Holds Barred: My Life in Politics* (Toronto: McClelland & Stewart, 1997); Erik Nielsen, *The House Is Not a Home* (Toronto: Macmillan of Canada, 1989); and Donald Johnston, *Up the Hill* (Montreal: Optimum International, 1986).

58 Francis Fukuyama, "What Is Governance?," *Governance: An International Journal of Policy, Administration, and Institutions* 26 (July 2013): 359.

59 James Q. Wilson makes this point in his *Bureaucracy*.

60 This point was made by a former secretary to the Treasury Board in "PS Modernization Exercise Shows Bureaucracy 'Hived Off' from Government," *Hill Times* (Ottawa), 19 May 2014, 24.

61 Ibid., 39.

62 See, among others, "America in Decay: The Sources of Political Dysfunction," *Foreign Affairs* (September/October 2014): 8.

63 "Wayne Wouters: Public Service Reform Means Fixing Sick Leave Too," *Ottawa Citizen*, 22 May 2014, http://ottawacitizen.com/news/national/wayne-wouters-public-service-reform-means-fixing-sick-leave-too.

64 Josh Wingrove, "Public Servants' Sick Days Immaterial to Ottawa's Bottom Line, Report Says," *Globe and Mail*, 16 July 2014, http://www.theglobeand mail.com/news/politics/public-servants-sick-days-immaterial-to-ottawas-bottom-line-report-says/article19630559/.

65 "Unions Launch Grievance against New Federal Rules on Employee Perfor-
    mance," Canada.com, 6 April 2014, http://www.canada.com/business
    /Unions+launch+grievance+against+federal+rules+employee+performance
    /9706290/story.html; and Kathryn May, "PS Unions Sign Pledge to Oppose
    Government Sick Leave Changes," National Newswatch, 26 January 2014,
    http://www.nationalnewswatch.com/2014/01/26/ps-unions-sign-pledge-to-
    oppose-government-sick-leave-changes/#.VBoL1xbkFm4.
66 Bob Murphy, "Canadian Forces Dentists' Productivity Questioned," CBC
    News, 20 March 2014, http://www.cbc.ca/news/canada/nova-scotia/canadian-
    forces-dentists-productivity-questioned-1.2579134.
67 See, among others, Savoie, *Court Government and the Collapse of Accountability*.
68 See, among others, Savoie, *Whatever Happened to the Music Teacher?*
69 See, among many others, Schuck, *Why Government Fails so Often*.
70 See, among many others, "PM Seeks to Tie NDP's Name to Moncton Demon-
    stration," *Globe and Mail*, 9 May 1988; see also "Angry Crowd Demand
    Cochrane's Resignation," *Times-Transcript*, 24 June 1986.
71 Quoted in Savoie, *Politics of Public Spending in Canada*, 257.
72 "Via Rail to Repair Northern New Brunswick Rail Line, Halifax Route to
    Montreal Saved," *Truro Daily News*, 13 May 2014.
73 Konrad Yakabuski, "How Long Does Ontario Need to Turn Around a Bloat-
    ed Utility?" *Globe and Mail*, 12 December 2013.
74 "Permanent Revolution," *Times*, 9 July 2013; and "Whitehall to Adopt Busi-
    ness Style in Unified Management Overhaul," *Financial Times*, 10 July 2013.
75 B. Guy Peters, "Government Reorganization: A Theoretical Analysis" (paper
    presented at the 1991 meeting of the Canadian Political Science Associa-
    tion, June 1991, Kingston, ON), 1.
76 One only has to look at various public opinion surveys to see evidence of
    this. See also, among others, Savoie, *Whatever Happened to the Music Teacher?*
77 B. Guy Peters and Donald J. Savoie, "Civil Service Reform: Misdiagnosing
    the Patient," *Public Administration Review* 54, no. 6 (1994): 416–25.
78 The overload problem in government has been well debated in the litera-
    ture. See, among many others, Richard Simeon, "The Overload Thesis and
    Canadian Government," *Canadian Public Policy* 2, no. 4 (1976): 541–52.

CHAPTER TWELVE

1 Alasdair Roberts, *The Logic of Discipline: Global Capitalism and the Architec-
   ture of Government* (Oxford: Oxford University Press, 2010), 16.
2 Jeffrey L. Pressman and Aaron Wildavsky, *Implementation: How Great Expec-

tations in Washington Are Dashed in Oakland (Berkeley: University of California Press, 1973).

3 Andrew Graham, "Pressman/Wildavsky and Bardach: Implementation in the Public Sector, Past, Present and Future," *Canadian Public Administration* 48, no. 2 (2005): 268–73.

4 Public Service Commission, *Annual Report* (Ottawa: Public Service Commission, 2013–2014). See also Katherine A. H. Graham and Gene Swimmer, "The Ottawa Syndrome: The Localization of Federal Public Servants in Canada," *Canadian Public Administration* 52, no. 3 (2009): 417–37.

5 "Blaine Higgs Blames Politics for Unbalanced Budgets," CBC News, 7 February 2014, http://www.cbc.ca/news/canada/new-brunswick/blaine-higgs-blames-politics-for-unbalanced-budgets-1.2527183.

6 David A. Good makes this point in his *The Politics of Public Management* (Toronto: University of Toronto Press, 2003), 182.

7 See, for example, "How to Fish for Votes with Local Spending," *Globe and Mail*, 6 September 2013.

8 See, among others, "Feds Spending up 23 Percent since Tories Won Office," *Hill Times* (Ottawa), 5 May 2014, 1 and 18. The information is based on Department of Finance documents and consultations with government officials.

9 Elizabeth Renzetti, "As Government Snoops, Canadians ... Take a Nap," *Globe and Mail*, 3 February 2014, http://www.theglobeandmail.com/globe-debate/as-government-snoops-canadians-take-a-nap/article16661040/; and Robert Benzie, "Provinces Urge Jason Kenney to Rethink Canada Jobs Grants," *Star*, 4 February 2014, http://www.thestar.com/news/canada/2014/02/04/provinces_urge_jason_kenney_to_rethink_canada_jobs_grant.html.

10 B. Guy Peters and Jon Pierre, eds., *Politicians, Bureaucrats and Administrative Reform* (London: Routledge, 2004).

11 Peter Aucoin, "New Political Governance in Westminster Systems: Impartial Public Administration and Management Performance at Risk," *Governance* 25, no. 2 (2012): 181.

12 "Public Servants Asked to Promote Conservative Tax Proposal on Twitter," *Globe and Mail*, 21 November 2014, http://www.theglobeandmail.com/news/politics/public-servants-asked-to-promote-conservative-tax-proposal-on-twitter/article21705733/.

13 Ibid.

14 Peter Aucoin, "Influencing Public Policy and Decision-Making: Power Shifts," notes for presentation to the 2004 APEX Symposium, "Parliament, the People, and Public Service, Ottawa, 6–7 October 2004, 4.

15 Carl Dahlström, B. Guy Peters, and Jon Pierre, "Steering Strategies in Western Democracies," in *Steering from the Centre: Strengthening Political Control in Western Democracies* (Toronto: University of Toronto Press, 2011), 271.

16 Chrétien, *Straight from the Heart*, 18.

17 I note that there are now important post-employment guidelines that politicians and public servants must respect.

18 See, for example, Shaun P. Young, ed., *Evidence-Based Policy-Making in Canada* (Don Mills, ON: Oxford University Press Canada, 2013).

19 *Wilson, Bureaucracy.*

20 See, for example, Manion, *How Lucky I've Been.*

21 Savoie, *Court Government and the Collapse of Accountability*, 176–7.

22 Wilson, *Bureaucracy*, 133.

23 Les Metcalfe and Sue Richards, *Improving Public Management* (London: Sage, 1987), 63.

24 R.A.W. Rhodes, "Recovering the Craft of Public Administration in Network Governance" (paper presented to the International Political Science Association World Congress, Montreal, 19–24 July 2014), 3.

25 Christopher Pollitt and Geert Bouckaert, *Public Management Reform – A Comparative Analysis: New Public Management, Governance, and the Neo-Weberian State* (Oxford: Oxford University Press, 2011).

26 Ross Douthat, "Obamacare, Failing Ahead of Schedule," *New York Times*, 19 October 2013, http://www.nytimes.com/2013/10/20/opinion/sunday/douthat-obamacare-failing-ahead-of-schedule.html?_r=0.

27 Oliver Moore and Kaitlyn McGrath, "Ice-Storm Gift Cards Run Out Again as Resentment Mounts in Toronto," *Globe and Mail*, 2 January 2014, http://cached.newslookup.com/cached.php?ref_id=123&siteid=2115&id=427 5136&t=1388692436.

28 Consultations with Ed Clark, Fox Harbour, Nova Scotia, July 2013.

29 See, for example, Donald F. Kettl and James W. Fesler, *The Politics of the Administrative Process* (Washington, DC: CQ, 2009).

30 As every student of public administration knows full well, there is a growing body of literature on this issue. See, among many others, W.A. Niskanen, *Bureaucracy and Representative Government* (New Jersey: Transaction, 1974).

31 See, for example, J. Raadschelders and K. H. Lee, "Trends in the Study of Public Administration: Empirical and Qualitative Observations from *Public Administration Review*, 2000–2009," *Public Administration Review* 71, no. 1 (2011): 19–33.

32 Bevir, *Democratic Governance*, 80.

33 Manion, *How Lucky I've Been*; and Ian D. Clark and Harry Swain, "Distinguishing the Real from the Surreal in Management Reform: Suggestions for Beleaguered Administrators in the Government of Canada," *Canadian Public Administration* 48, no. 4 (2005): 458.

34 Auditor General, *Evaluating the Effectiveness of Programs*, Fall Report of the Auditor General of Canada (Ottawa: Office of the Auditor General, 2009), 24.

35 See Wilson, *Bureaucracy*, 221.

36 Ibid., 131 and 217.

37 See, among others, Savoie, *Breaking the Bargain*.

38 James G. March and Johan P. Olsen, "The New Institutionalism: Organizational Factors in Political Life," *American Political Science Review* 7, no. 3 (1984): 734–49.

39 Pressman and Wildavsky, *Implementation*, xvi.

40 P.A. Hall and R.C.R. Taylor, "Political Science and the Three New Institutionalisms," *Political Studies* 44, no. 3 (1996): 936–57. Principal-agent theory constitutes an important part of the political science literature. See, among many others, Hussein Kassim and Anand Menon, "The Principal-Agent Approach and the Study of the European Union: Promise Unfulfilled?," *Journal of European Public Policy* 10, no. 1 (2003): 121–39.

41 Savoie, "Perfect Storm in Reverse."

42 Savoie, *Whatever Happened to the Music Teacher?*, 103.

43 See, among others, ibid.

44 Jordan Press, "Revenue Agency Too Timid about Big-Time Tax Cheats," *Ottawa Citizen*, 2 July 2014, http://ottawacitizen.com/news/national/revenue-agency-too-timid-about-big-time-tax-cheats-report.

45 Mark Kennedy, "NDP Leader Tom Mulcair Vows Not to Raise Personal Taxes if He Becomes Prime Minister in 2015," *National Post*, 19 May 2014, http://news.nationalpost.com/2014/05/19/ndp-leader-tom-mulcair-vows-not-to-raise-personal-taxes-if-he-becomes-prime-minister-in-2015/.

46 David Reevely, "Horwath Pledges to Trim $600m in Government Waste," *Ottawa Citizen*, 15 May 2014, http://www.ottawacitizen.com/Reevely+Horwath+pledges+trim+600m+government+waste/9838259/story.html; and Adrian Morrow and Kaleigh Rogers, "Battle Lines Drawn with Hudak's Vow to Cut 100,000 Jobs," *Globe and Mail*, 9 May 2014, http://www.theglobeandmail.com/news/politics/hudak-vows-to-cut-100000-public-sector-jobs-if-tories-win/article18580284/.

47 Scott Stinson, "Wynne's Empty Promises: Ontario Liberals Vowing to Balance Budget but Party Lacks Plan to Slay Deficit," *National Post*, 25 May

2014, http://fullcomment.nationalpost.com/2014/05/25/scott-stinson-ontario-liberals-vowing-to-balance-budget-but-party-lacks-plan-to-slay-deficit/.

48 Quoted in Savoie, *Court Government and the Collapse of Accountability*, 193.

49 Quoted in Kirk Makin, "Access to Justice Becoming a Privilege of the Rich, Judge Warns," *Globe and Mail*, 10 February 2011, http://www.theglobeand mail.com/news/national/access-to-justice-becoming-a-privilege-of-the-rich-judge-warns/article565873/.

50 "Despite Conservative Win, Electoral Data Shows Fort McMurray Voted Liberal," *Fort McMurray Today*, 8 July 2014, http://www.fortmcmurraytoday .com/2014/07/08/despite-conservative-win-electoral-data-shows-fort-mcmurray-voted-liberal.

51 Jon H. Pammett and Lawrence LeDuc, *Explaining the Turnout Decline in Canadian Federal Elections: A Survey of Non-Voters*, Elections Canada Online Report, March 2003, http://data.library.utoronto.ca/datapub/codebooks /utm/can_nonvote_03/TurnoutDecline.pdf.

52 Samara, *Lost in Translation or Just Lost?*, 1.

53 Perlin, "Malaise of Canadian Democracy," 155.

54 Larry Diamond, *Developing Democracy towards Consolidation* (Baltimore: Johns Hopkins University Press, 1999).

55 Samuel P. Huntington, *American Politics: The Promise of Disharmony* (Cambridge, MA: Belknap, 1981).

56 Perlin, "The Malaise of Canadian Democracy," 154–75.

57 Francis Fukuyama, "America in Decay: The Sources of Political Dysfunction," *Foreign Affairs* (September/October 2014): 10.

Index

Abella, Rosalie, 79
Aboriginal/Treaty rights, 83
Acadian movement, 23–5
access to information: interest
    groups and, 241; and Lac-Mégan-
    tic derailment, 225–6; and lobby-
    ists' activities, 91–2; ministers
    and, 186; MPs and, 94; and pro-
    gram managers, 273; and trans-
    parency, 241; whistle-blowing
    and, 186. *See also* information
    requests
Access to Information Act, 94
accountability: and accounting offi-
    cer concept, 125, 130; of ACOA,
    151; administrative vs perfor-
    mance, 137–8; for budget, 65–6,
    67–8; Canada School of Public
    Service and, 160, 161–2; collegial-
    ity vs personal, 134; deputy min-
    isters and, 129–30; financial
    audits and, 133; and government
    ability to hold persons to
    account, 118, 119; of government
    to Parliament, 53, 58, 67–8; and
    growth of public service, 202;
    hierarchy and, 132; management

and, 122; and ministerial respon-
    sibility, 122–3; PCO clerks'
    vision/review exercises and,
    126–7; to performance measures,
    127; performance vs procedural,
    15, 118, 121, 132, 133; permanent
    election campaigns vs, 63–4; of
    politicians, 101; in private vs pub-
    lic sector, 9, 117–18, 121, 129; and
    program delivery, 268; of public
    servants, 100–1; public servants
    above fault line and, 175–6; rules
    vs values approach and, 135; SOAs
    and, 125
Accountability Act. *See* Federal
    Accountability Act
accounting officer, 125, 130
adversarial politics: dangers of, 247;
    media vs Parliament and, 63
advocacy associations: access to gov-
    ernment, 86–7; minority-language
    associations and, 25–6; volun-
    teerism and paid, 24. *See also*
    interest groups
Alboim, Elly, 41–2
Alcock, Reg, 175
Alexander, Chris, 81

Al-Mashat crisis, 181
Ambulance New Brunswick, 40
André, Harvie, 89
Apple, 243
Armstrong, Sir Robert, 98–9
Association of Professional Execu-
    tives of the Public Service of
    Canada, 190
Atlantic Canada: ACOA as making
    difference in, 147–8, 151–2;
    Atlantic Investment Partnership
    and, 150; Chrétien on, 152; DREE
    and, 141–2; DRIE and, 141, 142;
    economic development agency
    for, 142–4; economic growth pre-
    dicted for, 140–1; economy in,
    141, 152; federal budgets and,
    149–50; IRDP and, 141; Mulroney
    and, 142–4, 152; PCO report on
    future cooperation among
    Atlantic provinces, 89; regional
    economic development in, 139,
    140–1
Atlantic Canada Opportunities
    Agency (ACOA): and 1988 elec-
    tion, 147–8; accountability of,
    151; Action Program, 148–9, 150;
    announcement of, 139, 143–4;
    and Atlantic Investment Partner-
    ship, 150; cash grants, 143, 144,
    148–9; as catalyst, 143; Chrétien-
    Martin program review and,
    148–9; Chrétien's priorities and,
    149; concept development vs
    implementation in, 273–4; con-
    sultant status, 89; deputy minis-
    ter as head of, 143; DRIE and, 143;
    economic development agree-
    ments with provinces, 149; and

entrepreneurial development,
    143; establishment of, 140; FED-
    NOR compared to, 146; funding,
    143, 147; as generous, 148; goal-
    accomplishment gap in, 252;
    Harper program review and, 151;
    impact on Atlantic Canada
    regional economy, 147–8, 151–2,
    252; mandate, 143; McPhail and,
    166–7; media and, 144; Mulroney
    and, 140, 143–4, 152, 252; Murray
    on, 165–6; overhead manage-
    ment, 151; PCO consultant use
    and, 89; and principal-agency
    theory, 167; and private sector,
    143; reliance on existing vs new
    programs, 147; size/growth of,
    139, 143, 147, 148, 149, 150–1,
    166, 273; tax incentives vs cash
    grants for, 143, 144; Treasury
    Board Secretariat MAF and, 151;
    WD's similarity to, 145
Atlantic Investment Partnership, 150
Aucoin, Peter, 180
Auditor General, Office of the
    (OAG): and assessment/evaluation
    of program spending, 182–3;
    audit of evaluation function in
    Environment Canada, 272; and
    blame game, 132, 183; and
    bureaucracy as monolithic body,
    182–3; *Evaluating the Effectiveness
    of Programs*, 131–2; and evalua-
    tions, 210; and Lac-Mégantic
    derailment, 221, 223–4; opposi-
    tion and, 132; and performance
    assessment/evaluation, 131–2,
    210; and regulatory regime, 217;
    and reporting requirements, 115

Axworthy, Lloyd, 257
Axworthy, Tom, 207

Baar, Carl, 76
Bagehot, Walter, 57
Baird, John, 177–8
Baldwin, Robert, 214
Banting, Keith, 37–8
Bazowski, Raymond, 77–8
Beck, Ulrich, 71
Benedict, Wayne, 228
Bevir, Mark, 71, 101
BlackBerry, 7, 243; journalism, 40–1
Blair, Tony, 5, 42
Blais, André, 36
blame: 2008 financial crisis and, 223; and decision-making, 9–10; evaluation reports and, 187; fault line and, 15; and implementation issues, 261; Lac-Mégantic derailment and, 223–5; ministerial responsibility vs, 207; and ministers vs bureaucrats, 180–1; OAG and, 132, 183; and partisan staff vs career public servants, 102; politicians and, 223, 224; prime ministers and, 128; as priority, vs shrinking middle class, 38; in private vs public sector, 120; and program managers, 260; public servants above fault line and, 167, 177, 179, 182, 195; public servants and, 68–9, 83, 115; reforms vs, 275; and risk avoidance, 189, 194; Second World War and, 239; senior government officials and, 116; senior public servants and, 128, 167, 248; as stifling creativity, 254; temporary

foreign worker program and, 175
Bloomberg, 245
Bok, Derek, 206
Boothe, Paul, 213
bottom line: governments and, 115; oversight managers as, 128–9; performance/evaluation reports as, 128; private sector and, 5, 249; and thickening of government operations, 128–9
Bouckaert, Geert, 269
Bourgault, Jacques, 110, 130; *Managing Publicly*, 104–5
Bourgon, Jocelyne, 135
Bowling Alone (Putnam), 22–3
Bridges, Sir Edward, 104
Britain. *See* United Kingdom
British North America, party government in, 56
British North America Act (BNA Act), 57
Bron, Ian, 228
Bronfman, Edgar, 231
Brunetta, Frank, 162
Bryce, Bob, 27, 155, 271
budget: 1968 changes to process, 67–8; 2013 omnibus bill, 68; accountability for, 65–6, 67–8; elections and, 64–5; Parliament and, 58; and spending estimates, 66–7
bureaucrats/bureaucracy: "bureaucratic" as label, 8; and common good, 48–9; elites, and interest groups, 241; general theories of, 172; and implementation, 97; irrelevance of, 280; as looking inward, 205; as monolith, 171–2, 182; neutrality of, 49; politicians'

attacks on, 268; qualities of, 199;
and representative democracy, 48;
size/growth of, 7, 166, 202, 204,
259–60, 273–4; as tax-eaters, 7.
See also public servants; public
service
business community: governments
turning to, 90–1; as inspiration
for governments, 8; and management, 101; in Nova Scotia,
169–70; and organized groups,
250–2; regulation and, 217–18;
self-regulation by, 219. *See also*
private sector
businesses: bad calls, 8–9; departments as, 7; hidden regulatory
costs for, 216; multinational
firms, 45, 215; regulations and,
213, 215; relocation by, 45
Butler, Sir Robin, 69, 122

Cabinet: changing role of, 73; committees, 176; as focus group, 253;
government, court government
and, 90; House of Commons
and, 57; partisan political staff
attending committee meetings
of, 109–10
Cameron, David, 5, 8
Camp, Dalton, 167
Canada Revenue Agency: function
of, 171; pursuit of wealthy vs
smaller tax cheats, 275
Canada School of Public Service:
accountabili-
ty/evaluation/performance
reports, 160, 161–2; action vs fundamental research in, 157; advisory board vs board of directors,

155; announcement of, 139;
board of governors vs advisory
board, 158; budget, 158, 161; as
centre of excellence, 159, 163;
concept development vs implementation, 273–4; controversies,
162–3; costs, 154, 158–9; curriculum, 157; funding, 155, 157; goal-
accomplishment gap, 161, 252;
government departments compared to, 158; independence of,
154–5, 164; legislation establishing, 156; Manion as principal,
155, 157; naming and name
changes, 154–5, 158, 252; NPM
vocabulary in, 160; orientation
course, 157; and principal-agency
theory, 167; and private sector,
160, 161; programs, 159–60; publications, 157; research, 158, 159,
165; Savoie as deputy/acting principal, 156; as school vs centre,
158; senior public servants as
staff, 156, 159, 162–3, 165; senior
public servants managing, 159;
size/growth of, 139, 157, 273–4;
staff, 154, 157, 158, 159, 160, 161,
162–3; universities compared to,
161, 163
Canada Transportation Act, 229
Canadian Association of Petroleum
Producers, 92
Canadian Bankers Association, 92
Canadian Cattlemen's Association,
92
Canadian Centre for Management
Development (CCMD). *See* Canada
School of Public Service
Canadian Centre for Management

Studies (CCMS). *See* Canada School of Public Service

"The Canadian Centre for Management Studies" (CCMS) (Savoie), 153–5

Canadian Chamber of Commerce, 93

Canadian Council of Chief Executives, 93, 250, 251–2

Canadian Federation of Independent Business, 92

Canadian Federation of Students, 8

Canadian Heritage, Department of, 171, 183

Canadian Manufacturers and Exporters, 93

Canadian National Railway (CN): lobbyists for, 225; PCO clerk as head, 136; privatization of, 258; selling of lines, 229; shops closure in Moncton, 257–8

Canadian Nuclear Safety Commission, 214

Canadian Pacific Railway (CP), 225, 229

Canadian Public Administration, 153

Canadian Radio-television and Telecommunications Commission (CRTC), 216

Canadian Research Data Centre Network, 106

Capitalism, Socialism and Democracy (Schumpeter), 48–9

Cappe, Mel, 135–6

Carney, Mark, 39

Carrera, Leandro, 204

Carroll, Barbara, 184, 197

Carty, Ken, 36

caucus, MPs and, 64

C.D. Howe Institute, 229–30

census, cancellation of mandatory long-form questionnaire, 71, 106–7

central agencies: attraction to new public servants, 166; and campaign commitments, 65; and departments, 108; deputy ministers drawn from, 48, 104; duties/responsibilities, 185; growth of, 185; and ideas vs implementation, 15; and information requests, 185–6; and line managers, 200–1; and management, 104, 115; number of, 186; and partisan political staff, 102; and policy issues, 185; and union negotiations, 268

centre, governing from: and distance between policy-makers and front-line program managers, 262; and implementation, 262; and policy, 265; politicians and, 253; prime ministers and, 103, 252–3; public servants and, 253; and response to controversies, 265; as stifling creativity, 254

Charles I, King, 56

Charter of Rights and Freedoms, 214; and constitutional limitations on government, 77; and courts, 57, 74, 77, 78, 94; cruel and unusual treatment under, 81; and judiciary, 75; and transfer of policy-making power to courts, 76

checks and balances, 55

Chong, Michael, 59

Chrétien, Jean: acceptance of responsibility vs blame, 120, 207;

and accounting officer, 125; and ACOA, 152; appointment of PCO clerk, 125; and Atlantic Canada, 252; and Gomery Commission, 120; on government as force for good, 14; and ministers' chiefs of staff, 103; streamlining of Cabinet committee system, 176; on superiority of private sector management, 5; on "survival game," 182, 265

Chrétien, Raymond, 119–20

Chrétien-Martin program review: across-the-board spending cuts, 274–5; effect of cuts on ACOA, 148–9, 151; majority mandates and expenditure reduction, 65; prime ministers and spending reductions, 116, 202; and regulatory agencies/processes, 217; results of, 200–1

churches: Anglican, 22; decline in attendees, 40; government organizations compared to, 30; and machinery of government, 30; membership, 21; and public sector programs, 21, 23; United Church, 21–2. *See also* Roman Catholic Church

citizens/individuals: access to courts, 85–6; access to government, 94, 278; access to justice system, 277–8; assessment criteria of government efficiency, 262; community vs individuals, 73; as consumers/customers, 101, 127, 135; disconnection from processes/influence, 261; global economy and, 278; government above

fault line and, 279; government and, 16; government below fault line and, 279; government hierarchy and access to government, 74; interest groups compared to, 241; MPs and, 86, 94; Parliament as ally of, 278; participation, 3–4, 33–6; political party disconnection from, 240; and public interest, 241, 249; public service below fault line as ally of, 278; public value and, 3–4; ranking on most influential/important, 105–6; regulations and, 213; in Tait report, 135; and voting, 277

civil society: social cohesion and, 33; weakening of organizations, 37

Clark, Ed, 14, 127, 250, 270

Clark, Joe, 207

Clement, Tony, 162

clerks of the Privy Council (PCO): 2013 vision exercise, 126; ambassadorial appointments, 136–7; and controversies, 175; deputy ministers' accountability to, 130; influence/importance of, 106; and management issues, 175; numbers and terms of office, 127; and policy, 103, 232; reform initiatives, 205; vision/review exercises, 126–7

Clinton, Bill, 5

Cohen, Andrew, 119

collective bargaining: government executives and, 196; introduction into public service, 209; labour laws and, 84; and non-performers, 198; private vs public sector and, 196; and public service sectional interests, 113. *See also* unions

command-and-control bureaucracy, 227

common good: bureaucracy and, 48–9; complexity of, 71; global economy and, 45, 112; government and, 46; government and public good initiatives, 244–5; House of Commons and, 62; media and debates over, 47; policy issue complexity and, 47; politicians and, 49; public service and, 167; special interest groups and, 48–9; voters and, 48–9. *See also* public interest

Commons. *See* House of Commons

comparative advantage, 3

Conservative Party: and Cabinet decisions, 253; and foreign workers program, 175; and middle class, 38; and power of prime ministers vs MPs, 59; and regional economic development, 141, 165. *See also* Harper, Stephen; Mulroney, Brian; political parties

Constitution Act (1982), 57. *See also* Charter of Rights and Freedoms

consultants: and decision making, 86–9; as former politicans/advisors/senior public servants, 265; government departments and, 88; for government spending cuts, 201–2; growth of firms, 88–9; influence of, 105; PCO and, 88–9; and policy, 102; politicians and, 102; and power, 88; and program evaluations,

131; reporting of communications with government officials, 92; spending on, 88

controversies/problems: and blame game, 175; Canada School of Public Service and, 162–3; lobbyists avoiding, 90; MPs and, 266; and permanent election campaigns, 177; PMO and, 110; politicians and, 164; prime ministers and, 128, 175, 181, 253–4; in private vs public sector, 264; public servants above fault line and, 177–8, 253–4; public servants and, 206; scientists and, 163–4; senior public servants above fault line and, 263–4; strength of centre and, 265; wicked, 241–2, 245, 276

Copps, Sheila, 246

Corrections Canada, 172; and courts, 83

Corus Entertainment, 230

court government: access to, 267; and access to prime minister, 267; Cabinet government vs, 90; decision-making by, 253; distance from senior program managers, 267; economic elites and, 207; efficiency of, 267; and government below fault line, 12; and political survival, 238; public servants above fault line in, 179

courts: Charter of Rights and Freedoms and, 57, 74, 77, 78, 94; and constitutionality of legislation, 57; and decision making, 86; and economic elites, 85–6; and expansion of scope of government,

267; and government, 94; and
government's ability to shape
policies/programs, 80–1; and
Harper's "tough on crime" agenda, 80; and implementation,
79–80, 82, 94–5; individual citizens' access to, 85–6; interest
groups and, 75, 85–6; judicial
activism, 75, 76; and machinery
of government, 78–9, 83, 267;
and management issues, 83–6,
196; and non-performers, 84; and
policy, 74, 75, 82, 86, 94–5; and
political compromise, 82; politi-
cal/economic elites' pursuit of
agenda before, 11; and politics,
75–6; power of, 76, 77, 94; prime
minister and, 94; and public
interest, 241; and public servants,
82–3; and public service terminations, 196, 197–8; as replacing
public debates, 82; and social
agenda, 75; special interest
groups and, 78; unions and, 83,
269
courts of appeal, and policy-making, 76
Coyne, Andrew, 239
Crick, Bernard, 95
crises: consensus regarding, 239;
and empowerment of managers,
266; government efficiency in,
230, 239; regulations and, 225;
regulatory regime and, 233;
response to, 220–1. See also con-
troversies/problems; financial crisis of 2008; Second World War
Crossman, Richard, Diaries of a Cabinet Minister, 99

Crown corporations, privatization
of, 258
Customs and Revenue Agency, 125
Cutting Red Tape and Freeing Business to Grow (Red Tape Reduction Commission), 217

Dahrendorf, Ralf, 33
Dalton, Russell, 34
decision making: and blame-avoidance, 9–10; changed locus of, 73;
collegiality vs personal accountability in, 134; consultants and,
86–9; courts and, 86; and fault
line, 266; by heads of govern-
ment/advisors vs government
departments/agencies, 9–10; hori-
zontality of, 194; interest groups
and, 88; by line departments,
128; lobbyists and, 90; management discretion and, 270–1; management layers and, 194; ministerial responsibility and
accountability for, 207; MPs and,
64; multiple involvement in, 94;
power and, 270; by prime ministers and courtiers, 253; in private
vs public sector, 188, 266, 270; by
regional ministers, 253; shift
away from government, 87; slow-
ing of, 271; thickening of, 88;
upstairs vs downstairs, 267–8
Defence, Department of. See
National Defence, Department of
(DND)
Delacourt, Susan, 46, 62–3
Deloitte Touche, 201–2, 274
democracy: anti-elite bias/ethic of,
279; civil society erosion and, 33;

commitment to, 278; as contest vs common good, 71; criticisms of, 54–5; and democratic deficit, 33; and democratic satisfaction, 6; direct, 54; establishing public interest in, 113; in Greece, 54, 55; participatory, 33; politicians and, 246; public service and, 112; sober second voice for, 55, 58; social capital and, 22–3; in United States, 54–5. See also representative democracy

Department of Regional Economic Expansion (DREE), 141, 146

Department of Regional Industrial Expansion (DRIE), 141–2, 143, 145

departments: as businesses, 7; central agencies and, 108; competition among, 188–9; and consultant firms, 88; decision making by heads of government and advisors vs, 9–10; deputy ministers and, 104; developmental mandates, 171; diversity among, 171–2; and economic elites, 93; Harper program review cuts to, 201; interdepartmentality among, 103–4, 267; lobbyists and, 93; mandates conflicting among, 172; ministerial offices and, 110; not good at adjusting to changing circumstances, 268; program evaluation units, 200, 201; SOAs in, 124–5. See also line departments

deputy ministers (DMs): and accountability, 129–30; accountability to prime minister, 129, 130; career public servants becoming,

48, 183; and centre of government, 104; collegiality of, 104; as drawn from central agencies, 48, 104; earnings, 208; of Finance, 106; influence/importance of, 106; and interdepartmental policy process, 103–4; and management, 104; and ministers, 110, 130; ministers' chiefs of staff and, 109; and own departments, 104; PCO clerk and, 130; pensions, 208; performance awards, 208; and performance measurements, 129; and policy, 103; prime ministers and, 105, 129, 193; and public servants below fault line, 183–4; role of, 104–5; SOAs and, 124–5; and values/ethics, 136

deregulation. See regulation(s); regulatory regime(s)

Deschamps, Marie, 80

Dexter, Darrell, 169, 276

Diamond, Larry, 278

Diaries of a Cabinet Minister (Crossman), 99

Dicerni, Richard, 195

Discover Canada, 108

divine right to rule, 54, 56

division of powers, between levels of government, 57

DND. See National Defence, Department of (DND)

Docherty, David, 61

Dodd-Frank Wall Street Reform and Consumer Protection Act (2010), 220–1

Dodek, Adam, 81

Doern, G. Bruce, 213–14, 215–16, 229, 230

Dominion Institute, 74
Doughty, Howard, 33
Douglas, Heather, 164
Drucker, Peter, 13
Drummond, Don, 107
Duffy, Mike, 49, 120
Dunleavy, Patrick, 204
Dunn, John, 55

Eaton's catalogue operations, 257, 258
Economic Advisory Council, 91
economic classes: and access to government, 278; divide between, 36; religion and bond between, 31–2; wealthy vs middle classes, 36. *See also* income disparity/inequality; middle class
economic crisis of 2008. *See* financial crisis of 2008
Economic Development for Canada in the 1980s, 140
economic elites: access to policy-/decision-makers, 231, 261; and courts, 85–6; departments and, 93; and policies/initiatives, 11–12; and political/bureaucratic elites, 265–6; and prime minister's court, 207; and public interest, 95; and regulatory regime, 231; and senior public servants, 207
Economist: on businesses vs bureaucracies for growth, 8; on government–business relationship, 95; on House of Commons, 58
economy: competitiveness and, 45; governmental roles in sectors of, 28; government and, 249–50; government and future, 245;

national governments and management of, 44–5; NEP and, 250; private sector and, 45; regulatory regime and, 232. *See also* global economy/globalization; regional economic development
Edward III, King, 56
EKOS Research, 34
election campaigns/elections: attack ads in, 63; and budget process, 64–5; and composition of House of Commons, 57; elites in, 34; MPs and, 64; party leaders/advisors and, 62; personal attacks/ruthlessness in, 246; policies appealing to voters in, 247; political parties and, 57; promises, 64–5; representative democracy and, 48; and whiz-bang ideas, 241; winning of, 64–5, 240, 247. *See also* permanent election campaigns; voters/voting
Elections Canada, on low voter turnout, 34–6, 278
elites: and democracy, 279; economic vs political/bureaucratic, 265–6; in elections, 34; and policies/initiatives, 11–12; pursuit of agenda, 11–12. *See also* economic elites
empowerment, 127–8, 181, 192
entrepreneurship: ACOA and, 143; in Nova Scotia, 169–70; NPM and sponsorship scandal, 136; public sector and, 121; risk avoidance and, 189
Environment Canada, OAG audit of evaluation function in, 272
Estey, Willard, 76

estimates. *See* spending estimates
Evaluating the Effectiveness of Programs (Office of the Auditor General [OAG]), 131–2
evaluations/performance reports: and blame game, 187; Canada School of Public Service and, 160, 161–2; growth of, 271; negative, 187; in private vs public sector, 188; senior public servants and, 115–16. *See also* performance measurement/evaluation; program evaluations
Exit, Voice, and Loyalty (Hirschman), 3–4
expenditure. *See* spending

fault line(s): and decision making, 266; growth of, 173; and managing up vs down, 173; and policy vs implementation, 15; in private vs public sector, 193; theory, and implementation, 12. *See also* government above fault line; government below fault line; public servants above fault line; public servants below fault line
Federal Accountability Act, 120–1, 126, 130, 131
Federal Economic Development Initiative for Northern Ontario (FEDNOR), 146, 152
Federalist Papers (Madison), 13, 54–5
Federal Open Market Committee, 219
Ferguson, Niall, 23
Finance, Department of: and changing regional economic balance, 140; function of, 171; and funding of ACOA, 144; lobbyists/interest groups and, 93
Financial Administration Act, 182–3
financial crisis of 2008: and blame game, 223; global economy and, 277; and government use of senior private sector executives, 91, 251–2; national R&D investment and outcomes from, 244; and private sector weakness, 91; regulatory regime and, 219–21, 239; and social cohesion, 39; and trust in institutions, 39; in United States, 219–21, 223
Finer, Herman, 30
Finer, Sam, 53–4
Fisheries and Oceans, Department of (DFO), 82
Flaherty, Jim, 91, 201–2
Flanagan, Tom, 247
Fonberg, Rob, 119
Food Inspection Agency, 125
Ford, Gerald, 42
Foreign Affairs, Department of: ambassadorial appointments of Privy Council clerks and, 137; division from Foreign Affairs and International Trade, 119–20; exceeding expectations, 192–3; lobbyists/interest groups and, 93
Franks, Ned, 59
Fraser, Sheila, 66, 132
Fredericton Daily Gleaner, on ACOA, 144
free-trade agreements, 214, 218, 226, 231
French Canada, Trudeau and, 25–6

front-line managers/workers:
    delegation to, 270; duties/
    responsibilities, 184–5; freedom/
    discretion for, 270; performance
    evaluations, 197. *See also* line-
    department directors/managers;
    public servants below fault line
Frum, David, 43
Fukuyama, Francis, 254, 279
Fulton Commission, 101, 117
fusion energy, 242–3

Galbraith, John Kenneth, 90
Giddens, Anthony, 31
Gidengil, Elisabeth, 36
Gilbert, Anne, 82
Glassco Commission, 101, 117
Glass-Steagall Act (1933), 219, 221
global economy/globalization: and
    2008 financial crisis, 220, 277;
    and citizens, 278; and common
    good, 45; competition in, 45, 46;
    and income inequality, 38; and
    job loss, 37; politicians and, 45–6;
    and private vs public sector, 256;
    and public interest, 112; and pub-
    lic sector, 277; and regulatory
    regime/regulation, 211–12, 213,
    220, 226, 230, 231, 275; rise of, 45;
    and unions, 37, 208, 209
Globe and Mail: on Canada School
    of Public Service, 162; on Cana-
    dian ambassador's residence in
    Rome, 136–7; on protection of
    Parliament, 69; ranking of prof-
    itable companies, 5–6
Gomery Commission, 120, 198
Google, 243
Gore, Al, 9

Governing from the Bench (Macfar-
    lane), 76
Governing from the Centre (Savoie),
    253
government above fault line: and
    citizens, 279; government below
    fault line vs, 260; and interest
    groups, 265; and lobbyists, 265
government below fault line: and
    citizens, 279; disbelief culture in,
    268; functions of, 266; govern-
    ment above fault line vs, 260;
    prime ministers and, 269; prime
    ministers' court and, 12; and pro-
    gram delivery, 279; quality of,
    266; reforms and, 259, 268. *See
    also* line departments
government(s): accountability to
    Parliament, 53, 58, 67–8; as active
    players, 11; budget accountabili-
    ty, 65–6; business community as
    inspiration for, 8; and citizens,
    16; complexity of structure of, 74;
    courts and, 94; and crises, 239;
    division of powers in, 57; and
    economy, 245, 249–50; establish-
    ment of circumstances for, vs
    management of success, 245, 258,
    259; global economy and, 46;
    granting of power to Parliament,
    53; growth of, 26, 27–8, 30,
    259–60, 276–7; hierarchy in, 74,
    94; and horizontal issues, 73;
    House of Commons and, 57; and
    long term, 245; as model employ-
    er, 209, 257; and national interest,
    277; by networks, 73, 267; over-
    load of, 15, 25–9; prime ministers
    in charge of, 277; public opinion

on, 278; reduction of role, 4; role of, 16; and rules/procedures, 270–1; during Second World War, 9, 26–7, 28, 209, 239; service to ruler, 54; three branches of, 55; and Trudeau's vision of French Canada, 25–6; trust in, 6, 278; turning to business community, 90–1; and visionary investments, 242–6, 276; and wicked problems, 241–2, 245, 276

Grace review, 100

Graham, Andrew, 261–2

Gramm-Leach-Bliley Act, 219

Gray, Herb, 66

Great Depression, 26, 27, 44, 219

Great Society, 4, 46

Greece, democracy in, 54, 55

Greene, Ian, 76

Greenspan, Alan, 219

Grey, Earl, 30

Griffith, Andrew, 107–8

gross domestic product (GDP), 28

"Guide for Ministers" (PCO), 180

Guité, Chuck, 136

Gulick, Luther, 194

Hadfield, Chris, 242

Haida decision, 82–3

Harding, Mark, 77

Harper, Stephen: acceptance of responsibility, 207; and accounting officer, 125; and ACOA, 152; addition of positions to public service, 202; appointment of PCO clerk, 125; on bureaucracy/public service, 107; and Canadian Nuclear Safety Commission, 214; and consultants, 88, 203; and FED-NOR, 152; and government spending, 263; and middle class, 38; and MPs, 59; and national interest, 49; and private sector, 201–2, 274; program elimination, 263; and regulation, 212, 214, 217–18, 232; and Senate scandal, 120; and spending reductions, 116, 203, 274; and "Strong Families" tax measures, 264; "tough on crime" agenda, 80

Harper program review: about, 201–3; across-the-board spending cuts, 274–5; and elimination of deficit, 201; elimination of public service positions, 173; and executive-level public service positions, 195; launching of, 151, 201; majority mandates and, 65, 151, 200; PM's signing off on spending cuts, 202; and spending reductions, 65, 116, 151, 200

Hatfield, Michael, 108–9

Hatfield, Richard, 142

Health Canada: and regulation, 233; scientists speaking out on health issues, 117

health care, refugee claimants and, 81

Heintzman, Ralph, 116, 117, 125, 157, 159

Henry VIII, King, 54

hierarchy: and accountability, 132; advantages of, 74; as non-functional, 94

Hill Times: on "broken" Parliament, 69; on most influential in government, 105–6

Hillwatch.com, 87

Himelfarb, Alex, 119, 135

Hirschman, Albert, *Exit,Voice, and Loyalty*, 3–4

Homer-Dixon, Thomas, 164

Hood, Christopher, 157, 206, 214

Hoover Commission, 101

House of Commons: and Cabinet, 57; and government, 57; history of, 56, 57; lobbyists and, 89–90; "people" represented in, 57; short-term political gain vs public good, 62; and sovereign, 57; Speaker, 56; spin specialists and, 58

How Lucky I've Been (Manion), 271–2

Hudak, Tim, 196

Hungarian refugee crisis, 108

Huntington, Samuel, 279

Hutchinson, Allan, 76

ideas: generation of, 263, 265; implementation vs, 15, 95, 263, 270, 275, 280; and political survival, 265; and visionary investments, 242–6; whiz-bang, 177, 241, 249, 263, 280

Ignatieff, Michael, 41, 42, 81, 246, 247

implementation: announcement of new initiatives/programs vs, 166; blame game and, 261; bureaucrats and, 97; of centres of excellence, 164; courts and, 79–80, 82, 94–5; disbelief culture and, 268; of election promises, 64–5; elites' agendas vs, 12; fault-line theory and, 12; governing from centre and, 262; ideas vs, 15, 95, 241,

263, 270, 275, 280; lack of resolution of issues, 261; machinery of government and, 241; in McCain Foods, 170; of new initiatives, 166–7; of Obamacare, 269; of policy, 109, 261–2; policy vs, 15, 273; politicians and, 269–70; politicians/senior public servants and, 273; prime ministers and reform of, 269; prime ministers' priorities vs, 273; program managers and, 166–7; public servants above fault line and, 166, 167; by public servants below fault line, 166; recommendations regarding policy vs, 251; and success, 166; Supreme Court and, 83, 85

Implementation (Pressman; Wildavsky), 261–2, 273

income disparity/inequality, 8, 9, 37–9, 50

Increased Ministerial Authority and Accountability initiative, 126

individuals. *See* citizens/individuals

Industrial and Regional Development Program (IRDP), 141

Industry Canada, lobbyists/interest groups and, 93

information gathering: in regulatory regimes, 214; socioeconomic data, 106–7

information requests: central agencies and, 185–6; management levels and, 194; public servants below fault line and, 185; senior public servants and, 116. *See also* access to information

information technology: and growth of bureaucracy, 204; and

interest groups, 87; Internet, 41–2; and productivity, 204; and regulatory regime, 230. *See also* social media

initiatives: elites and, 11–12; implementation of new, 166–7; political/economic elites and major, 11–12; politicians and visibility of new, 165–6; reliance on existing vs new programs for development of, 147; risk avoidance and, 189; spending on low- vs high-priority, 252; spending on new vs old, 254

institutions: checks and balances for, 55; global financial crisis of 2008 and trust in, 39; irrelevance of political, 280; public opinion on, 59–60; trust in, 6, 39, 71. *See also* government(s)

Integrated Service Delivery Project, 169–70, 181, 189, 270

interest groups: and access to government, 86–7; and access-to-information legislation, 241; and access to policy-/decision-makers, 261; blocking change, 279; citizens compared to, 241; and courts, 75, 85–6; and decision-making, 88; evidence-based policy advice and, 265; government above fault line and, 265; information technology and, 87; and key government officials, 241; and PMO, 92–3; and political/economic elites' pursuit of agenda, 12; and power, 92–3; and public interest, 95, 241; public service detachment from, 96; transparency and, 241

International Federation of Accountants, 226

Invest More, Innovate More, Trade More, Learn More (Savoie), 169

Irving Oil, 221

Jacobs, Jane, 232

job classification system, 120

job creation: global economy and, 45–6; national governments and, 44; private sector and, 232, 251; regional incentive programs and, 152

job loss: globalization and, 37; Moncton closures and, 257; private sector efficiency and, 37; regulation and, 212, 232

Johnson, Al, 153; "The Role of the Deputy Minister," 29

Johnson, Nevil, 247

Johnston, Richard, 36

Johnstone, R., 23

justice system, 277–8

Justinian, Emperor, 55

Just Society, 4–5, 23, 46, 47

Kelleher, James, 146

Kennedy, John F., 9

Kenney, Jason, 107, 175

Kent, Tom, 152

Keynes, John Maynard, 10–11, 26–7, 100

Keystone pipeline, 177–8

Knopff, Rainer, 76, 77

Kroeger, Arthur, 29, 200

Krueger, Alan, 37

Lac-Mégantic derailment, 221–2, 223–6, 227, 228, 233

Lalonde, Marc, 257
Lambert, Allen, 155
laws: absolute rulers/monarchs and, 55; labour, 84; principles of justice and, 74–5, 81; Rome and, 55
Learning Disability Association, 79
LeBel, Louis, 80
LeBlanc, Dominic, 64
LeBlanc, Roméo, 84–5, 257
Lexchin, Joel, 233
Liberal Party: and Cabinet decisions, 253; and foreign workers program, 175; in postwar power held by, 44; and regional economic development, 165; and "Strong Families" tax measures, 264. See also Chrétien, Jean; Martin, Paul; political parties; Trudeau, Justin; Trudeau, Pierre E.
line-department directors/managers: central agencies and, 200–1; constraints upon, 195; and ministers' offices, 193–4; and organizational culture, 188; private sector counterparts compared to, 195. See also front-line managers/workers; public servants below fault line
line departments: Chrétien-Martin program review and cuts to, 200–1; competition among, 188–9; and decisions, 128; lawyers in, 82; levels of management in, 255; ministerial responsibility for, 47; public servants above fault line vs, 262; and shaping of new policies/programs, 47; values/ethics office, 136. See also

government below fault line
lobbyists: access-to-information legislation and, 91–2; activities of, 91–2; and controversy, 90; and decision making, 90; and departments, 93; and elites' pursuit of agenda, 12; former political advisors as, 90, 265; former public servants as, 90, 93–4, 265; former senior government officials as, 231; government above fault line and, 265; groups as leading private sector associations, 92; and House of Commons, 89–90; influence/power of, 105, 106; and Lac-Mégantic derailment, 225–6; and lobbying as lucrative business, 90; media and, 90; and ministers, 92, 225–6; and MPs, 89, 90; numbers of, 89, 92; and oil industry, 92; and PMO, 92–3; and policy, 102; politicians and, 102; and power in government, 92–3; and public interest, 241; and railway regulation, 227; and regulations, 215; reporting of communications with government officials, 92; senior public servants and, 207; services provided by, 90; spin doctors as, 63
Lougheed, Peter, 250
loyalty: to government of day vs public interest, 116; of public servants to government of day, 110–11, 135
Lumley, Ed, 141
Lynch, Kevin, 130

MacEachen, Allan J., 99, 107, 250

Macfarlane, Emmett, *Governing from the Bench*, 76
machinery of government: churches and, 30; complexity of, 186–7; components of, 178; courts and, 78–9, 83; growth of complexity of, 48; growth of government and, 277; and implementation, 241; limited knowledge of, 74; ministerial responsibility and, 30; overloading of, 49–50, 267; PCO and, 29–30; permanent election campaigns and, 277; phases in development of, 10–11; prime minister and, 29–30; as risk-averse, 194; size of, 178; thickening of, 26, 194; and transparency, 15
Mack, John, 215
MacKay, Elmer, 119
MacLean, Vince, 144
Maclean's, on most important in Ottawa, 105, 106
Mactavish, Ann, 80–1
Madison, James, *Federalist Papers*, 13, 54–5
Maioni, Antonia, 76
Mallory, James, 215
management: and accountability, 122; central agencies and, 104, 115; courts and issues of, 83–6; of departments as businesses, 7; deputy ministers and, 104; discretion of, 270–2; education/training for, 153–63; and elimination of organizational waste, 202; empowerment of, 127–8, 181, 192, 266; and government spending, 114; and human resources

issues, 272; incentives to promote good, 203; layers/levels of, 193–5, 255, 262, 267; oversight bodies and, 260; PCO clerks and, 126–7, 175; prime minister and issues regarding, 175; in private vs public sector, 3, 4, 5–6, 100–1, 102, 114, 124, 126, 129, 187, 188, 192–3, 259; public servants and, 101–2; and quality of government operations, 116–17; result-orientation in, 101; rewards for, 272; senior ministers and, 175; senior public servants and, 97–8, 100, 114–17; Thatcher's five critical issues of, 123; transparency and, 260; up vs down, 135, 173. *See also* implementation
management reform(s): expectations vs achievement in, 114, 126; and growth of public service, 202–3; ineffectuality of, 271; and ministerial responsibility, 134; objectives of, 114; private sector and, 208; and regulatory regime, 225. *See also* program reviews
managerialism, 113–17
Managing Publicly (Mintzberg; Bourgault), 104–5
Manfredi, Christopher, 75, 76
Manion, John L. "Jack," 67–8, 108, 109, 110, 155, 156, 157; *How Lucky I've Been*, 271–2
March, James G., 172
Marchand, Jean, 146
Marchi, Sergio, 58
Marleau, Robert, 70
Martin, Keith, 62
Martin, Lawrence, 174

Martin, Pat, 93–4

Martin, Paul: and Atlantic region, 150; on decline of middle class, 36–7; and division of Foreign Affairs and International Trade, 119; and partisan advisors attending Cabinet committee meetings, 109–10; as succeeding Chrétien, 149. *See also* Chrétien-Martin program review

Massé, Marcel, 113

May, Kathryn, 206

Mazankowski, Don: and ACOA, 145–6; and CCMD, 153, 155, 158–9, 162; Western agenda, 145–6

McCain, Harrison, 5, 14, 170, 196

McCain Foods, 170, 243–4

McCaughey, Gerald, 127

McCormick, Peter, 76

McGuinty, David, 224

McHardie, Dan, 40–1

McKenna, Frank, 144

McLachlin, Beverley, 74–5, 77, 85–6, 277–8. *See also* Supreme Court of Canada

McNeil, Stephen, 170

McNish, Jacquie, 228

McPhail, Don, 166–7

media: and ACOA, 144; and adversarial politics, 63; changes in, 46–7; and controversies, 175; and decline of Parliament, 58; and importance of issues, 264–5; lobbyists and, 90; and management issues, 175; MPs and, 175; and national debates about national interests/common good, 47; news cycle and journalism, 40–1; news-

papers, 40; new vs traditional, 40–4; as oversight body, 10; partisan appointees and, 264; politicians and, 46; and public service, 205; and responses to questions, 194; Second World War and, 239

Meech Lake Accord, 144

Meisel, John, 62

members of Legislative Assembly (MLAs), in community, 21

members of Parliament (MPs): and 2013 omnibus bill, 68; and access-to-information legislation, 94; accountability for budget, 65–6; as antidote to permanent government, 266; in caucus meetings, 64; Chong's bill on powers of, 59; and citizens' access to government, 94; in community, 21; constituency representation and local projects, 61–2; and decision making, 64; and decline of Parliament, 58–9, 60; election promises, 64–5, 86; and estimates, 66; and lobbyists, 89, 90; and management issues, 175; media and, 175; as ombudsman, 86; and public servants, 61; role of, 60–2, 63, 266; running on tracks/not creating problems, 266; senior public servants on, 68–9; speaking on behalf of citizens/constituents, 86; support for political parties, 61; training/orientation of, 60; trust in, 6, 69; understanding of Parliament/government, 60. *See also* ministers; politicians

Mendelsohn, Matthew, 62

middle class: and income inequality, 38–9; shrinking of, 36–7; and social cohesion, 38, 39

Mikisew decision, 83

Mining Association, 92

ministerial offices/staff: and changes to political–public service landscape, 179–80; contact with line-department directors, 193–4; and departments, 110; and information requests, 193–4

ministerial responsibility: accountability and, 122–3; and accountability for decison-making, 207; blame vs, 207, 224; changes in, 180; decline in, 120; for estimates, 67–8; history of, 30; and Lac-Mégantic derailment, 224; for line departments, 47; and machinery of government, 30; management reform and, 134; PCO and, 29–30; reform measures and, 138; in Tait report, 134–5

ministers: advisors to, 179–80; chiefs of staff for, 102–3, 109, 179–80; and deputy ministers, 110, 130; executive assistants, 179; and information requests, 186; lobbyists and, 92–3, 225–6; and management issues, 175; and policy, 97, 108; regional, and decision-making, 253; and shaping of new policies/programs, 47

Mintz, Jack, 91

Mintzberg, Henry, 157, 187; *Managing Publicly*, 104–5

Montreal, Maine and Atlantic (MMA) railway, 224

Moore, Mark, 3

morale: in government, 4; of public servants/service, 189–90, 205, 248, 255, 275

Morton, F.L., 76

Mulcair, Thomas, 38, 223, 276

Mulroney, Brian: and 1988 election, 146; and ACOA, 140, 143–4, 152; and Atlantic Canada, 142–3, 252; and bureaucracy, 102, 107; and Cabinet committee system, 176; and Canada School of Public Service, 155, 156, 159, 162; and chiefs of staff in ministerial offices, 102–3; and free-trade agreement, 214; and Meech Lake Accord, 144; and ministerial responsibility, 138; and Mulroney-Tellier reforms, 123–5; and NEP, 250; and Nielsen task force, 216–17; and politician–public servant relationship, 109; and power of MPs, 59; and program reviews by private sector executives, 100; and public service influence over policy, 103; and regional industrial assistance, 141; and regulation, 214, 218; and West, 145–6. *See also* Nielsen task force/review

multiculturalism, 107–8

multinational firms: and creation of global economy, 45; and regulations, 215

Murphy, Mike, 78

Murphy, Shawn, 66

Murray, Lowell, 66, 165–6

Myles, John, 37–8

Nadon, Marc, 84

National Capital Region, public service in, 173, 174, 202, 263

National Defence, Department of (DND), 132, 133

National Energy Program (NEP), 249–50

national interest: government and, 277; permanent election campaigns vs, 63–4; voters vs non-voters and, 277. *See also* public interest

National Science Foundation, 243

Natural Resources, Department of, 93

Nessen, Ron, 42

networks/networking: deputy ministers and, 105; government by, 73, 267

neutrality, 71

Nevitte, Neil, 22–3, 36

Newall, Ted, 155

New Brunswick: CN closure of shops in Moncton, 257–8; early French immersion program, 78; Eaton's closure in Moncton, 257–8; health-care services delivery, 78

New Democratic Party (NDP): and middle class, 38; and "Strong Families" tax measures, 264; two main political parties vs, 44. *See also* Mulcair, Thomas; political parties

New Public Management (NPM): and empowerment of government managers, 127–8, 181; and entrepreneurship, 136; expectations vs achievement in, 114, 126, 262; and growth of public service, 203; inability to duplicate private sector conditions in public service, 114; and irreconcilability of roles, 114–15; and managing up vs down, 173; old public service values vs, 135; and performance measurement, 130; and public-private partnerships, 134; and public servants, 126; and public service terminations, 117; and re-allocation of resources, 167–8; risk avoidance and, 189; and shift to private sector notions, 134; and size of public service, 201; and sponsorship scandal, 136; studies on, 11, 122; and unchanged attitudes toward public sector, 138; vocabulary in Canada School of Public Service, 160

Newsom, Gavin, 7

Newton, Kenneth, 33

Nielsen task force/review, 100, 216–17

Nike, 45

Nixon, Gordon, 127

non-performers: courts and, 84, 196, 197–8, 269; lack of change in dealing with, 116–17, 151; managers and, 151; and morale, 199; in private vs public sector, 278–9; responsibility for, 255; as takers, 199; unions and, 84, 196, 197–8, 269, 278–9

Normand, Martin, 24

Norris, Pippa, 33

Nova Scotia: as business-friendly, 169–70, 182; Court of Appeal, 80; economic development in, 169–70, 181, 189; increased taxation in, 276; Integrated Service

Delivery Project, 169–70, 181, 189, 270; risk-avoidance approach in, 189; school construction for French-language students, 80
Now Discover Your Strengths, 3

Obama, Barack, 9, 269
Obamacare, 269
OECD, on social cohesion, 39
OECD countries: income inequality in, 37; tax reductions in, 37
Office of Privatization and Regulatory Affairs, 217
Office of the Auditor General (OAG). *See* Auditor General, Office of the (OAG)
Office of the Commissioner of Lobbying, 91–2
officers of Parliament, 178
Olson, Mancur, 34
Ontario Power Generation (OPG), 258
opposition: and 2013 omnibus bill, 68; goal of, 70; and OAG, 132
Osbaldeston, Gordon, 103
O'Toole, Barry J., 7–8, 134
oversight bodies, 10, 128–9, 260

Paine, Thomas, *Rights of Man,* 55
Pammett, Jon, 36
Parliament: accountability for budget, 65–6, 67; and accountability of government, 53, 58; and adversarial politics, 63–4; as ally of citizens, 278; and budget, 58; decline of, 58–9, 69–70; and division of Foreign Affairs and International Trade, 119; division of powers between levels of government

and, 57; golden age of, 58; and government accountability, 67–8; history of, 56–8; majorities vs support of Crown, 56–7; media and decline of, 58; need for repair, 59–60; political power of, 53, 56; politicians' attitudes toward, 70; purpose of, 53; senior public servants and, 70; sessions, 59; trust in, 6, 69; Westminster model, 56–8, 94
Parliament Hill 2014 shooting, 167–8
partisanship: of appointments at centre, 264; and blame game, 102; and Cabinet committee meetings, 109–10; and common good, 240–1; expansion of, 102; and policy, 102, 103; public service and, 111–12, 180; senior public servants above fault line and, 264
Paulson, Hank, 219
pensions: of deputy ministers (DMs), 208; of public servants, 94, 199, 278; of senior public servants, 162, 163, 231; unions and, 278
performance: accountability for, 118, 137–8; in private sector, 127; procedure/rules vs, 15, 118, 127–33, 270–1; as qualitative, 131; Supreme Court and assessment of government, 80
performance measurement/evaluation: accountability to, 127; auditor general and, 131–2; as bottom line, 128; consultants and, 131; deputy minis-

ters and, 129; front-line managers'/
workers' appraisals, 197; growth
of personnel and spending on,
131; and layers of bureaucracy,
128–9; in private vs public sector,
5–6, 127, 210

permanent election campaigns:
accountability vs, 63–4; and
adversarial politics, 63–4; controversies and, 177; and machinery
of government, 277; national
interest vs, 63–4; political parties
and, 240; politicians and, 41; politics as, 63; and reaching outside,
206–7; social media and, 41, 43

Perry, J.L., 121

Peters, B. Guy, 111, 157, 259

Peters, Tom, 193

Piketty, Thomas, 38

Pitfield, Michael, 153

policy advice: career politicians
and, 248; evidence-based, 106,
248, 265; ideology- vs evidence-
based, 180; public servants and,
87, 108, 248; public service and,
111, 126

policy-making: career public servants and, 48; complexity of,
87–8; concept development vs
implementation, 167; courts and,
86; courts of appeal and, 76; hori-
zontality of, 194; politicians and,
97; public service and, 106, 110;
senior ministers and, 97; and
understanding what government
is good at, 11

policy/policies: anecdotal evidence
for, 108; central agencies and, 185;
changes in shaping new issues,

47; clerks of the Privy Council
(PCO) and, 232; and common
good, 47; complexity of, 47, 48;
consultants and, 102; courts and,
74, 82, 94–5; deputy ministers
and, 103; de-statization of state as
locus of, 87; in election campaigns, 247; elites and new, 11–12;
governing from centre and, 265;
governing party and, 102; growth
of complexity of process, 48; by
heads of government and advisors, 10; ideas vs implementation
in, 95; implementation of, 109;
implementation vs, 15, 261–2;
lobbyists and, 102; ministers and,
108; ministers' chiefs of staff and,
103; organized groups and,
250–2; partisanship and, 102, 103;
politicians and, 101, 102–5, 103,
106, 232; prime ministers and, 97,
103; private sector and, 102,
249–50; and public interest,
111–12, 240; public servants
above fault line and, 179; public
servants and, 107; public service
and, 103, 107, 205; recommendations vs implementation of, 251;
and regulation, 231; regulatory
regime and, 233; science and, 164;
senior public servants and, 29, 97,
98, 99, 100, 101, 103, 232; socioeconomic data and, 106–7;
Supreme Court and, 75, 76, 77–8;
university-based management
programs and, 153; visibility vs,
165

polis, 54

political parties: in community, 21;

diminishing role of, 62; discipline, 61; disconnection from population, 240; and elections, 57; history of, 56–7; as leader-centric, 62, 278; leaders/advisors and election campaigns, 62; leaders' power, 240; marketing strategy, 63; membership, 3, 62–3, 240, 278; MPs' support for, 61; permanent election campaigns and, 240; politics and responsible government, 56–7; in postwar period, 44; and public interest, 56–7, 70, 240–1; and public opinion, 62, 240

political power. *See* power

politicians: accountability of, 101; and blame game, 207, 223, 224; and bureaucracy, 268; and campaign spending commitments, 65; career, 248; and change, 101, 269; and common good, 49; and consultants, 102; and controversies, 164; and democracy, 246; difficulties in serving as, 248; global economy and, 45–6; and governing from centre, 253; and ideology- vs evidence-based policy advice, 180; and implementation, 269–70; and lobbyists, 102; and media, 46; and middle class, 38; and new initiatives/programs/money, 165–6; and new taxes, 276; and Parliament, 70; and partisan political staff, 102; and permanent election campaigns, 41; and policy, 97, 101, 102–5, 106, 232; and program managers running on

tracks, 273; and public interest, 113; public opinion on, 60, 63, 246; and public servants, 99, 109, 111–12, 207, 249; and regional economic development, 152, 165; and regulations, 213; and responsibility vs blame, 207; and senior public servants, 100–1; social media and, 42–3, 248; as tax-eaters, 7; and visibility, 144, 165–6; and voters, 277. *See also* members of Parliament (MPs)

politics: as alternative to government by coercion, 246; in community, 21; courts and, 75–6; judges and, 77–8, 85; and management of perceptions, 238; as marketing strategy vs public service, 62; personal attacks in, 247; religion and, 23; ruthlessness in, 246, 247–8; social media and, 40; as survival game, 182, 265; and voters, 247–8

The Politics of Public Spending in Canada (Savoie), 131

Pollitt, Christopher, 157, 206, 269

population. *See* citizens/individuals

power: consultants and, 88; of courts, 76, 77; courts and, 94; and decision-making, 270; in Greek polis, 54; and history of parliamentary system, 56; interest groups and, 92–3; judicial, 75; lobbyists and, 92–3, 105, 106; of MPs, 59; of Parliament, 53; party leaders and, 240; PMO and, 180; prime ministers and, 53, 59, 128, 252–3; priorities of, vs shrinking middle class, 38; rulers/monarchs

and, 53–4, 55, 56; of Supreme
Court, 76
Pressman, Jeffrey L., *Implementa-*
tion, 261–2, 273
Priest, Margot, 229–30
prime ministers: advisors to, 179–80;
and blame game, 128; chief of
staff, 105–6; court of (*see* court
government); and courts, 94; and
decisions on machinery of government questions, 29–30; deputy
ministers and, 129, 130, 193;
duties of, 174–5; empowerment
of managers, 128; goal-setting by,
252–3; as governing from centre,
103, 202, 252–3; and government
below fault line, 269; and implementation reform, 269; influence
of, 105, 106; and management
issues, 175; and PCO, 174; and policy, 97, 103, 253–4; power of, 53,
59, 128, 180, 252–3; priorities and
deputy ministers, 105; and prob-
lems/controversies, 128, 175, 181;
public opinion and, 253; and
public servants above fault line,
174–5; and public servants below
fault line, 181; and regulations,
214; social media and, 43; and
spending cuts, 200, 201, 202, 274;
and Supreme Court judicial
appointments, 84; wife of, 105;
workload, 253
Prime Minister's Office (PMO): communications staff in, 116; concentration of power in, 180; and
ideas vs implementation, 15; lob-
byists/interest groups and, 92–3;
ministerial staff and, 179–80; par-

tisanship of, 102; and political
problems, 110; Supreme Court
vs, 85
Prince, Michael, 213–14, 229, 230
principal-agency theory, 167, 201
private sector: ACOA and, 143; and
bottom line, 5, 249; Canada
School of Public Service and,
160, 161; economic interests, 91;
and economy, 45; emulation of,
205, 208; financial crisis of 2008
and, 91; former senior government officials in, 90, 93–4, 231,
265; golden age of, 8–9; government activities hived off to, 280;
government spending cuts and,
201–2, 274; language training in,
158; and National Energy Program (NEP), 249–50; NPM unable
to duplicate conditions, 114; perception as more dynamic/
successful, 8; performance/
performance measurement in,
5–6, 127; and policy, 249–50; privatization of Crown corporations
and, 258; public opinion of, 8–9;
and public policy, 102; public
sector reforms borrowed from,
10; public service activities transferred to, 275–6; regulation
enforcement and, 216; regulatory
regime turned over to, 232; and
shareholders, 91; and smart
regulations vs regulatory regime,
275; socioeconomic data/
information sources, 106–7; values associated with, 6; and
wicked problems, 242. *See also*
business community

private vs public sector: in accountability, 9, 121, 129, 133; accountability in, 117–18; and adversarial
politics, 63; appeal of, 5–6; and
budgeting, 65; and campaign
commitments, 65; collective bargaining and, 196; comparative
advantage in, 3; in competition,
121; and consequences for job
done poorly, 255–6; controversies
in, 264; cost-effectiveness in, 256;
culture/outlook clash, 208; decision-making in, 188, 266, 270;
efficiency in, 15, 258; and exit vs
voice, 4; fault lines in, 193; in
functions performed, 208; fundamental differences between, 10;
in getting things done, 188; global economy and, 208–9, 256;
implementation in, 12; line-
department directors and, 195;
management in, 3, 4, 5–6, 100–1,
102, 114, 124, 126, 129, 187, 188,
192–3, 259; mutual criticisms,
251–2; non-performers in, 196;
and operations management,
123; performance measurement
in, 127, 188, 210; performance vs
procedural/administrative
accountability in, 133; and procedural accountability, 132; productivity in, 204–5, 256; in provision
of public services, 5; "publicness"
and, 138; and public vs private
value, 3; in purposes, 121; responsibility vs blame in, 120; rewards
for competence in, 188; salaries
in, 208; Thatcher and, 8, 97, 114,
259; transparency in, 9; unions

in, 196, 208–9, 256, 278–9; values
in, 232–3; work incentives in, 188
privatization: of Canadian National
Railway, 136; of Crown corporations, 258; management revolution and, 114
Privy Council Office (PCO): and
ACOA, 89; and Cabinet committees, 176; clerks of the, 126–7;
communications staff in, 116;
and consultants, 88–9; and decisions on machinery of government questions, 29–30; deputy-
minister-level classification in,
185; deputy ministers drawn
from, 48; "Guide for Ministers,"
180; and ministerial responsibility, 29–30; and ministers' chiefs of
staff, 109; and prime minister,
174; role/mandate, 89; secretariats, 176; service areas of, 176; and
social media, 44
productivity: information technology and, 204; lack of incentives
for, 203; measuring of, 204; in
private vs public sector, 204–5,
256; and program reviews, 204;
unions and, 203
program delivery: accountability
and, 268; government below
fault line and, 279; public sector
reforms and, 15; public servants
and, 98; time spent on, vs evaluation, 272; transparency requirements and, 268
program evaluations: above fault
line, 183; assessment of success,
238; consultants and, 131; growth
of personnel and spending on,

131; OAG and program spending, 182–3; percentage of time spent on, vs program delivery, 272; regulatory regime and, 217; units in departments/agencies, 200, 201

program managers: access-to-information legislation and, 273; blame game and, 260; constraints upon, 272; distance from prime minister's court, 267; duties/responsibilities, 184–5; and implementation, 166–7; and staff running on tracks, 273. *See also* front-line managers/workers

program reviews: and bureaucratic growth, 260; private sector executives and, 100; productivity and, 204; and public service growth, 209–10; and regional/field vs National Capital Region offices, 263; and spending reductions, 116, 209–10, 255; and staff cuts/reallocations, 150. *See also* Chrétien-Martin program review; Harper program review

PS 2000 initiative, 126

public consultation(s): problems regarding, 33–4; social media and, 43; special interest groups and, 34

public good. *See* common good; public interest

public interest: access of citizens vs interest groups to, 240–1; checks and balances and, 55; citizens and implementation of politics in, 249; citizens defining, 55; complexity of, 71; courts and, 241; in democracy, 112, 113; de-statization and, 87; economic elites and, 95; evidence-based policy advice vs elites talking to elites and, 265; global economy and, 112; history of, 54–5; interest groups and, 95, 113, 241; lobbyists and, 241; loyalty to government of day vs, 116; national governments and, 44; partisanship and, 240–1; pluralism and, 112–13; policy and, 111–12, 240; political parties and, 56–7, 70, 240–1; politicians and, 113; public sector and, 14; public servants/service and, 97, 110–14, 179; regulation(s) and, 210, 212–13, 215–16, 218, 223; rights revolution and, 46; Second World War and, 239; self-regulation and, 229–30; social cohesion and, 32; Supreme Court and, 79; taxes and, 56; values/ethics and, 112. *See also* common good; national interest

public opinion: on government not caring about citizens' opinions, 279; and limited knowledge of machinery of government, 74; partisan appointees and, 264; on performance in government, 276, 278; on political institutions, 59–60; on political parties, 62, 240; on politicians, 60, 63, 246; prime ministers and, 253; of private sector, 8–9; on public service, 205; on response to crises, 220–1; on Supreme Court, 85; on trust in federal government, 6, 278

Public Policy Forum, 250
public-private partnerships, 10, 134
public sector: and accountability, 121, 133; bias for action, 121; churches and, 21, 23; credibility of, 121; defining characteristics, 73; downsizing of, 5; emulation of private sector, 10, 205, 208; and entrepreneurial spirit, 121; global economy and, 277; golden age of, 4–5; perceptions of, over fifty years, 4–6; performance measurement in, 6, 133; and public interest, 14; public participation as central to, 3–4; public support for, 9; reforms as reconciliation of irreconcilable, 121; traditional qualities associated with, 3; values associated with, 6. *See also* private vs public sector
public servants: accountability of, 100–1; avoidance of paper trail, 82–3; benefits, 190, 199; and blame, 68–9, 83, 102, 115, 207, 248, 255–7; and budgets vs efficiency, 256; bureaucrats vs takers among, 199; as Canada School of Public Service teachers, 159; career politicians and, 248; challenges facing, 88; conditions for reaching outside, 206–7; and controversies, 206; courts and, 82–3; criticisms of, 99–100; declining value of work, 189; experience/knowledge of particular field/department, 104; fault line between, 173; and governing from centre, 253; as lobbyists, 90; loyalty of, 110–11, 116, 135, 271;

and management, 101–2; in middle of public service, 206; misconduct by, 136; morale of, 189–90, 205, 248, 255; MPs and, 61, 68–9; in Mulroney-Tellier reforms, 123–5; in National Capital Region, 173, 174, 263; neutrality, 71, 110–14, 134, 271; and parsimonious culture in government, 255; pensions, 94, 199, 278; percentage dealing with general public, 174; and policy, 48, 87, 107, 108, 248; politicians and, 99, 109, 110–12, 207, 249; and program/services delivery, 98; and public interest, 110–14; and reputation of government, 255–7; and result-orientation, 101, 114; as risk-averse, 244; role of, vs politicians' role, 111; sick leave, 190, 199, 205, 256; and social media, 42–3; and spending reductions, 255; and standing committees, 68–9; terminations of, 116–17, 196–9; turnover in regional/local vs National Capital offices, 186; UN code of conduct for, 112; visibility vs anonymity of, 206; workload, 198–9. *See also* bureaucrats/bureaucracy; senior public servants
public servants above fault line: about, 178; and accountability, 175–6; below fault line vs, 183–4; and blame game, 177, 179, 182, 195; and conflicting goals, 182; and controversies, 177–8; functions of, 178–9; and implementation, 12, 166; and new policies/

measures, 165–6; numbers of, 178; and policies/programs/issues running on tracks/not creating problems, 253–4; and policy, 179; prime minister's agenda and, 174–5; in prime minister's court, 179; and progress of projects, 181; and public interest, 179; public servants below fault line vs, 262; qualities of, 179; as self-governing, 175–6; and whiz-bang ideas, 177. *See also* senior public servants

public servants below fault line: above fault line vs, 183–4; as ally of citizens, 278; and deputy minister's agenda, 183–4; duties/responsibilities, 184–5; implementation by, 12, 166; and information requests, 185–6; and Integrated Service Delivery Project, 181; limited upward mobility for, 272; performance of, and citizen mistrust, 278; prime minister and, 181; public servants above fault line vs, 262. *See also* line-department directors/managers

public service: altruistic, 32–3; anonymity, 134; as under attack, 113; characteristics of, 111; and common good, 167; corporate culture, 153; and democracy, 112; detachment from interest groups, 96; diversity in services providers, vs monopoly of, 5; empowerment in, 192; golden age of, 7–8, 26, 33, 205; growth of, 131, 202–3, 209–10; hiring through merit sys-

tem, 111; ideal vs private gain, 134; job classification system, 120; media and, 205; monopoly over services, 5; morale problem, 275; neutrality of, 180; NPM and irreconcilability of roles, 114–15; and partisanship, 111–12; partisanship of, 180; and policy, 103, 107, 205; and policy advice, 111, 126; and policy-making, 106, 110; and public interest, 97; public opinion on, 205; rules vs values approach in, 135; as serving government of day, 135; special interest groups vs, 113; staff cuts/reallocations, 150; values/ethics exercise for, 112, 134–6. *See also* bureaucrats/bureaucracy

Public Service Commission (PSC): as "audit" agency, 128; and Canada School of Public Service, 158; and managerialism, 115; on public service pride in service, 153; and reporting requirements, 115

Public Service Labour Relations Board (PSLRB), 199

Public Service Modernization Act, 197

public value, 3, 50

Putnam, Robert, *Bowling Alone*, 22–3

Quebec, private health-care insurance in, 79–80

Question Period, 174

railways: dangerous goods transport, 221–2, 227–8; regulation of, 221–2, 223–6, 227–8

Rainey, H.G., 121
Raitt, Lisa, 224, 225–6
Ranger, Louis, 130
Rayner review, 100
Reagan, Ronald, 100, 102
reallocation of resources: for ACOA, 147, 150; for Canada School of Public Service, 161; government competence at, 252; human resources, 147, 150, 166; lack of incentives for, 167–8; by managers, 125; NPM and, 167–8; program reviews and staff cuts, 150; regulatory agency uses vs, 216; and wicked problems, 242
Red Tape Reduction Commission, 217–18; *Cutting Red Tape and Freeing Business to Grow*, 217
reforms: blame game vs, 275; borrowing from private sector for, 10; to government below fault line, 259; and ministerial responsibility, 138; packaging new policies vs, 275; and program delivery, 15. *See also* management reform(s)
regional economic development: agency creation, 141–2, 145–6 (*see also* Atlantic Canada Opportunities Agency [ACOA]); in Atlantic Canada, 139, 140–1; changing balance in, 140; combatting disparities in, 141; and DREE, 141–2; and DRIE, 141–2; expectations vs achievement in, 238; and FEDNOR, 146; and job creation, 152; in Nova Scotia, 169–70, 181, 189; politicians and, 144, 152, 165; senior public servants and, 152;

and thickening of government, 152; and visibility, 144, 165; WD compared to ACOA in, 145–6
regulation(s): alternatives to, 217; assessment of proposed new, 217; auditing of, 224; balance in number of, 213, 215; and business community, 215, 217–18; command-and-control bureaucracy and, 227; cost of enforcement, 216; and crises, 225; dangerous goods transportation and, 221–2, 223–5, 225–6; and economic competitiveness, 216; enforcement, 216, 225, 229; enforcement vs compliance, 216; globalization and, 213, 226, 231; impact assessments, 217; as job killers, 212, 232; lobbyists and, 215; of marine transportation, 228; as necessity for governments, 212–13; Nielsen task force and, 216–17; one for one rule, 218, 227; and oversight, 224–5; policy and, 231; on political agenda, 211–12; politicians and, 213; prime ministers and, 214; program evaluation, 217; and public interest, 210, 212–13, 215–16, 218, 223; of railways, 221–2, 223–5, 225–6, 227–8; reduction in, 212; reform of, 215; and report-writing vs on-site inspection, 266; self-, 219, 223, 229–30; and self-inspection vs enforcement, 229; smart, 216, 227, 275; weak, 219
regulatory regime(s): 2008 financial crisis and, 219–21, 239; business-

friendly vs sectoral/public interest, 215–16; changes to, 215–18, 233–4; control theory in, 214; cost, 216–17; crises and, 233; economic elites and, 231; and economic growth, 232; enforcement in, 215; and enforcement vs spot audits, 215; free-trade agreements and, 218, 226; globalization and, 218, 230, 274–5; independence from political control, 215; information-gathering and, 214; information technology and, 230; management reforms and, 225; numbers of public servants in, 216; OAG and, 217; and policy, 233; quality of, 225–30; regulatory advisory committee and, 218; and regulatory affairs branch creation, 217; resource reallocation vs other uses in, 216; scorecard for, 217–18; self-inspection in, 226; self-regulation and, 230; standard-setting in, 214, 215; theory of regulatory control and, 230; time taken to review, 275; turned over to private sector, 232; in United Kingdom, 232; in United States, 219–21, 239

Reid, Scott, 116

La Relève, 9

representative democracy: BNA Act and, 57; bureaucracy and, 48; decline in credibility of, 48–9; and elections, 48; history of, 53; purpose of, 53; stability in, 245. See also democracy

research and development (R&D), 243–6

results-orientation: in management, 101; public servants and, 101, 114

Revenue Canada, 187

Rhodes, Rod, 114

Ricardo, David, 3

Rights of Man (Paine), 55

risk avoidance: blame game and, 189, 194; and entrepreneurship, 189; reaching inward vs outward and, 205

Robertson, Gordon, 29, 89

Robertson, Grant, 228

"The Role of the Deputy Minister" (Johnson), 29

Roman Catholic Church: changes in, 31–2; and community, 50; crisis in, 21; government organizations compared to, 30; health/social services transferred to public sector, 23; management layers/levels in, 193, 262; membership, 21; parish priests, 20, 21, 31

Rome, government in, 55

Rothstein, Henry, 214

Royal Canadian Mounted Police (RCMP), 168

Russell, Peter, 82

Saint Lawrence Seaway, 244

Samara, 36, 59, 60, 62, 70

Samuelson, Paul, 3

Sarkozy, Nicolas, 45–6

Savoie, Donald: "The Canadian Centre for Management Studies" (CCMS), 153–5; as CCMD deputy/acting principal, 156; Governing from the Centre, 253; Invest More, Innovate More, Trade More,

Learn More, 169; *The Politics of Public Spending in Canada,* 131; *Thatcher, Reagan, and Mulroney,* 173

Schuck, Peter H., 7

Schultz, Richard, 213–14, 215, 229, 230

Schumpeter, Joseph, 34; *Capitalism, Socialism and Democracy,* 48–9

science/scientists, 163–4, 167, 206

Second World War: and blame game, 239; government during, 9, 26–7, 28, 209, 239; media and, 239; politician–senior public servant relationship during, 100; and public interest, 239; and social cohesion, 44

secretariats, 176

secularization, 21–2, 47

Segal, Hugh, 62

self-inspection, 226, 229, 232

self-regulation, 219, 223, 229–30

Senate: establishment of, 57–8; and regional perspective, 58; spending scandal, 49, 120, 133

senior public servants: and blame game, 128; and Canada School of Public Service, 159; career rise through ranks, 108; CEOs meeting with, 91; and competition among departments, 188–9; depression among, 189–90; dismissal/termination of, 165, 198–9; economic elites and, 207; and evaluations/performance reports, 115–16; growth of executive category, 194–5; as lobbyists, 93–4, 231; lobbyists and, 207; and management, 97–8, 100, 114–17;

and Parliament, 70; pensions, 162, 163, 231; and policy, 97, 98, 99, 100, 101, 103, 232; and policy vs administrative issues, 29; politicians and, 100–1; post-retirement, in private sector, 207, 231; and program managers running on tracks, 273; and regional economic development, 152; traditional career rise, 104. *See also* public servants above fault line

senior public servants above fault line: and blame game, 167; and controversies, 263–4; and implementation, 167; as promiscuously partisan, 264

Shepody potato, 243–4

Siegel, David, 184, 197

Simon, Herbert A., 172, 210

Simpson, Jeffrey, 196

Smith, Adam, *Wealth of Nations,* 3

Smith, David E., 59

Snowden, Edward, 71

social capital: about, 49; decline of, 22–3; volunteerism and, 25

social cohesion: about, 49; charitable giving and, 39; and civil society, 33; decline in, 36–7; defined, 32; global financial crisis of 2008 and, 39; income inequality and, 39; middle class and, 38, 39; in postwar period, 44, 46; social media and, 40; studies on, 32; volunteerism and, 39

social media: government monitoring/analysis of content, 43–4; and journalism, 40–1; and national debates about national interests/common good, 47; and news, 41–2; as oversight body, 10; PCO and, 44; and permanent election campaigns, 41, 43; and politicians, 42–3; and politics, 40; and prime minister and advisors, 43; and private lives of public figures, 248; and public consultations, 43; public servants and, 42–3; and public values conflicts, 50; and social cohesion, 40; and special interest groups, 43

La Société de l'Acadie du Nouveau-Brunswick (SANB), 23, 24

La Société Nationale des Acadiens (SNA), 21, 23, 24

Songer, Donald, 75, 84

special interest groups: and courts, 78; and public consultation, 34; and public good, 48–9; public interest vs, 113; public service vs, 113; social media and, 43

special operating agencies (SOAs), 124–5, 126

spending: management and, 114; on new vs old initiatives, 254; on overhead functions, 271; prime ministers and, 200, 201; program reviews and reductions in, 209–10, 255; RCMP and, 168; and reallocation of resources, 252; on regulation, 216; regulatory regimes and, 216–17; and retail politics, 263; rise in, 9, 28. *See also* Chrétien-Martin program review; Harper program review; visionary investments

spending estimates: budget and, 66–7; complexity of, 66; minister-ial responsibility for, 67–8; MPs' scrutiny of, 66

spending reductions: across-the-board, 274–5; consultants for, 201–2; incentives for, 200; majority mandates and, 65, 200, 201; prime ministers and, 116, 202, 274; productivity and, 204

spin specialists: and adversarial politics, 63; history of use of, 116; and House of Commons, 58; as lobbyists, 63; numbers of, 116; and permanent election campaigns, 63; and social media, 41

sponsorship scandal, 120, 136, 198

Stagg, Jack, 177

Statistics Canada: and cancellation of mandatory census long-form questionnaire, 106–7; reduction in funding for, 106–7; and voter turnout, 36

Steele, Graham, 63

Stewart, Ian, 250

Strathy, George, 86

supply (appropriations), 66, 67

Supreme Court of Canada: and Cabinet secrets, 84; Haida and Taku River decision, 82–3; and implementation, 83, 85; influence/importance of chief justice, 106; influence of, 76; judicial appointments to, 84; Mikisew decision, 83; and Nova Scotia school construction for French-language students, 80; party appointing, and judicial ideology/policy preferences, 84; and performance assessment in government, 80; performance report,

84; PMO vs, 85; and politics, 76; power of, 76; and private health-care insurance, 79–80; and public interest, 79; public opinion regarding, 85; and public policy, 75, 76, 77–8; and social agenda, 75; and special-needs student programs, 79; workload, 84. See also McLachlin, Beverley Szablowski, George, 76

Tait, John: report, 112, 134–6, 173; and values/ethics exercise, 112, 134–6, 157, 159
Taku River decision, 83
taxes: and income inequality, 38; new, 276; in public interest, 56; reductions in, and income inequality, 37; rulers and, 56
taxpayers: and global financial crisis of 2008, 39; tax-eaters vs, 7
Tellier, Paul, 123–4, 153, 155, 181, 264
temporary foreign worker program, 107, 175
Thatcher, Margaret: and account-ability, 122; on bureaucrats, 97; cuts to government, 97; emula-tion of reforms in Canada, 123; and management issues in gov-ernment, 123; and ministerial responsibility, 138; and private vs public sector, 8, 97, 102, 114, 259; and program reviews by private sector executives, 100; and public interest, 97; and public sector policy vs management, 107; and public service influence over pol-icy, 103; reforms, 9, 121–3; and

size of civil service, 97, 98–9
Thatcher, Reagan, and Mulroney (Savoie), 173
Thériault, Joseph Yvon, 82
thickness/thickening: of decision-making, 88; of machinery of gov-ernment, 26, 194; of operations, and bottom line, 128–9; and pro-gram managers, 271–2; regional economic development and, 152
Thomas, Martin, 76
Thomas, Paul, 132
time allocation, 68
Tomkins, Adam, 56
Touraine (QC) orientation/training centre, 153–4, 155, 157, 158, 160
Trade and Development, Depart-ment of, 93. See also Foreign Affairs, Department of
transparency: access-to-information legislation and, 241; interest groups and, 241; machinery of government and, 15; and man-agement, 260; in private vs public sector, 9; and program delivery, 268
Transportation Safety Board, 222, 223, 224–5
Transport Canada: and Lac-Mégan-tic derailment, 221–2, 223–5, 227; as reactive, 228; spending at, 133
Travers, Jim, 189
Treasury Board: and Canada School of Public Service, 160, 161–2; Chrétien's streamlining of Cabi-net committees and, 176; and evaluation of direct program spending, 182–3; and Harper program review, 201–2; inappro-

priate cards incident, 192; and Increased Ministerial Authority and Accountability initiative, 126; numbers of decisions, 128; and reduction in regulations, 212; study on compensation, 199

Treasury Board Secretariat: cutting of executive-level jobs, 194–5; Management Accountability Framework (MAF), 151, 160; and reporting requirements, 115; and values/ethics, 136, 162–3

Trudeau, Justin, 38

Trudeau, Pierre E.: and Cabinet committee system, 176; and Charter of Rights and Freedoms, 214; and French Canada vision, 25–6; and governing from centre, 103; and Just Society, 47; Pitfield and, 153; and politician–senior line-department public servant relationship, 109; and regulation, 214

trust: in charities, 39; in government, 6, 278; in institutions, 6, 39, 71; in MPs, 69; in Parliament, 69; in public sector, 6–8

unions: avoidance of, 150; and courts, 83, 269; disciplinary action and, 198, 199, 268–9; global economy and, 208, 209; globalization and, 37; labour relations approach/model, 255, 268; and non-performers, 84, 255, 269, 278–9; and pensions, 278; in private vs public sector, 196, 256, 278–9; and productivity, 203; purpose of, 203; and terminations, 197–8. See also collective bargaining

United Kingdom: civil service, 97, 98–9, 205–6; executive agencies in, 124; regulatory regime in, 232; sale of High Commission property, 137; Westminster model of Parliament in Canada vs, 57–8. See also Thatcher, Margaret

United Nations code of conduct for public servants, 112

United States: 2008 financial crisis in, 219–21, 223; democracy in, 54–5; federal system, 57; and fusion energy, 242–3; regulatory regime in, 219–21, 239

upstairs-downstairs approach, 261, 262–3. See also fault line(s)

Usher, Dan, 152

values/ethics: Canada School of Public Service and, 162–3; code, 136; counsellor, 136; deputy ministers and, 136; fault line and, 173; income inequality and, 50; and leadership, 136; private sector, 6; private vs public sector, 232–3; and public interest, 112; public sector, 6; public service, 112, 134–6; social media and, 50; and sponsorship scandal, 136; Tait/Tait report and, 112, 134–6, 157, 159, 173; Treasury Board Secretariat and, 136, 162–3

Veilleux, Gérard, 153, 155

Via Rail train-bus crash (September 2013), 227

visionary investments, 242–6, 276. See also ideas

voluntary sector: government activities hived off to, 280; transfer of public service activities to, 275–6

volunteerism: about, 39–40; and advocacy associations, 24; in community, 20–1; decline of, 39–40; and social capital, 25; and social cohesion, 39

voters/voting: citizen participation and, 34, 277; and common good, 48–9; and efficiency in private vs public sector, 258; election campaign policies and, 247; and national interest, 277; political ruthlessness and, 247–8; politicians and, 277; responsibility for state of government, 257–8; turnout, 4, 34–6, 48, 247, 277, 278

Waddell, Chris, 40

Walker Consulting Group, 275

Wallin, Pamela, 120

Wall Street Journal, on regulation, 213

Waugh, Rick, 127

Wealth of Nations (Smith), 3

Weber, Max, 34, 111, 171, 172, 192–3, 271

Welcome to Parliament: A Job with No Description, 60

Weller, Patrick, 87

Western Economic Diversification (WD), 145–6, 159

Westminster model of Parliament, 56–8, 94

whistle-blowing, 71, 186

wicked problems: government and, 241–2, 245, 276; private sector and, 242

Wildavsky, Aaron, *Implementation,* 261–2, 273

Williams, Shirley, 99

Wilson, James Q., 172, 186, 187, 188

Wilson, Michael, 147

Wilson of Dinton, Lord, 26

Wouters, Wayne, 127, 256

Wright, Nigel, 49, 120

Wynne, Kathleen, 276

Yes Minister, 99–100, 109

Young, Donald, 243